WISE LEADERSHIP

Wise Leadership provides current and emerging leaders with a grounded, intuitive framework to help them understand and master multiple leadership identities, allowing them to adapt seamlessly to different leadership settings and challenges.

Anchored in a wisdom-based approach, Kessler digs into leadership's philosophical core to uncover the six fundamental challenges leaders face and presents the corresponding set of six synergistic competencies or tools that readers can develop to solve them. Bridging scholarship with practice, each part of this leadership toolbox is outlined in a clear and consistent way so that readers can learn exactly when, why, and how to use it. The user-friendly format also eases comparison and customization of the different approaches along with a consideration of their strengths and dangers.

Incorporating colorful examples and practical guidelines, this book will equip both students and professionals with a dynamic repertoire of flexible leadership skills that will help them succeed in any situation.

Eric H. Kessler is a Distinguished University Professor and Henry George Scholar in the Lubin School of Business at Pace University, New York City, USA. He is a recognized authority in global leadership and organization management and the worldwide General Editor of the *Encyclopedia of Management Theory*. Dr. Kessler has worked with a wide range of business and government practitioners, authored over 120 academic papers, instructed over 4,000 students, overseen numerous international field studies and community service projects, and published seven critically acclaimed books appearing in over 70 countries. Designated a public opinion leader, he has been quoted in major news outlets and praised for his achievements in research (Choice Book Award), education (Kenan Teaching Excellence Award), service (Jefferson Public Service Medal), and practice (Fulbright Specialist Grant). He is also a past President of the Eastern Academy of Management as well as the recipient of numerous honors and distinctions in the fields of business, economics, forensics, management, and psychology.

WISE LEADERSHIP

A Toolbox for Sustainable Success

Eric H. Kessler

NEW YORK AND LONDON

First published 2021
by Routledge
52 Vanderbilt Avenue, New York, NY 10017

and by Routledge
2 Park Square, Milton Park, Abingdon, Oxon, OX14 4RN

Routledge is an imprint of the Taylor & Francis Group, an informa business

© 2021 Taylor & Francis

The right of Eric H. Kessler to be identified as authors of this work has
been asserted by him in accordance with sections 77 and 78 of the
Copyright, Designs and Patents Act 1988.

All rights reserved. No part of this book may be reprinted or reproduced or
utilized in any form or by any electronic, mechanical, or other means, now
known or hereafter invented, including photocopying and recording, or in
any information storage or retrieval system, without permission in writing
from the publishers.

Trademark notice: Product or corporate names may be trademarks or
registered trademarks, and are used only for identification and explanation
without intent to infringe.

Library of Congress Cataloging-in-Publication Data
Names: Kessler, Eric H., author.
Title: Wise leadership : a toolbox for sustainable success / Eric H. Kessler.
Description: 1 Edition. | New York : Routledge, 2020. | Includes
bibliographical references and index.
Identifiers: LCCN 2020011567 (print) | LCCN 2020011568 (ebook) |
ISBN 9781138498808 (hardback) | ISBN 9781138498839 (paperback) |
ISBN 9781351015516 (ebook)
Subjects: LCSH: Leadership–Psychological aspects.
Classification: LCC HD57.7 .K4775 2020 (print) | LCC HD57.7 (ebook) |
DDC 658.4/092–dc23
LC record available at https://lccn.loc.gov/2020011567
LC ebook record available at https://lccn.loc.gov/2020011568

ISBN: 978-1-138-49880-8 (hbk)
ISBN: 978-1-138-49883-9 (pbk)
ISBN: 978-1-351-01551-6 (ebk)

Typeset in Bembo
by Wearset Ltd, Boldon, Tyne and Wear

With sincere respect to the giants whose shoulders I am privileged to stand on,
With warm gratitude to the many who have supported me in this undertaking,
And with keen hope to those who might find its insights useful for navigating their personal and professional leadership journeys.

CONTENTS

List of Figures		*xi*
List of Tables		*xii*

Introduction   1
 Seeing and Not Seeing 1
 Hiding in Plain Sight 2
 Our Guiding Principles 3
 Our Intended Path 4
 A Word of Caution 5

PART I
Discovering Your Leadership Wisdom   **7**

1   The PROBLEM: Stupid Smart People   9
 Leadership Idiocy Abounds 10
 Let's Stop 'K.I.D.'-ding Ourselves 12
 What Wisdom Is … And What It Is Not 15
 Connecting Wisdom and Leadership 17
 A Disheartening and Deteriorating Disequilibrium 19
 Wise and Shine 21
 A Roadmap for 'Wise Leadership' 25

2   The JOURNEY: Paths for Exploring Leadership   28
 Exploring Leadership 29

viii Contents

(Good) Path 1: Leadership Chronologies – A Punctuated
Progression 31
(Better) Path 2: Leadership Categories – Two Fundamental
Questions 32
(Best) Path 3: Leadership Competencies – Key Insights from
Leadership Theory 34
So ... Essential Leadership Roles 40
With ... Core Leadership Identities 45
Okay, What Does This All Mean? 47

3 The SOLUTION: A Model of 'Wise' Leadership   48
From Philosophy 49
To Leadership 56
A Model of Wise Leadership 60
Being – Head and Heart Challenges 63
Seeing – Inside and Outside Challenges 65
Doing – Pull and Push Challenges 66
A Preview of Part II 67

PART II
Assembling Your Leadership Toolbox   71

4 The MIND of a Leader: How to Use Your Leadership
Scientist (Logic) Tools   73
When Facing and Thinking and Understanding
Challenges 76
Activate Your Leader 'Logic' Tool 81
Be a Leadership SCIENTIST 86
To Use Your Head 88
And with Extraordinary Intellectual Prowess 95
Lead with Sagacity 103

5 The HEART of a Leader: How to Use Your
Leadership Artist (Aesthetics) Tools   105
When Facing Emotional and Motivation Challenges 108
Activate Your Leader 'Aesthetics' Tool 113
Be a Leadership ARTIST 116
To Use Your Heart 117
And with Extraordinary Emotive Capacity 125
Lead with Spirit 134

Contents **ix**

6 Looking Deep INSIDE Yourself: How to Use Your
Leadership Icon (Ethics) Tools 136
When Facing Moral and Value Challenges 139
Activate Your Leader 'Ethics' Tool 144
Be a Leadership ICON 147
To Look Deep Inside Yourself 148
And with Extraordinary Introspective Insight 158
Lead through Character 166

7 Looking Far OUTSIDE Yourself: How to Use Your
Leadership Advocate (Metaphysics) Tools 168
When Facing Meaning and Commitment Challenges 171
Activate Your Leader 'Metaphysics' Tool 175
Be a Leadership ADVOCATE 178
To Look Outside Yourself 180
And with Extraordinary Meaningful Objectives 189
Lead through Purpose 197

8 PULLING People Together: How to Use Your
Leadership Maestro (Epistemology) Tools 199
When Facing Harmony and Teamwork Challenges 202
Activate Your Leader 'Epistemology' Tool 206
Be a Leadership MAESTRO 213
To Pull People Together 214
And with Extraordinary Collaborative Orientation 224
Lead with Unity 231

9 PUSHING People Forward: How to Use Your
Leadership General (Politics) Tools 232
When Facing Execution and Implementation Challenges 235
Activate Your Leader 'Politics' Tool 239
Be a Leadership GENERAL 245
To Push People Forward 246
And with Extraordinary Functional Application 256
Lead with Functional Value 263

PART III
Leveraging Your Leadership Success **265**

10 A SELECTION Guide for the Wise Leader:
Customizing your Leadership Approach 267

x Contents

The Importance of Agility and Customization 268
Sizing Yourself Up 274
Summoning the Skill and the Will 277
What Happens When You Are the 'Wrong'
    Type of Leader 279
Taken Together: Aligning the Gears 286
Implications and Issues Going Forward 289

11 An OPTIMIZATION Guide for the Wise Leader:
    Growing your Leadership Strengths   290
    Dynamic Leadership Competencies 291
    Growing Oneself: Maximizing Your Toolbox 291
    Growing Others: An (Organizational) Talent Management
        Program 297
    Implications and Issues 307

12 A MAINTENANCE Guide for the Wise Leader:
    Trouble-Shooting your Leadership Exposures   309
    Erosion versus Evolution 310
    Major Forces – Opportunities and Threats 311
    Technology and Leadership 315
    Globalization and Leadership 320
    Institutions and Leadership 326
    Your Personal Trouble-Shooting Checklist 331

Appendix A: Bibliography   334
Appendix B: Summary of Core Wise Leadership Tools   349
Appendix C: Sample Syllabus for a Wise Leadership Program   350
Appendix D: Exercises to Practice Wise Leadership   351
Index of Names   353
Index of Subjects   357

FIGURES

1.1	The Supply and Demand of Wisdom	20
1.2	Snapshot: Climbing the Wisdom Ladder	22
1.3	Cinema: Mastering the Wisdom Cycle	23
3.1	A Model of Wise Leadership	61
4.1	Focus: Logic and the Leadership Scientist	78
5.1	Focus: Aesthetics and the Leadership Artist	110
6.1	Focus: Ethics and the Leadership Icon	140
7.1	Focus: Metaphysics and the Leadership Advocate	172
8.1	Focus: Epistemology and the Leadership Maestro	203
9.1	Focus: Politics and the Leadership General	237
10.1	Customizing Your Approach (Aligning the Gears)	286

TABLES

2.1	Chronology of Major Leadership Theories	31
2.2	Categorization of Major Leadership Themes	33
3.1	Wise Leadership Tools	59
4.1	Tools for Developing the MIND of a Leader	88
4.2	Becoming a Leadership Scientist	103
5.1	Tools for Developing the HEART of a Leader	116
5.2	Becoming a Leadership Artist	135
6.1	Tools for Looking Deep INSIDE Yourself	148
6.2	Becoming a Leadership Icon	167
7.1	Tools for Looking Far OUTSIDE Yourself	180
7.2	Becoming a Leadership Advocate	197
8.1	Tools for PULLING People Together	214
8.2	Becoming a Leadership Maestro	231
9.1	Tools for PUSHING People Forward	246
9.2	Becoming a Leadership General	264
10.1	So … Where Do You Stand?	274
10.2	Do You Have the Skill and the Will?	277
10.3	(Mis)Matching Leadership Tools to Leadership Challenges	280
11.1	So … How Sharp Are Your Tools?	292
11.2	Strengthening Your Leadership Wisdom 'Talent'	300
12.1	So … Where Are You Exposed (and What are the Dangers)?	312
12.2	A Trouble-Shooting Checklist	332

INTRODUCTION

Imagine summertime in Tuscany.

To many, especially those who have been, this is quite a pleasant picture. Filled with luminescent landscapes of rolling green hills and sun-splashed blooms. Above them a blindingly blue sky speckled with wispy white clouds. Below them vines of plump purple grapes meandering amidst the breeze-blown trees. And intermingled among them glistening statues of nuanced expression as well as masterfully painted, symphonic frescos depicting the dramas of human theater that we retrospectively call history and colloquially call life.

Yet this picture is often truncated by another that is not so pleasant. Yes, tourists.

The warm season invariably ushers in clamoring hoards that flock to cities like Florence by the busload. Aggressively elbowing through the cobblestone corridors they seek to approximate (or at least pose for a good photo with) the age of renaissance and its spirit of rebirth.

One of the most popular targets of their lenses is the Galleria dell Accademia, the home of Michelangelo's soaring sculpture *David*. Most people are familiar with The David, and rightly so. It is one of the world's most famous figures. As such it is placed at the end of a long hallway so that the gazes of its visitors are instantly met by the larger-than-life figure.

Almost unavoidably, here is where their attention will hover. However, this is precisely the WRONG place for it.

Do you know why?

Seeing and Not Seeing

People seem compelled to rush through the museum corridors to view this iconic masterpiece. As if the statue is a powerful magnet and they are mindless ball-bearings.

2 Introduction

And this can make the experience seem like a track meet that rewards the swiftest selfie-seekers. But the funny thing is that, in doing so, visitors often race past four smaller works positioned to the side that are easy to miss amidst the grandeur of David. Yet these works are, quite paradoxically, perhaps even more important in representing its renaissance philosophy.

The *Unfinished Prisoners* are, in the words from guidebook impresario Arthur Frommer, perhaps Michelangelo's most fascinating works. "Like no others", he says,

> these statues symbolize Michelangelo's theory that sculpture is an 'art that takes away superfluous material.' The great master saw a true sculpture as something that was already inherent in the stone, and all it needed was a skilled chisel to free it from the extraneous rock.
>
> *(Moretti, 2010: 160)*

The modern-day visitor will, if they know where and why to look, witness in these works the timeless human dynamic – struggling, twisting, and fighting to escape their trappings and limitations. The *St. Matthew* bursting through his rocky walls. The *Bearded Slave* casting off his stony shackles. The *Awakening Slave* rising from his boulder's bondage. And *Atlas* removing the burden of his oppressive marble confines.

It is said that any way of seeing is also a way of not seeing. If this is so, and if we are able to resist the visual temptation of fixing our stares only on the *David* (as well as all the proverbial 'Davids' in our life), then we will behold the most lucid landmarks to this mysterious, awesome thing we call 'wisdom' and its relation to leadership.

Interested?

Hiding in Plain Sight

All too often we see what is easiest to see, what we are directed to see, and perhaps what we are hard-wired to see. The prisoners are not tucked away in some dark corner or placed in an isolated back room. For those without the skill or the will to notice them they are hiding in plain sight.

The same is true for leadership. Our attention is drawn to bright and shiny things, larger-than-life figures, and breaking news. But the finished product seldom reveals the secrets of its composition. The fact of the matter is that the David was not given to the marble. It was always in the marble. As Michelangelo said, he did not create the statue but instead simply revealed it (or, if you will, released it from its gritty sedimentary penitentiary).

It is my contention that just as there are monuments residing deep inside the marble, the potential for wisdom is inside each and every one of us. And its principles have been hiding in plain sight for ages. Yet we too often choose to rush past them in search of the latest fad, fashion, or focus.

Wisdom is not found on the top of some distant, ephemeral mountaintop. It is not a singular far-off prize set at the end of some regal hallway.

Wisdom is nuanced. It is dynamic. And it is found within.

If we can learn how to access this wisdom in our daily lives, then we can also learn how it might be deployed to elevate ourselves, and elevate others, to achieve personal as well as professional success.

To be better.

To see better.

And to do better.

So please allow this introduction to serve as a tour guide, setting the stage as you venture forth to explore, extract, and enhance the wisdom within you.

Our Guiding Principles

What makes this book different from all the others about leadership?

A few things.

WISE LEADERSHIP is built on several principles.

- Firm Grounding: It utilizes a deep wisdom-based perspective.
- High-Level Synergy: It ties together the diverse insights from the major theories of leadership.
- Solid Framework: It constructs a dynamic contingency model of tools and tasks.
- Relatable Examples: It illustrates the model by drawing from the greatest real and idealized leaders of humankind.
- User Customization: It presents guided opportunities for personal reflection and development.
- Usefulness: It communicates clear, practical success strategies for walking the talk.

Here we separate our discussion from others that are content with superficial considerations of the topic without sufficient theoretical foundation. Or paying selective attention to one or two 'friendly' parts of the vast leadership literature and landscape. Or advancing simplistic formulas that champion a favorite 'one best way' of leading. Or discussing narrowly framed examples from one focal era or culture or domain without ways for generalizing or personalizing them. Or avoiding the hard work of forging practical tools that might actually help a reader address real-world challenges.

More specifically, the book is written with the optimistic objective that, after reading it, you will say the following …

'It is deep' – Our book does not get caught up in myopic analyses, what is hot-at-the-moment considerations, and short-term unsustainable solutions plaguing much of the leadership conversation. Instead it goes back to the source, to the deepest and most profound ideas of history's greatest sages, to match the seriousness of

4 Introduction

the topic with the soberness of the dialog. In doing this it sets a solid context for contextualizing and exploring what leaders can and should do across the spectrum of their responsibilities.

'It is rigorous' – Our book is based on a sound scholarly base. It is not simply a single viewpoint on the topic or a biased tome that professes an exclusive channel into wisdom. Indeed, this book builds on established research and a decades-long expansive investigation to understand wisdom as it relates to leading. The result is a clear model that captures the essence of the issue.

'It is integrative' – Our book does not seek to add to the cacophony of opinions and pontifications that fill the leadership landscape. It does not seek to advocate a favorite aspect of the field or narrow model of the literature. Instead it brings the pieces together so that the parts can be understood in light of the whole. As such it produces not an either-or mentality but instead a contingent framework that, in the spirit of Newton, 'stands on the shoulders of giants' to combine the gamut of their collective insights.

'It is alive' – Our book does not wallow in the static and the staid, nor confine itself to the technical language of the academic. Rather, it breathes life into the model by drawing upon colorful cases of the most accomplished real as well as fictional characters of our history. These illustrations include historical figures and modern experts for sure but also literary and cinematic characters who exemplify its principles and guidelines.

'It is developmental' – Our book does not profess wisdom as an unattainable ideal but instead as something everyone can pursue in his or her own way as per their own circumstances. It attempts to lay bare this critical but mysterious idea of wisdom. And it speaks to a process and offers instruments for how we might become wiser people and build wiser organizations.

'It is applied' – Our book does not consider wisdom in the abstract but expressly relates it to the real-life challenges of leading and managing. Contained herein are specific practices and overarching strategies for using the book as a means, not as an end, to facilitate personal and professional success.

Our Intended Path

In a nutshell, this is what you will find in the coming pages.

Part I of the book outlines the nature and need for wise leadership, summarizes the paths that have been pursued to understand it, and then pieces them together to present a generalized as well as dynamic model of leadership wisdom.

Part II of the book describes the six core wisdom-based elements that comprise the model. Each will be shown to be a necessary but not sufficient part of a larger 'Leadership Toolbox'. Utilizing a rich set of illustrations across a variety of contexts, it will also show how each element can be used to address different fundamental leadership challenges.

Part III of the book constructs a roadmap for using the tools. More specifically, they provide actionable strategies for each reader (yes – this means you!) to customize, leverage, and maintain their leadership toolboxes.

As such, this book will endeavor to partner with you to achieve several learning objectives:

> … To appreciate the nature of wisdom, and how it is fundamentally different from simply amassing more data, processing more information, and even creating more knowledge.
> … To comprehend wisdom's key characteristics and how they relate to each other.
> … To gain through concrete examples how they translate into a set of practical tools or best leadership practices.
> … To then take these tools and use them in developing and sustaining your own leadership wisdom.

In sum, to share a set of straightforward principles so that you can match core leadership competencies to your primary leadership challenges,

And lead successfully in any situation.

A Word of Caution

Constructing a model such as this takes time and perseverance. This is why for years I have resisted book offers on this topic … until now. This is why I finally feel that it is ready to share. Not because it is a comprehensive or unassailable product. To the contrary, any such claims would be profoundly unwise. Instead, it is because the template ultimately puts us on the right course for unleashing our wisdom potential. And its core principles have been shown to be extraordinarily useful – across times, tasks, and domains – in explaining and enhancing leadership success.

In a word, it works.

In addition, and insofar as the gap between the demand for and supply of wisdom seems to be growing faster than ever, our world can be particularly well served by wiser leadership. As such, this model is timed to make a critical difference in the success of leaders and their organizations.

So please excuse any flaws and tolerate any shortcomings in what you are about to read. It is admittedly not perfect. Let us dismiss this false notion from the start.

But have the conversation we must. Because wisdom is a journey, not a destination. And although it is a critical one it is not always easy or without queries and challenges. This recalls the words of wisdom by Will Durant (2014: 11) in his book *Fallen Leaves*: "So, brave reader, you have fair warning: proceed at your own risk. But I shall be warmed by your company."

Let us then venture into the proverbial breach feeling confident that this is worthy of our engagement, our customization, and our refinement as we work together to improve our common lot. For ourselves. For our fellow travelers. And for future travelers.

PART I

Discovering Your Leadership Wisdom

1

THE PROBLEM

Stupid Smart People

There is a better way to lead …
And it is hiding in plain sight

We are drowning in data.
Overflowing in information.
Awash in knowledge.
And we are starving for wisdom.

In this first chapter you will be confronted with a paradox. How can leaders, and by extension the organizations and institutions they run, (1) have more data and more information and more knowledge at their fingertips, yet (2) at the same time, despite the exponentially expanding powers they bring, continue to do so many dumb things?

Fortunately there is an answer. There is a way out of this dilemma.

And as you now know, it is hiding in plain sight.

It is found not from traveling the same path faster but instead by rethinking the path itself. Not from fancier leadership bells and whistles but instead from going 'back to the future' and applying classic (but contemporary relevant) leadership insights. In a word, it comes from the ancient concept of wisdom.

Specifically, this introductory chapter will be framed as follows:

- Leadership Idiocy Abounds
- Let's Stop 'K.I.D.' ding Ourselves
- What Wisdom is … and What it is NOT
- Wisdom and Leadership
- A Disheartening and Deteriorating Disequilibrium

10 Discovering Your Leadership Wisdom

- Wise and Shine
- A Roadmap for 'Wise Leadership'

Leadership Idiocy Abounds

We live in an age of many wicked contradictions. And none is wickeder than the following. It is the ultimate oxymoron. It haunts us as we try to best navigate our life course. And it constrains the success of our leaders as they try to do the same for our organizations.

Here it is.

On the one hand, the world is 'smarter' than it has ever been.

We are witnessing an unparalleled upward trajectory of human capacity and potential. This is axiomatic to a point that it has become practically a truism. If you don't believe me then simply put the book down for a moment and look around. You will no doubt see, dwelling behind nearly everything in your visual field, the potent engine of basic scientific progression fueling remarkable technological and functional advancements. Together this potent cocktail is enabling us to channel, and even alter, the world's mechanics to go farther, deeper, and faster than ever before. Explore land, sea, sky, and space. Discover the building blocks of matter and the systems of our bodies. Access any fact or connect with any person with just the swipe of a finger. It is remarkable to see how the science of today is scarcely recognizable from that of ten, two, or even one generation past.

According to Buckminster Fuller's famous 'Knowledge Doubling Curve' our accumulated expertise is on a path to double every year, and as recently amended this will soon be reduced to every 12 hours. Just think about it. Picture all that humans have ever known in their roughly 100,000-plus years of existence and now imagine the process repeating, and its pile replicating, each half-day. If true, then, at midnight when an uber-guru managed to learn everything ever codified, they would still be ignorant of about half of what is known by the next noon. A daunting image for sure.

This progression has created an unmistakable trend in the arc of history. Each generation successively leapfrogging its previous, cumulative iterations in the basic realization and mastery of how things work. And it continues to penetrate almost every corner of human activity. To paraphrase Isaac Newton's famous rejoinder from a 1675 letter, we continue to stand on the upwardly rising shoulders of giants in our collective faculties or 'smarts'.

This is the good news.

Yet, on the other hand (yup, here it comes) … the world is also 'dumber' than it has ever been.

Notwithstanding the aforementioned growth in our knowledge, the daily news is, seemingly without pause or exception, filled with countless examples of human idiocy. With a range and scope too numerous to mention. Whichever examples I could choose to punctuate this would surely be surpassed by countless others in the brief time it takes for the book to go to print, or even in the time it takes for the reader to progress from chapter to chapter, or perhaps even the time it has taken me to type this paragraph.

The *Merriam Webster Dictionary* prompts us to consider idiocy as acts that display (synonyms) absurdity, asininity, fatuity, folly, foolery, foppery, imbecility, inanity, insanity, lunacy, stupidity … and/or (related words) absurdness, craziness, foolishness, inaneness, madness, senselessness, witlessness; buffoonery, shenanigans, drivel, nonsense, twaddle; blunder, bungle, flub, goof.

Think about it: How much idiocy have you read about recently in our political, business, social, recreational, academic, government, economic, ecological, etc. organizations and their varied pursuits?

To put it bluntly there are just too many smart people doing too many stupid things.

It is overwhelming, it is constant, and strangely enough it is just as predictable as the previous discussion on the advancement of knowledge. And it is characteristic not only of some people but also, alas, of the very 'best and brightest' whom we have entrusted to lead our cherished public and private institutions. This is in large part because we have become so preoccupied with more information and knowledge, so infatuated with and reliant on superficial analyses and quick fixes, that we tend not to focus the same energy on developing and deploying deep-seeded leadership wisdom.

This is discussed with particularly lucidity in the book *Sapiens*, where Yuval Noah Harari's historical analysis reaches the conclusion that (2015: 415–416):

> Seventy thousand years ago, homo sapiens was still an insignificant animal minding its own business in a corner of Africa. In the following millennia it transformed itself into the master of the entire planet and the terror of the ecosystem…. We have mastered our surroundings, increased food production, built cities, established empires, and created far-flung trade networks. But did we decrease the amount of suffering in the world? Time and again, massive increases in human power did not necessarily improve the well-being of individual Sapiens…. Moreover despite the astonishing things that humans are capable of doing, we remain unsure of our goals and we seem to be as discontented as ever. We have advanced from our canoes to galleys to steamships to space shuttles – but nobody knows where we're going. We are more powerful than ever before, but have very little idea what to do with all that power.

In other words our collective wisdom has not kept up with our burgeoning knowledge. We have gotten so smart in so many ways but at the same time we remain mired in impenetrable cycles of stupidity. And our leaders and our organizations too often seem lost despite the availability of sophisticated tools for finding their way. Hence Will Durant's (2014: 36, 158) clarion call: "A wise man can learn from other men's experience; a fool cannot learn even from his own … (thus

12 Discovering Your Leadership Wisdom

pleading) Who will now arise to harness our knowledge to wisdom, our science to conscience, our power to human purpose?"

Upshot: There is an imbalance in the demand for, and supply of, wise leadership. And more than this the demand–supply imbalance is reaching a critical mass where the consequences present critical, far-reaching challenges to us as individuals and we as a people.

This prompts us to answer the critical question of WHY. Why is this happening? Or in more prosaic terms, 'Why do leaders fail?' As I will argue later in this book it is primarily because they lack the wisdom to either (1) develop the right tools for the different parts of the job and/or (2) learn when or how to correctly use them. As a result, they do not target and engage their leadership approaches to meet the increasingly complex (short-term snapshot) and dynamically changing (long-term cinema) leadership realities.

It is precisely through this realization that we can begin to chart a path towards wise leadership. Leaders exert great power to shape their organization's destinies – be they countries, companies, and even families – and thus bear a heavy responsibility when things do not go well. And just like any other role, we can analyze its requirements and then trace the requisite competencies needed to meet them.

We can change the situation. We can become better, wiser leaders.

But to do this we must stop kidding ourselves....

Let's Stop 'K.I.D.'-ding Ourselves

Just as in the book's opening example, we often travel the path of life with great distraction. We do not always see, or esteem, or prioritize, what is most important. We frequently do not apply our best time and energies to the most significant and valuable issues that, ironically, are the very factors that determine our fates.

And today the distractions are multiplying to dizzying proportions. We are increasingly overwhelmed by endless streams of data. Blinded by new technologies. Overloaded by incomplete and skewed information. Enamored by dubiously collected and zealously professed chunks of decontextualized or incomplete knowledge. And as the aphorism goes, this can be a very dangerous thing.

Ironically it is our expanding capacity for, and socially sanctioned system of, data-information-knowledge processing at the same time that makes us both smarter and dumber than ever. With the acceleration of rote-based training masquerading as education, agenda-based social commentary imitating news, and myopic skewed experimentations sounding the false trumpet of truth, we are losing our way.

It is getting harder and harder to determine what is core. To separate (pick your metaphor) ... the masterpiece from its marble. The truth from the trivia. The wheat from the chaff. The music from the static. Thus we increasingly find ourselves managed by, instead of strategically managing, our environment. And in its wake we are actually perpetuating a system that impedes rather than facilitates our progress.

But enough of the abstract. Let's get personal.

Here is a quick quiz.

Please answer True or False to the following:

Q1: The smarter you are … the more successful you are?
Q2: The smarter you are … the happier you are?
Q3: The smarter you are … the better person you are?
Q4: The smarter you are … the more effective leader you are?

Okay, now here is the answer key.

Ready:
False, False, False, False!

These are cold hard facts. Raw intelligence is NOT a very accurate predictor of success, or happiness, or even other desirable things like depth of spirituality, engagement and citizenship, and sustained leadership effectiveness. Neither are things that can be used to grow our supposed 'smarts' like having more money or possessing better technology.

As the movie character Forrest Gump famously quipped, "stupid is as stupid does." Correspondingly smart, well-resourced people should act smartly – right? But time and time again what we define and measure as smart – our IQ, the degrees hanging on our wall, how well we do on Jeopardy!, number of websites or cable channels we view, Twitter followers we acquire, the size of our bank accounts, etc. – simply do not seem to mesh well with the outcomes we would hope for.

Think about the following examples (the names have been obscured to protect the 'guilty' and also because there are just too many instances to keep current):

Politician 'A' rises to a high office in the land, a supposed paragon of leadership and boundless expectations, but: (1) makes a dumb policy decision, (2) commits a dumb ethical error, (3) miscalculates the political, economic, military, or public implications of their agenda, (4) all of the above.

Corporate executive 'B' is selected to lead their company to greatness but (1) crafts a strategy that undermines the culture and alienates the workforce, (2) reaches for financial gain but does great harm to local environments and peoples, (3) makes a dumb merger, acquisition, or venture, (4) all of the above.

Superstar athlete 'C' is predicted to be the next great thing in their sport but (1) takes performance-enhancing drugs believing that they will never get caught, (2) overestimates their role on the team and winds up undermining its success, (3) becomes so enamored by the fame, fortune, and celebrity of their position that they forget their roots and lose the love of the game, (4) all of the above.

Scientific wunderkind 'D' creates a new theorem for their field and gets showered with accolades but cannot (1) keep a happy family, (2) balance their own checkbook, (3) achieve spiritual, social, or personal peace, (4) all of the above.

14 Discovering Your Leadership Wisdom

Or how about asking yourself these equally wicked questions …

Can you be smart … and miserable?

Fabulously rich (pick one) trust-fund baby, tech-pioneer, or old-money patriarch 'E' has every need provided for but (1) does not truly appreciate what they have, (2) does not use their resources to help others, (3) is so preoccupied with the zeroes at the end of their net worth that they do not escape their castle/prison to learn new things, see beautiful places, or meet amazing everyday people, (4) all of the above.

Can you be smart … and evil?

Talented student 'F' is able to see more and do more than any of their peers but (1) pursues the veritable 'dark side' of their creations, (2) acts solely to benefit themselves but actually does as much harm to their psyche as suffered by the victims of their malice, (3) otherwise misuses, confuses, or abuses their power, (4) all of the above.

Can you be smart … and inept?

Closet virtuoso 'G' has everything going for them but (1) lacks the focus to realize their objectives and aspirations, (2) lacks the fire to motivate their action and hard work, (3) lacks the perspective to balance their efforts, account for their drawbacks, and evolve their strategies, (4) all of the above.

So what does this all really mean? In our age of enlightenment, of powerful technology and limitless information, of ever-growing knowledge and access, when it seems things should be so much clearer and easer, idiocy abounds.

And remember that it is not always the 'other guy' who does these things. We are not immune to this analysis ourselves. Funny how many drivers feel that everyone else on the road has a problem and does not drive as well as he or she does. Or how many people think that it is the other person who is dancing out of step or singing off-key. We cannot look at others if we do not also look critically at ourselves.

These are just a small sample of the examples of 'Idiocy' that we might read about in a single newspaper on a single day. Smart people doing stupid things. In a way this is unexpected. We were taught that the more <u>K</u>nowledge, <u>I</u>nformation, and <u>D</u>ata (K.I.D.) you acquire, the more success you would have. Better decisions. Better lives. More impact. More success. Well … not so fast. Not necessarily. It turns out that in doing this we are just 'K.I.D.'-ding ourselves. They are often necessary but seldom sufficient. And without the requisite guidance they can even lead us farther and faster astray.

Today there is a general belief that it is desirable to collect more data. Absorb more information. Gain more knowledge. These can certainly be good things or increase our potential to do good things. However, neither is necessarily so. Something needs to guide its development – or this K.I.D.-ding can hinder us, blind us, even harm us, and move us backward. Something needs to focus its energies – or this K.I.D.-ding can confuse us, disorient us, distract us, and again move us in the wrong direction. Something needs to apply it productively – or this K.I.D.-ding can obsess us, consume us, even enslave us, and sit idly as a false end or terminal (versus instrumental) goal in isolated towers of self-satisfaction and complacency.

There must be something more. Something that drives the system to truly become stronger; that provides the lens to sincerely see clearer; and that provides the vehicle to effectively do better. Fortunately for us there is. And, as the example of Michelangelo's *Prisoners* from our book's Preface suggests, it has been hiding in plain sight.

We are talking about the big 'W' word: WISDOM.

What Wisdom Is ... And What It Is Not

Oooh, Wisdom.

Perhaps I should cue the fog machine or classical soundtrack to create a majestic, mysterious mood.

Yet this thing we call wisdom is really not as haunting or elusive as some would have us believe. It is also not as exclusive and privileged.

Wisdom is definitely not reserved only for a select elite but for anyone willing to do the work. If you follow the prescriptions in this book then you can be, see, and do things wisely. You can become a wise leader. Upshot: This book is saying something different – you should pay attention.

Moreover, there is perhaps nothing more important in the conduct of human affairs than wisdom. Wisdom is indeed indubitably the Uber-Factor for Success. If you enhance your wisdom then you can enhance your life course and the success of those who you lead. Upshot: The messages in this book can be incredibly important – you should care about them.

So let's take a moment to break things down.

Wisdom is not just more data, more information, or more knowledge. Yes, it builds upon all of these. But in doing so it transfigures their combination and elevates the creation in a way that is fundamentally different from the mere sum of its parts. This further explains the KID-ding ourselves problem and is elucidated within the following simple hierarchy (from Kessler & Bailey, 2007):

Data < Information < Knowledge < Wisdom.

Data are raw facts. Bits and bytes. Nearly everything in the world generates data. And we are collecting more if it than ever. Sorted and studied they allow us to better categorize and recognize daily phenomenon. However, without an overlying framework, accompanying codebook, or embedded template, a data-only approach to leadership renders but a cacophony of meaningless ever-streaming noise.

Information is the processing of data to make it meaningful. It is created when we attach labels to the conditions and patterns that the aforementioned observations reveal. Information technology (IT) 'systems' thus allow us to organize

16 Discovering Your Leadership Wisdom

(form) and enhance (function) related practices. However, without an understanding of the circumstances in which the patterns emerge and their embedded assumptions, an information-only approach to leadership is extremely limited and carries the potential to obscure thought and confuse action.

Knowledge is the further refinement of information to ascertain axioms and reveal justified true belief. It analyzes as well as synthesizes the aforementioned information into conceptual frameworks for discerning their relationships. However, it is inherently conditional and incomplete insofar as almost everything we 'know' is contingent upon a host of varying factors that change across dynamic, interdependent systems. Moreover, a knowledge-only approach to leadership does not require prudence or principle and is therefore very dangerous. Its models and modes may provide great power but do not necessitate commensurate perspective or responsibility.

Wisdom continues to build upon these levels oriented towards achieving and enabling a good life. Wisdom is thus not a simple coagulation of its manifest subordinate dimensions but is instead a metamorphosis from them. It thereby represents the epitome of human development and conduct … facilitating more formidable understanding and affect, more penetrating insight and volition, and more effective harmonization and functioning.

To drive the point home please consider the following simple example (from The Rubik Zone, 2019): There are 43,252,003,274,489,856,000 possible positions on a classic Rubik's cube. This is a big number. Almost incomprehensible. Especially for a $3 \times 3 \times 3$-inch toy. In words: 43 quintillion, 252 quadrillion, 3 trillion, 274 billion, 489 million, 856 thousand. Yet from any given position a person is never more than 20 moves from solving it. Lesson … 'Working Hard' is not the same thing as 'Working Smart'. Perspective, experience, motivation, intuition, prudence, composure, and execution – these things matter!

However, what makes wisdom particularly elusive is our predominant tendency to like easy answers, clear paths, spoon-fed solutions, and quick fixes. The solution to the wisdom quest is not just more schooling. Said plainly, when pedagogy is dominated by data-, information-, and knowledge-based training paradigms we exacerbate rather than ameliorate the problem. The solution is also not just more experience. Said plainly, we cannot simply expect wisdom to come automatically with age, for as Mohandâs Gandhi explained, it is not a function of experience per se but is instead derivative of the attitude and outlook brought to that experience. There can be more or less foolish adults as well as more or less prescient progenies.

Yet, if properly pursued and applied, discovering the 'love of wisdom' offers powerful tools for addressing the fundamental challenges of leadership. People can subject any field of human activity, such as leadership, to fundamental questioning that completes its science in the synthesis of wisdom (Durant, 1961). Later in this book I will argue that wisdom comes from three basic philosophic dynamics. First, by BEING better through extraordinary intellectual prowess (head) and emotive capacity (heart), which represent the essential sagacity and spirit that enable it.

Second, from SEEING better, through extraordinary introspective insight (seeing inside) and principled objectives (seeing outside), which represent the essential character and purpose that guide it. Third, from DOING better, which represents the extraordinary collaborative orientation (pulling things together) and functional application (pushing things forward), which represent the essential unity and value that drive it.

But this is later. For now, though, before we go any further, just a brief word on the question of how the book relates not only to philosophy but also to the domains of spirituality and religion. To be clear, this book makes no claim and passes no judgment on people's personalized paths. Regardless of the routes one pursues towards being, seeing, and doing better, our model is inclusive insofar as it ascribes to the principles of (1) equifinality and (2) pragmatism. First, that there are many ways of conceptualizing and communicating its tools so that one size (or set of terminology) does not necessarily have to fit all. Thus you should feel free to adapt the dialog to your creed or code accordingly. Second, that as long as the core elements are solid then the vehicles through which they are processed can vary. In a word, that the model can be used in a manner consistent with whatever works best for you, your followers, and your surroundings. Thus you should feel free to choose or emphasize whichever parts of the toolbox that can help you the most in your conditions and context.

So, to paraphrase philosopher Lao Tsu as discussed by theorist management Karl Weick (from the 2007 Foreword to the *Handbook of Organizational and Managerial Wisdom* on pp. ix–xiii): "In pursuit of knowledge, every day something is acquired; In pursuit of wisdom, every day something is dropped." Please take the model you are about to read about and consider its insights in the light of your circumstances and preferences. Then tailor them to make them your own. And then evolve them into your unique way to thrive and to lead others to thrive.

Connecting Wisdom and Leadership

Leadership, like wisdom, is also a cool word worthy of drumrolls or similar stage-setting crescendos.

We have placed an aura around the ideal of leadership, and rightly so. Leaders, by the nature of the role, often bear an asymmetrical burden and exert an outsized impact upon the course of their organizations' events. It is this dynamic that has inspired countless models, modes, and methods for describing its relationships and professing its secrets. Indeed, a Google search (conducted in July 2019) of the term 'leadership' garnered over 6.5 billion hits (plus over four million research documents) and a similar Amazon search turns up over 60,000 related books on the subject. In addition, a brief survey of popular textbooks on leadership – e.g., those authored by respected scholars Daft (2014), DuBrin (2018), Northouse (2018), and Yukl (2012) – reveals that leadership has been defined in ways too numerous to catalogue coherently.

18 Discovering Your Leadership Wisdom

As a result the leadership literature is difficult to coalesce. And this creates problems. Conceptually, what is its true definition? Practically, what is its best method? Pedagogically, how does one teach it and develop it?

Perhaps instead of perpetually muddying the waters with new studies and terminology we need instead to become still for a moment. This way we can avoid getting caught up in its torrents but instead see deeper and clearer the foundation of its streams of thought.

It is my contention here that this foundation lies in wisdom.

Wisdom and leadership are necessarily yet abstractly symbiotic. For example, there are at least three discernible genres of recent investigations as to their intersection. They can be characterized as the 'integrative' approach of Ardelt, the 'developmental' approach of Baltes and colleagues, and the 'balanced approach of Sternberg.

Monika Ardelt (2000, 2004) suggests that wisdom embodies an *integrative* leadership dynamic. At its essence this means that wise individuals are able to synthesize cognitive (knowing and comprehending), reflective (perspective and introspection), and affective (compassion and empathy) dimensions. Wisdom, as compared to knowledge, therefore involves a more fundamental understanding of one's world and one's place in it.

Paul Baltes and colleagues (2000, 2004) suggest that wisdom embodies a *developmental* leadership dynamic. At its essence this means that wise individuals are able to process several antecedent conditions and perform along emergent criteria. Based on contextual-, domain-, and person-specific factors, people and collectives can become wiser. Wisdom, as compared to knowledge, therefore involves an evolving metaheuristic to orchestrate mind and virtue in the fundamental pragmatics of life.

Robert Sternberg (1990, 2003) suggests that wisdom embodies a *balancing* leadership dynamic. At its essence this means that wise individuals are able to utilize their intelligence, creativity, and knowledge, as mediated by core values, to adapt to, shape, and select environments and reach a common good. Wisdom, as compared to knowledge, therefore involves a higher order juxtaposition and operation to satisfy relevant stakeholder interests over the short and long terms. Taken together, wisdom can be seen to involve different competencies, combinatory dynamics, and uses.

These have been since supplemented by a number of promising lines of inquiry. For example, Christopher Peterson and Martin Seligman's (2004) conceptualization of 'Character Strengths' corresponds to the above both directly – in their identification of wisdom – and indirectly – in the delineation of other wisdom-based attributes in complementary categories. Further to this, Susan Bluck and Judith Gluck (2005) reconcile wisdom as a conglomeration of component categories, and Ursula Staudinger and colleagues (2005) see it as a desirable yet rare quality for those rising to leadership positions. John Shotter and Haridimos Tsoukas (2014) see it as a practical (i.e., "phronesis") application of capacity to judgment.

Paul Bierly and colleagues (2000) see it as a hierarchical learning dynamic. Bernard McKenna and colleagues (2009) see it manifest in a set of principles used to navigate organizations in a complex world.

Each of these efforts, though distinct, combines to highlight the need to dynamically integrate different dimensions of wisdom. Together they point to the need to return to leadership's philosophical core, and so to clearly and consistently synthesize relevant insights and contingencies. As per Joullie's (2016) sentiment: "Managers ... benefit from an appreciation and at least rudimentary understanding of philosophy, and that no management education is complete if it is not anchored in its understanding." This discernment is intensified when applied to leadership.

However, we need to overcome several challenges first before arriving at the synthesis.

Among the biggest of them, in words of the economist, is the pesky imbalance between the supply and demand of wisdom.

A Disheartening and Deteriorating Disequilibrium

The intersection of wisdom and leadership is elusive. As suggested earlier, there is a general misunderstanding about wisdom and, as a result, an expanding misalignment of the supply and demand curves of its development and deployment. This imbalance is both perpetuating and exacerbating a dangerous disequilibrium where leaders look to meet an increasingly complex and dangerous set of challenges with a limited set of tools. In a word, at a time when we need leadership wisdom the most, we are traveling a path that compromises rather than evolves it.

It doesn't get any more basic, any Economics 101-ish, than supply and demand. Wisdom is in high demand ... and our need for wisdom is growing. Wisdom is also in short supply ... and our capacity for wisdom is stunted if not outright shrinking. As indicated in Figure 1.1, this is an (im)perfect storm indeed.

First, there is a high demand for wisdom. In a word, we very much need wisdom at every level of our leadership. It is ubiquitous. It relates to us performing and growing as individuals. To enhancing our interactions at work and in families, friendships, and communities. To enhancing our organizations and businesses. To enhancing our states and societies, and in our social, governmental, and economic programs. To enhancing our world and in our international, environment, geopolitical, and cultural endeavors. In short, where there are humans and collections of people, there is a need for wisdom.

The need for wisdom is also critical. Insofar as wisdom relates to BEING, SEEING, and DOING (discussed later in the book in great detail), it enhances leadership performance and differentiates winners from the also-rans. Wisdom connotes superior intellectual and emotional capabilities, sharper internal and external insight, more productive deployment of resources. As such, it drives

20 Discovering Your Leadership Wisdom

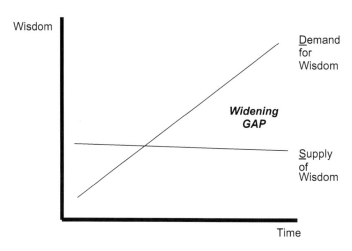

FIGURE 1.1 The Supply and Demand of Wisdom.

bottom-line results. It also facilitates 'softer' metrics of success such as satisfaction and well-being.

But more than this, the curve suggests that not only is there a high demand for wisdom in our leadership, it is also growing. In our age of dynamism, with rapidly evolving and frame-breaking changes, we cannot simply rely on what has worked in the recent past. In our age of complexity, with the exponentially expanding range and interaction of a multiplicity of forces, we cannot myopically and stoically manage single leverage points. In our age of interdependence, with emerging and intensifying networks of linkages, we cannot isolate divergent issues and impacts. In our age of empowerment, with pronounced flattening of dispersed nodes of influence, we cannot push univocal agendas. In our age of uncertainty, with a pronounced lack of familiarity and predictability, we cannot lock in or double down too much.

As such, the demand for leadership wisdom can be seen to be high and growing.

Second, there is a (relatively) low supply of wisdom. We often lack enough wisdom in our leadership to deal with these challenges because, frankly, it requires a lot of work, as well as the breaking of old habits and the discarding of outmoded crutches, and this does not appeal to many. We also tend to lack wisdom in our leadership because, well, it is nuanced. This runs counter to general preferences for simple and pre-packaged solutions. However, in a world that is increasingly less simple, straightforward, one-dimensional, or amenable to the quick fix or magic bullet, this is problematic. Moreover, we often lack wisdom in our leadership because it is intangible. That is to say its properties tend not to be easily defined by simple numbers or common language.

Not only is there a relatively lower supply of wisdom, the curve suggests that it is also in many ways shrinking. That is to say we are becoming relatively less prepared and insufficiently rewarded for wisdom. Our systems and schools are decreasingly designed to inspire or develop it. Blind memorization and mechanical rote do not help approximate wisdom. Our institutions and (social) networks are decreasingly not set up to esteem or reward it. Clever banters and divisive rhetoric do not help or approximate wisdom. Instead they stereotype versus educate; obscure versus illuminate; fracture versus unify, and limit versus liberate our capacities.

As such, the supply of leadership wisdom can be seen to be low and shrinking.

This disequilibrium begets and is subsequently exacerbated by a particularly cruel irony. Reminiscent of Plato's (as per Jowett, 2008: see Plato's Republic) cave, we do not necessarily esteem those who are wisest among us. The educational and vocational paths that build wisdom are not in any systematic way related to those that offer the most pay, power, fame, or fortune (for a particularly poignant example consider the earnings of philosophy majors and teachers). Those who are the most far-sighted, moral, and uniting are often dismissed in favor of, or even at the behest of, those who are more short-term, selfish, and acrimonious. It is a paradox that perplexed Plato and continues to haunt us today. Why do we not promote the very thing that we need the most? Will Rogers was right – common sense isn't always common practice.

So what to do … Weep? Give up? Tune out? Simply settle?

NO!

The imbalance of high demand and low supply of wisdom presents not only a problem but also a wonderful opportunity. We cannot stop or slow the demand curve for wisdom in our leaders, but we can and must rise up to meet its slope by increasing the supply. In doing so we need to break from the K.I.D. prison and find a different way. Consistent with developments in the field of 'positive psychology', we can focus not on what is wrong (the problem or disease) but what can be right (how to get healthier). And in line with the spirit of what has become known as 'positive management', we can utilize proven frameworks and time-tested approaches not only for critique but also for enhancement. To create the capacity. To crystalize the vision. To enable the execution. We need to refocus on wisdom in order to meet our challenges, embrace our opportunities, and foster personal and professional success of ourselves as leaders and for those who we lead.

In some of my notorious pun-laden language, which when I speak about the topic has received some of the most enthusiastic responses (as well as the loudest groans), we need to 'Wise and Shine'!

Wise and Shine

There are at least two major implications of the above imbalance. The first is in the here-and-now. This explains the gap. The second is over time. This explains why the gap is growing.

The Here-And-Now Gap (Leadership 'Snapshot')

First, in the hear-and-now, we too often obscure the nature of wisdom, and our leadership is therefore missing the mark.

In examining modern organizational and institutional trends, knowledge management can be seen as a dominant force in the foundational business landscape. We see this in the 1980s and 1990s with the emergence of the Chief Knowledge Officer (CKO) and derivative leadership training programs. We see this in the 1990s and 2000s with the emergence of the Chief Information Officer (CIO) and derivative leadership IT systems and related initiatives. We see this in the 2000s and 2010s with the emergence of the Chief Data Officer (CDO) where 'big data' is penetrating nearly every discipline in the business school and deliberation in the corporate boardroom.

We have partially traversed the ladder. But there is one more important step we must take (as indicated in Figure 1.2). To a Chief Wisdom Officer (CWO).

Yet, as the aforementioned trend suggests, as our questions get bigger and bigger our thinking seems to get smaller and smaller ... and hence more removed from the foundationally philosophical inquiries that enable the very competencies and contingencies required to succeed in the modern landscape. Thus as per the above we are in many ways moving down, not up, the hierarchy – i.e., going in precisely the wrong direction – and as such moving further away from wisdom.

To reiterate, wisdom is not just more training but instead reaped from true education. After all, education comes from the ancient Greek term 'educari' or to draw forth (just like Michelangelo did with his sculptures, versus artificially inserting something from outside).

Training is at best about increasing our knowledge. Typical of traditional pedagogies. And it has its use and its place. But when applied to leadership it tends

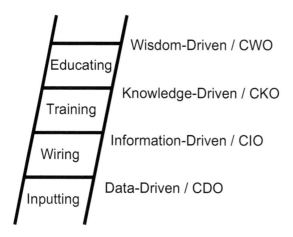

FIGURE 1.2   Snapshot: Climbing the Wisdom Ladder.

to rely too much on rigid dicta like: Memorize names and dates. Methodize theories and models. Rehearse algorithms and techniques. Training thus tends to produce minions and middle-managers. Tools and technicians. Accessories and automatons. Resources and robots. Limited in growth, bounded by schema, and fearful of change.

By contrast, education is about increasing our wisdom. Creating and illuminating experiences. Wisdom is found in the process of how to think and how to feel. In seeing who we are, and where we are, and what we should be doing. In big-picture marshaling and effective deploying of capabilities. True education can thus produce engaged, elucidated executives. Visionaries and value-enhancers. Lovers and leaders. Creators of new systems. Elevating lives. Constantly growing, breaking frames, and shaping change.

It is true that most do not ever turn their marble into masterpiece. By educating for wisdom, we can change the situation.

The Growing Gap (Leadership 'Cinema')

Second, over time, we are institutionalizing a system that gets us further and further afield from bridging this gap.

As indicated in Figure 1.3, wisdom can be understood as simultaneously both a state of being and as a way of engaging. The former, which is more common, recognizes that one can have more or less cumulative wisdom. However, in the

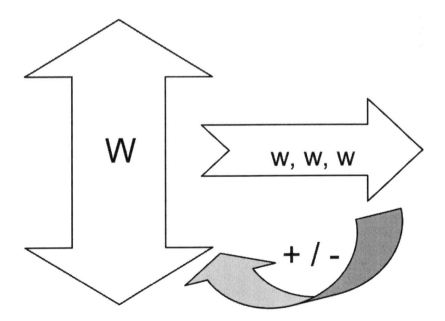

FIGURE 1.3 Cinema: Mastering the Wisdom Cycle.

24 Discovering Your Leadership Wisdom

latter, insofar as wisdom is also a process, we can use or misuse it, direct or mis-direct it, and grow or lose it, through our behavior in various situations over time. Thus we must realize that wisdom, akin to energy, is potential and kinetic. One must be able to build potential capacity (being), realize and connect that capacity (seeing), and kinetically engage it appropriately (doing) for immediate and long-term progress. Any breaks in the cycle (see Figure 1.3 from Kessler & Bailey, 2007) disable the system. Without sufficient potential for it we cannot be strong enough. Without exercising discerning vision of it we cannot see well enough. Without effective action with it we cannot do well enough. It is this fundamental interplay between acquiring and utilizing wisdom that powers its cumulative, sustainable development.

To further explain the above, consider Rafael's masterpiece *School of Athens* (which is one of my favorite paintings ... and incidentally includes the likeness of Michelangelo as one of its characters). In it you will see depictions of 'wise men' Plato and Aristotle having what looks like an important conversation. Plato is pointing upward arguing that there are universal, carved-in-stone capital 'T' Truths in the world. These are absolute. They are ideal truths towards which we can only hope to aspire, whether in our thinking and science, faith and prayers, reflections and medications, etc. Plato's semi-rebellious student Aristotle is point-ing down to the ground making the case that lowercase 't' truths are in fact more relative to the situation. Sometimes an approach will work but other times, in other places, or with other people or problems, the same approach will fail miser-ably. Thus what is true for some cultures, in some industries, or at some points in your life will not be the case in others. These truths vary based on the particular circumstance.

Me, I think both have a point. C'mon, we are talking about Plato and Aristotle here. My approach however, when encountering seemingly contradictory ideas such as these, is usually to search for the way in which they can be blended. What unites them. The bigger issue or system of which the views are a part. Here are my two cents (or, to keep in character, drachmas) on the matter.

There is something beyond our immediate concept that seems to underlie how things are and how things work. Einstein spoke of this as his quest to understand the laws of the universe, or, as he put it, to know but a small piece of the mind of God. But in our daily lives we must act. We must survive. Here-and-now we must eat, talk, navigate, negotiate, perform, and produce. And for these there are rules that work. They are usually contingent rules, which is to say that 'it depends', and the trick is to then find out what things depend on. If the light turns green then go. But if you are in London you drive on a different side of the street than if in New York. If your partner says 'yes' then the deal is done. But if you are in Tokyo the reply might merely be a courtesy or a signal of understanding, not agreement. So perhaps there are Truths to aspire towards but the path might be processed through the many nuanced truths we confront and learn from.

Now what does all this have to do with wisdom? Well, the same arguments hold and we must account for the duality that there is both a capital Wisdom and lowercase wisdoms. One can have more or less cumulative wisdom. This is the potential from which we can draw. It is also a process. At any time we can use (leverage) or misuse it (ignore). We can find (see) or miss it (be blind). We can build (grow) or lose it (regress). Thus we must stay focused on the big picture but at the same time succeed in the smaller scenes that define our engagements. This is the wisdom cycle. It represents both snapshot and cinema. The inseparable interplay between acquiring and utilizing wisdom. And the virtual or vicious cycles that result.

As another example, consider the accumulated insights of *Time Magazine*'s annual 'Most Influential' lists. In analyzing the more than one thousand people whose influence has been deemed most lasting and significant, the following results, if you will forgive yet another pun, jump off the page: Over 90 percent of the most influential leaders have appeared only a single time. One and done. Moreover, when one examines the 'pioneer' subcategory of leaders – the truest of visionaries – only 2 percent have found their way back onto the list in more than a single instance. We can conclude from this that, among other things, although it is hard to approximate wise leadership it is even harder to continuously grow and sustain it. As argued previously this will continue to be a challenge in increasingly complex and dynamic times.

So what to do?

We need to RISE up the wisdom ladder.

We need to SHINE our wisdom on our worlds and turn its vicious cycles into virtuous ones.

We need to 'wise and shine'.

A Roadmap for 'Wise Leadership'

It is one thing to identify the problem. It is another to figure out a way to solve it.

If one strips away the increasingly opaque terminologies and mythologies that tend to obscure more than they clarify then we might reveal that, because leadership is inherently a job, it entails a discernible set of activities and requisite competencies which are differentially malleable across context. As such, like any other job, and as per classical contingency perspectives, an individual needs to use the right 'tools' applied in the right way and in the right circumstances to succeed at it.

Thus through this book you will discover several things. How to identify the six primary CHALLENGES that leaders face. How to then assemble and use a set of core leadership TOOLS to solve each challenge. And, by doing this continuously and cumulatively, how to set out on a path to continuously grow your strengths, fix your weaknesses, and put yourself on that rare arc of sustained leadership success.

These six tools comprise what we call the 'Leader's Toolbox'.

They have been forged from the strongest steel of history's greatest wisdom – the philosophical foundations that define the major challenges of our collective journey. They have also been time-tested in the hottest fire of humanity's greatest successes – the profound achievements of the most influential real and idealized leaders who have proven themselves across a multitude of eras, tasks, and locations.

Here is a more detailed description of the book's plan for approximating them.

First, as begun in the introduction, we outline the nature and need for wise leadership. Wisdom is profoundly different from data-, information-, and knowledge-based leadership paradigms. Central to this book is that we need to 'dig deeper' by rediscovering leadership's foundational philosophical core.

Second, the tools for wise leadership are sourced from primary questions crystallized by the different branches of philosophic (philos-sophia – 'love of wisdom') inquiry and manifest in the subsequent competency sets that asymmetrically impact the fundamental contingencies of humankind's collective journey. Leaders can therefore be more or less wise in enacting multiple identity domains: Logic, and being a leadership scientist; Aesthetics, and being a leadership artist; Ethics, and being a leadership icon; Metaphysics, and being a leadership advocate; Epistemology, and being a leadership maestro; and Politics, and being a leadership general.

Third, these tools are mapped onto the range of leaders' primary challenges. These callings provide the guideposts for utilizing the aforementioned tools: Through the solving of intellectual- and inspirational-related challenges; through the solving of character- and purpose-related challenges; and through the solving of collaboration and execution-related challenges. Together they offer insights into the complementary, contingent leadership capacities that leaders must leverage to be sustainably successful in and across situations. Effective leaders adapt to fit the demands of the different situations they face. The more effective the leader the more (1) comprehensive their range and (2) precise their application.

Fourth, we will reconcile the framework with existing academic theories of leadership to stitch them together. For example, each theory of leadership identified in the reader's guide of the *Encyclopedia of Management Theory* (as per Kessler, 2013b) will be related to the aforementioned tools and challenges to show how readers should not ask themselves 'which theory of leadership is best' but instead 'when is each theory of leadership most useful'.

Fifth, we will illustrate the model by weaving in diverse, prominent examples of leadership success. Here we will overlay our lens onto our 'greatest' leaders as revealed in (1) REAL (evidenced via *Time Magazine*'s 'Most Influential' lists) and (2) IDEALIZED (evidenced via the American Film Institute's 'Greatest Movie Heroes' lists) archetypes that hold across multiple leadership contexts and domains of engagement.

Sixth, we will then describe how modern leaders can understand, customize, and then use the best practices of the above. The coming pages will detail these tools – their features, their fundamentals, and the best practices for using them efficiently and effectively. More than this they will show you exactly what each tool does and why they do it, help you understand when and where the tools should be used, and through a collection of colorful examples and practical guidelines see how each can be developed and applied so that you can succeed as a leader no matter what challenges you are confronted with.

Bottom Line – You can learn how to be an effective leader in any situation. This book will show you how.

2

THE JOURNEY

Paths for Exploring Leadership

Leadership is complex and confusing
But its essence can be boiled down
To a few key components

Much has been written about leadership. And many people – academics, executives, coaches, administrators, politicos, pundits, etc. – have attempted to map its territory.

Yet taken together these efforts are so varied that they tend to obscure more than they elucidate.

But this doesn't have to be the case.

In this chapter you will first be taken on a bird's-eye tour of the many different approaches that have been taken in the search for answers about leadership.

Here we will characterize three different types of paths – good, better, and best – that have been blazed through its proverbial jungle for making sense of the vast research literature.

You will then be shown how they can be combined and clarified to suggest a common way forward.

Specifically, the journey will be framed as follows:

- Exploring Leadership
- (Good) Path 1: Leadership Chronologies – A Punctuated Progression
- (Better) Path 2: Leadership Categories – Two Fundamental Questions
- (Best) Path 3: Leadership Competencies – Key Insights from Theory to Practice
- So … Essential Leadership Roles
- With … Core Leadership Identities
- Okay, What Does This All Mean?

Exploring Leadership

When we are faced with a confusing, growing imbalance between the demand and supply of leadership wisdom (see Chapter 1 for more about this), we are forced to look for help.

What has been said about the matter that can be used to make sense of this incredibly important but at the same time incredibly confusing field?

The most natural place to turn to for answers is what is normally termed the leadership 'literature'. This is essentially a catalog or record of the different scholarly as well as professional approaches where many have entered to study the topic. The problem is that by doing this the leadership literature has grown incredibly vast and become incredibly diverse. As a result, its explanations tend to run past each other and champion contradictory callings.

We will therefore turn to a creative methodology for figuring it out. In his famous 1972 book *Essence of Decision* Harvard political historian Graham Allison retells the story of the Cuban Missile Crisis using three increasingly sophisticated lenses to explain the same series of events. In doing this he helps his readers break their shackles of traditional ways of thinking and supersede traditional, overly simplistic templates. This in turn shows them how to uncover unseen but fundamental principles that lie beneath the familiar story that, when they are revealed, help explain, predict, and ultimately manage these forces.

Here I adapt Allison's approach and focus it on the highly familiar but existentially elusive phenomenon of leadership. As such this will not be just another tome on leading but instead something entirely different. Not one that stops at a basic, surface survey. Not one that even stops at a rudimentary thematic template. Instead it will be one that digs deeper to actually uncover the hidden principles that drive (or, if misunderstood and misapplied, undermine) leadership success.

Thus, similar to Allison, we will tell the story of leadership through three increasingly revealing lenses.

First, we will briefly touch upon the simplest but at the same time the most numbing of templates, the CHRONOLOGICAL map of leadership thought.

This is a good place to start. It is also a bad place to finish. As such the chronological approach has become regarded as a classic straw-man (i.e., a flimsy construction meant to collapse under the slightest of critical winds) that is all too common in traditional leadership dictionary descriptions but rarer in more advanced thinking circles. If someone attempts to explain leadership to you through this chronological approach, then they are simply taking the easiest trail by marking the temporal lineage of who said what when. It is essentially a one-dimensional timeline that is meant for acolytes to abide by. Students to memorize. Or historians to pinpoint and plot major eras, movements, and figures. There is some descriptive value here for sure but little else in terms of analysis, evaluation, or synthesis.

Second, from this we will move to the slightly more advanced, but correspondingly more dangerous, CATEGORICAL approach of leadership thought.

30 Discovering Your Leadership Wisdom

This is the most common circuitous trail taken in conventional leadership textbooks and academic readers. If someone attempts to explain leadership to you through this approach then they are simply comparing and contrasting different theoretical models of leadership based on one or more surface characteristics. For example, typical classroom schemas of this ilk focus on trait- versus behavior-focused theories and/or universalistic- versus contingency-oriented theories. As such the discussion usually devolves into a boiled-down two-dimensional descriptive schematic. The limitations of such an approach are numerous and include the tendency to pile conceptual terminology upon even more conceptual terminology with confusing disclaimers and boundary conditions resembling the small print found at the bottom of impenetrable legal contracts.

More than this, though, an even greater danger to the true learner of leadership is that they present leadership models as competing paradigms. That is, the reader typically leaves with the suggestion that they have to select a preferred model over other models and then abide by its prescriptions alone to achieve wonderful results. However, and as will soon be shown, it more often than not fails to appreciate the value of looking at theories as complementary pieces, instead of competing paradigms, where each offers limited yet corresponding insights into constructing a more complete and accurate picture of what it means to lead.

Third, we will raise the bar and conclude with a less traditional but infinitely more useful COMPETENCY-based method.

If someone attempts to explain leadership to you through this approach, they are taking a proverbial machete to the leadership jungle to clear the brush and uncover a better way forward – namely, how the aforementioned perspectives are really synergistic lenses that combine with each other to form a path towards an integrated leader toolbox. That is, instead of getting lost among alternate frameworks or getting caught between warring factions where one must choose sides and give loyalty to one theory or another, our accumulated leadership insights are instead treated as offering complementary resources that both diagnose and solve a wide range of core challenges which leaders tend to come across.

In this sense such a multi-dimensional mapping is both considerably more progressive and practical insofar as it builds on the previous methods and is broadly useful for the actual (or prospective) leader. In doing so, and as teased out earlier in this book, it seeks to delineate a discrete set of higher-order integrative 'meta'- or 'mega'-competencies in terms of (1) identifying what these precise capabilities are and (2) how to synergistically align and deploy their corresponding tools depending on the context. It thus bears emphasizing that this approach is most consistent with the idea that a key skill of leaders is making sense of the different situations that confront them and drawing upon the appropriate leadership identities, roles, and behaviors to overcome the obstacles to success.

This is where we are going. But we must get there first.

(Good) Path 1: Leadership Chronologies –
A Punctuated Progression

There have been many false starts for sure in the research into leadership. There have also been many accumulated arcs and departures in the highly fragmented field. Compounding this there has been a plethora of diverse perspectives overlaid onto the field that render any meaningful timeline of leadership nonlinear and highly disjunctive.

If we turn to one of the many texts that new students of leadership might be asked to read – such as Daft, DuBrin, Northouse, or Yukl – then we might find convenient, easily packageable ways for introducing some of the most generic movements in the field. For example, tables of contents might group and present the evolution of ideas about leadership under the era labels of 'Traits, Behaviors, and Relationships' and 'Contingency Approaches to Leadership', or perhaps 'Leadership Behaviors, Attitudes, and Styles'.

Such a retrospective accounting of the general eras of leadership models may be of most interest to historians or those who wish to construct a movie documentary on the field's growth (good luck selling tickets for this yawner!). For example, using information by which to chronicle the major theories of leadership in the order in which they popularly emerged in the mainstream literature (Kessler, 2013b), we might find something like that shown in Table 2.1.

TABLE 2.1 Chronology of Major Leadership Theories

Year	Theory
Pre-1950s	Charismatic Theory of Leadership
	Trait Theory of Leadership
1950s and 1960s	Leadership Continuum Theory
	Theory X and Y
	Managerial Grid
	Contingency Theory of Leadership
	Leader–Member Exchange (LMX) Theory
	Situational Theory of Leadership
1970s	Path–Goal Theory of Leadership
	Servant Leadership
	Transformational Theory of Leadership
	Substitutes for Leadership
	Attribution Model of Leadership
1980s	Leadership Practices
	Cognitive Resource Theory
Post-2000s	Level-5 Leadership
	Authentic Leadership
	Competing Values Framework

32 Discovering Your Leadership Wisdom

Do you feel knowledgeable about leadership by reading this? Probably not.

Will memorizing and then parroting it back on an exam, at a job interview, or at a board meeting help you or the organization succeed? Again, probably not.

It is nice to know what people have done. However, a precursory familiarity with names and dates might be at times necessary but it is certainly never sufficient. A timeline is a tad more useful than the more generic 'leadership eras' approach simply by virtue of its increased granularity and greater detail. But this still does not help us see where theories came from, or how they fit together, or reasonably project where their totality might take us. Moreover, a chronology does not convey a sense of essential message or overall integration. Pay attention to it in order to pass your class or dazzle at the department cocktail party ... but feel able to quickly discard it thereafter and free up valuable neurons for more interesting, and useful, analyses.

(Better) Path 2: Leadership Categories – Two Fundamental Questions

As the preceding text suggests, it is not much use or fun navigating the jungle of personalities, professionals, and pundits that peddle their different advice on leadership. In fact, this is getting worse with the explosion of narrowly derivative academic studies (for example, testing these models for each and every demographic, cultural, and otherwise incident variable that will allow a research to publish a technical article and one day get tenure) and poorly grounded how-to stories (for example, the lessons of every manager, coach, organizer, and the like who feel that their personal styles and circumstances should be the standard for you to admire and emulate). As a result, it can be downright dizzying wandering through the leadership lists populating bookstores, texts, and websites that propagate and promote a seemingly endless stream of competing 'here today, gone tomorrow' leadership theories and trends.

A clear, coherent, time-tested model that is both firmly grounded in research and readily applicable to real-world practice is hard to come by. However, by examining the competing perspectives that prior research stakes out we can take a proverbial machete to this jungle and better understand how the subject of leadership has been explored. When push comes to shove, leaders influence organizational performance and that of their members in a myriad but finite number of ways. A review of the vast literature on leadership reveals several broad-based patterns. More specifically, two primary dimensions can be seen to underscore the primary research to date on the topic of leadership. This is captured in Kessler (2010.)

First, consider this following question: Is leadership a noun or a verb? This is an effort to figure out where leadership resides – in a person as a function of their characteristics, or instead as a derivative of their actions. The former (leadership seen more as a noun) suggests that it is essentially a composite or amalgam

The JOURNEY: Exploring Leadership **33**

of more or less optimally arranged character traits that are largely intrinsic and innate. That is to say, some leaders possess the proverbial 'right stuff', and the best leaders possess it in greater degrees, whereas others are hopelessly destined to be less proficient. The latter (leadership seen more as a verb) suggests that it is essentially a process or interrelated set of skilled behaviors that can be executed more or less ably. Thus leaders can be shown how to lead better.

Second, consider this corresponding question: Is leadership universal or contingent? This is an effort to figure out what type of leadership is called for in a given context. The former option (universal) suggests that there is 'one best way' to lead and this applies anywhere, at any time, with anyone, and on anything. That is to say, there is a universal playbook that, if properly followed, differentiates better from worse leaders. The latter option (contingent) suggests that leaders must skillfully diagnose and adapt to complex, situation-specific sets of factors for becoming more or less successful. Thus there is an art as well as a science to leaders who must be able to diagnose relevant circumstances – e.g., varying across cultures, eras, followers, tasks, and the like – and execute appropriate interventions in order to succeed in the short term as well as remain sustainably successful over time.

When the two aforementioned questions are operationalized and plotted against one another a 2×2 diagram can be constructed (see Table 2.2) that encapsulates the main thrusts of leadership thought. These quadrants are both logically as well as temporally distinct.

In Quadrant 'A' we locate Universal Trait approaches to leadership. These are among the oldest in the literature and are exemplified by what have been colloquially termed 'great-man' theories. They appeal primarily to those who cling to concepts of genetically based or physiologically enhanced uber-leaders. In recent times they have often been referenced in tandem with research on personality (e.g., Big-5, HEXACO theories), intelligence (e.g., cognitive and emotional), and charisma insofar as these are conceptualized as inherently trait-based and related

TABLE 2.2 Categorization of Major Leadership Themes

Context Person	Universal	Contingent
Trait	Quadrant A Assumption: Leaders are born Key Implication: How to find them	Quadrant C Assumption: Leaders are fit Key Implication: How to place them
Behavior	Quadrant B Assumption: Leaders are skilled Key Implication: How to train them	Quadrant D Assumption: Leaders are dynamic Key Implication: How to educate them

34 Discovering Your Leadership Wisdom

to leadership performance. Here leaders are ultimately seen as born, or in modern times perhaps cloned, and as a result the key success factor is to find these precious diamonds in the rough.

In Quadrant 'B' (coincidentally but not without irony, this is the predominant approach ascribed to by B-Schools) we locate Universal Behavior approaches to leadership. These represent the gaggle of models that propose leadership recipes for constructing and acting like a leader – for example, with regard to task and relationship competencies as well as other proficiencies. Specific theories of this ilk tend to focus on particular manifest patterns or advocated styles such as servant leadership, level-5 leadership, or authentic leadership. Here leaders are ultimately seen as sufficiently skilled and, as a result, the key success factor is to train them on the aforementioned dimensions.

In Quadrant 'C' we locate Contingent Trait approaches to leadership. These spring from classic work by Fiedler and colleagues who put forth that we possess durable leadership preferences and profiles that may be a better or worse fit in different situations. Here leaders are ultimately seen as fit and, as a result, the key success factor is to place them appropriately so that their inflexible profiles match their unchangeable situations.

In Quadrant 'D' we locate Contingent Behavior approaches to leadership. These are among the most complex but also the most useful theoretical approaches insofar as they chart if-then decision points that leaders must navigate, such as with regard to the differential demands of diverse followers, tasks, domains, and corporate as well as national cultures. They are represented by frameworks such as Hersey and Blanchard's situational theory of leadership and House's path-goal theory of leadership. Here leaders are ultimately seen as sufficiently dynamic and, as a result, the key implication is to educate them on how to read situations and dynamically adapt their behavior to fit them.

All in all, the different categories of leadership theories present a better resource than simple chronologies … but still it falls short of what we need in a number of critical ways. Right off the top, it still does little to resolve the fragmented face put on the leadership literature. However, most central to these shortcomings is the fact that they portray an either-or adversarial ethos between the different approaches to model leadership. There remains the manifest need for a unifying paradigm, a methodology for weaving their lessons together, and a set of complementary principles that can provide the modern leader with a more complete but understandable template for making sense of their environment and doing their job well within it.

(Best) Path 3: Leadership Competencies –
Key Insights from Leadership Theory

As per the reasoning articulated by physicists such as the late great Stephen Hawking (Hawking & Mlodinow, 2010: 8, 58) and later applied to the field of management, a grand understanding of leadership reality: (1) appreciates that our models are cumulative approximations that build from and on each other but in different directions, (2) identifies each aspect of their domains of influence, and (3) embraces systems mentality whereby each theory applies to a complementary aspect of leadership. More specifically (as per Kessler & Bartunek, 2014: 238):

> [A] grand understanding of our reality weaves different models to harmoniously integrate the small maps into a larger, more comprehensive one. The Hawking and Mlodinow presentation of M-theory is based in the belief that "most laws of nature exist as part of a larger, interconnected system of laws" (p. 28). As per Hawking and Mlodinow: M-theory is not a theory in the usual sense. It is a whole family of different theories, each of which is a good description of observations only in some range of physical situations. It is a bit like a map.... To faithfully map the entire earth, one has to use a collection of maps, each of which covers a limited region. The maps overlap each other, and where they do, they show the same landscape. M-theory is similar. The different theories in the M-theory family may look very different, but they can all be regarded as aspects of the same underlying theory ... applicable only in limited ranges.... But just as there is no flat map that is a good representation of the earth's entire surface, there is no single theory that is a good representation of observations in all situations.... Each theory in the M-theory network is good at describing phenomena within a certain range. Wherever their ranges overlap, the various theories in the network agree, so they can all be said to be parts of the same theory.
>
> What might scholars do to adapt a physics based M-theory to management? We suggest, following Kessler, that it would involve the creation of a hierarchical series of maps. These maps would be based on "stitching" different management theories together in ways that (1) across multiple layers of theorizing, present a more panoramic perspective of their complementary, interrelated landscapes and then (2) combine to synthesize these layers and their evolutions over time in a way that eventually reveals one all-inclusive metamap.

From a pluralistic or meta-theoretical perspective (see Campbell, 1969; Tsoukas, 1994) different research models that fall within the above purviews are best seen not as irreconcilable alternatives but instead as considering different pieces of the larger leadership picture. Accordingly, to embrace a pluralistic approach to leadership we must resist the temptation to obscure the topic by dividing it up into atomized, segmented tribes (re: chronology) and camps (re: categories), each focusing on parts of the big picture. This causes us to lose the holistic grasp of leadership as a complex professional practice. In other words, an integrative leadership framework would preserve all the richness of existing theories but provide

36 Discovering Your Leadership Wisdom

the means for stitching together the plurality of their 'micro' theoretical maps into a unified, overarching 'macro' shared sphere.

A key take-away for both leadership scholars and practitioners is thus to discover how various leadership theories complement each other. For example, when leaders are unidimensional and good at one thing – i.e., the proverbial 'one-trick ponies' – then personal adaptability is relaxed and they must be placed correctly. When contexts are unidimensional and demand one critical skill – i.e., basic 'single-issue' problems – then contextual adaptability is relaxed and leaders must be trained correctly. Notwithstanding, these circumstances are exceptions to the generalized need for global leaders who can adapt to diverse and fluid circumstances.

That is to say, because of a preponderance of evidence (cf., Yukl, 1989) that favors a contingent-behavior approach to leading, we henceforth default to its maxims that (1) leaders must be developed and that (2) this development should be deep- as well as wide-reaching insofar as there are many factors that can impact leadership effectiveness. In short, that modern global leaders are charged with identifying the key challenges they face at different points in time and then activating the appropriate tools to best address them.

One way to delineate these challenges is to combine the major theories of leadership, versus plotting one against the other in a timeline or two-by-two and then arguing which one is better. We do this here by organizing their insights into several themes. Indeed, if leadership is behavioral and contingent, and if these actions can be boiled down into essential types of leadership problems and roles, then we should be able to make sense of the major models of leadership across a discrete set of categories.

To do this we will again turn to the *Encyclopedia of Management Theory* (EMT) but in a different way than when merely considering chronology or methodology. In this 1,000-plus-page compendium of the major theoretical frameworks in the management field there are 18 primary theories of leadership identified in its reader's guide. If you recall, they were listed earlier in this chapter. Each of these theories' core messages is encapsulated in its 'Appendix B – Central Management Insight' and are now reproduced here in the following discussion and graphics, with appropriate emphases added. Together they can be reconciled (albeit imperfectly – these are complex theories with many elements – therefore we use primary themes rather than comprehensive categorizations to highlight similarities) into a general rubric of BEING, SEEING, and DOING.

To movie fans the above labels might be repackaged as Lights-Camera-Action.

BEING better, or enhancing your proverbial LIGHTS, can be seen in theories that discuss both the cognitive as well as emotive aspects of leadership.

First, regarding logic, several core leadership theories can be seen to articulate *cognitive*-oriented messages. These include: (1) Cognitive Resource Theory (Fiedler & Garcia, 1987; Sternberg, 1995) with its emphasis on leader 'smarts', and (2) Trait Theory of Leadership (Bass & Stogdill, 1990; Zaccaro, 2007) with its emphasis on characteristics such as leader intelligence. For example, the

Cognitive Resource Theory emphasizes how leaders can use generalized as well as domain-specific intellectual capacities to make better decisions.

Cognitive Resource Theory	Leaders tend to use their raw *intelligence* to make decisions; however, in some situations, leaders' relevant *experience* strongly contributes to effectiveness.
Trait Theory of Leadership	Leadership emergence and effectiveness is a function of the *exceptional qualities, abilities, or traits* – such as personality and intelligence – which one possesses.

Second, regarding aesthetics, several core leadership theories can be seen to articulate *affective* or emotion-oriented messages. These include: Charismatic Theory of Leadership (Conger & Kanungo, 1998; Weber, 1968) with its emphasis on intrinsic activation; Path-Goal Theory (House, 1996; Wofford & Liska, 1993) with its emphasis on motivational dynamics; and Transformational Theory of Leadership (Bass, 1985; Judge, & Piccolo, 2004) with its emphasis on inspirational processes. For example, regarding the latter, the Transformational Theory of Leadership emphasizes the value of truly inspiring employees rather than relying on transaction-based compliance from rewards and punishments.

Charismatic Theory of Leadership	*Charismatic* leadership is an attribution based on followers' interpretations of their leader's behavior; a set of distinct behaviors leads to this attribution.
Path-Goal Theory of Leadership	Situational factors determine the choice of optimal leader behaviors designed to help remove obstacles and *motivate* employees as they strive to achieve work-related goals.
Transformational Theory of Leadership	Inspiring employees is a better way to achieve your goals than motivating them with rewards and punishments; this power comes from idealized influence, *inspirational* motivation, intellectual stimulation, and individualized consideration.

SEEING better, or enhancing your proverbial CAMERA, can be seen in theories that discuss both the internal as well as external aspects of leadership.

Third, regarding ethics, several core leadership theories can be seen to articulate *internally* oriented messages. These include: Theory X and Y (McGregor, 1960; Schein, 2011) with its emphasis on values; Servant Leadership (Greenleaf, 1977; Liden, Wayne, Zhao, & Henderson, 2008) with its emphasis on humanism and morality, and Authentic Leadership (Gardner, Avolio, Luthans, May, & Walumbwa, 2005; George & Sims, 2007) with its emphasis on genuineness. For example, Authentic Leadership maintains that leaders who remain true to their beliefs and

38 Discovering Your Leadership Wisdom

convictions and display consistency between their words and deeds will foster elevated levels of follower trust and performance.

Theory X and Y	Managers' *assumptions* about human behavior, whether pessimistic (theory x) or optimistic (theory y), tend to result in corresponding patterns of behaviors; managers should assist employees in reaching their full potential.
Servant Leadership	Leaders must make their top priority that of providing followers with the tools and support they need to develop *mutual trust* and reach their *full potential*.
Authentic Leadership	Leaders who remain true to their personal values and convictions and display *consistency* between their words and deeds will foster elevated levels of follower trust and performance.

Fourth, regarding metaphysics, several core leadership theories can be seen to articulate *externally* oriented messages. These include: Competing Values Framework (Cameron, Quinn, DeGraff, & Thakor, 2006; Quinn & Rohrbaugh, 1983) with its emphasis on organizational ideals and intentions as well as Level-5 Leadership (Collins, 2001a, 2001b) with its emphasis on higher order goals and objectives. For example, the importance of vision and mission is integral to messages from both of these models.

Competing Values Framework	In every organization competing and contradictory *values* exist; the most effective organizations, as well as the most effective leaders, are paradoxical – they simultaneously represent and display competing values.
Level-5 Leadership	The pinnacle of executive leadership styles is that of a Level-5 leader who embodies personal humility and strong and willful persistence in pursuing common *goals and objectives*.

DOING better, or enhancing your proverbial ACTION, can be seen in theories that discuss both the pulling- as well as pushing-aspects of leadership.

Fifth, regarding epistemology, several core leadership theories can be seen to articulate unification or *pulling*-oriented messages. These include: Attribution Model of Leadership (Green & Mitchell, 1979; Martinko & Gardner, 1987) with its emphasis on shared explanations, Leader–Member Exchange (LMX) Theory (Graen & Uhl-Bien, 1995; Wayne, Shore, & Liden, 1997) with its emphasis on mutuality and relationships; and Leadership Continuum Theory (Tannenbaum & Massarik, 1950; Tannenbaum & Schmidt, 1973) with its emphasis on parameters of participation and involvement. For example, implicit as well as explicit communicative processes play critical roles across these models.

Attribution Model of Leadership	Leaders' and employees' causal *explanations* for employee performance uniquely and interactively influence performance responses, including future expectations and behaviors.
Leader–Member Exchange (LMX) Theory	A leader develops different exchange *relationships* with his or her subordinates which vary in quality and impact important outcomes.
Leadership Continuum Theory	The range of managerial choices during decision-making efforts can be conceptualized along a continuum, from autocratic to *democratic* approaches, and are more or less appropriate under different conditions.

Sixth, regarding politics, several core leadership theories can be seen to articulate execution or *pushing*-oriented messages. These include: Situational Theory of Leadership (Hersey, Blanchard, & Johnson, 2009; Thompson & Vecchio, 2009) with its emphasis on effectiveness; Contingency Theory of Leadership (Fielder, 1967; Strube & Garcia, 1981) with its emphasis on behavioral fit; Leadership Practices (Kouzes & Posner, 2011, 2012) with its emphasis on practical skills; the Managerial (Leadership) Grid (Blake & Mouton, 1964, 1982) with its emphasis on success criteria; and Substitutes for Leadership (Kerr & Jermier, 1978; Podsakoff, MacKenzie, & Bommer, 1996) with its emphasis on critical performance factors.

Situational Theory of Leadership	Managers can best lead and develop subordinates by using specified leadership *styles* to match a subordinate's level of ability and commitment.
Contingency Theory of Leadership	Leadership *behaviors* will not necessarily yield the same results in all situations; a fit between leadership style and contingency variables is positively related to leadership effectiveness.
Leadership Practices	Leadership is a set of identifiable *skills* and abilities that are available to anyone; leadership is not about who you are; it's about what you do.
Managerial (Leadership) Grid	There are two primary dimensions or orientations in leaders' behavior – concern for production and concern for people – and this resultant leadership style impacts organizational *effectiveness*.
Substitutes for Leadership	There are multiple contextual *factors* that enhance, neutralize, or substitute for relationship-oriented versus task-oriented leadership across three categories: subordinate, task, and organizational characteristics.

All in all, when taking the above theoretical insights into account within a synergistic, competency-based, meta-theoretical framework the leadership jungle can be boiled down into the following truths:

40 Discovering Your Leadership Wisdom

- Leading involves several different types of ROLES, with the effectiveness of these roles dependent on the degree to which they fit the challenge at hand, and
- Leaders must be able to invoke the appropriate IDENTITY to carry out these roles – i.e., to successfully match the right tool to the right job.

Each of these points will now be elaborated.

So ... Essential Leadership Roles

> Leading involves several different types of ROLES with the effectiveness of these roles dependent on the degree to which they fit the challenge at hand.

Leadership is a role. An extremely complex one, comprising several complementary components or 'sub-roles'. Here I attempt synchronicity between models to present a more coherent, comprehensive picture of this. To blend comparable elements between studies – even those that vary across a wide range of methods, mores, and modes – to find a common ground.

So, what are the dimensions of leadership role(s)? Let's start with the classics.

The Classics

What has now been termed 'classic' research on leadership behavior focused on two types of activities – Tasks and Relationships. They are coalesced from several different models, for example: (1) the 'Michigan' stream of Job-Centered and Employee-Centered behaviors, and (2) the 'Ohio State' stream of Initiating Structure and Consideration behaviors. They also relate to Robert Blake and Jane Mouton's as well as Paul Hersey and Ken Blanchard's well-known frameworks described above. All in all, these categories put forth that the leadership role consists of these general dimensions.

As per Andrew DuBrin (2018), task-oriented, production-related role behaviors are characterized by their aim to organize and define jobs by engaging in such activities as assigning specific tasks, specifying procedures to be followed, scheduling work, and clarifying expectations for team members. They embody attitudes and behaviors such as: Adaptability to the situation, direction setting, high performance standards, risk taking and a bias for action, hands-on guidance, asking tough questions, and organizing. In contrast, relationship-oriented, people-related role behaviors are characterized by their aim to create an environment of emotional support, warmth, friendliness, and trust by being friendly and approachable, looking out for members' personal welfare, and doing favors. They embody attitudes and behaviors such as: Openness to opinions, creating inspiration and visibility, satisfying higher-order needs, providing emotional support and encouragement, and promoting principles and values.

The JOURNEY: Exploring Leadership **41**

Supporting the above is Gary Yukl's (2002) consolidating of research on leadership behaviors, or 'what leaders do', to develop a 'hierarchical taxonomy' of what he terms 'metacategories' that are grounded in past scholarship. These essentially reinforce classic ideas of task and relationship roles along with adding consideration of change-oriented behaviors that extend task actions across both operational and innovative dimensions of action.

The Mainstream

Building on these classics are more recent leadership role models. And like their predecessors they can be seen to voice views which, when aggregated and integrated, are highly consistent and gel with those set out in this book. Here are two examples.

Tom Rath's 2007 'StrengthsFinder' model, later extended in 2009 with Barrie Conchie to the domain of 'Strengths-Based Leadership', proposes different domains of leadership. Whereas they posit leadership strengths as relatively fixed within individuals (which runs counter to the developmental approach of this book but might ring true for those less flexible, lower growth-oriented individuals), they do recognize that effective team leadership must contain all of the elements in a balanced, complementary manner. Although they recognize but four of these domains of leadership, the others come into view when accounting for what they term the basic needs of followers. Witness the overlap:

	HERE	THERE
1.	Head	The 'strategic thinking' domain
2.	Heart	The 'influence' domain and 'compassion' need
3.	Inside	The 'trust' need
4.	Outside	The 'hope' need
5.	Pull	The 'relationship building' domain and 'stability' need
6.	Push	The 'execution' domain

For instance, in their model: (1) Strategic thinking involves intellectual and analytic-related strengths. (2) Influence involves inspiration and persuasion related-strengths, and satisfying the compassion need involves caring and 'having a heart'. (3) Satisfying the trust need involves honesty, respect, and integrity. (4) Satisfying the hope need involves direction, faith, and guidance. (5) Relationship building offers the 'social glue' to keep people together, and satisfying the stability need involves providing security and support. (6) Execution involves getting things done via discipline- and achiever-related strengths.

James Kouzes and Barry Posner's '2012 Leadership Practices' model, through its survey of personal-best leadership experiences, proposes five clusters of behaviors identified as practices of exemplary leadership. Even though they posit five

42 Discovering Your Leadership Wisdom

types of behaviors, a sixth can be gleaned that can be seen to emerge from a common foundation:

	HERE	THERE
1.	Head	(Embedded in others)
2.	Heart	Encourage the Heart
3.	Inside	Model the Way
4.	Outside	Inspire a Shared Vision
5.	Pull	Enable Others to Act
6.	Push	Challenge the Process

For instance, in their model: (1) Embedded across several of the following dimensions are behaviors related to learning and ideating. (2) Encourage the Heart involves reward, recognition, celebration, and appreciation. (3) Model the Way involves ensuring adherence to principles and standards. 4) Inspire a Shared Vision involves imagining a common future and speaking about the higher meaning and purpose of work. (5) Enable Others to Act involves creating cooperative mechanisms and supportive relationships. (6) Challenge the Process involves project management via plans and measurable as well as innovative improvements.

Related Research and Popular Press

Related literatures offer similar consolidations that, interestingly enough, also fall into line with the book's framework.

For example, the 2017 San Diego Wisdom Scale (SD-WISE) integrates the 'six most commonly included components of wisdom' with neurobiological and statistical evidence to propose the following metrics (which similarly align):

	HERE	THERE
1.	Head	Knowledge of life, social advising, and decision-making
2.	Heart	Emotional regulation and stress management
3.	Inside	Insight, reflection, and self-understanding
4.	Outside	Tolerance for divergent values, openness to diversity
5.	Pull	Pro-social behaviors (e.g., empathy, altruism and social cooperation)
6.	Push	Decisiveness, effectiveness dealing with uncertain, ambiguous events

The popular press literature on leadership is even more flooded, and some would say deluged to the point of incomprehensibility, with different frameworks of leadership roles. It has gotten to the point where armies of consultants and pundits are pitching their cleverly labeled products with scarcely a cite, reference, or attempt at reconciliation with those of others. Notwithstanding with a little effort

The JOURNEY: Exploring Leadership 43

these can also be seen to evidence a strong implicit reliance on the book's six tools or subsets of them. For example, in Loren Appelbaum and Matthew Paese's 2001 'What Senior Leaders Do: The Nine Roles of Strategic Leadership' we can plot an overlap of the following:

	HERE	THERE
1.	Head	Integrates information and data from all sources
2.	Heart	Captivates, builds passions and commitment
3.	Inside	Upholds interests, takes responsibility
4.	Outside	Aligns vision with enterprise, sub-units, and shareholders
5.	Pull	Attracts, develops, and retains talent in the right place at the right time
6.	Push	Mobilizes stakeholders for getting things done quickly

In David Miller's 2002 'Successful change leaders: What makes them? What do they do that is different?' from the *Journal of Change Management* we can plot an overlap of:

	HERE	THERE
1.	Head	Sees problems in a fresh, unconstrained way. Enjoys uncertainty and ambiguity.
2.	Heart	Optimistic: Upbeat, optimistic view of the world. Does not dampen enthusiasm.
3.	Inside	Self-assured: High self-esteem. Confident. Feels in control of events.
4.	Outside	Purposeful: Clear understanding of priorities. Sense of direction and purpose. Maintains focus.
5.	Pull	Collaborative: Draws upon others. Structures and organized, methodical approach to work. Maps out what needs to be done. Uses systems.
6.	Push	Proactive: Seizes opportunities. Thinks and acts rapidly.

In Alan Belasen and Nancy Frank's 2008 'Competing values leadership: quadrant roles and personality traits' from the *Leadership & Organization Development Journal* we can plot a partial overlap of the following:

	HERE	THERE
1.	Head	Analyzer
2.	Heart	Motivator
3.	Inside	–
4.	Outside	Vision setter
5.	Pull	–
6.	Push	Taskmaster

44 Discovering Your Leadership Wisdom

In Shelley Kirkpatrick and Edwin Locke's 1991 'Leadership: do traits matter?' from the *Academy of Management Executive* we can also plot a partial overlap as follows:

	HERE	THERE
1.	Head	Decision making, problem solving
2.	Heart	Motivating with specific, challenging goals as well as with rewards and punishments
3.	Inside	–
4.	Outside	Creating and implementing a vision
5.	Pull	Structuring; Team building; Selecting and training
6.	Push	Promoting change and innovation

Contemporary

These contemporary perspectives are frequently drawn upon, knowingly or not, when leadership is discussed in the popular press.

Circling back to modern research efforts, a content analysis of key ideas and terms of articles across the spectrum reveals a similar structural basis. For example, a content analysis of more than 25 of the most relevant recent reported studies on leadership (see Appendix A) reveals the following trends and consistencies with the approach of this book.

- One, when referring to the leader's HEAD, or cognition-related roles, the most frequently found references were to possessing critical information, knowledge, and the capacity for decision making. They were often described as analysts or detectives.
- Two, when referring to the leader's HEART, or emotion-related roles, the most frequently found references were to passion, inspiration, and the capacity for caring. They were often described as cheerleaders or energizers.
- Three, when referring to the leader's INSIDE, or character-related roles, the most frequently found references were to honesty, transparency, and seeing the core of their organizations. They were often described as historians or servants.
- Four, when referring to the leader's OUTSIDE, or meaning-related roles, the most frequently found references were to objectives, missions, and seeing the future of their organization. They were often described as visionaries or navigators.
- Five, when referring to the leader's PULL, or teamwork-related roles, the most frequently found references were to cooperation, coordination, and building a context and culture of cohesion. They were often described as communicators, architects, or designers.
- Six, when referring to the leader's PUSH, or performance-related roles, the most frequently found references were to execution, action, and getting results. They were often described as directors, overseers, or pioneers.

To summarize, the above integration of classics, mainstream, related and popular press, and contemporary leadership writings reveals that there may indeed be a core set of leadership role dimensions and tools.

With … Core Leadership Identities

> Leaders must be able to invoke the appropriate IDENTITY to carry out their roles – i.e., successfully match the right tool to the right job.

Leaders are people. As people they have personal identities. It is the syncing of the self with the demands of the leadership role that provides the final key to Wise Leadership. In this section I provide a roadmap to this line of research below with three station stops: self-concept, identity, and roles.

Self-Concept

Stanford psychologist Roderick Kramer provides a wonderful summary of the theory of the self. He describes that, as per social psychologist Mark Leary, *selfhood* connotes the aggregate thoughts, feelings, and behaviors that arise from people's awareness of themselves as possessing a self that operates as both subject (being seen) and agent (doing the seeing). As per social identity theorist Marilynn Brewer, our individual-level self-concept therefore includes the collection of attributes that we associate with ourselves as unique individuals. Because it is inherently multi-dimensional, social psychologist Kay Deaux offers us the metaphor of the self as a kaleidoscope. We are *kaleidoscopic* – or, as evolutionary psychologists have proposed, modular – insofar as our self-experiences display plasticity. That is, our selves are shifting, varied, and multi-faceted across differing contexts and under differing task needs. Through better awareness and regulation we can navigate effectively in the world by strategically changing our self-expressions to respond to different experiences and demands.

If we are able to raise our behaviors to the level of environmental needs, then, according to renowned psychologist Albert Bandura and his social cognitive theory, we demonstrate efficacy in our personal agency by bringing ourselves to bear on what we can control. As per Bandura (2013: 715) when they cultivate the talents and adaptability necessary to thrive in a complex world, "people can influence how they play the hand that fortuity deals them".

Self-Concept and Identity

According to Jan Stets and Peter Burke (2000), "the core of an identity is the categorization of the self as an occupant of a role, and the incorporation, into the self, of the meanings and expectations associated with that role and its performance". Thus our self-identities are influenced by "the match between

46 Discovering Your Leadership Wisdom

the individual meanings of occupying a particular role and the behaviors that a person enacts in that role when interacting with others". It is through this process of self-categorization or identification that our identities are formed. More than this, though, they highlight that our set of identities have different saliences insofar as there are unequal probabilities that a person will activate one particular identity rather than another in a particular situation. When we play out an identity actuality, and if it fits the identity standards – i.e., the meanings and norms that the person associates with the role – then we experience self-verification.

These insights are reinforced, and extended, by Michael Hogg (Hogg, Terry, & White, 1995; Hogg, 2001) in his discussion of identity theory and social identity theory. Identity theory explains individuals' role-related behaviors within a "multifaceted and dynamic self that mediates the relationship between social structure and individual behavior". That is to say, the self is (1) complex – it contains multiple components based on role identities; (2) hierarchical – because some identities have more relevance than others. Role identities are organized hierarchically in the self-concept … "those positioned near the top of the hierarchy are more likely to be invoked in a particular situation … thus people with the same role identities may behave differently in a given context because of differences in identity salience"; and (3) dynamic – where they are a result of "a process of labeling or self-definition" derived from the role and its relationship with its larger social context where situational factors may entail the construction and reconstruction of roles. As a result different people will experience interpersonal (across different individuals' perceptions, because "the salience of a particular identity will be determined by the person's commitment to that role") as well as intra-personal (across a single individual's roles and the importance of each role in their portfolio) variability in role identities. Thus, leaders who remain leaders match their style to their dominant contexts.

Self-Concept, Identity, and Role Theory

As is evident from the above, the concept of role is critical to understanding the formulation and projection of self-identity. The notion of the role has been around for a while in the classic work of sociologists. Erving Goffman saw social life as resembling theater and Talcott Parsons added to this concept their contribution to larger social systems such as organizations. Daniel Katz and Robert Kahn further refined it in 1978 to describe the patterns of behavior in organizations as developed from specific task requirements. In their 2013 review of the concept, Steven Fellows and William Kahn define a role as "a socially constructed position or category" and people as 'role actors'. It is the interpretation of our roles and their expectations that lead us to construct 'scripts' for how to act in different situations. In a sense, we play different roles depending on the tasks and performance objectives that we associate with these roles.

Roles are not always static or simple. Instead role-occupants – especially those in higher, more abstract roles like 'leader' – engage in role making as well as role playing by taking part in the crafting of their roles to fit expectations and demands. In fact, it is not unusual for these types of role sets to be highly complex and fluid. Thus, it is critically important for leaders to avoid role mismatch (playing the wrong parts) and role strain (not fulfilling the parts well). If roles are set up in a manner that is complementary then they can enrich the role set. Recent work in role theory has focused on this dynamic constitution and reconstitution of roles as people modify their scripts to match their shifting contexts of demands and expectations.

To summarize, the above integration of self-concept, identity, and role theory reinforces that leaders are essentially charged with invoking the appropriate sense of self to carry out the varied aspects of their jobs. In a word, to successfully match the right tool to the right job.

Okay, What Does This All Mean?

The best way of understanding leadership is clearly through the competency lens. And through this lens we can see that, as per a contingent behavior approach to leadership, there are different aspects of the leadership role that must be met with different aspects of a leader's sense of self and related skill-sets.

Combining this with what we know about wisdom from Chapter 1 we can deduce that (1) each of the primary branches of philosophy asks a different fundamental question and, as such, (2) demands a different set of component competencies and alacrities of the leaders who seek to meet their varied roles by developing and deploying the appropriate identities.

The essential competencies and identities are: (1) Logic, as a leadership scientist; (2) Aesthetics, as a leadership artist; (3) Ethics, as a leadership icon; (4) Metaphysics, as a leadership advocate; (5) Epistemology, as a leadership maestro; and (6) Politics, as a leadership general.

These are not new ideas. I did not invent them. However, I do not ignore them. Instead this book asks that you embrace their insights and tools and then apply them to the challenge of modern leadership. Their tools offer invaluable lessons. They are laid out in the cumulative wisdom of the wisest thinkers of our history. They are also revealed in the newspapers and magazines chronicling how the most influential movers of our age operate through their intellect, and their inspiration. Through their character, and their vision. Through their collaboration, and their execution.

In the next chapter we will synthesize this into a single, simple, and useful model of wise leadership that today's leaders can use to be sustainably successful in whatever situations they face.

3

THE SOLUTION

A Model of 'Wise' Leadership

Wise leaders master and apply multiple leadership identities –
They match the right leadership tool to their dominant leadership challenge

In this chapter we apply the major historical/scientific approaches to wisdom to (1) construct a framework that integrates the main insights of leadership theory and (2) capture its core principles for furthering your personal and professional leadership success.

Each component needs to be developed on its own, but also balanced with the others so that they work in harmony.

Each of them is necessary on their own, but none are sufficient to address the gamut of challenges leaders face.

In a word, wisdom is not just one single thing.

And leadership wisdom is therefore not a single thing either.

For wise leaders to be sustainably successful they need to first master multiple leadership identities and then apply their characteristics in the right situation.

That is, to match the right leadership tool to their dominant leadership challenge.

Specifically, the journey will be framed as follows:

- From Philosophy
- To Leadership
- A Model of Wise Leadership
- Head and Heart
- Inside and Outside
- Push and Pull
- A Preview of Part II

From Philosophy

To start, let us recognize that wise leadership can be broken down into its two terms: wisdom (via philosophy) and leadership. Then it can be fused at its nexus. This is precisely what we will now do, starting with philosophy.

Why Philosophy

There is no shortage of self-help publications promising 'wisdom' (however loosely expressed) for nearly everything under the sun. Lamentably though there are just so many books, articles, etc. that use the word 'wisdom' but never explain what they actually mean by this word. To this point, in 2019 a simple search on google.com for the word 'wisdom' yielded nearly 500 million results and amazon.com listed over a quarter of a million books related to the topic.

Truth be told the term is more often than not carelessly tossed about and rarely, if ever, well defined. Try picking up one of the many pop management books promising the latest fad and you will see the word 'wisdom' cast so casually, perhaps to get your attention and money, but then just as quickly dropped as an aside to some other point. "Listen to the wisdom of the world's greatest X." "Words of wisdom by Y." "Z was the most/least wise." So vague and obfuscated are their suppositions that they might best be worthy of after-dinner fortune cookies. If the proverbial black box of wisdom is not opened we never become any wiser to what those slickly alluded-to magic potions, deep secrets, shimmering stars, right stuffs, etc. ever really are.

So what still remains is the central, simple, yet still unanswered question: What is this thing we call wisdom anyway?

Alas, the only way to truly answer it is to return to its source.

The word 'philosophy', as has been discussed earlier, is roughly translatable as 'love of wisdom'. Since wisdom is fundamentally different from data-, information-, and knowledge-based paradigms an elucidated approach to leadership wisdom must get beyond these elemental and intermittently trendy topics to consider the larger, deeper sphere of what it means for a global leader to be more or less wise. Indeed, there is nothing more seminal to the concept of leadership. As per the *Cambridge Dictionary of Philosophy* (Audi, 1999), wisdom represents an understanding of the highest principles of things that function as a guide for living, and facilitating in others, a truly exemplary human life. Thus, according to Will Durant (1961), "philosophy is essentially the completion of science in the synthesis of wisdom".

Following the publication of the *Handbook of Organizational and Managerial Wisdom* there have been streams of research looking to specifically apply the ancient concept of wisdom to modern organizational and leadership studies. Insofar as wisdom is a 'good thing' this is a positive development, especially given the previously discussed gap between its demand and its supply – the imbalance

50 Discovering Your Leadership Wisdom

between our growing need for leadership wisdom and its seemingly shrinking supply is evidenced by the cavalcade of modern leadership failures spanning public and private institutions too numerous to mention. However, a major impediment in the literature's advancement can be located, ironically, at the basic conceptualization of the construct. In a word there seem to be as many definitions of wisdom, and thus varieties of arguments, as there are authors and articles advancing them. Without a common paradigm or means of amalgamation, these, real as well as semantic, differences constrain theory development and its systematic application (Hitt, Beamish, Jackson, & Mathieu, 2007).

Wisdom by its very nature cannot be (1) artificially boiled down to a single dimension and, compounding this, (2) the different dimensions cannot be advanced in isolation. Philosophy provides the basis for a unifying paradigm – one that is simultaneously broad and deep, essentially abstract and applicable, dizzyingly complex and penetratingly profound, as well as differentiated and integrative – from which to extract fundamental principles about wise leadership and discern their relationships. The following discussion of philosophy is culled from many reference sources, including: *Encyclopedia Britannica*, *Oxford Dictionary of Philosophy*, *Routledge Encyclopedia of Philosophy*, *Stanford Encyclopedia of Philosophy*, and the *Cambridge Dictionary of Philosophy*.

What Philosophy

Philosophy is both descriptive and prescriptive. As per Stewart and Blocker (1987), it is a method for discerning what is true, distilling this truth to a set of principles, and from these establishing normative criteria on how best to think and act. Philosophy is unique insofar as it does not have a distinct area of interest. As per Plato, "Philosophy begins in wonder" and, without this wonder, "the unexamined life is not worth living".

At its essence, philosophy is thus a cumulative catalog of humanity's greatest thinkers tackling its most fundamental problems. And they (though perhaps not their theories or systems) are household names. Echoing through the ages are the names of its humble yet determined thinkers: Heraclitus and Socrates. Confucius and Lao-Tzu. Plato and Aristotle. Ibn Sina and St. Anselm. Niccolo Machiavelli and Thomas Moore. Francis Bacon and René Descartes. Thomas Hobbes and John Locke. Baruch Spinoza and Gottfried Leibniz. David Hume and Michel de Montaigne. Voltaire and Jean-Jacques Rousseau. Immanuel Kant and Johann Gottlieb Fichte. Adam Smith and Karl Marx. Georg Hegel and Arthur Schopenhauer. Auguste Comte and John Stuart Mill. Soren Kierkegaard and Friedrich Nietzsche. Gottlob Frege and Edmund Husserl. Alfred North Whitehead and G. E. Moore. Martin Buber and Bertrand Russell. Ludwig Wittgenstein and Martin Heidegger. Karl Popper and Jean-Paul Sartre. Albert Camus and Michel Foucault. Just to name a few.

So how to make sense of their rich ideas and insights? And put them together in a way that is useful without being overwhelming and overly complex?

We can pursue this through the following.

Though varying across texts and tomes there are at least six distinct areas of philosophic inquiry, or as some label them, branches, within its purview. In short they are as follows: Logic is concerned with the laws of valid reasoning and its soundness or fidelity. Ethics deals with problems of right conduct. Aesthetics attempts to determine the nature of beauty and the character of tastes and preferences. Epistemology investigates the nature of knowledge and the process of knowing. Metaphysics inquires into the nature and ultimate significance of what exists as real. Politics investigates social and systematized conduct to uncover proper principles of power, organization, and governance.

To put a little more meat on the bone....

1 LOGIC

First, the branch of LOGIC is at its foundation the study of inference and argument.

More broadly, its scholars and sages investigate ideal methods of thought by asking questions about what constitutes sound reasoning and what can be construed as rational. The central property of logic is 'soundness' or internal fidelity. As per Stewart and Blocker (1987: 57), logic is concerned with the 'life of reason' and, in this sense, overlaps with science and the scientist's quest for theory-based facts. An

> advantage to grounding your opinions in reason is that these opinions are more stable than those which are not supported by reason ... in addition, the rational ideal of the life of reason is the more likely means to be accurate, reliable knowledge about the world.

Thus, in essence, it is about working towards valid, reliable representations of how the world works. Through deduction (analyzing and determining specific instances) and induction (synthesizing and inferring general systems) the logical individual can explain, predict, and influence their world.

For example, here is a sampling of philosophic thinkers and their insights on logic.

From Aristotle, in his *Organon* (i.e., the 'instrument' for knowing and judging truth), he gives us a doctrine of categories for making sense of things as well as the syllogism for rationally determining what valid conclusions must be deduced from given premises. He also warns against a litany of common logical flaws to which less wise men often fall prey.

From Gottlob Frege we receive analytic philosophy, where he offers us methods for representing complex statements, studying inferences, deriving axioms, and formalizing 'proofs'. Related to this are the efforts of George Boole whose modern symbolic logic and Boolean algebra offered translations that are used in digital computing.

52 Discovering Your Leadership Wisdom

From Alfred North Whitehead we are enriched with mathematical logic and advancements in the philosophy of science. Along with collaborator Bertrand Russell, through their *Principia Mathematica* they harmonized math and logic both broadly and deeply.

So what might we take from this area of wisdom? Here are some genres of essential Logic questions:

- What is rational?
- What is true and valid?
- What constitutes sound reasoning?

2 AESTHETICS

Second, the branch of AESTHETICS is the study of ideal form or beauty, including the character of tastes and preferences. Its scholars and sages are concerned with questions such as what is enjoyable and why, linking design and art to objects, structures, experiences, and language. As per Stewart and Blocker, aesthetics is concerned with the nature of beauty and artistic expression as well as emotion and the artistic experience. Insofar as art communicates emotion, aesthetics seeks to understand the intrinsic/extrinsic sources of pleasure(s) and feelings. Thus, in essence, it is about considering and reconciling what we like and why we like it.

For example, here is a sampling of philosophic thinkers and their insights on aesthetics.

From Socrates and Plato we delve into beautiful forms, the nature and properties of beautiful things, the attractions they elicit, the inspirations they encourage, and even the feelings of love we develop towards them.

From Immanuel Kant we appreciate the notion of pure, objective beauty and the process of its influence based on subjective feelings of taste and pleasure.

From Arthur Schopenhauer we see why things such as art stimulate and charm us to different levels and degrees, and how we are drawn into aesthetic experiences with all their emotions and pleasures, and even how we experience enrapture within sublime yearnings of the heart.

So what might we take from this area of wisdom? Here are some genres of essential Aesthetics questions:

- Why do we like things?
- What is beauty?
- What is enjoyable?

3 ETHICS

Third, the branch of ETHICS is concerned with ideal conduct, the nature of ultimate value, and the moral standards by which human action can be judged. Its scholars and sages study what actions are 'right' and what ends are 'good', thereby deriving a method or code by which people should live. As per Stewart and Blocker, ethics is concerned with what we ought to do. Simply put, in the difference between good-and-bad. It deals with issues of objectivism and relativism – if there is a single universal standard of Good or instead situation-specific goods. It also deals with the nature of morality and human nature, as well as specific methods for codifying them – e.g., Results and utility versus motives and moral duty. Thus, in essence, it is about considering and reconciling the difference between right and wrong.

For example, here is a sampling of philosophic thinkers and their insights on ethics.

From Immanuel Kant's moral philosophy we hear that the general rightness or wrongness of one's actions is based on whether they are principled, or in his view meet 'The Categorical Imperative' – a supreme principle of morality where a person of goodwill and character seeks to act in ways that could be made into universal precepts and faithfully respects others' humanity as ends in and of themselves (versus merely means towards one's selfish gratifications).

From John Stuart-Mill and Jeremy Bentham we receive a more outcome-oriented view of virtuous action as meeting the standards of 'utilitarian' where one pursues the actions that result in the greatest good for the greatest number of people.

From Friedrich Nietzsche we are told that morality is something different from the above, more in line with a sequence of positive strivings towards a natural evolution and flourishing via 'higher men' that confidently create themselves and, by doing so, elevate society.

So what might we take from this area of wisdom? Here are some genres of essential Ethics questions:

- What ends are good?
- What actions are right?
- By what standards should we live?

4 METAPHYSICS

Fourth, the branch of METAPHYSICS is the study of ultimate reality and what constitutes the structure and content of what exists as real. Its scholars and sages consider complex systems and through this what it means to exist as a person in one's relation to the larger world. As per Stewart and Blocker, metaphysics, the most ancient branch of philosophy, is concerned with the distinction between surface, transient appearances and the nature of ultimate reality. It seeks to link the everyday with comprehensive and consistent views of the world. As such it seeks to tie together the tangible/visible and the overarching ideal/invisible. Thus, in essence, it is about considering and reconciling one's micro images of self with a more comprehensive, higher-order macro schemata.

54 Discovering Your Leadership Wisdom

For example, here is a sampling of philosophic thinkers and their insights into metaphysics.

From Georg Hegel there is a dynamic relationship between the infinite and the intimate, where the process of reconciling theses and their antitheses yields higher-order syntheses that unite conscious beings – through this we can bring all facets of ordinary existence into the realm of ideal and absolute reality.

From St. Anselm we receive a more theological view of reality that sees a divine nature where people of faith seek to know God and do his work in a world of freedom, sin, service, and redemption.

From Baruch Spinoza we delve into a 'modal' metaphysics where underlying substance fuses with our manifest patterns of natural life and its finite matter to form a geometric pattern imbued in the vast totality – here we humans are cosmically united with the infinite whole and everything within it.

So what might we take from this area of wisdom? Here are some genres of essential Metaphysics questions:

- What is the meaning and purpose of existence?
- Of overarching reality?
- Of self and our relation to the above?

5 EPISTEMOLOGY

Fifth, the branch of EPISTEMOLOGY focuses on the origin, nature, and limits of human understanding, both a priori (theory) and a posteriori (empiricism). Its scholars and sages concern themselves with what we know and how we know it as well as the question of whether objectively true and shared belief is even possible. As per Stewart and Blocker, epistemology is concerned with the basis of our collective discourse for how we sort out sentiments and beliefs to arrive at some shared certainty. It probes the different sources of people's (or, more accurately, peoples') sentiments, the way they weave them into views, why these views might differ, and methods for how they might be squared with each other. For example, in terms of disparities between peoples' senses and experiences. Thus, in essence, it is about considering and reconciling individualized experiences with group and organizational connections.

For example, here is a sampling of philosophic thinkers and their insights into epistemology.

From René Descartes' theory of knowing we first discover that we are (hence the famous 'cogito ergo sum') and that we are not alone dreaming; then, upon the recognition of viable others, through a circular process of orderly reconciling doubt with common notions and criteria for accepting their claims, we move towards credible shared views.

From John Locke we learn the importance of experience that etches perspectives on our 'tabula rasa' (i.e., clean slate) and the alignment of simple sensory perceptions with abstract ideas and their qualities – as argued in his *An Essay Concerning Human Understanding*, these are then accepted when they connect and agree with those of other peoples. David Hume further developed these notions of sensation, impressions, ideas, and the connections we create between things and how these customs guide life.

From more modern philosophers such as Karl Popper, Michel Foucault, and Ludwig Wittgenstein we receive ideas on: the importance of the empirical demarcation and reconciliation of ideas (Popper), the influence of political structure and historical representations on how ideas are viewed in different societies (Foucault), and the role of language games and communication in determining how we categorize things and negotiate our viewpoints (Wittgenstein).

So what might we take from this area of wisdom? Here are some genres of essential Epistemology questions:

- How do we make sense of things?
- What do we collectively know?
- How do we, or how can we, all know it?

6 POLITICS

Sixth, the branch of POLITICS investigates social and systematized conduct to uncover proper principles of power, influence, organization, and governance. It blends intellectual consideration with pragmatic implementation, or the abstract with the impact, so as to get things done effectively and efficiently. As per Stewart and Blocker, social and political philosophy is concerned with the establishment/ design of arrangements between peoples especially as they exist between peoples in formal organizations such as nations or states. More specifically, it examines the benefits and drawbacks of different types of arrangements and design dimensions – e.g., capitalistic, socialistic, communistic, etc. It also goes beyond the descriptive to evaluate the functionality of structural arrangements and their specific dimensions on various criteria such as effectiveness. Thus, in essence, it is about considering and reconciling the different ways of organizing activities to get things done and achieve goals.

For example, here is a sampling of philosophic thinkers and their insights into politics.

From Thomas Hobbes we are familiarized with 'social contract theory', were peoples voluntarily give power to organizations that can temper the states of our nature with governed authority and expertise to utilize resources more efficiently and to complete projects more effectively.

From Niccolo Machiavelli we learn about the practical maxims leaders can use for gaining and keeping power within these organizations, such as in *The Prince* where he offers advice on designing structures, shaping cultures, implementing objectives, overcoming opposition, and championing change.

56 Discovering Your Leadership Wisdom

From Jean–Jacques Rousseau we gain insights into constructing organizations that protect essential freedoms, encourage engagement and participation, facilitate learning and education, and the fulfillment of the general will of its legitimate stakeholder interests. These were extended by John Rawls in his 'four roles' of political philosophy (the first among them being the necessity of practical survival and performance) and championing of corresponding political progress and liberalism.

So what might we take from this area of wisdom? Here are some genres of essential Politics questions:

- What is the best way to organize?
- To distribute power and utilize resources?
- To practically, pragmatically govern and execute?

To Leadership

One thing leadership scholars can agree on, and a sad truth of the leadership literature, is that there remains a sore need for an overall template to help us better understand its big picture and guide leaders in their development.

And this sentiment has persisted for too long.

For example, in his 1974 magnum opus of leadership theory, *Handbook of Leadership: A Survey of the Literature*, Ralph Stogdill laments that "there are almost as many definitions of leadership as there are persons who have attempted to define the concept".

Nearly a decade later eminent leadership scholar Gary Yukl, in his 1989 *Managerial Leadership: A Review of Theory and Research*, similarly points to "the absence of broad theories that integrate the findings from different approaches".

And the song remains the same into the next era of leadership studies as prominent leadership guru Robert Lord reports in 2005 via the esteemed *The Leadership Quarterly* that still there "are no general models for the development of leadership skills".

This trend continues to the modern day where Day and colleagues, in their 2014 'Advances in leader and leadership development: A review of 25 years of research and theory', recognize that "despite the significant advances in understanding leadership development ... the field is still relatively immature". Jessica Dinh and colleagues, in their 2014 'Leadership theory and research in the new millennium: Current theoretical trends and changing perspectives', likewise conclude that "no unified theory of leadership currently exists".

However, hope is not lost.

The seeds for its solution can be found in what Day and colleagues also highlight as the importance of meta-identity and self-regulatory processes in effective leadership. This is further detailed by Lord and Hall in their arguments that a leader's self-identity provides (1) structure around which relevant leadership knowledge can

The SOLUTION: 'Wise' Leadership **57**

be organized and (2) direction for how a leader puts him- or herself out there to engage in the situation. Thus they propose that leadership skill is a function of how leaders access and use their information ... "thus increasing one's repertoire of leadership skills requires a concomitant change in developing identities and an increased willingness to voluntary assume a specific social role" (2014: 594).

In other words, to succeed, leaders must make sense of the situations that confront them and draw upon their 'meta-monitoring skills' to generate appropriate leadership behaviors. They discuss this as 'the ability to gauge progress' in different domains so to 'adjust the identities they enact' and 'adjust behavior accordingly'. In my vernacular, they need to have a broad leadership toolbox and know when and how to use each one.

So, before I formally present the proverbial toolbox, as a teaser, please consider the following (trick) questions:

> Q1: Who will make the best leader? The most (a) intelligent, (b) charismatic, (c) ethical, (d) committed, (e) unifying, or (f) political person?
>
> Q2: When faced with a leadership challenge one should choose: The most (a) rational, (b) elegant, (c) moral, (d) meaningful, (e) popular, or (f) practical solution?
>
> Q3: The most important job of a leader is to: (a) Make good judgments and provide a voice of reason, (b) Motivate their followers and provide inspiration, (c) Establish core values and provide a moral compass, (d) Create meaning and provide a sense of purpose, (e) Facilitate teamwork and provide a path for harmony, or (f) Get the job done and provide a means for execution?

Why are these trick questions? It is precisely because they present leadership as a false choice between alternative competency-based approaches. Instead the seminal thrust of leadership contingencies (proposed first by Fiedler and expanded since) suggests that different leadership tools are appropriate for different leadership challenges or situations. In a word: Wise leaders need to be able, and willing, to use the right tool for the job.

Along with James Bailey, in the 2007 *Handbook of Organizational and Managerial Wisdom*, I derived from its systematic exploration of wisdom dimensions the following 'best practices'. They are presented here with amended category labels.

(RE: LOGIC)

> ... to think. Think implies that the wisest individuals, teams, organizations, and strategies demonstrate extraordinary intellectual prowess. This is evidenced by characterizations of said actors as possessing highly developed intellectual capacity, keen insight, the ability for complex

58 Discovering Your Leadership Wisdom

deliberation, deep cultural intelligence, and a broad knowledge base. Thus, wise actors in the professional domain are smart. They use their heads. They get it. They deploy their resources to process issues and figure things out.

(RE: AESTHETICS)

… to feel. By feel, we mean that the wisest individuals, teams, organizations, and strategies demonstrate extraordinary emotive capacity. This is evidenced by characterizations of said actors as possessing profound spirituality, a fundamental prudence, the courage to do what is right, empathy and understanding of others, and an openness to differences between peoples and contexts. Thus, wise actors in the professional domain are intimately connected. They use their hearts. They deploy their empathy and sensitivity to be in touch.

(RE: ETHICS)

… to reflect. Reflect implies that the wisest individuals, teams, organizations, and strategies demonstrate extraordinary introspective insight. This is evidenced by characterizations of said actors as possessing contemplative understanding and appreciation of their values, needs, emotions, interpretations, and sense of being. Thus, wise actors in the professional domain are deep. They discover their identity. They deploy their insight and grounded base to realize and leverage the self.

(RE: METAPHYSICS)

… to aspire. Aspire implies that the wisest individuals, teams, organizations, and strategies demonstrate extraordinary principled objectives. This is evidenced by characterizations of said actors as possessing a concern for the public good, striving for a common purpose, establishing sustainability, promoting humaneness, and addressing profound and meaningful issues. Thus, wise actors in the professional domain are well-intentioned. They channel their will in positive directions. They deploy their humanity and citizenry to make themselves and their world better.

(RE: EPISTEMOLOGY)

… to synergize. To synergize implies that the wisest individuals, teams, organizations, and strategies demonstrate extraordinary collaborative orientation. This is evidenced by characterizations of said actors as possessing strong norms and systemic checks that balance, productive change, mutual collaboration, and collective coherence. Thus, wise actors in the professional domain are unified. They coordinate their efforts.

The SOLUTION: 'Wise' Leadership **59**

> They deploy their harmony and congruence to be on the same page and move to the same music.

(RE: POLITICS)

> ... to engage. Possessing the ability to engage implies that the wisest individuals, teams, organizations, and strategies demonstrate extraordinary functional application. This is evidenced by characterizations of said actors as possessing behavioral proactiveness, situational recognition, consistent experimentation, established networks, and practical experience. Thus, wise actors in the professional domain are active. They engage their world. They deploy their flexibility, energy, and acumen to adapt to their stage and cast.

Indeed, over the last decade these insights have proven to be remarkably resilient and useful. Here I further extend the framework to describe different fundamental leadership challenges as reconciled with Chapter 2's discussions on leadership and role identity and integrated with the previous philosophical analyses. They are summarized in Table 3.1.

All six dimensions are corroborated in several complementary streams of research. These were reviewed in Chapter 2 but two will be highlighted below.

For example, when looking back at Dinh and colleagues' review of the literature, they consider the following (with our framework's labels added): (1) Cognitive, thinking-centered theories of information-processing leadership; (2) Affective, feelings-centered theories of inspirational and motivational leadership; (3) Inside, character-centered theories of ethical leadership; (4) Outside, meaning-centered theories of visionary leadership; (5) Pull, synergy-centered theories of team, culture, and relationship leadership; and (6) Push, value-centered theories of strategic and performance leadership.

TABLE 3.1 Wise Leadership Tools

1.	Leadership **Logic** – Using your *head*, as a proverbial scientist, to address sagacity-related (thinking and understanding) cognitive challenges.
2.	Leadership **Aesthetics** – Using your *heart*, as a proverbial artist, to address spirit-related (feeling and inspiration) affective challenges.
3.	Leadership **Ethics** – Looking *inside* yourself, as a proverbial icon, to address character-related (moral and principle) integrity challenges.
4.	Leadership **Metaphysics** – Looking *outside* yourself, as a proverbial advocate, to address purpose-related (meaning and mission) significance challenges.
5.	Leadership **Epistemology** – Pulling people *together*, as a proverbial maestro, to address unity-related (integration and coordination) connection challenges.
6.	Leadership **Politics** – Pushing people *forward*, as a proverbial general, to address value-related (efficiency and effectiveness) execution challenges.

60 Discovering Your Leadership Wisdom

In addition, as a further example, when looking at Lord and Hall's arguments regarding essential leadership skills, they consider the following (again, with our framework's labels added): (1) Cognitive, technical and decision skills; (2) Affective, emotional and empathy skills; (3) Inside, authenticity and principle skills; (4) Outside, value and societal-focused skills; (5) Pull, social and group skills; and (6) Push, task and performance skills.

A Model of Wise Leadership

The core model of leadership wisdom is now formally presented using the aforementioned LIGHTS-CAMERA-ACTION metaphor.

> Lights = Being Better
> Head AND Heart
> To think like a leader.
> And to also feel like a leader.

> Camera = Seeing Better
> Inside AND Outside
> To see deep inside oneself.
> And to also see far beyond oneself.

> Action = Doing Better
> Pull AND Push
> To pull people together.
> And to also push people forward.

In a word … Wise Leaders are defined by the holistic as well as specific ways in which they choose to BE, to SEE, and to DO.

Within each of the three lights-camera-action categories the components are ideally both individually developed and synergistically deployed.

Then the categories themselves should be combined to work in harmony, each of them necessary but none by themselves sufficient, to optimize and enable the model.

This model is illustrated in Figure 3.1 (hint: It provides a nice photo-op for keeping the reference handy on your phone).

In summary, I have constructed this model to make the following argument: Depending on the dominant challenge you face, a different tool is required to successfully address it; the key is to MATCH YOUR LEADERSHIP IDENTITY TO THE SITUATION so that you can focus on the appropriate process to achieve the desired outcome.

This requires the (1) HOLISTIC, systematic development of each tool and (2) their SPECIFIC, dynamic deployment to solve the appropriate problem.

The SOLUTION: 'Wise' Leadership   61

FIGURE 3.1   A Model of Wise Leadership.

- Problem: When Facing Reasoning and Judgment Challenges
  Solution: Activate Your Leader 'Logic' Tool
  Identity: Be a Leadership SCIENTIST
  Method: To Use Your Head
  Focus: And with Extraordinary Intellectual Prowess
  Outcome: Lead with *Sagacity*

- Problem: When Facing Emotional and Motivation Challenges
  Solution: Activate Your Leader 'Aesthetics' Tool
  Identity: Be a Leadership ARTIST
  Method: To Use Your Heart
  Focus: And with Extraordinary Emotive Capacity
  Outcome: Lead with *Spirit*

- Problem: When Facing Moral and Value Challenges
  Solution: Activate Your Leader 'Ethics' Tool
  Identity: Be a Leadership ICON
  Method: To Look Inside Yourself
  Focus: And with Extraordinary Introspective Insight
  Outcome: Lead through *Character*

62 Discovering Your Leadership Wisdom

- Problem: When Facing Meaning and Commitment Challenges
  Solution: Activate Your Leader 'Metaphysics' Tool
  Identity: Be a Leadership ADVOCATE
  Method: To Look Outside Yourself
  Focus: And with Extraordinary Principled Objectives
  Outcome: Lead through *Purpose*

- Problem: When Facing Harmony and Teamwork Challenges
  Solution: Activate Your Leader 'Epistemology' Tool
  Identity: Be a Leadership MAESTRO
  Method: To Pull People Together
  Focus: And with Extraordinary Collaborative Orientation
  Outcome: Lead for *Unity*

- Problem: When Facing Execution and Implementation Challenges
  Solution: Activate Your Leader 'Politics' Tool
  Identity: Be a Leadership GENERAL
  Method: To Push People Forward
  Focus: And with Extraordinary Functional Application
  Outcome: Lead for *Value*

Characteristics of the Model

The multi-dimensionality and complementarity of leadership competencies are emphasized in none other than Plato's discussion of the nature and education of leaders, or 'philosopher kings'. First, that they are necessary. Plato sees philosophic wisdom as indispensable for the proper governance of organizations. Given the particular demands of the leadership position it must be filled by those who possess requisite competencies lest they fall into ruin.

Second, that they are learnable. Plato outlines a curriculum of sorts for the cultivation of wise leaders, which ironically is more resembling of a liberal arts (versus business) education. Areas of study are intended to attune the mind and cultivate elucidated perspectives of organizational praxis such as through math and geometry as well as music and gymnastics. Interesting elements of this process include (1) that leaders must have a certain level of age and experience and (2) that they can be either male or female – i.e., gender is not a prerequisite for wisdom.

Third, that they are synergistic. Effective leaders are not one-trick ponies. They must combine complementary elements requisite with their complex demands such as intelligence, bravery, temperance, tenacity, attractiveness, truthfulness, and munificence. Since the challenges of the position are multi-faceted and fluid a wise leader must be able to comprehend, cultivate, and then correctly apply these proficiencies towards the stable, sustainable execution of their role.

This is the good news.

Challenges of the Model

Yet the leaders we need tend not to be the leaders we get. True philosophers are rare. Not because their ways are too mysterious but rather because our current systems do not support them. For instance, we are inclined not to want leaders who are true philosophers. These are the people we often least relate to and identify with (cf., social identity theory). Because they are so different, see so different, and act so different they are ill-regarded and unpopular.

And it gets even worse. Even if by some chance or fleeting fancy a true lover of wisdom were to be chosen then their wise tenure would not remain for long. They would lamentably, but likely, be corrupted by the socially institutionalized nature of the role and seduced by vicious cycles of its dysfunctional rewards contingencies.

Does this sound like it was observed many millennia or merely minutes ago? This idea that we might hope for one thing but reward another is certainly not new to management scholars such as Steve Kerr (1975) and pundits such as Dilbert animator Scott Adams (1996). In essence, it highlights that what it takes to (1) be a leader is different from what it takes to (2) become a leader. The first query is one of effectiveness or execution. Alternatively, the second query is one of intention or electability. In theory the two should be aligned. In practice they are frequently not (see, e.g., George & Sims, 2007; George, 2015; Pfeffer, 2015). Thus Plato's steely mandate, with bracketed comments added (Sterling & Scott, 1985):

> Unless philosophers [truly wise individuals] become kings [leaders] in our cities [organizations] OR unless those who are now kings and rulers become true philosophers.... So that political power and philosophic intelligence converge ... I believe there can be no end to troubles.

This is the bad news.

The purpose of the remainder of this book is to propose a way out of this mess by showing exactly how leaders can execute their role wisely. The tools are based in the core dimensions of the leadership role as grounded in the corresponding branches of philosophy. Each is previewed below and detailed in the coming chapters.

Being – Head and Heart Challenges

The first set of philosophical fields – logic and aesthetics – reveal complementary 'BEING' tools leaders can use to strengthen people and organizations. They represent the proverbial luminosity of the lights that are developed/used when a leader is faced with (head) and will (heart) challenges.

64 Discovering Your Leadership Wisdom

Tool #1

You will learn (in Chapter 4) how to develop, discern, and deploy your Leadership **SCIENTIST**. Many of the challenges leaders face are essentially ones of understanding. In short, thinking problems.

This is addressed from what our greatest philosophical gurus term _logic_ where we must overcome barriers to sound reasoning and rationality to discover the hidden truth of situations.

Here leaders must open their inner _Scientist_ tool to complete three types of jobs – they are related to the challenges of: comprehension, assessment, and judgment. Comprehension via broad and deep sets of relevant knowledge. Assessment via keen attention and sharp perception. Judgment via rational and creative processing.

When doing this they can leverage the lessons of humankind's most influential scientific achievements to use their heads and tap into an extraordinary intellectual prowess to lead with _sagacity_.

Tool #2

You will learn (in Chapter 5) how to develop, discern, and deploy your Leadership **ARTIST**. Many of the challenges leaders face are alternatively ones of inspiration. In short, feeling problems.

This is addressed from what our greatest philosophical gurus term _aesthetics_ where we must overcome barriers to emotional well-being and joy to discover the hidden beauty of situations.

Here leaders must open their inner _Artist_ tool to complete three types of jobs – they are related to the challenges of: awareness, attitude, and motivation. Awareness via sensitivity and empathy. An attitude replete with positivity and pluralism. Inspiration stemming from mastery of motivation and influence.

When doing this they can leverage the lessons of humankind's most influential artistic achievements to use their hearts and tap into an extraordinary emotive capacity to lead with _spirit_.

Together

Of course it would be foolish to address matters of the heart with a logical scientist tool or to address matters of the head with an emotional artist tool. Leaders must have both of these tools and know when to use them. If you are just a brainy leader, or just a sensitive leader, then you might succeed when lucky enough to be in the right place at the right time, but this success will be one-dimensional (unbalanced) and short-lived (unsustainable). You will fail unless you are both capable and inspiring.

The SOLUTION: 'Wise' Leadership **65**

Therefore, the recipe for success is not head or heart, it is head AND heart. The tools do not compete. They do unique but complementary jobs that are appropriate in different situations to fix different problems. You must learn, master, and appropriately use both of them.

Seeing – Inside and Outside Challenges

The second set of philosophical fields – ethics and metaphysics – reveal complementary 'SEEING' tools leaders can use to orient people and organizations. They represent the proverbial resolution of our cameras on reality and are used when a leader is faced with character (inside) and purpose (outside) challenges.

Tool #3

You will learn (in Chapter 6) how to develop, discern, and deploy your Leadership **ICON**. Many of the challenges leaders face are essentially ones of integrity. In short, moral problems.

This is addressed from what our greatest philosophical gurus term *ethics* where we must overcome barriers to reflection by looking inside one's self to discover a greater sense of right and wrong and the nature of being good.

Here leaders must open their inner *Icon* tool to complete three types of jobs – they are related to the challenges of: morality, authenticity, and confidence. Morality via an ethical mindset and maturation. Authenticity in the cinema of ethical alignment and growth. Confidence from the derivation of ethical esteem and agency.

When doing this they can leverage the lessons of humankind's most influential iconic achievements to see deep and tap into extraordinary introspective insight to lead with *character*.

Tool #4

You will learn (in Chapter 7) how to develop, discern, and deploy your Leadership **ADVOCATE**. Many of the challenges leaders face are alternatively ones of significance. In short, meaning problems.

This is addressed from what our greatest philosophical gurus term *metaphysics* where we must overcome barriers to aspiration by looking outside one's self to discover a greater sense of mission and importance and the nature of one's place in the world.

Here leaders must open their inner *Advocate* tool to complete three types of jobs – they are related to the challenges of: mindfulness, collegiality, and transcendence. Mindfulness in the coalescing of ontology and perspective. Collegiality in the realization of inclusiveness and duty. Transcendence emerging from super-personal munificence and service.

66 Discovering Your Leadership Wisdom

When doing this they can leverage the lessons of humankind's most influential advocacy achievements to see far and tap into extraordinary principled objectives to lead with *purpose*.

Together

It is again critical to appreciate that leaders must have both of these tools and know when to use them. If not, then your leadership will be unbalanced and unsustainable.

Therefore the recipe for success is not inside or outside, it is inside AND outside. The tools do not compete. They do unique but complementary jobs that are appropriate in different situations to fix different problems. You must learn, master, and appropriately use both of them.

Doing – Pull and Push Challenges

The third and final set of philosophical fields – epistemology and politics – reveal complementary 'DOING' tools leaders can use to move people and organizations. They represent the proverbial force of energy activation and are used when a leader is faced with integration (pull) and value (push) challenges.

Tool #5

You will learn (in Chapter 8) how to develop, discern, and deploy your Leadership **MAESTRO**. Many of the challenges leaders face are essentially ones of organization and process. In short, pulling-together problems.

This is addressed from what our greatest philosophical gurus term *epistemology* where we must overcome barriers to communication and coordination to use a common language for achieving a synergistic system.

Here leaders must open their inner *Maestro* tool to complete three types of jobs – they are related to the challenges of: complementarity, interdependency, and harmony. Complementarity in the composition and alignment of parts. Interdependency through the communication and resolution of roles. Harmony from the connective architecture of structure and culture.

When doing this they can leverage the lessons of humankind's most influential coordination achievements to tap into extraordinary collaborative orientation to lead for *unity*.

Tool #6

You will learn (in Chapter 9) how to develop, discern, and deploy your Leadership **GENERAL**. Many of the challenges leaders face are alternatively ones of outcome and results. In short, pushing-forward problems.

The SOLUTION: 'Wise' Leadership **67**

This is addressed from what our greatest philosophical gurus term _politics_ where we must overcome barriers to efficiency and effectiveness to use pragmatic strategies for achieving 'real world' performance.

Here leaders must open their inner _General_ tool to complete three types of jobs – they are related to the challenges of: excellence, advantage, and innovation. Excellence via efficiency and effectiveness. Advantage via strategic operations and innovation. Sustainability via institutionalized learning and change.

When doing this they can leverage the lessons of humankind's most influential practical achievements to tap into extraordinary functional application to lead for _value_.

Together

Once more it is critical to appreciate that leaders must have both of these tools and know when to use them. If you cannot bring people together or push them forward, then your leadership will be unbalanced and unsustainable.

Therefore, the recipe for success is not pull or push, it is pull AND push. The tools do not compete. They do unique but complementary jobs that are appropriate in different situations to fix different problems. You must learn, master, and appropriately use both of them.

A Preview of Part II

Part I of the book (Chapters 1–3) has made the case for Wise Leadership and traced the varied paths that have led to its model. When taken together, the framework offers the reader a proverbial 'Leadership Toolbox' for leading in any situation: Logic, for being a leadership scientist; Aesthetics, for being a leadership artist; Ethics, for being a leadership icon; Metaphysics, for being a leadership advocate; Epistemology, for being a leadership maestro; and Politics, for being a leadership general.

In technical terms, the sustainably successful leader has the (1) meta-monitoring skills to identify/reconcile the dominant situational elements and role identities employed to confront them, and the (2) corresponding mega-heuristics to activate appropriate wise leadership competencies and behaviors for facilitating sustainable (personal and professional) success.

In more plainspoken terms, the successful leader (1) has a bigger toolbox and (2) a better set of directions to be more precise and adept in their application.

In Part II of the book (Chapters 4–9) we will detail these tools – their features, their fundamentals, and the best practices for applying them efficiently and effectively. They will also be punctuated by publicly available attributed aphorisms and common knowledge insights culled from numerous original as well as secondary sources, the latter including: _The Concise Columbia Dictionary of Quotations_ (Andrews, 1989), _The Home Book of Quotations: Classical and Modern_ (Stevenson, 1967),

68 Discovering Your Leadership Wisdom

The Oxford Dictionary of Quotations (1979), *The Ultimate Book of Business Quotations* (Crainer, 1998), *Great Quotes from Great Leaders* (Anderson, 1990), *The Great Thoughts* (Seldes, 1985) as well as compilations such as by MusicChoice.com, Goodreads.com, and Brainyquote.com. More than this, though, through a meticulous treatment you will learn exactly what each tool does and why they do it, understand when and where the tools should be used, and through a collection of colorful examples and practical guidelines see how each can be developed and applied so you can succeed as a leader no matter what challenges you are confronted with.

To further substantiate the tools, we will illustrate the model in action by weaving in diverse, prominent examples of leadership success. Here we will overlay our lens onto our 'greatest' leaders as revealed in REAL (as evidenced via *Time Magazine*'s 'Most Influential' lists) as well as IDEALIZED (as evidenced via American Film Institute's 'Greatest Movie Heroes' lists) archetypes that hold across multiple leadership contexts and domains of engagement.

However, we will do this differently. Not just a bunch of cases. And mercifully not another leadership laundry list or leadership Mount Rushmore.

Because this is boring and overdone. It is also not terribly useful.

Instead we adapt one of the most compelling models of personal development for enlivening the conversation and vitalizing its lessons. It is sourced from an all-time classic book originally published in 1937 by Napoleon Hill and posthumously updated in 2003, entitled *Think and Grow Rich*. Whereas I do not ascribe to all of Mr. Hill's ideas for evoking and applying history's greatest insights, his general method for creating an assembly of 'Invisible Counselors' is extraordinarily compelling.

In a nutshell, to use this technique, please do the following.

First, define a purpose for the meeting. For example, this would involve identifying the main leadership problem you are facing. As considered in this book they might be: (1) a reasoning and judgment challenge like better creating understanding; (2) an emotional and motivation challenge like better creating energy; (3) a moral and value challenge like figuring out what is right; (4) a meaning and commitment challenge like figuring out what is important; (5) a harmony and teamwork challenge like optimizing connections; or (6) an execution and implementation challenge like optimizing operational efficiency.

Then call a meeting of archetypes who excelled at addressing this type of problem. For example, these experts might come from those discussed in this book. Or they could also come from more personal examples.

Finally, preside over the meeting, allowing each participant time to provide their individual words of wisdom as well as interact with the others to approximate a group wisdom. For example, put the problem to the panel and solicit ideas. What would Socrates say? Oprah? Buddha? Gandhi? Queen Elizabeth I? Napoleon? You might also want to simulate conversations and posit interactions. How would these people interact? Argue? Find agreement? Offer advice?

The SOLUTION: 'Wise' Leadership **69**

So, for illustrative purposes, we will do some of this at the conclusion of each chapter. Not the actual simulations but setting them up at least. I cannot conduct your meeting for you – this must be done personally.

This is what I will do. I will (hypothetically) ask each to introduce themselves and provide a basic biographical profile. I will ask them what they 'bring to the table' – yes, pun intended! – with regard to the category of wisdom they are discussing. I may even prompt them to provide particularly relevant tips or advice they might highlight in reference to using this wisdom tool.

This is what I will not do. Try to emulate their speech patterns or style. Or try to pretend that I know each of them completely or at least as well as the armies of their dedicated biographers. All symbolic dialogs are just this – for illustrative purposes only. They are not intended to insinuate, invoke, or offend, and anything seen in this manner is both regrettable and unintentional (so sincere apologies in advance).

At the end of the day my hope is that they will inspire you not to quibble about affiliation or semantics but instead to (1) capture the nature of the exercise as applied to each Wise Leadership tool, (2) glean some illustrations or insights from the process, and (3) create your own customized councils with who you wish to put on them (famous or personal figures – e.g., perhaps an admired relative, boss, or coach) and enable you to preside over your own meetings. Who knows, perhaps after all is said and done you might even appoint a representative from each assembly to sit on your '(Leadership) Executive Committee' to integrate the advice across chapters at an even higher plane.

PART II

Assembling Your Leadership Toolbox

4

THE MIND OF A LEADER

How to Use Your Leadership Scientist (Logic) Tools

How does a leader think?

How can you develop the mind of a leader?

These are good questions in any age. They are especially pertinent in our age. This is because today's leaders face a perfect storm that is presenting them (you?) with unprecedented intellectual challenges.

Our organizations are growing increasingly complex with many moving parts. And these parts are moving incredibly fast as technology exponentially evolves to throw at us a continuously updating stream of new 'normals'. And these normals are getting harder to predict as they are embedded in increasingly uncertain, overlapping, and interconnected environments. And these environments are characterized by constantly evolving arrays of global players, each ratcheting up the competitive pressures as they vie for crowded revenue streams.

As the prior paragraphs reveal, we are often faced with environments characterized by the following: Complex. Dynamic. Uncertain. Hypercompetitive.

So, do you still want to be a leader? A wise leader?

Then you must learn to think like one.

One of the tools leaders must hone and wield is logic. Thinking and helping people think. Using your head and helping people use their heads. Elevating your and their thought processes.

But don't just take my word for it. Please consider the following insights.

Our life is shaped by our mind; we become what we think.
– Buddha

The mind is owned by the self and can make a hell of heaven or a heaven of hell.
– John Milton

---

74 Assembling Your Leadership Toolbox

> *I am not a product of my circumstances. I am a product of my decisions.*
> – Stephen Covey
>
> *Every now and then a man's mind is stretched by a new idea or sensation, and never shrinks back to its former dimensions.*
> – Oliver Wendell Holmes
>
> *Unless philosophers become kings (wise leaders) in our cities (organizations), OR unless those who are now kings and rulers become true philosophers so that political power and philosophic intelligence converge, I believe there can be no end to troubles.*
> – Adapted from Plato's Republic

Our world is, in the simplest of terms, ultimately a product of our mind. Our picture of reality is our experienced reality. And these pictures can be more or less developed. Just as Buddha's voice travels across the vast chasms of time to remind us, at the end of the day a person's world and their identity is essentially, unmistakably, and unwaveringly what they think it to be. Two people facing the same circumstances can have very different experiences based on what aspects they emphasize and how they frame it. This is because they actively make sense of it. And how they make sense of it will form their world and enable (or retard) their ability to navigate in it. There is always more data, information, etc. in a situation than anyone can possibly process. Therefore the way our brains effect and are affected by it will vary in proportion to the size of our proverbial sponges (how much we can absorb – more is usually better than less) as well as the quality of our filters (how strategically we can absorb – intentionally is usually better than haphazardly). In this way we become a product of our superimposed sense-making templates. We see or skew the world in a multitude of ways and, in doing so, we create our own realities and by extension our own identities within them. Our thoughts can also be more or less accurate in proportion to how we take in the input – the breadth and depth of our understandings – as well as how we use the input – the problem-solving methodology we employ. Thus, the more we expand and enlighten our horizons the better we will be equipped to deal with whatever falls within them. To lead ourselves and to lead others.

As thinking creatures we are therefore empowered, or limited, primarily by the reaches of our thoughts. This means that our thoughts are, in the end and perhaps without parallel, controlled ultimately by ourselves. And this is simultaneously emboldening and terrifying. As per John Milton this freedom of thought can be both very exciting and quite scary. Nobody else can decide for us what to think. They may attempt to guide or nudge us, but we ultimately have our hands firmly on the wheel. We determine what we see and how we see it. We determine our thoughts about it and how it impacts us. We can, through alternative perspectives or alternative choices, change our experienced realities. Even the most positive event can be spun in a negative light, and vice versa. Opportunities and threats are intellectually interchangeable. With the right mindset we can therefore lift ourselves, and the organizations we lead, to an existence of light. We can create heaven from hell. Or without it we might under-appreciate blessings, miss opportunities, and skew prospects to banish ourselves – and our followers – to a lesser existence of disappointment and darkness.

Think about it. Through better choices we can travel vastly different highways in the course of our lives. With better decisions we can set ourselves up for success or for failure. Of course circumstances differ and some can present more or less of a challenge. Ultimately though there are many forks in the road and they can lead us to very different tomorrows. Each choice also has a multiplier effect because it sets the stage for the next set of choices. Said technically, there are path dependencies in the arcs of our decisions. In the game of life each move has both short- and long-term implications, and it is how we navigate them that determines the success of our journey. This is especially true regarding our critical 'turning points' – the big decisions on one's journey that produce a lasting shift in the life course trajectory (see Elder, 1985). Steve Covey is right on point. We have 'agency'. We can influence our paths insofar as we react to, act upon, or proactively change the aspects of our life course. If we were more rational during one turning point or more creative during another, then our (and our organizations') fates might have turned out quite differently. Choice is power. And choice is a product of our mind.

As we learn to do this better, we increase our capacity of thought both in terms of what we understand and how we understand. Our present circumstances are improved by shining a stronger intellectual light on them. And our future circumstances can be improved by putting ourselves in better positions with such successive lights. It is a virtuous circle. A cumulative path. Learning improves position … that then enables more learning. Chief Justice Holmes' analogy is particularly useful for understanding this. Akin to a physical work-out in the gym which tears and (re)builds muscles, working out our brains through learning similarly activates the creative-destructive process of reshaping our intellect. When we 'work out' our mind we stretch its potential. We make it stronger. We give it more power to elevate our current and future trajectories. We are better positioned to help our organizations succeed.

Unfortunately, we do not always take these positive paths. Sometimes we are intellectual sloths that, instead of working out, rest on the proverbial couch of comfort and familiarity, never learning, developing, and growing. And we do not always (s)elect those leaders who take these positive paths, instead treading and re-treading along tired paths. As per Ralph Waldo Emerson in his 'Self Reliance' this "foolish consistency is the hobgoblin of little minds". Instead, and as Plato rightly articulates, our leaders especially must be thinking people. The most learned and learning among us need to occupy the very positions that most demand their cognitive acumen. If we do not develop and deploy our best minds or do not perpetually grow and utilize these minds, then we will not be able to keep pace with the challenges that face us. In other words, our leaders must use their brains well if we, and our organizations, are to prosper. Our leaders should lead us with the best possible of minds.

So here we are.

Chapter 4 explains how leaders THINK (i.e., use their HEAD). It is firmly grounded in the philosophical branch of LOGIC. Developing this tool enables the wise leader and their organization to become STRONGER at what they do. In this way it involves discovering, honing, and unleashing your inner leadership SCIENTIST.

However, the true nature of the leader's mind is often misunderstood. More than this, individuals' internal limitations and organizations' external barriers can prevent us from truly thinking like a proverbial leadership scientist.

So, what to do?

Coalescing what we know about leadership logic provides several tools to help us in this endeavor.

In short, to be a leadership scientist …

1. Building a better thinking core involves enlarging your breadth and depth of comprehension;
2. Crafting a better thinking process allows you to assess things better through sharper perception and keener intuition; and
3. Leveraging your thinking capacity involves exercising superior judgment through enhanced rational and creative competencies.

Taken together, the chapter's presentation of comprehension, assessment, and judgment will allow you to enhance this leadership tool and work towards EXTRAORDINARY INTELLECTUAL PROWESS.

When faced with reasoning and judgment challenges it will enable you to lead a personal and professional life infused with SAGACITY.

This chapter is therefore organized as follows:

*   Problem: When Facing Thinking and Understanding Challenges
*   Solution: Activate Your Leader 'Logic' Tool
*   Identity: Be a Leadership SCIENTIST
*   Method: To Use Your Head
*   Focus: And with Extraordinary Intellectual Prowess
*   Outcome: Lead with *Sagacity*

When Facing Thinking and Understanding Challenges

What is this Type of Problem?

One type of challenge leaders face is technical or cognitive in nature. It involves understanding. In essence it demands that you develop the 'head' or mind of a leader. That you think like a leader. This is because leaders need to figure things out. Technical things. Factual things. Mechanical things. Procedural things. And, more than this, leaders need to help their followers figure these things out too.

An appropriate analogy for thinking is the functioning of a human brain – or, as information technology (IT) and artificial intelligence (AI) capacities advance, perhaps an electronic brain.

A brain processes data. A brain converts this data into meaningful information. A brain then combines this information with concepts, categories, schema, and scripts to generate – or revise – our knowledge. And if we are fortunate it helps the mind soar to new heights and bring all those attached to it to similarly elucidated levels of understanding. It some ways this is akin to a computer. This is why humans have been so diligent at supplementing its power to 'figure things out' with increasingly sophisticated technological instruments. This is also why we are on the brink of what many see as a potential quantum leap in not just supplementing but also substituting artificially intelligent, or even one-day sentient, man-made brains. The research says that we still have a way to go but the popular press is rife with speculation on what such a world might look like.

So ask yourself: Do you appreciate and can you adequately tap into the power of your brain? Are you expanding it? Supplementing it? Stretching it? Transforming it?

Can you use it to develop a leadership mind?

To think like a leader?

Net-Net: The first core element of wisdom is to 'think'. Think implies that the wisest individuals, teams, organizations, missions, and movements demonstrate extraordinary intellectual prowess. Thus, wise leaders are smart. They use their heads. They get it. They deploy their resources to process issues better than the rest of us and figure things out.

This is depicted in Figure 4.1, with emphasis added in our model of Wise Leadership to highlight the current topic.

So how do you know when you are facing cognitive and thinking-related (understanding) challenges that require you to be a leadership scientist? And why are these problems so darned hard to solve?

These issues are addressed below.

How Do You Know When You Are Facing It?

You need to be a leadership scientist when you encounter cognitive and thinking-related challenges. More specifically, when you face: (1) Problems of Comprehension, (2) Problems of Assessment, and/or (3) Problems of Judgment. Each is now explained.

The Need for Bigger Sponges: Dealing with Problems of Comprehension

The foundation for building leadership logic tools involves expanding your comprehension. In technical terms, here you face challenges where you (and your

78 Assembling Your Leadership Toolbox

Tool # 1:
When there are cognitive and thinking (understanding) challenges...

FIGURE 4.1 Focus: Logic and the Leadership Scientist.

people, groups, organizations, etc.) do not have sufficient breadth and depth of background to make sense of your reality.

In plain speak, when you are struggling with questions of 'What do I need to know?' and 'What do I need to know about it?'

In these cases, they indicate that we have a problem of comprehension.

This is a Data > Information issue. Logical input never makes it on to your radar screen. You cannot lead because you cannot focus on the relevant data and translate it into good information.

Here are some examples: Facing you is a finance problem … and you need to know break-even models to make a good decision. Or perhaps facing you is an economics problem … and you need to know supply-and-demand models to make a good decision. Or instead facing you is a basic math problem … and you need to know probability models to make a good decision. Or maybe facing you is a basic physics problem … and you need to know wind friction models to make a good decision. Or maybe facing you is a behavioral change problem … and you need to know facilitator and resistor force models to make a good decision.

The key is comprehending what type of problem you are facing and what types of cognitive tools are available to solve it properly.

The best leaders can identify problems and the proper tools for solving them. They can soak it all up. They have bigger sponges.

Basically, to do this, you need to (1) have a general familiarity with or access to a broad spectrum of fields relevant to your area of leadership, and (2) be able to search across as well as within these fields as needed.

Fields overlap more and more, and not always in evident ways. Issues are encountered from all over the spectrum. And their answers often come from surprising areas. Technicians at the bottom or even the middle of the proverbial pyramid can get away with more narrow, focused areas of expertise. However, leaders at the top of the hierarchy need to see the big picture and this often involves many overlapping domains. They also need to be able to drill down to any/all to make deep-level connections, assess options, and even find/invent solutions.

Broader, deeper knowledge tilts the odds in your favor. When facing comprehension problems, leaders with bigger sponges are more likely to succeed.

The Need for Better Filters: Dealing with Problems of Assessment

Once your core is broadened and deepened, crafting a better logical process will allow you to pick up more, and higher quality, cues. If you cannot feed your core and supply it with the necessary inputs, then it becomes unused, malnourished capacity. It certainly will not expand. It may even wither and deteriorate if neglected for a prolonged period of time.

Constantly refueling and expanding their assessment capacity is exactly what thinking leaders do.

In technical terms, this problem arises when you do not have sharp perception and/or keen intuition. You do not discern the critical details (analysis) and/or their essential patterns and gists (synthesis).

In plain speak, you struggle with questions of 'What are the essential facts?' and 'How do they relate to each other?

In these cases, they indicate that we have a problem of assessment.

This is an Information > Knowledge issue. Logical input is not processed well. You cannot lead because you cannot separate, combine, and utilize available information to construct higher levels of appraisal.

Here are some examples: You assess that there are three real competitors … and you can discern that nine out of ten times the first mover will win. You assess that the negotiator kept looking up and fidgeting when pushed out of their comfort zone … and you can determine that more likely than not their arguments are ill-informed or overstated. You assess that the noises made by the machinery are exacerbated at certain times of the day … and you can surmise that there is a problem with resource capacity utilization.

The best leaders can assess situations and assess the underlying patterns and meanings in the situation that are hidden from the neophyte but become evident to the thinking leader. They can sort it all out. They have better filters.

Basically, to do this, you need to (1) be able to see what is out there and take in as much as possible, and (2) be able to sense what is relevant and prioritize what is more and less important and give them their due attention. We are bombarded

80 Assembling Your Leadership Toolbox

with stimuli at a rate that greatly outpaces our ability to sense and process it. The person with the bigger sponge can take in more. They get more evidence from the scene or more words from the page. However, the person with the better filter can accept/reject as well as alter focus to prioritize their intake. They are better at spotlighting the right evidence and the right words/arguments.

Sharper perception and keener intuition tilt the probabilities in your favor. When facing assessment problems, leaders with better filters are more likely to succeed.

The Need for Sager Choices: Dealing with Problems of Judgment

Once your logical core is constructed, and once your logical process is humming, then full integration of your logical leadership can take place. You can become rational and lead with reason. You can become creative and lead with originality.

In technical terms, these problems arise when you do not have rational and/or creative problem solving. When you cannot determine the most reasonable way to solve problems or the most inventive ways to reimagine them.

In plain speak, when you struggle with questions of 'What is the most rational way of dealing with this?' and 'What is the most creative way of reimagining this?'

In these cases, they indicate that we have a problem of judgment.

This is a Knowledge > Wisdom issue. Logical inputs and processes are not coupled to enable the most intellectually substantial conclusions. You cannot lead because you cannot utilize your knowledge to enable better realities.

Here are some examples: You can use PERT analysis to determine critical path … then analytically crunch the algorithm and select the highest expected value option. You can brainstorm alternatives … then creatively subject them to lateral reasoning exercises to expand solution sets and enable more imaginative, favorable futures.

The best leaders can judge what paths are best and judge how to best navigate them. They can generate better decisions. They make sager choices.

Basically, to do this, you need to (1) logically analyze the evidence within your broad/deep background, and (2) supersede this to synthesize the pieces of evidence across and beyond your background. Analysis generates logically consistent, tried-and-true rational solutions. It tells you, given the current situation, what is best to do. A leader needs to utilize available resources to organize, assess, and generate solutions to common problems. Synthesis generates logically consistent, new, and original creative solutions. It tells you how to rearrange things to alter the current situation and change its opportunity and constraint sets. A leader also needs to employ these resources within the parameters of their profession to deal with uncommon and unforeseen problems.

Rational and creative decision making tilts the probabilities in your favor. When facing judgment problems, leaders who make sager choices are more likely to succeed.

Taken Together

If we do not rise to meet Comprehension challenges then data never gets onto our radar screen and cannot be translated into information. This is dangerous. Leaders fail if they cannot comprehend well.

If we do not rise to meet Assessment challenges then information becomes twisted, misshapen, and misrepresented into incomplete or false knowledge. This is also dangerous. Leaders fail if they cannot assess well.

If we do not rise to meet Judgment challenges then knowledge is not utilized properly or capably – i.e., (unwisely), and we 'blow' our opportunities by taking wrong turns and making bad decisions. This too is dangerous. Leaders fail if they cannot judge well.

UPSHOT: Wise leaders identify when they are facing cognitive, logic-related challenges.

Activate Your Leader 'Logic' Tool

As expressed in the preceding section, the primary tool leaders use to understand and make decisions is sourced from the domain of logic.

It is necessary to know that you are facing a logic-related 'head' challenge. But it is not sufficient. You must also be able to solve it.

Without leadership SCIENTIST tools, leaders will be hard-pressed to have the basic comprehension, the means of assessment, and/or the facilities to make sound judgments.

If you cannot do these things, then you subject yourself to logical traps and shortcomings. You will not have the mind to deal with the cognitive challenges leaders inevitably face.

And your leadership will fail.

And your organization and people will suffer.

And you will get replaced.

Leaders are looked to as guides. Guides who take people and their organizations to a desirable place. And without a good map, without good senses, without good judgment, leaders will lead them astray.

If you want to lead, then you must know what you are doing.

This applies to both the immediate and extended terms. Comprehension must be sound but also ever-enhanced to deal with expanding realities and new advances in one's field. Assessment must be sound but ever-enhanced to deal with increasingly complex networks of knowledge. Judgment must be sound but also ever-enhanced to make the proper decisions and to deal with the unexpected. After all, problems that can be solved easily do not make it to the desk of a leader. With one's rise in the organization clear algorithms fade away and only the hardest issues with no clear precedents or paths occupy one's agenda.

This is why logical tools are not so easy to acquire and to employ. If they were, then all leaders would not have any rationality lapses and the world would not be

82 Assembling Your Leadership Toolbox

so rife with poor decisions. So, in the same economic terms used in the book's introduction but customized for this particular chapter, there is often an imbalance of the demand for logic and the supply of logic.

Here are some of the key barriers in ourselves (individual) and our environments (organizational) that impede us and our followers from addressing these types of issues.

Some Comprehension Challenges Leaders Must Overcome

First, people are notoriously bad at comprehending situations. If leaders do not address these things, then they and their followers will be severely compromised.

We tend to be prisoners of our own mental models and see only what our narrow training prepares us to see. Narrowness blinds us to everything else around us. Landscaped and panoramic lenses are better than myopic pinpoints. We also tend to be prisoners of our own tools. An overreliance on summary (Wikipedia, Cliffnotes), search (Google, Siri), and processing (spreadsheets, indexes) tools dumb us down and limit us to surface understandings. Appreciation of assumptions and the underlying logic of algorithms are critical for understanding what is really going on and how/why.

Common comprehension problems include:

- Heuristics – We often ignore established disciplinary-based models. Instead we use 'rules of thumb' to quickly and easily estimate things when in fact these so-called rules are often based on subjective, flawed assumptions. Yes they can sometimes prove useful. However, even when they succeed in approximating general patterns they open us up to systematic errors and biases.
  Leaders need to fight the tendency to blindly oversimplify.
  Leadership scientists do not rely on cheap shortcuts.
- Projection – We often ignore established culturally based models. Instead we artificially boil down complex things by assuming that everyone is like us, however egocentrically defined. Unfortunately in an ever-increasing diverse world people are less and less likely to be just like us.
  Leaders need to fight the tendency to treat everyone like themselves.
  Leadership scientists embrace variety.
- Stereotyping – We often ignore established sociologically based models. Instead we artificially boil down complex things by assuming that everyone is like 'their group', however idiosyncratically and prejudicially defined. When we assume that all people who share the same label (fill in the blanks: age, gender, ethnicity, religion, appearance, etc.) are the same we open ourselves up to serious problems.
  Leaders need to fight the tendency to see everyone as their labels.
  Leadership scientists reject typecasting.

Your Leadership Scientist (Logic) Tools **83**

- Confirmation – We often ignore established statistically based models. Instead we look for support rather than truth by giving our loyalty to what we want to be true instead of what is in fact true. We create our own truths and convince ourselves of them regardless of the facts.
Leaders need to fight the tendency to believe what they want versus what they should.
Leadership scientists open their minds.
- Framing – We often ignore established utility-based models. Instead we assess phenomena relative to some arbitrary or manipulated reference point rather than objective outcomes. For example, deeming things as 'gains' or 'losses' because they happen to fall above or below one's aspirations and expectations. Thus the same fact can be seen positively or negatively depending on one's aspiration or target level.
Leaders need to fight the tendency to shape facts with arbitrary casings.
Leadership scientists strive towards objectivity.

Some Assessment Challenges Leaders Must Overcome

Second, people are notoriously bad at assessing situations. If leaders do not address these things, then they and their followers will be severely compromised.

We tend to be flawed, limited sensors. We do not take in nearly as much as we could. Retrospectively rereading mysteries and saying 'how did I miss these clues' or looking at an inventor and saying 'how did I not see this it is so simple' are evidence of this.

We also tend to be flawed, biased sensors. We focus on the wrong things. We pore over tangential matters and occupy ourselves with trivialities to the exclusion of more pertinent and central stimuli. Good readers know what sections to skim and what sections to read five times. Good passers sense who will be open, good pitchers sense what will be received, and good foragers sense where will be fruitful.

Common assessment problems include:

- Selective Attention – We see and don't see things in our environment solely based on our personal likes, training, motives, etc. For instance, people of different political parties or organizational roles seeing only the parts of issues the way they are conditioned to see them.
Leaders need to fight the tendency to be boxed into overly constraining cutouts.
Leadership scientists evaluate fairly.
- Manipulated Salience – We see and don't see things in our environment based on how they are presented. We are lured and suckered by bright, shiny objects. Advertisers, sound-byte-promoting pundits, and professional illusionists/ magicians are masters at this.

84 Assembling Your Leadership Toolbox

Leaders need to fight the tendency to be led down false paths.
Leadership scientists evaluate purposefully.

- Emphasis – We are drawn to observations that fit our memory structures, that seem like they should be important, or that occur in a certain order. For example, people tend to be disproportionately influenced by first (primacy) or last (recency) impressions.
  Leaders need to fight the tendency to place too much emphasis on the wrong things.
  Leadership scientists evaluate consistently.
- Halo – We are drawn to single, sometimes arbitrary aspects of complex phenomena often to the exclusion of better ones. For example, people tend to be disproportionately influenced by one attribute or characteristic (e.g., handshake, eye contact, etc.) even though they are not systematically linked with critical outcome metrics.
  Leaders need to fight the tendency to take this easy yet flawed path.
  Leadership scientists evaluate broadly.
- Context – We are drawn to things, for better or worse, based on the degree to which they stand out from their context. For example, people tend to notice surprising outlier events more and misrepresent their nature or meaning, whereas they would be seen more/less or perhaps even better/worse if simply viewed against a different background.
  Leaders need to fight the tendency to be taken in by obscuring shadows.
  Leadership scientists evaluate objectively.
- Attribution – We make decisions on the meriting of credit and blame based on spurious criteria. For example, we often self-servingly take credit (internal attribution) for good things and deflect responsibility (external attribution) for bad things.
  Leaders need to fight the tendency to get consumed by the blame game.
  Leadership scientists evaluate constructively.

Some Judgment Challenges Leaders Must Overcome

Third, people are notoriously bad at making decisions. If leaders do not address these things, then they and their followers will be severely compromised. We tend to be poor analyzers. We do not act in accordance with economic models but instead slant our realities and sub-optimize our judgments. We also tend to be poor synthesizers. We do not do a good job of 'coloring outside the lines' to address situations we did not foresee, anticipate, and plan for.

Common judgment problems include:

- Rationalization – We make decisions 'backwards', starting with the outcome and then force-fitting the process to justify it. This is often referred to as the pet-project or implicit favorite error. It happens when we favor preferred paths regardless of their rational or creative merit (and regardless if other paths might be better).

Leaders need to fight the tendency to pre-ordain their paths.

Leadership scientists don't play favorites.

- Satisficing – We make decisions 'boundedly', artificially limiting the criteria, alternatives, and/or processes used to drive choices. This is often a good way to make trivial decisions but can have catastrophic effects for major ones. It happens when we determine that it is not worth the energy, effort, etc. to be more rational or creative.

  Leaders need to fight the tendency to artificially cap their paths.

  Leadership scientists don't do things half-baked.

- Escalation – We make decisions 'retroactively', with an over-emphasis on sunk costs and the desire to avoid taking responsibility for errors. Essentially it is a fear of being seen as a failure or a wishy-washy, flip-flopping indecisive decision maker who cannot stick to their guns. It happens when we double down on bad choices and do not alter our approach in the face of disconfirming evidence.

  Leaders need to fight the tendency to overcommit to bad paths.

  Leadership scientists know when to quit.

- Lack of Imagination – We are unable to see past hardened categories and fixed schema. This can take the form of narrow vision and compressed boundary assumptions, constancy and singularity in our approaches and thinking languages, and complacency in our laziness and lack of questioning. It happens when we remain within our comfort zones at the expense of exploration and growth.

  Leaders need to fight the tendency to visit only well-worn paths.

  Leadership scientists don't blindly rely on habit.

Taken Together

These aspects of cognitive challenges are well illustrated in Plato's 'Allegory of the Cave' in his *Republic*. Plato famously paints a picture of people where they live in a proverbial cave of shadows, shackled in the darkness and seeing only false images that are spoon-fed to them by those in power. Because the masses know only this world of shadows they do not trust those who actually 'see', regard them as lunatics, and are hostile towards their attempts at help. Fast-forwarding to present times, Plato's work can be interpreted as a condemnation of intellectual lethargy and languor. But more than this, it also attributes part of the blame to the social/political environment that corrupts potential thinkers, motivates them in the wrong way, and compels them to select the 'wrong' leaders.

Most people do not always see the truth. They do not see it because (1) They cannot, (2) They do not want to, and/or (3) They are not incentivized for it.

86 Assembling Your Leadership Toolbox

First, we can be myopic and limited in comprehension. We live in a cave of shadows and are only exposed to flickering manipulations of the truth. As such we develop the tools to deal with only these shadows.

Second, we can be lazy and limited in assessment. It is too hard to break our chains. It is too hard to leave our comfort zones. It is too hard to climb up and elevate ourselves. It is too hard to see the light (especially with retinas accustomed to shadows).

Third, we can be selfish and limited in judgment. It is better for us to stay in the light than go back down. It is better for us to line our own pockets than share the wealth. It is better for us to be appreciated by like-minded others than be ridiculed by those needy but reluctant learners.

What is needed to break this vicious cycle? A leadership scientist with the skill. Someone who can overcome cognitive barriers to break the chains of ignorance and ascend to the light. Through this education and elucidation they go beyond shadows and see the real truth – i.e., the call to wisdom. And also a leadership scientist with the will. Someone with a desire not to wallow in this enlightened state but, akin to the Eastern concept of *Bodhisattva*, go back down into the cave and return to the people – i.e., answering the call to wise leadership. And, in addition, a system that supports and even encourages such leadership scientists to institutionalize the processes and create a virtuous circle.

Plato tells us that being wise (seeing the light) is hard, and being a wise leader (showing it to others) is even harder. But he also reminds us that it is not impossible and gives us a way to do it. As a heads-up, I will elaborate further upon this point in Chapter 11.

So we should not lament the lack of logic in our leadership. We should instead work to approximate these ideals.

The thinking person is able to be logical in their comprehension, assessment, and judgment. The thinking leader is able to help others and steer their organization in logical ways.

UPSHOT: Wise leaders don't just identify but also address cognitive, logic-related challenges.

Be a Leadership SCIENTIST

The identity best befitting a logical problem solver is that of a leadership scientist.

Science, as per the *Oxford English Dictionary*, is the intellectual and practical activity encompassing the systematic study of the structure and behavior of the physical and natural world through observation and experiment.

In short, it is the primary vehicle available to us for developing and leveraging the power of our brain.

What are the areas of the major scientific fields that a leadership scientist should be familiar with?

From a physical perspective we can look at natural sciences (e.g., chemistry and physics), life sciences (e.g., biology and neurology), and earth sciences (e.g., geology, ecology, and meteorology). They are useful in illuminating our context. Briefly … Chemistry is the branch of science that deals with the elemental composition, structure, and properties of substances of which matter is composed and the transformations they undergo. Physics is the branch of science concerned with the nature and properties of matter and energy (e.g., potential, kinetic) and the way they act on each other within the infinitesimally small as well as across the epically immense. Biology is the study of living organisms and their vital processes. It can be divided into many specialized fields that cover their morphology, physiology, anatomy, behavior, origin, and distribution. Neuroscience has as its focus the structure or function of our network of nerve cells and the brain. Neurology is, at its core, the branch of medicine or biology that deals with the anatomy, physiology, and functioning of central and peripheral nervous systems, especially in relation to integrative behavior and learning. Ecology is the branch of science that deals with the relationships of organisms to one another and to their physical environments. Geology is the branch of science that deals with the history and structure of the earth's physical substance and its life, especially as recorded in rocks and soil. Meteorology is the branch of science concerned with the processes and phenomena of the atmosphere, especially as a means of understanding and forecasting weather patterns.

From a social perspective we can also include fields such as sciences of psychology, sociology, economics, and anthropology. Briefly … Psychology refers to the study of the mind and behavior, including the human characteristics, motives, and attitudes that influence their actions. Sociology expands the level of analysis to look at how groups, organizations, and other social institutions provide context for these. Anthropology extends the level of analysis even further to also examine how the arcs of cultures and climates influence the trajectories of human development.

From a foundational perspective we can consider the science of mathematics. This involves systems of identifying, measuring, and combining numbers and other symbolic forms. In this way math underlies all other disciplines.

The above fields are invaluable in illuminating human dynamics. Scientists, by extension, are those most skilled and engaged in using them for advancing the intellectual processing and understanding of our world.

When you picture a scientist what images come into your head?

Perhaps they are wearing a lab-coat,

Peering through thick glasses in a wing of a library,

Out in the field measuring and recording something,

Staring into space lost in contemplation,

Bent over a desk feverously working through a puzzle or problem,

Or maybe diligently outlining the specs for a new technology or machine.

These are poor stereotypes and pigeonholes for sure, but they can be used as a jumping-off point for capturing the character of the scientist. And as such they may suggest ways for modeling how scientists think and what leaders can learn from them to think better.

88 Assembling Your Leadership Toolbox

TABLE 4.1 Tools for Developing the MIND of a Leader

Better Core: Comprehension	Broader Breadth Deeper Depth
Better Process: Assessment	Sharper Perception Keener Intuition
Better Leverage: Judgment	More Rational More Creative

Put more systematically, and in a manner consistent with the book's model:

- Scientists comprehend better (Data > Information): Leadership scientists therefore have the breadth and depth of knowledge – the sponge – to comprehend their challenges.
- Scientists assess better (Information > Knowledge). Leadership scientists therefore have the attention to and perception of the world – the filter – to assess their challenges.
- Scientists judge better (Knowledge > Wisdom). Leadership scientists therefore have the rational and inventive solutions to make sage judgments – the decisions – amidst their challenges.

Leadership scientists develop their logic in these three fundamental ways.

The following offers a step-by-step map for doing this. For convenience these steps are summarized in Table 4.1. They are then illustrated as well as elaborated upon in the subsequent corresponding sections.

To Use Your Head

Step One – Building a Better Core

> *The difference between an educated and uneducated man is the same*
> *difference as between being alive and being dead.*
> – Aristotle
>
> *The man who never alters his opinion is like standing water, and*
> *breeds reptiles of the mind.*
> – William Blake
>
> *Fear an ignorant man more than a lion.*
> – Turkish proverb
>
> *Who is wise? He that learns from everyone.*
> – Benjamin Franklin

Aristotle tells us that education is critical in the foundational comprehension necessary for the living of life. The message mirrors his teacher Plato's – and even before this his teacher Socrates' – idea that the unexamined life is not worth living. Blake adds that this education must be continuously updated and enhanced. Education is therefore a process and not a destination. The subsequent Turkish proverb warns us that if we do not learn and do not grow we are dangerous to ourselves and to those who entrust us with their leadership. Finally, Franklin tells us that to do this we need to be constant, open-minded, broad-based learners.

The core to becoming a better leadership scientist, or if you will a strategy for developing your HEAD 'lights', is therefore expanding how much you understand and how much you understand about it. That is to say – breadth and depth of comprehension.

Breadth of Comprehension

Broader breadth of comprehension allows you to integrate and put things together. Deeper depth of comprehension allows you to analyze and break things down. Combine them and construct a truly formidable intellectual foundation.

To broaden your breadth of comprehension, focus on increasing your exposures, your experiences, and your contacts. Quantity is key.

Some strategies include reading up on a variety of subjects. These might include history, physics, philosophy, literature, religions, professions, and the arts. The key is to delve into divergent and potentially complementary sources. Go to the library. Explore used book sales and free download sites. Swap texts and tomes with someone in another field.

- Leadership scientists read broadly

Other strategies might take the form of travel to a variety of places. Itineraries might include focusing on different cultures, contexts, activities, and traditions. Or you can do this virtually through GoogleMaps and YouTube. Again the key is to delve into divergent and potentially complementary sources.

- Leadership scientists travel broadly

Still other strategies might take the form of networking with a variety of peoples. Priorities might emphasize having diverse and horizon-expanding conversations, interactions, and engagements with people who you do not typically meet in your personal and professional circles. Once more, the key is to delve into divergent and potentially complementary sources.

90 Assembling Your Leadership Toolbox

- Leadership scientists network broadly

Think of the top part of the letter 'T'. Broad breadth involves expanding the horizontal reach of your understanding.

Depth of Comprehension

To extend your depth of comprehension, focus on increasing your education, your expertise, and your resources. Quality is key.

Some strategies include reading intensely within a subject. These might include going back to school, taking part-time refresher courses, or even participating in self-study opportunities through online (e.g., MOOC or individualized) and traditional methods. Notwithstanding, it should be systematic and grounded, triangulated (e.g., touching on complementary aspects of issues that adds to their depth of exploration), rigorous, and inclusive of both classical as well as leading-edge topics.

- Leadership scientists study deeply

Other strategies might take the form of expertise-building focuses that include proficiency-enhancing workshops, practice, simulation and case methodologies, trial-and-error, general training, or even customized professional mentorships. There are so many windows we can use to develop another skill or ability.

- Leadership scientists train deeply

Still other strategies might be to add resources to your toolbox in the forms of support technologies, subscriptions, templates, and equipment. The power of these tools relative to their cost is historically inexpensive. Develop personal laboratories for your mind.

- Leadership scientists enterprise deeply

Think of the bottom part of the letter 'T'. Greater depth involves expanding the vertical sophistication of your understanding.

Taken Together

So what are you waiting for?

Drive out heuristic shortcuts and over-simplification.
Resist projection and stereotyping.
Reduce feel-good confirmation biases.
Rein in framing-induced manipulations.

Instead increase your breadth and depth of knowledge.
Be more systematic and comprehensive in your understanding.
Grow your leadership scientist tool.
Start enhancing your comprehension capacities.
UPSHOT:Wise leaders evoke their inner scientist to logically comprehend.

Step Two – Crafting a Better Process

> *It's not what you look at that matters, it's what you see.*
> – Henry David Thoreau
>
> *An optimist is a person who sees a green light everywhere, while a pessimist sees only the red stoplight. … The truly wise person is colorblind.*
> – Albert Schweitzer
>
> *We must have strong minds, ready to accept facts as they are.*
> – Harry S. Truman
>
> *For years I have been accused of making snap judgments. Honestly, this is not the case because I am a profound, military student and the thoughts I express, perhaps too flippantly, are the result of years of thought and study.*
> – George Patton

Thoreau tells us that perception is critical. The eyes look but the mind sees. Leaders see more and see better. Schweitzer adds that there is a fickle nature to the seeing. Some see what they want to see. Some see what they would be aided by seeing. The wise are different. They see what is. Regardless of inclination or benefit. This point is also reinforced by Truman. Our minds must be strong enough with the capacity to perceive accurately and with the learned intuition to understand clearly. Patton makes this point even more strongly. He can assess situations not because he is a superman but because he has meticulously prepared himself to do it. Overnight success is actually the product of lots of hard work. The football quarterback who quickly reads defenses or the chess-master who can walk around the park instantly reading game boards does so because they have both spent hours upon hours studying and deducing patterns.

HEAD-Lights are employed to illuminate our place and path in the world. A development strategy would therefore entail improving what to process and how to process it. That is to say – enhancing perception and enhancing intuition.

Sharper Perception

To sharpen your perception, focus on increasing your precision and having an accurate picture of things. This can be done by enhancing your physical senses

92 Assembling Your Leadership Toolbox

and the ability to discern salience. It is manifest in being able to see things better literally as well as figuratively.

Try doing this around the office, on the train, or while going for walks. Can you notice more sights? It is manifest in being able to hear, smell, etc. things better. Try tasting different ingredients in your food, drink, or wine. Can you notice more flavors? Try listening to things at lower volumes, at further distances, or among lots of background noise. Can you notice more sounds? Try examining different faces. Can you notice more expressions?

- Leadership scientists sharpen their sensing

This can also be done by enhancing interpretation. Can you not just see or hear things better but also discern their messages and their meanings? Is it increasingly evident what these sights, noises, tastes, and expressions do in fact reveal?

- Leadership scientists sharpen their deciphering

In addition, this can be done by enhancing attribution. Can you figure out what is causing what? Who to assign responsibility to? What to credit when things go well and what to blame when they go poorly? Is it increasingly easier to pinpoint the critical components of these processes?

- Leadership scientists sharpen their attributing

Keener Intuition

To extend the keenness of your intuition, focus on increasing your instinct and natural 'sense' of things. This can be done by enhancing categorization. It is manifest in the ability to put things in cognitive categories and to differentiate these categories. What is a threat and what is an opportunity? Who is an ally and who is an enemy?

- Leadership scientists hone their categorization

This can also be done by enhancing pattern recognition. In other words, to figure out and see chains of events before they become evident. What is the likely coupling of this announcement or this adjustment? How are these variables related? Who are the main players likely to be?

- Leadership scientists hone their pattern recognition

In addition, this can be done by enhancing trajectory projection. Can you see into the proverbial future and, like a seer or chess-master, that know moves before they are actually taken? Science helps you to understand but it can also aid in a priori prediction. Which customers are likely to default? Which applicants are likely to fail?

- Leadership scientists hone their dynamic forecasting

Taken Together

So what are you waiting for?
  Wean tendencies of overly selective attention.
  Resist being deceived by manipulated saliences and emphases.
  Avoid halo and context effects that make you lose focus.
  Take care to identify and reduce attribution errors of credit and blame.
  Instead increase your perception and intuition.
  Be sharper and keener in your understanding.
  Grow your leadership scientist tool.
  Start enhancing your assessment capacities.
  UPSHOT: Wise leaders evoke their inner scientist to logically assess.

Step Three – Leveraging a Better Capacity

> *When the only tool you have is a hammer, all problems begin to resemble nails.*
> – Abraham Maslow
>
> *Failure to prepare is preparing to fail.*
> – John Wooden
>
> *The world of reality has its limits; the world of imagination is boundless.*
> – Jean-Jacques Rousseau
>
> *The true sign of intelligence is not knowledge but imagination.*
> – Albert Einstein

Maslow puts his scientific chops to bear in making the honest, accurate observation that we are only as good as the tools which we quip ourselves with. It is hard to be rational with poor instruments or the wrong instruments. If we are learned in the components and steps of good process and good science, right method and right thinking, then we can solve problems within their domain. Wooden tells us that the bulk of this work is done before you face a problem. If you know your methods, then you can choose the right one. If you know your process then you can follow it well even under time pressure and duress. Rational planning sets you up for success. It increases the probability that things will go well and increases the options to deal with them in case they go poorly. However, Rousseau reminds us that we must continuously evolve our thinking and dare to push, prod, or

94 Assembling Your Leadership Toolbox

even reshape or destroy its understanding when faced with uncertain or daunting challenges. Whereas rationality works well in the known it is limited when looking into the abyss. The mind must then not only deploy rationality but evolve it. Einstein, the proverbial poster child of science and perhaps (and literally) the best-known face of science, reinforces that true intelligence lies not just in understanding the rules but superseding them. Thinking beyond the possible. When we have understood everything, then rationality will do. Until that date we also need imagination.

HEAD-Lights, used well, result not just in superior comprehension and assessment but also in superior judgment. There are thus multiple dimensions of judgment, hence different targets for a development strategy. Two of the most important are our capacity for systematic and imaginative thought. That is to say – logic and creativity.

Rational Capacities

To broaden your rational capacities, focus on increasing your systematic approach to problem solving. Some strategies include establishing clearly stated objectives and criteria. Know what you want to accomplish and how you will judge success.

- Leadership scientists optimize their decision targets

Other strategies might take the form of methodically compiled choices and contingencies. Know how to judge the value, importance, and impact of different choice scenarios.

- Leadership scientists optimize their decision processes

Still other strategies might take the form of optimally calculated evaluation and choice. Know how to crunch the numbers and generate mathematically superior outcomes. This is the domain of the 'hard' sciences and how they inform the leadership scientist. In doing these things you can become more methodical.

- Leadership scientists optimize their decision selections

Creative Capacities

To broaden your creative capacities, focus on increasing your flexible or even playful approach to problem solving. Some strategies include enhanced range of opportunity and alternative generation. Know how to add and even create paths that others do not see.

- Leadership scientists expand their decision targets

Other strategies might take the form of extended extrapolation of ideas and assessments. Know how to build on these options, piggyback them onto others, and by doing this grow them in unique, hard-to-replicate ways.

- Leadership scientists expand their decision processes

Still other strategies might take the form of inventive development of options, combinations, features, and solutions. Know how to creatively problem solve to find different angles and implementation strategies for making things happen. This is more in the domain of the 'soft' sciences and how they inform the leadership scientist. In doing this you can become more exploratory.

- Leadership scientists expand their decision selections

Taken Together

So what are you waiting for?
Even though it feels good try not to over-rationalize.
Even though it is easier try not to over-satisfice.
Even though it may make you look better try not to over-escalate.
Even though it is safer try not to under-imagine.
Instead increase your rational and creative instruments.
Be more systematic and comprehensive in your decisions.
Grow your leadership scientist tool.
Start enhancing your judgment capacities.
UPSHOT: *Wise leaders evoke their inner scientist to logically judge.*

And with Extraordinary Intellectual Prowess

Developing this logic-oriented tool enables the wise leader and their organization to become stronger at what they do. In a way it involves discovering, honing, and unleashing your inner leadership scientist. Sagacity is a core aspect of successful leadership. It is evidenced throughout history in both historical as well as legendary accounts of leadership scientists who have used their heads to address logical challenges.

As described in the opening section, the core tools of leadership wisdom can be seen to manifest themselves in the record of humanity's greatest successes – the achievements of the most influential real and idealized leaders who have proven themselves across a multitude of times, tasks, and locations. As such, in addition to modern relevant and complementary examples, we draw predominantly from two distinct yet complementary sources: *Time Magazine's* (TM) lists of the most influential, and American Film Institute's (AFI) lists of the most heroic.

96 Assembling Your Leadership Toolbox

We will do this via the vehicle of an imaginary assembly of 'Invisible Counselors'. A Leadership scientist conference table to provide insights on how to think like a leader.

So, let us call this meeting to order ...

The Gavel

Here ye, here ye. I now call this LEADERSHIP SCIENTIST council to order.

Our focus is addressing COGNITIVE leadership challenges of UNDERSTANDING.

Our purpose is to animate the tool of LOGIC and leading for SAGACITY. That is, EXTRAORDINARY INTELLECTUAL PROWESS.

The Real

So, who might be attending as some of history's most influential logic counselors? Let us ask them to introduce themselves (note: all biographical profiles are gleaned from many sources, including the *Encyclopedia Britannica*) and speak to the leadership tool of logic and leading for sagacity.

Seat One

Perhaps an archetype of a scientific approach to nature and the world.

Like ... Benjamin Franklin.

Boston born but a son of Philadelphia, I was one of the founding fathers of the United States revolution. In this capacity I was a delegate to the Constitutional Convention and a primary party in drafting the Declaration of Independence. More than this though, I have been a printer, publisher, author, diplomat, inventor, and scientist. Some have described me as embodying the American ideal of a learned 'Renaissance Man'. I have 'made important contributions to science, especially in the understanding of electricity'. I am also renowned for the 'wit, wisdom, and elegance' of my writing.

Like ... Aristotle.

A philosopher and scientist, I have been described as 'one of the greatest intellectual figures of Western history'. This is in part because I was the author of foundational philosophical and scientific systems that were vast, covering most of the sciences, including 'biology, botany, chemistry, ethics, history, logic, metaphysics, rhetoric, philosophy of mind, philosophy of science, physics, poetics, political theory, psychology, and zoology'. Perhaps most notably, I was the founder of formal logic and syllogistic reasoning.

Like ... Francis Bacon.

I carry many titles, including lawyer, statesman, philosopher, and author. Intellectually I viewed all knowledge as attainable and promoted new ways by which people might grasp and even command nature. The apex of this quest was my *Novum Organum* (or New Instrument) that describes a systematic, step-by-step method for expanding our ways of knowing and understanding. It provided a broad description of facts, a classification of these facts, and an assessment of the connection between the varied phenomena under investigation.

However, if hard-pressed, we would probably award this seat to … Leonardo Da Vinci.

I am best known as a painter but also am a draftsman, sculptor, architect, and engineer whose genius, perhaps more than that of any other figure, epitomized the Renaissance ideal of figuring out how the world works. I assessed natural and human characteristics with remarkable precision and processed them both rationally and creatively to pioneer achievements across the board of human endeavors. My notebooks reveal a spirit of scientific inquiry and a mechanical inventiveness that were centuries ahead of their time. The fame that I enjoyed rests largely on my unlimited desire for knowledge, which guided all my thinking and behavior. To me sight was man's highest sense because it alone conveyed the facts of experience immediately, correctly, and with certainty. Hence, every phenomenon perceived became an object of knowledge, and knowing how to see became the great theme of my studies. I applied my creativity to every realm in which graphic representation is used. Beyond this I used a superb intellect, unusual powers of observation, and mastery of the art of drawing to study nature itself, a line of inquiry that allowed my dual pursuits of art and science to flourish. If asked to elaborate upon the secrets of my success, according to author Michael Gelb in his 2000 book *How To Think Like Leonardo da Vinci*, it is proposed that there are seven principles to approximate my cognitive acumen: (1) Curiosita: An insatiably curious approach to life; (2) Dimonstratzione: A commitment to test knowledge through experience; (3) Sensazione: The continual refinement of the senses, especially sight, as the means to clarify experience; (4) Sfumato: A willingness to embrace ambiguity, paradox, and uncertainty; (5) Arte/Scienza: The development of the balance and whole-brain thinking; (6) Corporalita: The cultivation of ambidexterity, fitness, and poise; and (7) Connessione: A recognition of the connectedness of all things and phenomena; 'systems thinking'.

Seat Two

Plus maybe a master of theory construction.

Like … Sir Isaac Newton.

I have been described as 'the culminating figure of the scientific revolution of the seventeenth century'. My interests span many scientific disciplines. For example: Optics, through the science of light where my discoveries laid the foundation for modern physical optics. Mechanics, through my three laws of motion that laid the foundation for the principles of modern physics and the formulation of the law of universal gravitation. And mathematics, where I formulated a little thing

98 Assembling Your Leadership Toolbox

called calculus. My resumé is perhaps nowhere better exemplified than in my *Mathematical Principles of Natural Philosophy* which is regarded as 'one of the most important single works in the history of modern science'.

Like ... Plato.

I have become known as the central figure of Western philosophy, to which Alfred North Whitehead famously quipped: "The safest general characterization of the European philosophical tradition is that it consists of a series of footnotes to Plato." I am perhaps most proud of the conceptualization of entities that I called ideal forms. These are not surface manifestations accessible to the senses but instead ideas reachable only by the mind. They are indeed the most fundamental 'constituents of reality, underlying the existence of the sensible world and giving it intelligibility'.

However, if hard-pressed, we would probably award this seat to ... Albert Einstein.

I have led an interesting life. But for the purpose of this book and my place at this table let me focus on just one year of it. During 1905, often called my 'miracle year', I published several papers each altering the course of physics. One where I applied the quantum theory to light. A second where I offered the first experimental proof of the existence of atoms. And a third where I showed that relativity theory led to the harmonization of mass and energy via the famous equation $E = mc2$. What are the secrets to thinking like me? According to author Scott Thorpe in his 2000 book of the same title, he proposes that this involves "freeing yourself from your 'rule ruts' so you can dream up amazing (and doable) solutions to the seemingly impossible". Similarly, Daniel Smith argues in his 2015 book that "my name has become synonymous with the word 'genius'. My strong determination, visualized goals, and unique combination of rationality and imagination helped me to view each success as a stepping-stone for even greater understanding." And Walter Isaacson, who wrote what many deem my best biography, reveals that "It was Albert Einstein's tendency to rebel that was the source of his great creativity ... and his real genius was his ability to focus on mundane things that most people overlook".

Seat Three

Let us also add an embodiment of the creative method.

Like ... Nikola Tesla.

I am foremost an inventor and an engineer. I discovered and patented the rotating magnetic field, the basis of most alternating-current machinery. I also developed the three-phase system of electric power transmission then sold the patent rights to my system of alternating-current dynamos, transformers, and motors to George Westinghouse. I also invented the Tesla coil, which is widely used in radio technology.

However, if hard-pressed, we would probably award this seat to ... Steve Jobs.

I am famously regarded for my contributions to computer development, enhancement, design, and diffusion. I did this by uniquely comprehending the interplay of man and machine. This required extraordinary breadth as well as depth in a number of fields. As per Walter Isaacson's 2008 biography of me (yes, the same person who chronicled Dr. Einstein), I am a creative entrepreneur whose creative genius revolutionized six industries: personal computers, animated movies, music, phones, tablet computing, and digital publishing. Isaacson's portrait flattered me with the following attributions. ... I stand as the 'ultimate icon of inventiveness and applied imagination'. I was able more than anyone else to connect creativity with technology. I then built a company predicated on this connection where quantum leaps of imagination were combined with remarkable feats of engineering.

Seat Four

How about an embodiment of the rational Method.

Like ... Charles Darwin.

I am a naturalist whose scientific theory of evolution by natural selection became the foundation of modern evolutionary studies. I systematically formulated my theory from evidence, which was meticulously gathered and analyzed from a voyage around the world aboard the *HMS Beagle*. It was later published in the 1859 book *Origin of Species*, which revolutionized modern concepts of science and thought.

Like ... Marie Curie.

I am a physicist most noted for my work on radioactivity. I led the Physics Laboratory at the Sorbonne, was Professor of General Physics in the Faculty of Sciences, and directed the Curie Laboratory in the Radium Institute of the University of Paris. I was also the first woman to win a Nobel Prize, and the only woman to win the award in two distinct yet complementary fields – for Physics and for Chemistry.

Seat Five

And finally trailblazers in the application of mathematics and computational methods.

Like ... Alan Turing (perhaps the most non-famous famous person ever).

I have been described as a 'mathematician and logician, who made major contributions to mathematics, cryptanalysis, logic, philosophy, and mathematical biology and also to new areas later named computer science, cognitive science, artificial intelligence, and artificial life'. I revolutionized cognitive science by inventing a Turing Machine – an electronic computer – to break the Nazi Enigma code and help win the Second World War. And later on, if this was not enough, in my papers 'On Computable Numbers' and 'Systems of Logic Based on Ordinals',

100 Assembling Your Leadership Toolbox

I laid the groundwork for pairing this hardware with complementary brain-like software to exponentially expand the frontiers of understanding.

Like … Bill James.

Through my popularly labeled 'money ball' I revealed how numbers explain complex human phenomena. This is called analytics. Now everything is seemingly being measured. Processed. Tested. Compared. As per author Scott Gray in his 2006 book entitled *The Mind of Bill James: How a Complete Outsider Changed Baseball* … (I have) been called 'baseball's shrewdest analyst' … and (my) Baseball Abstract has been acclaimed as the 'holy book of baseball'. … Thirty years ago, (I) introduced a new approach to evaluating players and strategies, and now (my) theories have become indispensable tools for agents, statistics analysts, maverick general managers, and anyone who is serious about understanding the game.

The Idealized

So, who might be attending as some of cinema's most heroic logic counselors? The master thinkers who out-reason their foes.

Seat Six

Why not start with Indiana Jones?

'Indy' was first featured in the 1981 film *Raiders of the Lost Ark* that combines with subsequent sequels *Temple of Doom*, *The Last Crusade*, and *Kingdom of the Crystal Skull* to track fictional archeologist Dr. Henry 'Indiana' Jones (portrayed by Harrison Ford) in his pursuit of lost artifacts and ancient relics – here the biblical Ark of the Covenant. In short, he is portrayed as a well-educated archeology professor who is able to draw from deep knowledge bases to read a broad set of ancient clues that enable him and his teams to solve cryptic historical puzzles. For example, in using a staff and symbol to locate the burial site of hidden treasures. His logical prowess was also on full display in his maneuvering through booby traps, outwitting well-armed enemies, and navigating a variety of treacherous passageways. This bears some resemblance to the less iconic but compelling Tom Hanks' character Robert Langdon, a Harvard professor of religious iconography and symbology, who demonstrated similar attributes in the screen adaptations of the *The Da Vinci Code* series.

Seats Seven and Eight

Then maybe Clarise Starling.

And while we're at it, similarly let us add Virgil Tibbs.

Starling the FBI investigator and Tibbs the police detective are similarly portrayed as uniquely able to use their knowledge, wits, and wiles to solve complex criminal cases.

Starling is portrayed by Jodie Foster in the 1991 classic neo-noir film *Silence of the Lambs*. She plays a FBI Academy student tasked with debriefing the master criminal Dr. Hannibal Lecter to pursue an active killer with the nickname of 'Buffalo Bill'. Although relatively inexperienced, Starling makes up for this with her razor-sharp intellect, powerful deductive abilities, and ability to think on her feet. For example, in the reasoning of past deliberate red herrings and gleaning insights to determine critical truths about the criminal.

Virgil Tibbs is portrayed by Sidney Poitier in the 1967 film *In the Heat of the Night*. He plays a prominent black homicide detective who assists in the investigation of the murder of a wealthy businessman in the Deep South. Like Clarise Starling, Detective Tibbs is highly resourceful and observant of his surroundings. However, he leans on his considerable deductive abilities but also his experience to navigate the twists and turns of the case and rationally decipher the circumstances that led to the crime. For example, in the ruling out of wrongly accused suspects and focusing on overlooked clues to pinpoint the killer's identity.

Seat Nine

And we must not exclude the Batman (Bruce Wayne).

Featured in the 1966 film *Batman* as well as numerous sequels, reboots, and associated mass media projects and products, the mega-rich multi-millionaire Bruce Wayne is shown to leverage his considerable resources to become a master criminologist who, through his *alter ego*, employs advanced technology and superior guile to battle an assortment of scheming evildoers. Based on the legendary DC Comics character of the same name, the Batman uses his forensic accoutrements to methodically and a perpetually outthink even the cleverest of evil minds. For example, he designs and builds devices that both respond to and anticipate the moves of his opponents akin to the intellectual sophistication of a chess-master.

Seat Ten (my WILDCARD)

I take some publisher prerogative here and add a character that was not on the AFI list but has made a personal impression with regard to their logical lessons. There are surely many candidates for this seat. For example, the brilliant Sherlock Holmes. Or *Star Trek*'s uber-logical Mr. Spock. Or *Fargo*'s Marge Gunderson. Or MIT genius Will Hunting (of the punny 'Good Will Hunting'). However, here my vote goes to someone perhaps not as celebrated but certainly every bit as formidable. The character is: Mona Lisa Vito.

A best supporting actress winner for her role in the 1992 film *My Cousin Vinnie*, Marisa Tomei brilliantly portrays a stylish city woman who accompanies her partner to the Deep South in order to defend his nephews who have been wrongly accused of a crime. Constantly underestimated and negatively stereotyped, Ms. Vito supersedes others' categories to provide critical expert testimony.

102 Assembling Your Leadership Toolbox

For example, about automotive design and the logic of how cars with internal combustion engines (ICE) work, specifically their axle assemblies and limited slip differentials which provide more control to the driver under poor road conditions. She sees what others do not and logically connects as well as abstracts from them to educate the jury, correct the prosecution, establish the essential truths and logical connections related to the case, and ultimately exonerate the youths.

Even More

We might also staff our 'back-benchers' with additional most-influential nominees.

Though nobody is perfect, including the aforementioned, here are some additional examples of people found on *Time Magazine*'s most influential list who have used their HEAD-Lights to impact their, and our, world – feel free to look them up to learn more about their lives, their methods, and their impact:

- Sigmund Freud … and the challenges of human psychology.
- Alexander Fleming … and the challenges of biology.
- John Maynard Keynes … and the challenges of economics.
- Robert Goddard … and the challenges of engineering.
- Charles-Édouard Jeanneret (Le Corbusier) … and the challenges of architecture.
- Ludwig Wittgenstein … and the challenges of logical philosophy.
- Edwin Hubble … and the challenges of astronomy.
- Jean Piaget … and the challenges of child development.
- Enrico Fermi … and the challenges of nuclear energy.
- Louis and Mary Leakey … and the challenges of anthropology.
- Kurt Gödel … and the challenges of mathematics.
- William Shockley … and the challenges of physics and electronics.
- Jonas Salk … and the challenges of virology.
- James Watson and Francis Crick … and the challenges of genetics.

The Upshot

During the Meeting

So … put your cognitive challenge on the table. What do you envision these figures saying about using your head to solve it?

When do you see calling on them for their advice?

How do you see them interacting with each other?

What might Da Vinci, Franklin, or Bacon say about the cognitive challenge? How might Newton, Einstein, or Plato retort? Could Jobs or Tesla add anything useful? And would this be supported, refuted, or amended by Darwin or Curie? And perhaps extended by Turing or James?

Should we also consider the insights offered by Dr. Jones for thinking and increasing understanding? And Detectives Starling and Tibbs? And certainly we should not ignore the Batman. Nor should we discount the contribution of Vito.

In addition, would anyone from the back chime in – say, for example, Freud, Keynes, Wittgenstein, Fermi, Leakey, or Salk?

After the Meeting

Do you see how these cases illustrate the principles of logic-related, sagacity-driven leadership? Comprehension? Assessment? Judgment?

What do you glean from our council that might be helpful in leading like a scientist to address cognitive challenges that might arise in your life?

Going Forward

How might you customize the content of the council to fit your personal preferences as well as professional circumstances? Add, subtract, or amend its membership to best suit your style and needs?

How might you customize the process of the council to fit your idiosyncratic predilections and references? Use it or preside over it differently?

Lead with Sagacity

Taken together this chapter's presentation of comprehension, assessment, and judgment tools will allow you to enhance this aspect of your leadership and work towards EXTRAORDINARY INTELLECTUAL PROWESS.

When faced with reasoning and cognitive-related challenges it will enable you to lead a personal and professional life infused with SAGACITY.

This is summarized for your convenience in Table 4.2.

TABLE 4.2 Becoming a Leadership Scientist

Leadership SCIENTIST	
Challenge	Cognitive (Logic)
Focus	Head – Thinking
Building a Better Core (D > I)	Comprehension *Breadth* *Depth*
Crafting a Better Process (I > K)	Assessment *Perception* *Intuition*
Leveraging a Better Capacity (K > W)	Judgment *Rational* *Creative*
Outcome	Sagacity: Extraordinary Intellectual Prowess

104 Assembling Your Leadership Toolbox

Appropriately, the initial part of becoming a wise leader that is discussed in our book is to BE Better. And leading your organization and its people in a way so that they can also be better. We use the metaphor of (powerful, glowing) LIGHTS for capturing this foundation of wisdom.

This chapter focuses on the first step in wise leadership – THINKING. It is grounded in the philosophical branch of LOGIC. It enables the wise person or organization to become cognitively stronger and be more proficient at what they do.

In this way it involves unleashing your inner SCIENTIST.

However, thinking is often misunderstood and, more than this, internal limitations and external barriers often prevent us from truly thinking like a leader. So ...

- Building a better thinking *core* involves enlarging your breadth and depth of comprehension.
- A better thinking *process* involves improving your assessment through sharper perception and keener intuition.
- *Leveraging* your thinking capacity involves superior judgment through enhanced rational and creative competencies.

If you do this then you will develop the MIND OF A LEADER.

5

THE HEART OF A LEADER

How to Use Your Leadership Artist (Aesthetics) Tools

How does a leader feel?

How can you develop the heart of a leader?

Chapter 4 conveys some very important insights into how leaders use their heads and think. First among these is that it is important to be smart. But it is not enough to just be smart. Leaders must also know how to use their hearts. To feel. So, if you want to be a leader, then you must also learn to care like one.

A nice corollary of the prior discussion is that leaders must focus on what they and their followers 'can do'. Can they comprehend well? Can they assess well? Can they judge well? And these are important. But what about the 'will do' problem? What about emotion? Just because you can do something does not mean you are willing to do it. Sometimes people have plenty of smarts but not enough heart. They suffer not from a lack of understanding but from a lack of motivation.

Emotion and motivation relate to energy. And we have an energy crisis today.

The world is energy. Even the things that we see – i.e., mass and matter – are essentially forms of energy. Even in a cosmological sense the combined size of all the planets, stars, etc. is dwarfed by this unknown power of 'dark energy' permeating our places and spaces.

Energy in a physical sense is potential and kinetic. And this includes human energy. Potential energy needs to be activated. Kinetic energy needs to be channeled. Energy can also be measured by its strength, direction, and resonance. Its strength needs to be optimized. Its direction needs to be oriented. And its resonance needs to be sustained. Following from Newton's law of conservation of energy, the total energy of an isolated system is constant; energy can be transformed from one form to another, and it can be channeled from one pursuit to another.

106 Assembling Your Leadership Toolbox

Thus, leaders need to stream their and their peoples' energy properly.

This is consistent with the arguments of many organizational psychologists, including Jim Loehr and Tony Schwartz. In their 2005 book, *The Power of Full Engagement: Managing Energy, Not Time, Is the Key to High Performance and Personal Renewal*, they argue that managed well our emotional energy can result in positive outcomes of an active (calm, optimistic, challenged, engaged, invigorated) and passive (carefree, peaceful, relieved, mellow, receptive) nature. Conversely, managed poorly, our emotional energy can manifest actively negative (impatient, irritable, frustrated, angry, defensive, fearful, anxious, worried) and passively negative (exhausted, empty, depressed, sad, hopeless) problems.

One could argue that energizing is just as if not more important than learning. This is for several reasons. One is a mass diffusion of information access and computing power that has leveled the proverbial playing field. Another is the apathy and stagnation that has emerged from this when people have so much that they are no longer (literally as well as figuratively) hungry as they once were. The flip side of this is that, for those who are engaged, this engagement has been put into overdrive and brings threatening levels of stress and burnout. In addition, both of these extremes – apathy and burnout – have propagated unprecedented levels of disconnection and negativity in our society, and in our organizations, where our omnipresent screens are being used more for escaping and raging than they are for more positive purposes.

As the prior paragraphs reveal, we are often faced with environments characterized by the following ... Apathetic. Frustrated. Angry. Exhausted. Stressed. Depressed.

So do you still want to be a leader? A wise leader?

Then you must learn to feel like one.

One of the tools leaders must hone and wield is aesthetics. Feeling and helping people feel. Using your heart and helping people use their hearts. Elevating your and their feeling processes.

But don't just take my word for it. Please consider the following insights.

When dealing with people, remember that you are not dealing with creatures of logic, but with creatures of emotion.
– Dale Carnegie

The best and most beautiful things in this world cannot be seen or even heard, but must be felt with the heart.
– Helen Keller

Think enthusiastically about everything; but especially about your job. If you do, you'll put a touch of glory in your life.
– Norman Vincent Peale

> *If you want to be happy, be.*
> — Leo Tolstoy
>
> *We must combine the toughness of the serpent and the softness of the dove, a tough mind and a tender heart.*
> — Dr. Martin Luther King, Jr.

Leaders lead people. Not plants or pencils. People. And, as per Andrew Carnegie, people are emotional creatures. Even though we can think this is not all that we do. And more than this, we are not always ruled by our minds. Out complex thoughts often come in at a distant second to our convoluted emotions. We fear. We hope. We desire. We love. We hate. These emotions are real and they matter. So, it is not enough to have a high intelligence quotient, or IQ. You must also have high emotional intelligence, or EQ.

These lights, and the flames that they fan, will not always make sense. But they don't have to. If we can feel their heat. If others can feel it too. Then they can inspire and they can move. Logical challenges are the dominion of our thoughts. But emotional challenges are something different entirely. They cannot be addressed with the head but instead must be solved through the heart. Teaching someone who already knows does no good if the thing holding them back is their outlook and their attitude. We must forge emotional connections with others if we are to lead them. Helen Keller reminds us of this.

The good news about understanding and managing emotions is that we have choices. We can choose to locate ourselves within the vast gamut of its possibilities. Emphasizing positive or negative emotions. For instance, at the extremes we can opt for hate or for love. We can also move with trepidation or with joy. We can be blasé or enthusiastic. And, as per the prince of positivity himself, Norman Vincent Peale reminds us that passion infuses whatever it touches with a spark of delight. It animates. Even at work.

It then follows that that thing which we call happiness is largely within our control. We can find it in us and help others do the same. Happiness is not something you wish for. Instead it is something you create. Tolstoy is right. Just as the previous chapter showed how we have agency over our thoughts, his corollary reminds us that we also have control over our emotions. And with the right tools we can influence the arc of others' happiness upward.

Therefore, we must be leaders who can think and feel. Reason and inspire. Light a fire of ideas to illuminate technical problems and light a fire of passion to arouse people – real people with real emotions who matter in and of themselves – to follow. Leaders must have, as per Dr. King, not just a formidable brain but also a compassionate heart. And we must stand ready to use each depending on what is needed.

So here we are.

108 Assembling Your Leadership Toolbox

Chapter 5 explains how leaders FEEL (i.e., not only use their heads but also use their HEARTS). It is grounded in the philosophical branch of AESTHETICS. Developing this tool enables the wise leader and their organization to become INSPIRED in what they do. In a way it involves discovering, honing, and unleashing your inner leadership ARTIST.

However, the true nature of the leader's heart is often misunderstood. More than this, individuals' internal limitations and organizations' external barriers can prevent us from truly feeling like a proverbial leadership artist.

So what to do?

Coalescing what we know about leadership aesthetics provides several tools to help us in this endeavor.

In short, to be a leadership artist …

1. Building a better feeling core involves expanding your sensitive and empathetic awareness;
2. Crafting a better feeling process will allow you to approach things with a more positive and pluralistic attitude; and
3. Leveraging your feeling capacity involves greater inspiration through enhanced motivation and influence competencies.

Taken together the chapter's presentation of awareness, attitude, and inspiration will allow you to enhance this leadership tool and work towards EXTRAORDINARY EMOTIVE CAPACITY. When faced with emotional and motivational challenges it will enable you to lead a personal and professional life infused with SPIRIT.

This chapter is therefore organized as follows:

- Problem: When Facing Emotional and Motivation Challenges
- Solution: Activate Your Leader 'Aesthetics' Tool
- Identity: Be a Leadership ARTIST
- Method: To Use Your Heart
- Focus: And with Extraordinary Emotive Capacity
- Outcome: Lead with *Spirit*

When Facing Emotional and Motivation Challenges

What is this Type of Problem?

One type of challenge leaders face is affective in nature. It involves feeling. In essence, it demands that you develop the 'Heart' of a leader. That you feel like a leader.

An appropriate analogy for thinking is, as suggested by the above, the human heart. Not in a literal sense because, as we know from Biology 101, the anatomical heart is essentially a pump. But more akin to the spirit of this chapter, in a more poetic sense because the lyrical heart is the wellspring of emotion.

The heart feels. It is sensitive to one's sentiments and it is empathetic towards others' passions. It embraces, or rejects, to different degrees, the feelings of peace (versus wallowing in quagmires of stress and anxiety), positivity (versus projecting toxic vibes of pessimism and gloom), and pluralism (versus walling oneself off in prisons of egoism and self-absorption). The heartstrings are where people are inspired and motivated. They are where people are swayed and influenced. To be human is to have passions and sentiments. They are not to be ignored but rather to be embraced.

So, ask yourself – Do you listen to the music of your heartstrings? Do you manage your emotions or are they managing you? Do you manage others' emotions or are you distracted or dumbfounded by them? Can you complement a leadership brain with a leadership heart?

Can you use it to develop a leadership heart?

To feel like a leader?

Net-Net: The second core element of wisdom is to 'feel'. By feel, I mean that the wisest individuals, teams, organizations, and missions demonstrate extraordinary emotive capacity. Thus, wise actors in the professional domain are intimately connected. They use their hearts. They deploy their empathy and sensitivity to touch and be in touch.

This is depicted in Figure 5.1, with emphasis added in our model of Wise Leadership to highlight the current topic.

So how do you know when you are facing affective and feeling-related (energy) challenges that require you to be a leadership artist? And why are these problems so darned hard to solve?

These issues are addressed below.

How Do You Know When You Are Facing It?

You need to be a leadership artist when you encounter affective and feeling-related challenges. More specifically, when you face: (1) Problems of Awareness, (2) Problems of Attitude, and/or (3) Problems of Inspiration. Each will be explained below.

The Need for Emotional Attentiveness: Solving the Problems of Awareness

The foundation for building a better leadership heart involves expanding your emotional awareness. In technical terms, here you do not have sufficient sensitivity and empathy to detect emotional cues. In plain speak, you struggle with – What emotions are present? How are they effecting people?

In this first instance we have a problem of AWARENESS. The leader is not (1) sensitive enough to their own emotional state to pick up critical clues about

FIGURE 5.1 Focus: Aesthetics and the Leadership Artist.

what is affecting him/herself as well as others; and (2) not empathetic enough to self and others' emotional states to honor what is being experience by, and affecting, their followers. And this happens even with the easiest emotions to see – expressed emotions. Expressed emotions should be evident in a person's face, speech, and other mannerisms. Even children can tell what a classmate's tears or smiles tend to indicate. However, some leaders appear blind to even these most obvious of clues. Harder still is detecting the underlying emotions hidden by a good poker face or efforts at self-suppression or delusion. If a leader cannot see emotions that are outwardly expressed, then what chance do they have of seeing the deeper, latent emotions that are brewing below, such as concealed fear or covert resentment?

Upshot – When emotional data never makes it onto the radar screen then leaders cannot address their root causes or catalyze their dormant potential. In these cases, they indicate that we need to address emotional awareness.

This is a Data > Information issue. Aesthetic input never makes it onto your radar screen.

The key is becoming aware of what types of emotions you and others are facing. Basically, to do this, you need to (1) have a general familiarity with or access to the emotional wheel, and (2) be able to attune to these areas as needed.

Emotions range from the very positive to the very negative. They also range from the active/intense to the passive/mild. As famously depicted in 1988 by Robert Plutchik, his 'Wheel of Emotions' illustrates eight primary emotions, seen as four pairs of opposites. They are: joy and sadness; anger and fear; surprise and anticipation; and trust and disgust. Each of these can range in intensity and combine with other emotions to produce complex patterns. This provokes some interesting questions, such as: How do leaders create ecstasy, amazement, and engagement? How can they avoid rage, loathing, and grief?

Leaders then must become emotionally literate. To be able to identify what a person is feeling. Sensitivity to one's own emotion and empathy to the emotions of others tilts the odds in your favor and, when facing affective problems, makes success more likely.

The Need for Emotional Channeling: Solving Problems of Attitude

Once your emotional core is addressed, crafting a better aesthetic process will allow you to fully and productively experience the feeling dynamics or aesthetic relationships. Sensing the tides of emotions is one thing. Riding their waves is another.

In technical terms, if you do not bring requisite positivity and/or pluralism to the issues at hand you will fail at discerning the affirming dimensions (vitality) and/or their different dimensions of manifestation (diversity). In plain speak, you struggle with – How can I be at ease with my feelings? How can I see their potential? How can I respect their range and harness their power?

In this second instance we have a problem of ATTITUDE. The leader is not able to channel emotions to create an environment of (1) positivity, where emotions create vitality and energy rather than creating a distraction or sapping the energy out of the room, and (2) pluralism, where emotions are appreciated in all of their diversity versus imposed upon people across all of their differences and stakeholder positions.

This is an Information > Knowledge issue. Aesthetic input is not processed well.

The best leaders can attend to emotions and appropriately orient themselves to the underlying patterns and meanings of emotional states that are hidden from the neophyte but become evident to the feeling leader. Basically, to do this, you need to (1) stream emotions towards the positive, to infuse the organization with affirming energy, and (2) apply a pluralistic template to this, enabling a supportive and mutually reinforcing climate of overlaps and partnerships.

If a leader cannot frame feelings in a beneficial light, then their emotional leadership cannot channel the dynamics in a way that supports, versus impedes, themselves and their followers.

The Need for a More Spirited Workforce: Solving Problems of Inspiration

Once your emotional core and process are addressed, then full integration of your aesthetic leadership can take place. You can become motivational and lead with passion. You can become influential and lead with spirit.

112 Assembling Your Leadership Toolbox

In technical terms, here you do not have motivational and/or influential capacity. These are the aesthetic outcomes. In plain speak, you struggle with – What do people want (in other words, what makes them happy)? How do I get them to do what I want them to do?

In this third instance we have a problem of INSPIRATION. The leader is not able to manage emotions to (1) motivate themselves and their followers, which includes energizing them in a desired direction, and (2) influence people to act on their motivations in desired ways. In a word, they do not determine what folks need and want (to create happiness) and/or align this with larger goals and objectives (to actuate power).

This is a Knowledge > Wisdom issue. Aesthetic inputs and processes are not coupled to attaining the most emotionally satisfying conclusions.

If a leader cannot build on their emotional awareness and attitude to actually inspire themselves and their followers then the fire is not lit. When that flame withers so does the élan of the group and the success of the leader.

The best leaders can amplify or regulate as well as channel or amend emotions to support larger goals and objectives. Basically, to do this, you need to (1) motivate and (2) influence. Motivation comes from the root 'to move'. We need to move people. Ignite and arouse them. Through the understanding of their needs. The shaping of their goals. The shepherding of their actions. The reinforcing of their actions. Influence in its most basic form involves getting people to do what you want them to do. It ties in with motivation through the use power, politics, and authority.

Taken Together

It is easy to see that there is a failure of leadership in each of these three cases. And you may have experienced one or more yourself. This would not be surprising because they are increasingly common in the workplace. Thus we can say that there is both a high and an increasing demand for leadership artists.

You also probably noticed that the problems are very different from those highlighted in the previous chapter. This is because they are feeling-related versus thinking-related challenges. Emotions are something else entirely and they frequently do not follow the rules of logic. You cannot use your head to think your way out of them. So, you cannot solve them the same way. Being a scientist will not work here. The tool does not fit the task. Instead, you have to become a different type of leader to solve matters of feelings. In other words, you have to use your heart to become a leadership artist.

If we do not rise to meet these Awareness challenges we remain NUMB to our and other people's emotions.

If we do not rise to meet Attitude challenges we cannot manage these emotions and instead are DEPENDENT on them, or at their mercy.

If we do not rise to meet Inspiration challenges we do not tap into their powerful spirit and are LAME in our leadership.

UPSHOT: Wise leaders know when they are facing affective, emotionally related challenges.

Activate Your Leader 'Aesthetics' Tool

As expressed in the preceding section, the primary tool leaders use to address emotional, energy-related challenges and make decisions is sourced from the domain of Aesthetics.

Without leadership ARTIST tools leaders are hard-pressed to have the basic emotional awareness, attitude, and inspiration to lead with spirit. They might get compliance but will never get full commitment. And they will lose to those who can.

Leaders are not just guides, they are also supporters. They are not only teachers but must also often serve as counselors. To fan the flames that arouse and stimulate. This is why aesthetic tools are not so easy to acquire and to employ. If they were, then no leaders would have emotional lapses and the world would not be so full of stressed-out, angry, and self-absorbed people rife with the destructive energies of negativity and apathy. So, in the same economic terms used in the book's introduction but customized for this particular chapter, there is often an imbalance of the demand for aesthetics and the supply of aesthetics.

Without leadership artist tools leaders are hard-pressed to sustain personal productivity and happiness. If you do not have spirit, then your leadership is bland. If your organization does not have spirit, then your ethos is unenjoyable and your energy levels are anemic.

Here are some of the key barriers in ourselves (individual) and our environments (organizational) that impede us and our followers from addressing these types of issues.

Some Emotional Awareness Challenges Leaders Must Overcome

First, people have a notoriously poor awareness of their and others' own emotions. That is to say we can be emotionally numb or ambivalent. Emotions inspire complex, organic, and holistic reactions in their hosts. They have a real impact on peoples' performance and satisfaction levels. Therefore, they cannot be ignored.

Common awareness problems include:

- Lack of personal sensitivity – We don't see our own emotions. Instead we often turn a blind eye to our emotional existence. We do not notice when fear, anger, hunger, etc. are impacting our mental, physical, and spiritual states. Leadership artists identify their emotions.
- Lack of personal empathy – We don't validate our own emotions. Instead we often spurn and scorn our emotional existence. Instead we dismiss it as noise

in the machine rather than a fundamental, critical part of the machine itself. Leadership artists accept the cogency of their emotions.

- Lack of interpersonal sensitivity – We don't see our or others' emotions. Instead we often turn a blind eye to their emotional existence. They do not have, or need to have, feelings. They are objects rather than subjects.
  Leadership artists identify others' emotions.
- Lack of interpersonal empathy – We don't validate others' emotions. Instead we often spurn and scorn their emotional existence. It is distraction. It is not our problem. It needs to be removed from the situation.
  Leadership artists accept the cogency of others' emotions.

Some Emotional Attitude Challenges Leaders Must Overcome

Second, people are notoriously bad at managing their and others' attitudes. Attitudes are peoples' propensities to react to things in a stable way. As such they can be more positive or negative. They can also be more closed or open. If leaders do not address attitude formation and perpetuation they will be severely compromised. Perhaps Mean. Hostile. Fearful. Insecure. Moreover, if leaders do not address these things then their followers will also be significantly compromised. And the diffusion of their negativity can paralyze or even destroy their organization from the inside.

Common attitude problems include:

- Attitude Valence – We often become overly negative. Instead of embracing our work and all of its challenges there is a tendency to become rejecting, disparaging, and even despondent. This is a problem of the wrong type of attitude.
  Leadership artists are more emotionally positive.
- Attitude Magnitude – We often become overly ambivalent. Instead of bonding with our work and all of its challenges there is a tendency to become distant, detached, and even apathetic. This is a problem of the wrong scale of attitude.
  Leadership artists are more emotionally engaged.
- Attitude Myopia – We often become overly critical. Instead of harmonizing with others' outlooks there is a tendency to become impervious, selfish, and even reproachful. This is a problem of the wrong synchronization of attitude.
  Leadership artists are more emotionally pluralistic.

Some Motivational and Inspirational Challenges Leaders Must Overcome

Third, people are notoriously bad at motivating themselves and others. If leaders do not address these things they will be severely compromised.

Common motivation problems include:

- Poor matching – We do not target peoples' active needs. Instead we often design generic systems that may or may not be in tune with what we, and others, actually want and crave.
Leadership artists identify motivational needs.
- Poor goal setting – We do not set motivating goals. Instead we are often too vague, too random, too unstable, or too inconsistent with what we are asking for and what we are painting as desirable.
Leadership artists set motivating goals.
- Poor job design – We do not establish motivating climates. Instead we often propagate narrow or empty tasks, dead-end jobs, and paths with little appeal or excitement.
Leadership artists create motivating climates.
- Poor expectations – We do not facilitate motivating actions. Instead we often fail to connect resources with actions, actions with outcomes, and outcomes with purposes. This compromises peoples' efficacy, instrumentality, and valence.
Lea–dership artists bolster motivating linkages.
- Poor reinforcement – We do not respond in motivating ways. Instead we often reward or punish the wrong things in the wrong ways.
Leadership artists institutionalize motivating systems.

Taken Together

These aspects of cognitive challenges are well illustrated in Csikszentmihalyi's (1988) concept of flow. To achieve a flow state is to enter a highly active, intrinsically pleasurable aesthetic state of being completely enwrapped in a movement. Akin to that achieved via transcendental practices it enables a holistic and joyous engagement of complete involvement. Subsequent work in what has since been termed positive psychology or positive organizational scholarship has sought to identify the characteristics and triggers of flow. This would help people approximate it in themselves and leaders to facilitate it in others. The nine different dimensions that comprise the concept include: Challenge–skill balance, Action–awareness merging, Clear goals, Unambiguous feedback, Concentration on the task at hand, A sense of control, Loss of self-consciousness, Transformation of time, and Autotelic experience.

Leaders need to know how to find flow in their work and facilitate flow for others.

As you can see, the issues of aesthetics and leadership are inexorably intertwined. Thus, the feeling person is able to master the aesthetic aspects of their awareness, attitude, and inspiration. More than this, though, the leadership artist is able to help others in their awareness, attitude, and inspiration and steer their organization towards a mastery of the aesthetic.

UPSHOT: Wise leaders address aesthetic, emotion-related challenges.

116 Assembling Your Leadership Toolbox

Be a Leadership ARTIST

The identity best befitting an emotional problem solver is that of a leadership artist.

Art, as per the *Oxford English Dictionary*, is the expression or application of human creative skill and imagination, typically in a visual form such as painting or sculpture, producing works to be appreciated primarily for their beauty or emotional power.

Artists, by extension, are those most skilled and engaged in advancing the emotional appreciation and inspiration of our world.

When you picture an artist what images come into your head?

Perhaps they are dreaming or painting under a tree,

With their crazy hair and stylish clothes blowing in the wind,

Out in the field prodding or rebelling against something,

Or maybe composing poetry, painting, or prose,

Then perhaps whirling hypnotically down an idyllic pathway,

Enrapt in capturing, and even stirring, the rhythm of the human experience.

These are poor stereotypes and pigeonholes for sure, but they can be used as a jumping-off point for capturing the character of the artist and contrasting them with that of the scientist. And as such they may suggest ways for modeling how artists feel and what leaders can learn from them to feel better.

Put more systematically, and in a manner consistent with the book's model:

- Artists are more attuned to the rhythms of the heart (Data > Information). Leadership artists therefore have the sensitivity and empathy to address emotional challenges.
- Artists are more immersed within the processes of attitude (Information > Knowledge). Leadership artists therefore convey their positivity and pluralism to address emotional challenges.
- Artists are more inspirational (Knowledge > Wisdom). Leadership artists therefore channel their motivational and influential capacities to address emotional challenges.

Leadership scientists develop their aesthetics in these three fundamental ways.

The following offers a step-by-step map for doing this. For convenience these steps are summarized in Table 5.1. They are then illustrated as well as elaborated upon in the subsequent corresponding sections.

TABLE 5.1 Tools for Developing the HEART of a Leader

Better Core: Awareness	Greater Sensitivity
	Deeper Empathy
Better Process: Attitude	Sense of Positivity
	Sense of Pluralism
Better Leverage: Inspiration	More Motivational
	More Influential

To Use Your Heart

Step One – Building a Better Core

> *If you want others to be happy, practice compassion. If you want to be happy, practice compassion.*
> – Dalai Lama
>
> *There is only one way to happiness and that is to cease worrying about things which are beyond the power of our will.*
> – Epictetus
>
> *Let your heart feel for the afflictions and distresses of everyone.*
> – George Washington
>
> *The happiness of a man in this life does not consist in the absence but in the mastery of his passions.*
> – Alfred, Lord Tennyson
>
> *Follow your bliss.*
> – Joseph Campbell

The Dalai Lama highlights the importance of sensitivity to oneself and empathy towards others. Appreciating your emotions as well as appreciating peoples' diverse emotions. Epictetus relates this to the difference between worry and concern. Accepting what one cannot control and focusing on what one can control. This is a canon of stress management. Washington combines and applies these insights to develop a truly caring sentiment. A sentiment that is universal across others no matter their distinctions or dispositions. Similar or different. Friend and foe. Compatriot or competitor. Tennyson builds on this to emphasize both the importance of these emotions as well as their proper stewardship. Finally, Campbell caps this with the simple point of finding the most central source of pleasure and delight. For us as well as for those who we lead. We should seek to do what we love and love what we do. We should, during our brief existence on this tiny planet, engage in our greatest source of joy. We should follow our bliss. We should help others find and follow their bliss. And we should align the two for the good of our organization and their denizens.

Leadership artists are sensitive and empathetic.

Wise leaders can see their and others' emotions.

The core to becoming a better leadership artist, or if you will a strategy for developing your HEART-Lights is therefore to expand your sensitivity and empathy.

118 Assembling Your Leadership Toolbox

Greater Sensitivity

Some strategies include emotional self-awareness and emotional self-control. Actively take emotional snapshots of your self at different points in time. Examine what you are feeling and how these feelings are impacting how you think and how you treat others. Then retrospectively string these pictures together to form emotional film reels that reveal the trajectories of your emotions throughout the days and across days, seasons, etc. Are there any trends that you should be aware of? What are the key factors that drive and shape your emotions? How can positive experiences be amplified and negative ones mitigated?

Consider taking the 'marshmallow test'. In its literal form a yummy snack is placed on the desk of a hungry person and they are asked to identify and control their drives – i.e., delay gratification. Can you identify your temptations and triggers (i.e., your figurative emotional marshmallows)? Can you then manage them?

- Take emotional selfies
- Take emotional home movies
- Conduct appropriate emotional interventions

Some additional strategies include emotional appreciation and acceptance. Do you give yourself permission to be human and have feelings? Some techniques for doing this include the following:

- Create an emotional inventory. Seek to identify feelings. Don't push them down and act like a robot. Probe them. Investigate their sources. Trace their impacts. Recognize and legitimize them.
- Seek emotional feedback from others. Sometimes we cannot see our anger, our nervousness, etc. as well as those who are dealing with us. They are another source of learning and perspective. If we are 'hangry' (anger stemming from lack of food) or 'cangry' (ire from a need for coffee) then others might see this before we realize it.

Deeper Empathy

Some strategies include awareness and management of others' emotions. Make some space to not only assess others' behaviors but also their emotional states. Ask them how they are feeling. Probe their stories, their hopes and dreams, and their overall experiences. Consider how these states are impacted by their surroundings (including you!). Then in addition to forming emotional film reels of each employee or colleague also amalgamate them together to coalesce collective emotional waves that capture overall moods and trends.

Consider taking the 'poker test'. In its literal form each game player is asked not only to identify and hide any reactions from their collections of cards (good or bad) but also to identify and capitalize on the emotions of other players that might reveal the qualities of their hidden hands. Can you pick up on others' cues

Your Leadership Artist (Aesthetics) Tools **119**

(i.e., their figurative emotional tells or signals)? Follow their emotional waxes and wanes? Can you then manage them?

- Take emotional pictures
- Create emotional biopics
- Conduct appropriate emotional interventions

Some additional strategies include appreciation and acceptance of others' emotions. Do you give others permission to be human and have feelings? This relates to what has become known as humanistic management, or as per the International Humanistic Management Association, leading 'as if people matter'. Some techniques for doing this include the following:

- Increasing your emotional inquisitiveness. Don't just dismiss others' emotions, or even label or judge emotions, be genuinely curious about them. And don't just hear them – really listen to them.
- Playing out (literally or mentally) the roles of others. Some ways to do this include standing in their place, walking in their shoes, sitting in their seats, adopting their perspective or point of view, etc. The point is to seek emotional insights from the inside of them and not your outsider perspective. This can be a simple mental exercise or complex role-playing simulation. If you appreciate their feelings and see where they are sourced, then you can understand their emotions better.

Taken Together

So what are you waiting for? Grow your leadership artist tool. Through sensitivity and empathy. Start enhancing your emotional awareness.

UPSHOT: Wise leaders are aesthetically aware.

Step Two – Crafting a Better Process

> *If you can't stand the heat, get out of the kitchen.*
> – Harry S. Truman
>
> *What seems to us as bitter trials are often blessings in disguise.*
> – Oscar Wilde
>
> *He that knows patience knows peace.*
> – Chinese proverb
>
> *Hope is the thing with feathers, that perches in the soul, and sings the tune without words, and never stops at all.*
> – Emily Dickinson

120 Assembling Your Leadership Toolbox

Truman's iconic aphorism points out several things. First, that leadership is hard. And second, that leaders need to be positive and perseverant in its pursuit. If you are not, then you will not last. Emotional traps abound and wait for you at nearly every step on the road to success. You must keep your head up and keep smiling. Wilde is consistent here in his observation that we can see the good or the bad in almost anything. Stay positive. The above Chinese proverb extends this to account for frustrations and conflicts. A pluralistic attitude that embraces diversity is much healthier than one that is impatient with anyone who is different or anything that is foreign. Acceptance is better than dogma. Tolerance is better than prejudice. Dickinson in her poetic majesty links these ideas to that of hope, perhaps the most positive and inclusive affect of all. It is the sole survivor of Pandora's Box allowing humanity to deal with all of its ailments. Hope keeps us going. Helps us fly. Allows us to sing our song.

Leadership artists are positive and pluralistic.

Wise leaders can process their and others' emotions.

A strategy for crafting a better process and developing your HEART- Lights is therefore expanding your positivity and pluralism.

Sense of Positivity

To broaden your positivity, focus on increasing your thriving and flourishing.

This draws from the aforementioned fields of positive psychology and positive organizational scholarship. Positive Psychology (https://ppc.sas.upenn.edu/) is described as: "the scientific study of the strengths that enable individuals and communities to thrive. The field is founded on the belief that people want to lead meaningful and fulfilling lives, to cultivate what is best within themselves, and to enhance their experiences of love, work, and play." Further, as per Cameron and colleagues (2003: 4), it relates to Positive Organizational Scholarship (POS) that seeks: "to inspire and enable leaders to build high-performing organizations that bring out the best in people. We are a catalyst for the creation and growth of positive organizations ... (this) encompasses attention to the enablers ... the motivations ... and the outcomes or effects ... associated with positive phenomena."

Some strategies for doing this include realizing your strengths and finding your best self.

For example, the University of Michigan (where much work on positive psychology and organizational scholarship has been done) has produced 'The Reflected Best Self Exercise (RBSE)' – they describe this as "a feedback seeking exercise that helps you identify and understand your unique strengths and talents. After you gather feedback from significant people in your life, the RBSE guides you through the process of creating a portrait of your best self and an action plan for leveraging your strengths." It involves four basic steps:

- Gather insights from people all around you to develop a rich understanding of your strengths.

Your Leadership Artist (Aesthetics) Tools **121**

- Identify patterns and common themes emerging from this feedback.
- Create a 'self-portrait' that extrapolates conditions and completes the following phrase: "When I am at my best, I …".
- Redesign your job to optimize your personal and professional engagements and emotional well-being.

Sense of Pluralism

To broaden your pluralism, focus on increasing your emotional inclusiveness, caring, and supportiveness. With an open heart. And with open arms.

Some strategies include helping others realize their strengths and enabling their best selves. To create a positive emotional atmosphere that allows them to thrive and flourish.

For example, the Harvard Pluralism Project rightly observes that

> Pluralism is only one of the possible responses to this new diversity. Some people may feel threatened by diversity, or even hostile to it. Others may look forward to the day when all differences fade into the landscape.… For those who welcome the new diversity, creating a workable pluralism will mean engaging people of different faiths and cultures in the creation of a common society.

Pluralism is not the same as 'exclusion' (you are separate) or 'condescension' (you are worse). It is also not the same as 'assimilation' (you need to conform and be like us). Pluralism relishes differences and truly enjoys the kaleidoscope of others.

- Pluralism is welcoming. Invite others in.
- Pluralism is compassionate. Treat others well.
- Pluralism is enabling. Seek and support others' best selves.

Taken Together

So what are you waiting for? Grow your leadership artist tool. Through positivity and pluralism. Start enhancing your emotional attitude.

UPSHOT: Wise leaders are aesthetically attuned.

Step Three – Leveraging a Better Capacity

There is no end. There is no beginning. There is only the passion of life.
– Federico Fellini

An automobile goes nowhere efficiently unless it has a quick, hot spark to ignite things, to set the cogs of the machine in motion.
– Knute Rockne

> *Flattery is from the teeth out. Sincere appreciation is from the heart out.*
> — Dale Carnegie
>
> *The energy ... which we bring to this endeavor will light our country and all who serve it, and the glow from that fire can truly light the world.*
> — John F. Kennedy

With the right emotional awareness and attitude we can channel our feelings towards the affirmative and truly inspire. Fellini relates this to passion, the most intense of intrinsic emotions. Passion allows for the brightest of flames and the greatest of motivations. Rockne emphasizes the importance of motivation in life. A car with no gas goes nowhere. The rational engine is nothing, just a fancy paperweight, without the heat of its emotional ignition. Carnegie quips that the pro-forma motivation is not enough to really stir the heart. To influence, to power and empower others, this spark must be deep. Power flows from within. Kennedy goes full circle, uniting these ideas of energy and motivation with the inspiration of others in a glowing light of the heart. A light that lights the leader and those around them.

Leadership artists are motivational and inspirational.

Wise leaders can leverage their and others' emotions.

A strategy for leveraging a better outcome of your enhanced HEART- Lights is therefore expanding your motivational and influential capacities.

More Motivational

To broaden your motivation, focus on increasing the *arousal, direction,* and *persistence* of voluntary actions that are goal directed — to fill 'gaps' between where one is and where one wishes to be. To inspire someone is to get them to exert more energy, to direct that energy, and to sustain that energy.

Some strategies include (1) Strategic: Addressing Needs; (2) Proactive: Constructing Contexts; (3) Active: Guiding Behaviors; and (4) Reactive: Managing Outcomes.

First, leaders strategically find out what people want.

Hint — This is not as easy as it might seem. And even if you do help one person your approach will not necessarily be externally (there are differences between people) or internally (there are differences within a person's many needs) generalizable. Moreover, even if you do get a handle on your peoples' emotions, these do not necessarily stay constant because situational demands (circumstances) and individual growth (maturity) make them change over time.

The main theories of human needs are themselves a confusing hodgepodge. According to Abraham Maslow there are five (or more, depending on the iteration) levels of universal, prepotent needs: the physical, safety and security, social

Your Leadership Artist (Aesthetics) Tools **123**

and love, respect and esteem, and actualization. These are condensed into three flexible categories by Alderfer where people can slide up and down scales to pursue existence, relationships, and growth. They are also emphasized by McClelland insofar as people strive to satiate needs for power, affiliation, and achievement.

However, some commonalities can be extracted. First, that there are higher order and lower order needs. Second, that these needs are satisfied intrinsically and externally. And third, that (per the prior paragraph) these are moving targets that must be addressed diversely and dynamically. One size does NOT fit all.

- Customize your leadership as per people's needs
- Allow for dynamism for each person – changes in wants over time
- Allow for diversity between people – changes in wants across contexts

Second, leaders proactively design roles/jobs for success.

Hint – There is a better and a worse way to do this. You can focus on the extrinsic such as money. This is surface and short term. Alternatively, you can focus on the intrinsic such as meaningfulness. This is deeper and longer term. Extrinsic motivators get you mere compliance that is tepid and produces minimum required effort. Intrinsic motivators get you true commitment that is wholehearted and gains maximum enthusiasm.

A survey of motivational design theories similarly reveals the root of these patterns. First, extrinsic factors are useful. For instance, according to Taylor and others, money is a valuable tool. Second, extrinsic factors however have their limits. For instance, according to Hertzberg and others, contextual factors can reduce negative motivation and dissatisfaction but are less able to promote positive motivation and deep, sustaining satisfaction than actually enhancing the content of jobs. Third, intrinsic factors are needed to go the distance and truly inspire. For instance, according to Hackman and Oldham as well as Deci and colleagues, true motivation is achieved through things like empowerment, meaning, learning and growth, autonomy, and self-determination.

- Provide sufficient extrinsic factors
- However, don't lean on the extrinsic exclusively
- Instead inspire through the incorporation of intrinsically motivational elements

Third, leaders actively guide people on their paths.

Hint – They do this through motivational goals and expectancies. For example, Locke and colleagues have shown that people are motivated more when they are given a goal. Goals facilitate attention, effort, persistence, and planning. They are even more effective when set correctly: When they are (1) Challenging but not impossible; (2) Specific and quantified; (3) Integrated with feedback for learning and adjustment; and (4) participative set to gain commitment.

124 Assembling Your Leadership Toolbox

Similarly Vroom and colleagues found that goals should be used as part of a larger, logical system whereby people pursue actions that they believe (1) they can do – i.e., there is efficacy; (2) that will get them rewarded – i.e., there is instrumentality; and (3) that will provide rewards which satisfy personal goals – i.e., there is valence.

- Utilize well-set goals
- Establish well-set expectancies

Fourth, leaders respond to others' behaviors.

Hint – They do this by rewarding appropriately, equitably, and fundamentally. There are a few important lessons here to follow. Reinforce what you want and punish what you don't. This seems commonsensical but, as pointed out by Kerr and others, we often hope for one thing (e.g., teamwork or innovation) but instead reward its opposite (self-centeredness and conservatism). Reward fairly and equitably. This also seems commonsensical but, as pointed out by Adams and others, we are often unfair in how we determine and administer our reinforcements. Finally, and consistent with an ongoing theme here, be careful not to squeeze out the joy by turning play into work. Instead we should be doing the opposite and, as discussed previously, emphasizing intrinsic reinforcements.

- Reward what you want
- Reward it fairly
- Reward it deeply

More Influential

To broaden your influence, focus on increasing your ability to get people to do what you want them to do. Commitment (versus compliance or resistance) is key.

Some strategies include: (1) building positional sources of power. Other strategies might take the form of (2) building personal sources of power. Still other strategies might take the form of (3) playing offensive and defensive politics to enhance the aforementioned.

Here are some sources for leader power, discussed in terms of their influence as more positionally or personally based.

Positional power includes the following:

- Build your legitimate power – This involves gaining formal positions of authority that are higher in an organizational hierarchy, or elevating your current position upward in this formal hierarchy. If you are 'above' someone they are supposed to listen to you. This applies across all types of organizations (e.g., families, clubs, businesses, churches, military, governments, etc.), though the strength of the expectations for authority obedience might vary across cultures and areas.

Your Leadership Artist (Aesthetics) Tools **125**

- Build your reward and coercive power – This involves gaining the positional control to administer benefits and punishments. If you can give someone something that they want, then they are more likely to be influenced by you. Similarly, if you are seen as being able to threaten or harm someone they are also more likely to be influenced by you.
- Build your centrality and visibility – This involves enhancing the placement of your position so that it is needed more and seen more. If you become more essential to things your influence increases. Even if you are just seen as more essential to things then your influence increases.

Personal power includes the following:

- Build your expert power – This involves acquiring the knowledge, skills, and abilities (KSAs) to make people listen to you. If you can do the job, or are seen as being able to do the job, then you increase your voice and people's desire to listen to it.
- Build your referent power – This involves acquiring the charisma to make people want to listen to you. This might entail creating a personal 'magnetism' that attracts attention or respect, visualizing and communicating stories, self-promoting and being dramatic, and making people feel good about themselves to stir and arouse.

Politics can increase or decrease the aforementioned power bases. Politics is the informal leveraging of influence. It can take many forms, including the following:

- Play Offense – This involves informally accentuating the positives of the above. For example, by acclaiming (blowing your own horn), ingratiating (selling yourself to others, often through compliments and flattery), and building relationships and loyalties.
- Play Defense – This involves informally reducing the exposures of the above. For example, by hiding weaknesses, forming coalitions, and reducing negative impressions.

Taken Together

So what are you waiting for? Grow your leadership artist tool. Through motivation and influence. Start enhancing your emotional inspiration.

UPSHOT: Wise leaders are aesthetically inspirational.

And with Extraordinary Emotive Capacity

As described in the opening section, the six core tools of leadership wisdom can be seen to manifest themselves in the record of humanity's greatest successes – the

126 Assembling Your Leadership Toolbox

achievements of the most influential real and idealized leaders who have proven themselves across a multitude of times, tasks, and locations. As such, in addition to modern relevant and complementary examples, we draw predominantly from two distinct yet complementary sources: *Time Magazine*'s (TM) lists of the most influential and American Film Institute's (AFI) lists of the most heroic.

We will do this via the vehicle of an imaginary assembly of 'Invisible Counselors'. A Leadership Artist conference table to provide insights into how to feel like a leader.

So let us call this meeting to order …

The Gavel

Here ye, here ye. I now call this LEADERSHIP ARTIST council to order.

Our focus is to address AFFECTIVE leadership challenges and INSPIRATION.

Our purpose is to animate the tool of AESTHETICS and leading with SPIRIT. That is, EXTRAORDINARY EMOTIVE CAPACITY.

The Real

So, who might be attending as some of history's most influential leadership ARTIST counselors? Let us ask them to introduce themselves (note: All biographical profiles are gleaned from many sources, including the *Encyclopedia Britannica*) and speak to the leadership tool of aesthetics and leading for spirit.

Seat One

Perhaps an inspirational orator.

Like … Winston Churchill.

I have been characterized as a masterful speaker and author who as prime minister rallied the British people during the Second World War and inspired my country from the brink of defeat to victory. I have also been labeled "a romantic believer in his country's greatness …; a statesman who was master of the arts of politics …; a man of iron constitution, inexhaustible energy, and total concentration". Moreover, outside of politics, I was also "a gifted journalist … an amateur painter, a speechmaker of rare power, a soldier of courage and distinction … a romantic, a fervent patriot … (and) an indomitable fighter". When needed most I wore my heart on my sleeve, famously proclaiming: "I have nothing to offer but blood, toil, tears and sweat." And when faced with ruthless attacks I was defiant in that "If this long island story of ours is to end at last, let it end only when each one of us lies choking in his own blood upon the ground".

Like … Martin Luther King, Jr.

I was a Baptist minister, a social activist, and a Nobel Peace Prize recipient during one of the most emotional struggles in the United States – its civil rights movement. My charismatic leadership was fundamental to that movement's success in ending the legal segregation of African Americans. I rose to national prominence as head of the Southern Christian Leadership Conference, which promoted nonviolent tactics, such as the inspirational March on Washington where more than 200,000 gathered to rally for change. It was said that here the crowds were uplifted by the emotional strength and prophetic quality of my famous 'I Have a Dream' speech, in which I stirred the passions and desires that all men, someday, would be brothers. More than this, I was described as 'handsome, eloquent, and doggedly determined' and used the power of television and the media to magnify the emotions and power of our struggle. For example, my media-friendly tactics such as sit-ins, letters, speeches, and protest marches aroused the devoted allegiance of onlookers in all parts of the country, as well as gaining the support from the administrations of Presidents Kennedy and Johnson. Specifically, in my 'Letter From a Birmingham Jail', I masterfully managed the passions fueling our movement through the use of many emotional levers: positional power (legitimate – based on legal responsibilities; reward – ability to provide desirable things such as peace and justice; coercive – ability to punish such as through revolt and disruption) and personal power (expert – acumen in the relevant matters; referent – a desirable and inspiring image, status, and overall reputation). In addition, I leveraged political tactics to add to their influence through such means as: developing contacts, keeping informed, creating a compelling vision, adapting to the audience, and making a quick showing as well as by displaying loyalty, managing impression, asking satisfied allies to support you, and being courteous and polite.

Seat Two

Plus maybe an inspirational writer.

Like … Leo Tolstoy.

I am a Russian author of realistic, evocative fiction and one of the world's greatest novelists. Through such emotion-filled novels as *War and Peace* and *Anna Karenina*, as well as shorter works such as *The Death of Ivan Ilyich*, I was able to see and depict the highs and lows of life's lusts. It has been said that I was unparalleled in my powers to capture the human spirit and titanic in my portrayal of its struggles to escape the limitations of the human condition. Some characterized my writing as the embodiment of the pure vitality of nature.

Like … the Brontë Sisters.

As per Emily Brontë, I am a stirring novelist and poet whose novel *Wuthering Heights* was a moving work of passion and hate set on the Yorkshire moors. As per Charlotte Brontë, I am a novelist noted for *Jane Eyre*, a resonant narrative of a woman in conflict with her natural desires and social condition.

128 Assembling Your Leadership Toolbox

However, if hard-pressed, I would probably award this seat to … William Shakespeare.

I am a poet, author, and actor considered by many to be the greatest dramatist of all time. Some describe me as supremely able to capture the emotional crescendos of human spirit. This allowed me to produce such a broad catalog of arousing, captivating works filled with intense 'pathos and mirth' such as *Hamlet*, *Macbeth*, and *Romeo and Juliet*. Chief among my abilities for doing this includes my use of words and images in a way that instills energy in the characters and rebounds it in the reader. I did this by empathizing with the plights of human situations and its full expression across the gamut of stimulations. As if this were not enough, the art form into which my creative energies went involved vivid stage productions, poignantly conveying feelings such as sympathy and joy, and actively compelling audiences to vicariously participate in its affect.

Seat Three

Let us also add an inspirational musician who literally as well as figuratively played the strings that moved the human heart.

Like … Wolfgang Amadeus Mozart.

I am widely recognized as one of the greatest composers in the history of music. It was said that my palate, my command of form, my melodic mastery, and my range of expression established me as among the most vividly and sophisticatedly emotional of all musicians. It is also said that my music was at once appealing to the specific tastes of different peoples as well as generally appealing to any and all audiences. I relished combining elegance and playfulness in ways that inspired unparalleled harmonies and dramatic transitions, creating an elixir of moods and movements that enrapt the listener.

Like … Ludwig van Beethoven.

I am widely regarded as the most passionate composer who ever lived. My art reaches out to encompass the highest spirit of humanism in all forms, and particularly nationalism with its zealous concern for the freedom and dignity of the individual. I revealed more vividly than any of my predecessors the power of music to convey a philosophy of life without the aid of spoken word or penned subtext; and my compositions convey the strongest assertion of the human will in all music, if not in all art. Thus I became the fountainhead of much that characterized the work of the Romantics … especially in my ideal of program or illustrative music, which I defined in connection with my Sixth Pastoral Symphony as 'more an expression of emotion than painting'.

Like … John Lennon and Paul McCartney.

From John: In The Beatles I assumed the role of the outspoken provocateur. I was a pretty good rock rhythm guitarist and paired this with my strong, gut-based singing. I patterned much of this approach on the rockabilly singers which I admired, with a frantic, bluesy masculinity but also with an impishly high voice

Your Leadership Artist (Aesthetics) Tools **129**

deployed to humorous and even emotional effect. From Paul: I am a vocalist, songwriter, composer, bass player, poet, and painter who helped transform popular music into a highly appealing art form. Feelings of all ilks resound from my evocative ballads and melodic love songs, and I was also responsible for many of The Beatles' grittier hard rock anthems.

Now together, as the heart of The Beatles. As per the Business Insider:

> Beatlemania conjures up a vivid image of frenzied fans ... with facial expressions that look more like they'd witnessed a gruesome murder ... hanging on for dear life as their owners attempted to push past overwhelmed human police barricades. Lots of tears and lots of screaming.... And what about music can make us tap our toes, lulls babies to sleep, well up with emotion, dance around or stir up furious mosh pits? ... Music is a personal preference, and although we know that it brings us pleasure.

And as per *Rolling Stone* magazine:

> The Beatles' momentous American debut on The Ed Sullivan Show ... would help incite something stronger in American youth that night – something that started as a consensus, as a shared joy, but that in time would seem like the prospect of power. Their impact was about something more than fad or celebrity; it was about laying claim to a brand-new kind of youth mandate.

Seat Four

And let us add an inspirational businessperson.

Like ... Sam Walton.

I am a retail magnate who founded Wal-Mart and developed it into the largest company and private employer in the United States and later the entire world. By popular accounts people tell me that I am an extremely charismatic leader. I inspired awe and affection, beloved by a great many of my followers (but, as is the case for all charismatics, not all of their emotions towards me were positive due to the unavoidably polarizing effects of charisma), and I empowered people and built up their esteem, their confidence, and their loyalty. My leadership approach was perfectly portrayed as one of 'projecting love on a mass scale'.

However, if hard-pressed, we would probably award this seat to ... Oprah Winfrey.

I am a television personality, actress, and entrepreneur who uses modern media as highly evocative vehicles for my extraordinary empathy, expression, inspiration, and encouragement. My syndicated daily talk show was among the most popular of the genre and I became one of the richest and most influential women in the United States. In addition, I appeared in several movies and started an on-air book

130 Assembling Your Leadership Toolbox

club that was extremely influential. As per FastCompany, conversations about me "are full of terms like disciples, sacred, moral compass, and spiritual leader … (people work for her) not just because she's the boss, but because she is the heart and soul, and the spiritual leader of this organization." Oprah sees herself in precisely this way: "I feel that my role here on earth is to inspire people, and to get them to look at themselves. My genuine wish is to do better and be better to everybody. That's not just some kind of talk for me. That's who I am."

Seat Five

And finally, an inspirational visualizer and storyteller.

Like … Stanley Kubrick.

I am a motion-picture director and writer whose films are characterized by a dramatic visual style, meticulous manipulation of detail, and perspectives that do not impose but instead invite the emotional reaction of its viewers. To this end I love exploring complex emotions in stunning, dramatic, and even dystopian-like shocking ways through vehicles such *Lolita* (seduction), *Dr. Strangelove* (war), *A Clockwork Orange* (violence), *The Shining* (fear), and *Full Metal Jacket* (anger). For example, my *2001: A Space Odyssey* sought an impact that would transcend language and reason. This was facilitated by eerily but also inspiringly developing crescendos as in the stunning pairings with classical composition such as Strauss' *Thus Spoke Zarathustra*. This powerful application of music to amplify atmosphere, character, and story was said by some to be a signature of my filmmaking.

However, if hard-pressed, we would probably award this seat to … Steven Spielberg.

I am a motion-picture director and producer whose diverse films – which ranged from science-fiction fare, including such classics as *Close Encounters of the Third Kind* and *E.T.: The Extra-Terrestrial* to historical dramas, notably *Schindler's List* and *Saving Private Ryan* – enjoyed unprecedented popular appeal. For example, my *Schindler's List* was shot in black and white with raw emotional detail. Also, my *Saving Private Ryan* re-creates realistic battle scenes, especially the extended opening sequence of the D-Day invasion. In addition, few movies have been as just plain scary as my classic shark thriller, *Jaws*. It was so evocative that it actually changed beach-going habits around the world. It has been said (in the book *Shoot Like Spielberg: The Visual Secrets of Action, Wonder and Emotional Adventure*) that:

> Spielberg makes his audience feel something, whether he's shooting a kids' adventure, a dramatic chase, or the darkest war scene. The auteur always employs a core set of techniques that make each shot crystal clear and evoke the most intense emotions from the audience…. From tension to tearjerker, these moves will make your scenes memorable enough to be talked about for years to come.

It is also critical to understand that a leader must first feel the emotion before they can make others feel it. As per *Wired* magazine, when choosing a movie, I need to "test how emotionally involved I want to be. I'm getting married to a movie. I've got to know it's true love." And emotion is most powerful when it is centered on purity, and particularly in my case on childhood fascination. Thus my observation that:

> Somehow, the magic of childhood lies in its formlessness, its squishiness – the ease with which emotions surge into one another and up to the surface, how subtly imagination washes over reality. Nothing's hardened yet. It's all still beautifully weak, for better and for worse.

The Idealized

So who might be attending as some of cinema's most heroic leadership artist counselors? The figurative indomitable souls who impel, inspire, and even out-gut their foes.

Seat Six

Why not start with Rocky Balboa?

Rocky Balboa, in the 1976 film *Rocky* and numerous sequels, is the overmatched but kind-hearted boxer who simply wills his way to fiercely battle the champ. Written and portrayed by Sylvester Stallone, the character rises from his humble beginnings to overcome a lackluster career and live up to his nickname the 'Italian Stallion'. Rocky uses emotion to fuel his passionate training regime. In the film's climactic scheme he 'guts it out' to tenaciously go the distance with a much more polished champion. And in the decision's aftermath he cares less about the judges and more about embracing his love Adrianne. All in all, Rocky symbolizes the fighter who does not necessarily have world-class talent but does most definitely possess world-class heart. The heart to embark and persevere through grueling self-imposed training schedules. The heart to stand in front of one's foe no matter the risks. The heart to tenaciously 'keep moving forward' no matter the obstacles. The heart to 'go the distance' no matter the difficulty. The heart of a champion. And the heart to declare his love for his wife in his greatest moment of glory.

Seat Seven

Then maybe we should invite Shane.

Shane in the 1953 film *Shane* (portrayed by Alan Ladd) is the western gunfighter who courageously stands up to greedy land barons. He had every reason and opportunity to run. But his heart would not allow it. Love. Loyalty. Caring. These are but some of the emotions keeping him there even when his head said no.

132 Assembling Your Leadership Toolbox

Despite his calm demeanor Shane's passion is unquestionable as he bigheartedly decides to get involved in a conflict that should otherwise have been irrelevant to him. He then single-handedly takes on a gang of hooligans to protect the powerless. And even the film's final scenes are strewn with the emotions of a pleading child hearkening for his hero to 'come back'.

Seat Eight

Further, let us add to the mix Jefferson (Mr.) Smith.

Jefferson (Mr.) Smith in the 1939 film *Mr. Smith Goes to Washington* is the hometown leader of the Boy Rangers and neophyte congressman who by sheer force of will filibusters the manipulative bill of greedy politicos. As a fledgling Junior Senator, Smith is an unlikely hero who does battle with a powerful, underhanded political machine. Smith argues his case for over 24 hours and faints – a superhuman, spirited effort fueled by his positive energy and unmatched empathy for the children who need him. Jeff would not allow weariness, weakness, or frustration to stop him. He would make a stand – figuratively as well as literally. And in doing so he would inspire those around him to stand with him and do the same.

Seat Nine

And also Mr. Chips.

Charles Edward (Mr. Chips) Chipping in the 1939 film *Goodbye, Mr. Chips* is the kind-hearted teacher who dedicates himself to the care of his students. Portrayed by Robert Donat, the character goes through a cycle of emotionless disciplinarian to compassionate educator. Broken out of his shell by the love of his life, her spirit proves to be contagious as he spurns the cold-hearted, factory-like mechanical training and regimented techniques characteristic of the day for something more intrinsically inspirational – humane thoughtfulness, warming compassion, and personalized consideration. He listens to people's problems. He nurtures those who entrust him. His kind nature gains the affection of his peers and protégés. Showing that a sense of humor is just as important as a sense of profit, he shows feeling and compassion for his students. Where they are not seen as faceless numbers but instead as expressive people, even family. Though never having biological children, through the kindness of this leader's heart towards his adoring followers he is shown in actuality to have 'thousands of them'.

Seat Ten (WILDCARD)

I take some publisher prerogative here and add a character that was not on the AFI list but that has made a personal impression with regard to their emotional, heart-related lessons. The character is: well, the amalgamated or prototypically classic Bill Murray movie character.

Bill Murray is widely recognized as one of the funniest actors in the business, perhaps most notably stemming from his television work on *Saturday Night Live* and continuing through a successful film career. Later his portrayals of 'serious' emotions gained equal acclaim. Notwithstanding, a link through many of his portrayals is the hardened cynic or aloof wanderer finally finding his heart. Such as in the 2014 *St. Vincent*, 2005 *Broken Flowers*, 2003 *Lost in Translation*, 1993 *Groundhog Day*, 1988 *Scrooged*, 1984 *The Razor's Edge*, 1981 *Stripes*, and 1979 *Meatballs*. For example, in *Scrooged*, Murray plays heartless television executive Frank Cross who is warmed by love and by compassion to show sympathy for the homeless, gratitude towards his cast and kin, compassion for a down-and-out employee, and tenderness toward his sweetheart. As quoted on IMDB, Murray comments on the emotional core that defines his characters:

> Melancholic and lovable is the trick, right? You've got to be able to show that you have these feelings. In the game of life, you get these feelings and how you deal with those feelings. What you do when you are trying to deal with a melancholy. A melancholy can be sweet. It's not a mean thing, but it's something that happens in life – like autumn.

Even More

We might also staff our 'back-benchers' with additional most-influential nominees such as:

- Igor Stravinsky   … and inspiring through composition.
- Charlie Chaplin   … and inspiring through film.
- Andrei Sakharov   … and inspiring through peace and humanist initiatives.
- Martha Graham   … and inspiring through dance.
- Lucille Ball   … and inspiring through laughter.
- Frank Sinatra   … and inspiring through music.
- Marlon Brando   … and inspiring through acting.
- Jim Henson   … and inspiring through puppetry.
- Fred (Mr.) Rodgers   … and inspiring through kindness and television.
- Bob Dylan   … and inspiring through song and songwriting.
- Aretha Franklin   … and inspiring through song and songwriting.
- Diana Spencer (Lady Di)   … and inspiring through grace and compassion.

The Upshot

During the Meeting

So … put your affective, emotional challenge on the table.

134 Assembling Your Leadership Toolbox

What do you envision these figures saying about using your heart to solve it? When do you see calling on them for their advice?

How do you see them interacting with each other?

What might Martin Luther King, Jr. or Winston Churchill say about the emotional challenge? How might William Shakespeare, Leo Tolstoy, or the Brontë Sisters retort?

Could Wolfgang Mozart, Ludwig Beethoven, or John Lennon and Paul McCartney add anything? And would this be supported, refuted, or amended by Oprah Winfrey or Sam Walton? And perhaps extended by Stanley Kubrick or Steven Spielberg?

Should we also consider the insights offered by Rocky Balboa for feeling and increasing spirit? Plus how about Shane? Or Jefferson Smith. And certainly we should not ignore Arthur Chips. Nor should we discount the contribution of the 'Bill Murray' character.

In addition, would anyone from the back chime in – say, for example, Chaplin, Sakharov, Graham, Ball Brando, Dylan, or Franklin?

After the Meeting

Do you see how these cases illustrate the principles of aesthetics-related, spirit-driven leadership? Awareness? Attitude? Inspiration?

What do you glean from our council that might be helpful in leading an artist to address affective challenges that might arise in your life?

GOING FORWARD

How might you customize the content of the council to fit your personal predilections as well as professional circumstances? Add, subtract, or amend its membership to best suit your style and needs?

How might you customize the process of the council to fit your idiosyncratic predilections and references? Use it or preside over it differently?

Lead with Spirit

Taken together, this chapter's presentation of awareness, attitude, and inspiration will allow you to enhance this leadership tool and work towards EXTRAORDINARY EMOTIVE CAPACITY.

When faced with emotional and affective-related challenges it will enable you to lead a personal and professional life infused with SPIRIT.

Appropriately, the second tool in a wise leader's toolbox is summarized for your convenience in Table 5.2.

This chapter focuses on the second step in wise leadership – FEELING. It is grounded in the philosophical branch of AESTHETICS. It enables the wise person or organization to become affectively stronger at what they do.

TABLE 5.2 Becoming a Leadership Artist

Leadership ARTIST	
Challenge	Affective (Aesthetics)
Focus	Heart – Feeling
Building a Better Core (D > I)	Awareness *Sensitivity* *Empathy*
Crafting a Better Process (I > K)	Attitude *Positivity* *Pluralism*
Leveraging a Better Capacity (K > W)	Inspiration *Motivational* *Influential*
Outcome	Spirit: Extraordinary Emotive Capacity

In this way it involves unleashing your inner ARTIST.

However, feeling is often misunderstood and, more than this, internal limitations and external barriers often prevent us from truly feeling like a leader. So ...

- Building a better feeling *core* involves enlarging your sensitivity and empathy of emotional awareness.
- A better feeling *process* involves improving your attitude through greater positivity and pluralism.
- *Leveraging* your feeling capacity involves superior inspiration through enhanced motivational and inspirational competencies.

If you do this then you will develop the HEART OF A LEADER.

6

LOOKING DEEP INSIDE YOURSELF

How to Use Your Leadership Icon (Ethics) Tools

How does a leader see deep inside their self?

How do you develop the reflective capacity and moral compass of a leader?

These are different types of questions than those from the last two chapters.

Different from matters of logic and being a leadership scientist.

Different from matters of aesthetics and being a leadership artist.

Those previous questions focused on being better. By brightening your proverbial head-lights and your heart-lights. Now we mix things up a bit and speak about the next part of the model. Not being better per se but seeing better. By focusing your inner-camera and your outer-camera.

We will begin this discussion here, in this sixth chapter, by looking INSIDE and developing extraordinary introspective insight.

How we see inside ourselves is vitally important to how we lead. And despite the technological advances to our ability to scan our bodies we walk around day-by-day remaining largely blind to our inner core. For example, people are frequently so focused (many would say hyper-focused bordering on obsession) with what we 'can' do that we ignore what we 'should' do. This is akin to the proverbial 'Jurassic Park' problem – just because scientists can clone dinosaurs does not mean that they should clone them. Similar issues rebound when speaking of modern-day DNA coding, leaps in nanotechnology and artificial intelligence, and in data mining. Just because leaders build their logical and inspirational capacities and expand what they can do, it is a separate issue entirely if and how it is right to use them.

People also tend to be overly focused on what will help and harm them in the immediate term. So much so that higher order covenants and principles are too often sacrificed at the altar of instant, selfish pleasures. Just because things feel good does not mean that they are good. Overindulgence and avarice are not higher order or long-term strategies for happiness. Just like in food consumption, where sayings such as 'a minute on the lips but forever on the hips' remind us to reflect upon the implications of transactional choices. And just like when considering personal privacy and freedom issues where deeper concerns must be balanced with our increasing capacities for generating targeted sales and customized playlists.

And more than this, there is a prevailing 'fakeness' filtering throughout the mechanisms of our interactions that it is becoming increasingly hard to know who and when to trust. As per Jean-Paul Sartre, or more popularly the reflective superhero Spiderman, with great (logical and emotional) power comes great (ethical) responsibility. To resist power for the sake of power. To rein in the arrogance and conceit, the selfishness and self-absorption, that tempts us when we become more powerful. To provide an internal check against our external sways. Yet a quick perusal of the headline and business news feeds will reveal that leaders are hard-pressed to resist such lures.

As the prior paragraphs reveal, we are often faced with environments characterized by the following. ... Moral blindness. Immaturity. Inauthenticity. Self-absorption. Distorted confidence.

So do you still want to be a leader? A wise leader?

Then you must learn to reflect like one.

One of the tools leaders must hone and wield is ethics. Reflecting and helping people reflect. Looking deep within yourself and helping people look deep within themselves. Elevating your and their character.

But don't just take my word for it. Please consider the following insights.

> *The only tyrant I accept in this world is the voice within.*
> – M. K. Gandhi
>
> *Ability may get you to the top, but it takes character to keep you there.*
> – John Wooden
>
> *If you want to test a man's character, give him power.*
> – Abraham Lincoln
>
> *Honesty is the first chapter in the book of wisdom.*
> – Thomas Jefferson
>
> *Without courage all other virtues lose their meaning.*
> – Winston Churchill

We are constantly barraged by others' messaging in our life, seemingly from the moment we rise (because most people sleep near and immediately check their mobile phones upon waking) to the moment we retire. So many opinions. So many influences. However, these outside voices must be filtered through one's

138 Assembling Your Leadership Toolbox

inner voice. To prioritize. To evaluate. To act. We can certainly listen to others but we must not be ruled by others. Cutting through the cacophony of noise must be the clarion call of one's core. Ethics must be important. It must be seen. It must be overlaid onto reality to make sense of it and to guide it. To live a principled life. This is the message of Indian statesman and icon M.K. Gandhi.

If we do this, if we ground ourselves firmly on a solid foundation built from within, then we can withstand all of the pressures and demands that seek to move us off of this base. For it is often harder to maintain success than to achieve it. When you are rising you are a moving target somewhat under the radar. But when you have arrived you are dead center on peoples' radars (and perhaps their targeting scopes). People seeking to forward their agendas and their interests no matter the costs and the implications. Leaders must maintain their standards. They must grow their standards. They must share their standards. They must live their standards. This is the message of legendary coach John Wooden.

Not only must you deal with other people's agendas, you must also deal with your own. Temptations tend to increase as one gains the means to attain them. With nothing one is not lured into such traps because there is little currency for realizing them. Yet with the leverage of power and the money that often comes with it leaders are presented with many options for which to spend them. It is here that one tests their mettle. It is here that one sees their core. Is challenged to stay true to their core. When temptation is greatest character must also be greatest. This is the message of Abraham Lincoln.

So in proportion to the leader's leverage they must strive for a clear conscience. Transparency in their dealings (even, or especially, when such dealings seem to be easily hid). Genuineness in their intentions. Fidelity in their processes. Faithfulness in their strivings. Anchored steadfastly to one's principles and values. For although it is certainly bad to lie to others it is even more dangerous to lie to oneself. Character matters. Trust matters. This is the message of Thomas Jefferson.

Of course, the above is more easily said than done. I can write and you can speak about being true to your core but in reality there are risks. What is good is not always what is expedient. What is noble is not always what is effective. What is right is not always what is popular. Nice guys might not always finish last, as per baseball savant Leo Derosher, but it is no doubt sometimes more difficult and more risky to be ethical. It often requires a harder path. In short, it takes courage. Confidence. A fidelity to your code. A responsibility to live through and within it. This is the message of Winston Churchill.

So here we are.

Chapter 6 explains how leaders REFLECT (i.e., look INSIDE). It is grounded in the philosophical branch of ETHICS. Developing this tool enables the wise leader and their organization to see DEEP within themselves. In a way it involves discovering, honing, and unleashing your inner leadership ICON.

However, the true nature of the leader's reflection is often misunderstood. More than this, individuals' internal limitations and organizations' external barriers can prevent us from truly reflecting like a proverbial leadership icon.

So what to do?

Coalescing what we know about leadership ethics provides several tools to help us in this endeavor.

In short, to be a leadership icon …

1. Building a better reflective core involves examining the overall mindset as well as the system of ethical assessment that gives you your morality;
2. Crafting a better reflecting process will allow you to see yourself in a more authentic way through personalized alignment and trust; and
3. Leveraging your reflective vision brings greater confidence through enhanced esteem and agency.

Taken together the chapter's presentation of morality, authenticity, and confidence will allow you to enhance this leadership tool and work towards EXTRAORDINARY INTROSPECTIVE INSIGHT.

When faced with moral and prudence-related challenges it will enable you to lead a personal and professional life infused with CHARACTER.

This chapter is therefore organized as follows:

- Problem: When Facing Moral and Value Challenges
- Solution: Activate Your Leader 'Ethics' Tool
- Identity: Be a Leadership ICON
- Method: To Look Inside Yourself
- Focus: And with Extraordinary Introspective Insight
- Outcome: Lead through *Character*

When Facing Moral and Value Challenges

What Is this Type of Problem?

One type of challenge leaders face is moral in nature. It involves reflection. In essence, it demands that you develop the 'integrity' of a leader. That you look inside, or see deep within, like a leader.

Some appropriate analogies for reflecting are the mirror and the microscope. Leaders look at themselves. Not just to fix their hair but to stare into their eyes and see their soul. And they seek to be at peace with the person in the mirror who is staring back at them. They also dissect themselves with a proverbial finer grained microscope to get under the skin, beyond surface images, and isolate different aspects of their character for subjecting them to similar inspection. In today's world this is done rather effectively with Magnetic Resonance Imaging (MRI) to produce three-dimensional detailed anatomical images. When something seems out of sync in one's inner compass then a leader may turn to similarly revealing reflective practices that probe beneath the surface to detect misalignments.

So ask yourself – When looking in the mirror do you like the person that you see? Are you afraid to look deeper at the different parts of yourself, even the ones that you are not strongest or most assured in?

Can you conduct a leadership MRI?

To reflect like a leader?

Net-Net: The third core element of management wisdom is to 'reflect'. Reflect implies that the wisest individuals, teams, organizations, and strategies demonstrate extraordinary introspective insight. Thus, wise actors in the professional domain see DEEP inside themselves. They discover their identity. They deploy their insight and grounded base to realize and leverage their inner self.

This is depicted in Figure 6.1, with emphasis added in our model of Wise Leadership to highlight the current topic.

So how do you know when you are facing conscience- and moral-related (integrity) challenges that require you to be a leadership icon? And why are these problems so darned hard to solve?

These issues are addressed below.

How Do You Know When You Are Facing It?

You can tell if you are facing this type of challenge if you see conscience and integrity-related challenges. More specifically, (1) Problems of Morality, (2) Problems of Authenticity, and/or (3) Problems of Confidence. Each will be explained below.

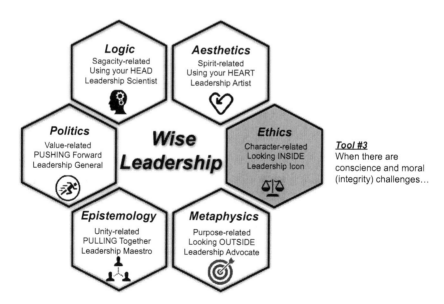

FIGURE 6.1 Focus: Ethics and the Leadership Icon.

The Need for an Ethical Outlook: Dealing with Problems of Morality

The foundation for building a better reflective core involves recognizing that ethics is important. If you do not know or care what values you seek to support or how you should seek to support them, then the ethical anchor is adrift and the moral core of your leadership is compromised. It seems almost self-evident to say that there is a moral component to leadership. However, if history is our judge then there are far too many transgressions and violations of even this basic axiom to necessarily assume it is so.

In technical terms, when these types of failures occur, you do not have an interest in or alacrity for seeing the world in terms of ethics. In plain speak you struggle with recognizing and addressing, even at the most basic level, the issues of what is the right thing to do and what is the right way to do it. In these cases they indicate that we face a challenge of integrity, more specifically one based in moral frames.

This is a Data > Information issue. Ethical input never makes it onto your radar screen.

Some examples: When addressing an issue in an ethical 'gray area' there is a blind overreliance on numbers and measurables even when they threaten to pull you into dubious moral directions. There may even be a summary dismissal of ethical codes of conduct or viewing them as irrelevant constraints based on pure ignorance or rampant arrogance.

The key is recognizing the ethical dimension to the issues you are facing and then having a means of reflecting upon it. Of course it is not my place in this book to tell you where you should locate your moral core. Many seek guidance from religious systems. Others from different types of spiritual journeys. And others from social or communal dialogs. It is however my contention that without this core one can become adrift.

Thus the best leaders can identify moral issues and the proper tools for solving them.

Basically, to do this, you need to (1) develop a moral mindset, and (2) grow your moral maturity.

A moral or ethical mindset, as per psychologist Howard Gardiner, is one that sees the existence and relevance of ethical issues as important and beneficial to oneself, one's organizations, and the larger society in general. Without it one is like a color-blind person who is systematically oblivious to select hues in the spectrum. A leader of this ilk is morally blind and cannot even see ethical issues. They are in danger of acting in an amoral manner.

Moral maturity, as per Lawrence Kohlberg, is a hierarchy of development that describes the level of processing ethical issues. For a leader at the lowest levels of the hierarchy this may be negligent or rudimentary at best – such as a pure ego-driven hedonist. A leader at moderate levels of the hierarchy is better but may be constrained – such as the blind social conformer. A leader at the most prominent

142 Assembling Your Leadership Toolbox

and enlightened echelons of the maturity hierarchy is deeply reflective – such as the highly principled actor.

The Need for Ethical Practices: Dealing with Problems of Authenticity

Once your ethical core is prioritized and matured, crafting a better reflective process will allow you to see yourself in a more authentic way through personalized alignment and inherent trustworthiness. A moral mindset and moral maturity must be translated into moral processes and practices. So, if you cannot just manage and support your core, but also build upon your core, then your moral anchor becomes moored and stagnant. It may even become overwhelmed and decay.

In technical terms, the problem here is that you do not have an authentic orientation and development trajectory. In plain speak, you struggle with what is the truest, best fit for the current and for the future self as well as for those whom you represent.

In these cases they indicate that we have a problem of authenticity. Authenticity refers to fidelity to oneself and in relationships with others.

This is an Information > Knowledge issue. Ethical input is present but is not processed well.

Some examples: You act in a way that runs counter to your idealized intentions. You are a shape-shifter extraordinaire, the proverbial flag flapping in the prevailing wind, the chameleon on steroids. This causes a person (per self-monitoring theory – see Snyder, 1979) to lose a sense of true self and the trust of others. If you are not true to yourself then who are you? If you flip-flop constantly then how can you be trusted? Of course exploration and evolution is important for leaders, but when they are seen as merely superficial and opportunistic then this is where problems of identity and trust set in.

Thus, the best leaders can reconcile their ethical core and create a sense of responsibility.

Basically, to do this you need to cultivate (1) personal alignment, and (2) interpersonal trust.

First, personal alignment is key to developing an ethical authenticity. If you cannot align with your core then you are a phony. A charade. Even if others do not see it. This schism between true and projected selves creates tension and a deep disconnect with the work of leadership both fundamentally as well as practically. As per Bill George, in his 2011 article 'Why Leaders Lose Their Way', self-reflection is a critical component of leadership development:

> Leaders who lose their way are not bad people; rather, they lose their moral bearings, often yielding to seductions in their paths. Very few people go into leadership roles to cheat or do evil, yet we all have the capacity for actions we deeply regret unless we stay grounded.… Before anyone takes on a leadership role, they should ask themselves, "Why do I

want to lead?" and "What's the purpose of my leadership?" These questions are simple to ask, but finding the real answers may take decades.

Second, as a leader you must also project alignment if you have any hope of people following you anywhere. Without followers you are not a leader. And you will not have followers, at least loyal and committed ones that last past the next paycheck or favor, if you are not trusted. Put simply, authenticity walks hand in hand with trust. Trust is a small word with big implications. Essentially it refers to the degree that people can rely on your intentions as well as the ability to act and foster outcomes according to these intentions. In other words, there is the attribution of both (1) a goodwill (trust that you will pursue the right ends) dimension to trust, as well as (2) a high competency (trust that you can achieve these ends) dimension to trust. Indeed, there is much research – for example, by Den Hartog, Posner, and Treviño – that points to the central role of trust in ethical leadership. Basically, if you are trusted then you will be followed. If not, then you might be temporarily abided but cannot lead in a way that instills sustainable fervor or lasting loyalty.

The Need for Ethical Courage: Dealing with Problems of Confidence

Once your core is clarified and matured, and once your reflective process is aligned and grown, then full integration of your ethical leadership can take place. It is only then that you can take that necessary third step to finding and fulfilling your inner character.

In technical terms, the problem here is that you do not have sufficient esteem and agency to carry through on your ethical intentions. In plain speak, you struggle with what you as a person can actually do in the here-and-now to be ethical. This is especially problematic when doing the right thing is not easy. Whether due to a general meekness, to a case of nerves, or related obstacles that prevent you from fully expressing yourself, fear impedes your inner character from emerging and you never become a leadership icon.

In these cases they indicate that we have a problem of ethical cowardice, a moral timidity or a lack of courage.

This is a Knowledge > Wisdom issue. Ethical inputs and processes are not coupled with confidence to attaining the most morally satisfying conclusions.

Some examples: Someone bows to peer pressure and goes along with the crowd to violate their code and perpetrate unethical acts. Or instead someone gives up or tunes out when bad things are happening, choosing to hide in dark corners rather than to stand firm in the light. Or maybe someone sees the right road to follow but does not take it because it is just too darn hard. Instead they take ethical short cuts. Lean on ethical excuses. Or make ethical compromises.

Thus, the best leaders can lead with character.

Basically, to do this, you need to evoke healthy senses of (1) esteem, and (2) agency.

144 Assembling Your Leadership Toolbox

First, esteem is a colloquial but useful metric for how comfortable you are in your own skin. When applied to ethics it captures the degree to which you can do the right, versus the easy or unpopular, thing. It assesses ethics from within. It allows you to go against what is widespread when that norm is morally wrong. Versus doing only what is most expedient. Versus doing only what is most profitable. It essentially allows you to make unpopular but morally justified decisions. It affords you the courage to act with integrity.

Second, agency is a metric for how much you are willing to accept accountability and take personal charge for impacting a situation. When applied to ethics, it represents the degree to which you can hold yourself morally responsible during as well as after the fact. It embraces versus shuns responsibility and duty. It recognizes the force and energy you apply to situations and your capacity to impact them. It sheds a helpless 'poor-me' mentality to take the proverbial wheel and, in the words of Gandhi, "be the change that you hope for in the world". It further affords you the courage to act with integrity.

All Together

If we do not rise to meet Morality challenges then we will not be coherent or grounded in our leadership. We cannot tell right from wrong.

If we do not rise to meet Authenticity challenges then we will not be true or trustworthy in our leadership. We cannot separate real from fake.

If we do not rise to meet Confidence challenges then we will not be comfortable or assured in our leadership. We cannot distinguish courage and poise from fearful timidity.

UPSHOT: Know when you are facing ethical, character-based challenges.

Activate Your Leader 'Ethics' Tool

As expressed in the preceding section, the primary tool leaders use to address integrity challenges is sourced from the domain of ethics. Ethical leadership, as per Brown and colleagues (2005), is the personal demonstration as well as organizational promotion of normatively appropriate conduct.

Without leadership ICON tools leaders are hard-pressed to gain personal productivity and happiness. If you cannot look deep within yourself then you subject yourself to ethical traps and shortcomings. You will not have the character to deal with integrity challenges.

Without leadership icon tools leaders are also hard-pressed to help others and their organization gain productivity and happiness. If your organization cannot look deep within itself then it will not have the character to deal with integrity challenges. For example, in promoting ethical strategies, employment practices, human rights initiatives, environmental protections, and societally beneficial policies and positions.

Let us be clear: leaders have a moral imperative to lead with character. By virtue of the social contract and the corresponding responsibilities that accompany their increased power. And they should also have a functional interest in ethics, say, for enhancing reputation. Thus, it is essential for leaders to not just have 'logos' and 'pathos' but also, as per Hannah and Avolio's (2011) consideration of leadership within the context of ethics, the 'ethos' to summon an inner strength to drive virtuous behavior. But alas these are not easy tools to acquire and employ. If they were then all leaders would not have any character concerns and the world would not face integrity issues. Here are some of the key barriers in ourselves (individual) and our environments (organizational) that impede us and our followers from addressing these types of issues.

Some Ethical Outlook Challenges Leaders Must Overcome

First, people are people. Inherently imperfect. They are sometimes greedy and entitled. They have conflicting and sometimes ill-aimed desires. They have self-interests and sometimes obsess on them. They have personal agendas and sometimes focus only on them. And they have temptations and sometimes succumb to them. And these lures can grow larger with rising leadership trajectories and the power that comes with it. As will be discussed below at greater depth, we vary in moral mindset and moral maturity. We do not often see things in ethical terms. And even when we do, we do not always approach them in an elucidated, principle-oriented way. Leaders need to look deep inside themselves.

- Leadership icons strive to see things in a moral light

Second, ethical codes are not always consistent. For example, what is prescribed by one's profession (e.g., being a doctor) may actually be proscribed by one's employment (e.g., job description formalized in one's hospital or clinic). And even more than this, their philosophic foundations themselves are not always consistent. What is good or right from one perspective (e.g., utilitarianism) might be wrong from another (e.g., justice). It is not my place to tell you how to form your code. But it is entirely within my purview to prompt you to do so. Leaders need to find, form, and galvanize their set of moral principles.

- Leadership icons strive to amplify this inner light with a principled-oriented approach

Some Ethical Process Challenges Leaders Must Overcome

Third, ethical standards vary. Between groups, between teams, between organizations, and between countries. This is partly due to the diversity of cultural and

146 Assembling Your Leadership Toolbox

societal norms. In this vein, there is a debate about whether there is a universal, 'capital-E' Ethic or contingent, 'lowercase-e' sets of ethics. In technical terms, whether ethics is an 'etic' (general) or an 'emic' (case-by-case) issue. Leaders therefore need to harmonize their ethics not just with themselves but also with their environments. And in doing so being agile and adaptive while simultaneously retaining their ethical center.

- Leadership icons attempt to align ethics with the situation

Fourth, contexts vary in their support for ethics. Unethical behaviors are notoriously more prevalent with high stakes and financial implications. For example, it is one thing to act ethically in a classroom or simulation where temptations are artificial and peripheral. But when things 'get real' the pressure to violate trust builds. It might be easy to pass up ten play dollars in a case study but less so to pass up ten million actual ones. To take a pretend hit in a video game and reset it versus suffer an actual job or status loss. Moreover, when leaders are increasingly measured and assessed on everything they achieve (or fail to achieve) no matter the morality of the actions needed to achieve them, and where compensation is linked to increasingly challenging and competitive goals regardless of how they are met, and when violating tacit or even explicit covenants are seen as shrewd practices rather than wrongful acts, then these outside pressures can dramatically erode trustworthiness. Bottom line: you are less likely to get ethical behavior if you do not reward it. Even if this means that values are compromised, corners are cut, agreements are dishonored, and others are harmed.

- Leadership icons attempt to earn trust by being consistently ethical (even when ethics are not rewarded)

Some Ethical Courage Challenges Leaders Must Overcome

Fifth, when things get confusing people too often turn into sheep that follow the crowd. As a result they can lose themselves in the moment. This is especially true in morally ambiguous situations or ethical gray areas that are not well defined and lend themselves to interpretation. As discussed earlier, it is hard to remain comfortable in one's own skin when you are doing something unpopular, even though it is the right thing to do. This is the essence of John F. Kennedy's treatise *Profiles in Courage* that lauds leaders who put the interests of their organizations ahead of parochial concerns.

- Leadership icons summon the requisite esteem to be confident in their character, especially when this is not popular

Sixth, people like to hide when things get tough. Pretending that someone else will do something about it. Looking to unload responsibility. This is the easier path. This is also the more low-risk, politically expedient path. However, it is not the right path. It embodies weakness and imbues cowardice. We should all run to the fight, run up the stairs (as per the heroic rescuers during the World Trade Center attack), and face down problems. Speak the hard truth. Confront the bully. Talk about the failure. However, as is lamentably evident, this is less often the case than not. Bravery should be a norm but, alas, it is all too uncommon.

- Leadership icons embrace the agency to be resolute in their character, especially when this is not easy

Taken Together

As you can see, the issues of ethics and leadership are inexorably intertwined. So, with so many shortcomings, so many temptations, so much variability, and so much confusion, leaders must be proactive in developing their character.

UPSHOT: Wise leaders address ethical, integrity-related challenges.

Be a Leadership ICON

The identity best befitting an ethical problem solver is that of a leadership icon.

Icon, as per the *Oxford English Dictionary*, is a famous person or thing that people admire and see as a symbol of a particular idea, way of life, etc. Icons, by extension, are those most representative of and admired for their adherence to a well-regarded characteristic. And with regard to ethics, leadership icons are those that emblemize the most good and decent of our pursuits as well as the organizations and associations that pursue them. In a word, icons have character. They embody and enact their ethical principles. From a strong moral foundation. Through authenticity and trust. With courage and confidence.

When you picture an icon what images come into your head?

Perhaps they are sitting beneath a dome or atop a pillar?

Rapt deep in meditation?

Holding a scale of justice or amidst a glow of righteousness?

Caring beyond the normal experiences of life's pulls and tugs?

Or maybe just being plain old decent, nice, and polite folk?

These are poor stereotypes and pigeonholes for sure, but they can be used as a jumping-off point for capturing the character of the icon. And as such they may suggest ways for modeling how icons reflect and what leaders can learn from them to reflect better.

148 Assembling Your Leadership Toolbox

TABLE 6.1 Tools for Looking Deep INSIDE Yourself

Better Core: Morality	Moral Mindset
	Moral Maturity
Better Process: Authenticity	Tighter Alignment
	Enhanced Trust
Better Leverage: Confidence	Appropriate Esteem
	Appropriate Agency

Put more systematically, and in a manner consistent with the book's model:

- Icons are more ethically attuned. Leadership icons therefore have the moral mindset and moral maturity to address ethical challenges.
- Icons are more authentic. Leadership icons also have the alignment and trust to address ethical challenges.
- Icons are more confident. Leadership icons additionally have the esteem and agency to address ethical challenges.

Leadership icons develop their ethics and their character in these three fundamental ways.

The following offers a step-by-step map for doing this. For convenience these steps are summarized in Table 6.1. They are then illustrated as well as elaborated upon in the subsequent corresponding sections.

To Look Deep Inside Yourself

Step One – Building a Better Core

> *No man is justified in doing evil on the basis of expediency.*
> – Theodore Roosevelt
>
> *You are never wrong to do the right thing.*
> – Mark Twain
>
> *If a man hasn't discovered something that he will die for, he isn't fit to live.*
> – Dr. Martin Luther King, Jr.
>
> *The quality of an individual is reflected in the standards they set for themselves.*
> – Ray Kroc
>
> *Right is more precious than peace.*
> – Woodrow Wilson

Teddy Roosevelt tells us that the easy path is not always the best path. Evil can be active and it can be passive. Active transgressions are easily seen, although sometimes only with the benefit of hindsight. To wrongly take property. Take liberties. Take advantage. Passive indiscretions are harder to spot. Doing nothing when the above occur. Not stopping someone wrongly stealing, exploiting, or manipulating. The hard things in life are hard for a reason. That is why they take character. Like Roosevelt charging up a hill. Easy is not the only metric for assessing situations. Right matters. Yet we are frequently admonished or even condemned for doing the right thing. This is a great irony. It is also a convoluting of the very words themselves. Right should mean right. It should not necessarily mean easy (as discussed above) or just profitable or just availing. Right should have a moral tone. An ethical lens. We may not be appeased or enriched or advanced by an action. But these are different than right. And this is what Mark Twain is telling us. So how does one calibrate right? Ultimately it is by looking deep inside and finding one's principles. As Dr. King shares, there are several useful vehicles for exploring these. Here the metaphor is 'willing to die for'. Searching for something greater than oneself. We all need to find a way to look past all the barriers to reflection and see one's core. Of course there are other vehicles. For example, as espoused by Immanuel Kant, what would you will to be a universal law? Or the more colloquial question how would you act if your grandparents were watching you or a New York Times reporter would put it on the front page of tomorrow's paper? It is this core, these principles, these standards, that begins to define the core of one's character. Greater maturity begets a better reputation and merits more renown. Aim lower and live lower. Aim higher and set the stage for greater character. It is not sufficient (as the rest of this chapter attests) but it is a necessary foundation from which to build one's ethical edifice. Ray Kroc and Harry Truman were right about this.

The core to becoming a better leadership icon, or if you will a strategy for developing your INNER 'Camera', is therefore expanding your moral mindset and moral maturity.

Moral Mindset

To develop your moral mindset, focus on seeing things in ethical terms.

One strategy includes the application of a moral lens.

That is, to prioritize and engage in ethical questioning …

Using the word 'should'.

First and foremost this involves developing and supporting moral imagination. Standing in the shoes of the stakeholder and asking how a proposed decision might impact a customer or supplier, a manager or worker, or even a community or ecosystem. This is because decisions are not always straightforward and easy to frame. Thus, leaders need to practice empathy and view situations from their multiple perspectives and histories. For example, when faced with ethical

150 Assembling Your Leadership Toolbox

dilemmas – situations in which none of the available alternatives seems ethically acceptable. Regarding work and human rights, such as in the case of living standards, safely, and privacy. Regarding environmental use and care, such as regarding pollution of air, land, and water. Regarding corruption, such as the facilitation of business by questionable means.

Another strategy might take the form of moral prompts and checks. That is, to draw and respect ethical boundaries, factoring in these issues in formal deliberations, and allowing the room to think, see, and act morally. For example:

- Using 'decision trees' and 'checklists' to structure moral issues. Whereas most people are familiar with logical trees that guide them along a given path with if-then rules, such as "if the product sells excessively fast then consider adjusting the price point" or "if the team plays four wide receivers then consider bringing in more defensive backs", moral trees formalize ethical considerations in the same way so that they cannot be easily ignored. This resembles the checklist approach used in places such as airplane cockpits and hospital operating rooms. In a similar manner leaders can use trees or checklists to better see ethical issues by looking at 'who gets hurt', 'is this legal', 'does this support our core values and mission' and 'will future generations look back kindly upon what we did'?
- Using ethical 'nudges' to increase moral mentality and conviction. Consistent with the Nobel prize-winning work by Richard Thaler (Thaler & Sunstein, 2009), if we design ways for rewarding moral considerations then they are more likely to occur. This incentivizes the moral mindset as opposed to societal, business, and other organizational systems that incentivize win-at-all-costs or money-is-everything mentalities.
- Using 'smell tests' and warning signs. This is akin to installing smoke alarms in your house or texting alarms in your car, but here they are moral alarms that look for certain signals and alert you when they are detected so that morally questionable situations can be faced and addressed before they get too far.

When doing the above you might find that the most profitable paths are not always the most ethical ones. And tough choices ensue. Thus, leaders need to also develop and foster moral courage. The ability to walk away from a decision that is lucrative but wrong. The ability to resist a superior who teaches or commands employees to pursue unethical actions. The moxie to go public to the media and call out persistent unethical behavior.

Still other strategies might take the form of moral conversations.

That is, to engage in ethical exchanges and explorations …

Discussing and debating these living issues in formal deliberations.

This can be done via practices such as:

- Institutionalizing the space and time for ethics … prioritizing morality.
- Designing jobs so that their ethics is entrained in their standards … integrating morality.

- Evaluating performance using ethical criteria … supporting morality.
- Leading by example … displaying morality.
- Establishing written codes of ethical conduct … formalizing morality.
- Developing mechanisms for dealing with ethical problems … guiding morality.
- Accepting whistleblowers … legitimizing morality.
- Providing training in ethics and social responsibility … practicing morality.

Moral Maturity

To develop your moral maturity, focus on putting principles at the forefront of your ethical mindset.

As per Lawrence Kohlberg (1969), model leaders need to move beyond low levels of pre-conventional morality (based on egocentric hedonism – right is defined as what avoids pain and gains pleasure). They also need to move beyond merely conventional morality (based on the law – right is defined as concordance with rules and norms). Instead they need to move towards a principled view of morality. To recognize that what is pleasurable is not always ethical. To recognize that what is legal or popular is not always ethical. This is where integrity is found. This is where character resides.

Some strategies include the active identification and resistance of lower level moral drivers. For example:

- To go from a base lower level to a conforming moderate level try, for instance, resisting a leadership style of pure hedonics and pleasure at any cost (to oneself and to others). Instead differentiate activities stemming from … higher versus lower order drives, long- versus short-term goals, prudent versus materialistic activities, and benevolent versus selfish worldviews.
- To go from a moderate level of conformity to a higher level of principles try, for instance, resisting a leadership style of pure submission and blind obedience to rules and regulations. Instead differentiate laws based on … deep versus shallow grounding, principled versus transactional criteria, whether they treat people as people versus objects (according to Martin Buber), and whether they institutionalize sameness versus differences (as per Dr. Martin Luther King, Jr.).

Complementary strategies would then seek to define such principles. This includes a priori exploring different systems and criteria sets. For example, consider the following guiding principles. Perhaps, as per Kant and Locke, your principles should be based on INPUTS into the ethical decision. This is about 'Rights'. Fundamental entitlements and privileges such as life, liberty, pursuit of happiness. Paramount here is considering issues of respect for values and humanity. Perhaps, as per Aristotle and Hobbes, your principles should be based on conducting the ethical decision PROCESS. This is about 'Justice'. Fair, equitable and objective

152 Assembling Your Leadership Toolbox

methods. Paramount here is considering issues of rule and law. Perhaps, as per Bentham and Mill, your principles should be based on the OUTCOMES of the ethical decision. This is about 'Results'. Utilitarianism. Achieving the greatest good for the greatest number. Paramount here is considering issues for comparison and optimization.

Maybe one of them will appeal to you? Or perhaps you can combine aspects or invent options to work best for your code? And institutionalize it so that it runs through your leadership and your life?

Taken Together

So, what are you waiting for? Grow your leadership icon tool. Start enhancing your moral core.

Drive out base-level hedonics.

Resist the selfish, short-term lures of instant gratifications and moral amnesia.

Reduce the crutch that legal (or accepted, popular, etc.) and ethical are always the same.

Rein in a pure focus on possible and profitable to the exclusion of the ethical.

Instead increase your level of moral maturity.

Be more principled.

Grow your level of moral reflection and consideration.

Start enhancing your character.

UPSHOT: Wise leaders develop a moral mindset and their moral maturity.

Step Two – Crafting a Better Process

> *Happiness is the full use of your powers along lines of excellence in a life affording scope.*
> – John F. Kennedy
>
> *Love your enemies, for they tell you your faults.*
> – Benjamin Franklin
>
> *The way to gain a good reputation is to endeavor to be what you desire to appear.*
> – Socrates
>
> *It takes twenty years to build a reputation and five minutes to ruin it.*
> – Warren Buffett
>
> *I hope I shall always possess firmness and virtue enough to maintain what I consider the most enviable of all titles, the character of an honest man.*
> – George Washington

Authenticity matters. And some of its synonyms are: Real. Sincere. Genuine. Consistent. Trustworthy.

Kennedy speaks to being real. Real is putting your character to moral use in the 'real' world. Using it to make a positive difference. Nicer. More good. More just. Aligning it in a manner consistent with one's context. Franklin speaks to being sincere. When living one will meet friends and foes. Friends are often too nice. Don't get me wrong, nice is good. But only if nice doesn't prevent one from being straight and frank about what one is doing and its moral overtones. Foes typically have fewer qualms for calling you out. For revealing your shortcomings. And in this sense they are wonderful foils for growing and aligning one's character to the circumstances at hand. Socrates speaks to being genuine. Be what you desire to be and how you desire to be seen. Match the deep-within to what you say and what you do. Alignment of intentionality and deed. Buffett speaks to being consistent. In doing so he and Socrates are of one voice. For if you are not then you will have an internal misalignment of core and process. Seeing one way but doing another. And this inconsistency can be ruinous to one's repute and good name. It is colloquially said that you are preceded by your reputation. Or, put another way, that your reputation is the thing that walks in the door before you do (colloquialized by Damon John on 'Shark Tank'). However, a reputation can be lost when the aforementioned inconsistencies occur. Finally, Washington speaks to being trustworthy. When character emerges. From (and not surprisingly) being consistently real, sincere, genuine, and honest.

As is evident from the above, authenticity is essential to processing ethical leadership.

The art of crafting your INNER Camera is defined by alignment and trust. Being real allows you to be true to yourself and to your organization. Being in touch with and aligned with your figurative snapshot. The picture of you. Being real also allows you to do these things in more and more consistent ways. Being in touch with and aligned with your figurative cinema. The movie of you.

A strategy for crafting a better process and developing your authenticity is therefore expanding your alignment and trust.

Ethical Alignment

Ethical alignment allows you to reconcile morality with your surroundings. For example, as per Archie Carroll's (Carroll & Shabana, 2010) 'pyramid' of ethics, leaders must simultaneously embed their ethics in the realities of the world in which they operate. For example, in the economic and societal contexts in which they operate. If you do this then you will be ethically aligned. And people will trust you.

Some strategies include integrating ethics with:

- Your colleagues. Make morality central to how you treat people. Ethics should be a part of your exchanges. They should define your relationships, not be external or alien to them. Seek alignment by promoting shared codes and conscience.

- Your criteria. Make morality central to how you measure success. Ethics should be a part of your standards. They should define your choice processes, not be external or alien to them. Seek alignment by promoting desired codes and conscience.
- Your circumstances. Make morality central to how you define situations. Ethics should be a part of your environment. They should define your atmosphere, not be external or alien to them. Seek alignment by promoting enacted codes and conscience.
- Your time. Make morality central to how you deal with tasks throughout the day. Ethics should be a part of your schedule. They should define your priorities, not be external or alien to them. Seek alignment by promoting evolved codes and conscience.

Enhanced Trust

Trust (as per Mayer, 2013) is a "fundamental building block of such working relationships both within organizations and between people, groups, and organizations themselves". It evidences both a willingness and ability to do what is expected. It is defined by a readiness to be vulnerable to another in the pursuit of a particular action or goal. As such it enables full emersion and commitment. And it covers all the 'gray areas' that cannot be anticipated by the cleverest contracts or most potent enforcements. Without trust there is no leadership. And without leadership there is no organization. And without organization there arises an immense ethical hazard.

You cannot sustainably, successfully lead if you cannot be trusted.

To develop your trustworthiness, perhaps focus on a few select things. Some strategies include the following:

- Bring into line your ethics and your words. Say what you mean. There should not be a gap between what you intend and what you convey.
- Bring into line your ethics and your deeds. Do what you say. There should not be a gap between what you convey and what you display.
- Doing the above instinctively. Make the above second nature to you. Your default setting. It should come naturally. If you have to work at it a lot – to actually say what you mean and actually do what you say – then inevitable seductions and temptations are more likely to derail you.

Taken Together

So, what are you waiting for?

Drive out ethical misalignments.

Resist making ethics peripheral to your life, your goals, and your environments.
Reduce gaps in trust.
Rein in contradictions and temptations.
Instead increase your ethical approach.
Be more morally integrated.
Grow your consistency and reliability.
Start enhancing your trustworthiness.
UPSHOT: Wise leaders are ethically authentic.

Step Three – Leveraging a Better Capacity

> *All dreams can come true if we have the courage to pursue them.*
> – Walt Disney
>
> *Cowards can never be moral.*
> – M. K. Gandhi
>
> *Whether you think you can or think you can't you are right.*
> – Henry Ford
>
> *Self-confidence is the first requisite to great undertakings.*
> – Samuel Johnson
>
> *To know what is right and not do it is cowardice.*
> – Confucius

Walt Disney tells us that to achieve we must have the courage to achieve. This is because life is hard. There are roadblocks. There are temptations. There are saboteurs and provocateurs. It is easier to be ethical in a vacuum or when considering cases within a contrived bubble. It is harder to do when real money is on the line. Not only abstract numbers on paper but when you can see and smell the gold. When privilege is offered. When it is your job, career, and bank account. When trade-offs become personal. Mohandâs Gandhi echoes this notion that this is precisely why courage is intertwined with practical morality. Not idyllic or theoretical morality. But morality amidst the pulls and tugs of politics and of business and of competition. Where the easy way is not always the right way. This can become real. Ingrained. Even second nature. As per Henry Ford, you can will yourself to higher plains and these in turn can unlock even higher ones. This involves enhancing your ethical esteem. And this is necessary to be an iconic leader. As per Samuel Johnson, you must believe in yourself before anyone else will. This involves enhancing your ethical efficacy and agency. Thus, it is a self-reinforcing cycle. Character requires courage and courage enables character. Confucius emphasizes the importance of such intestinal fortitude. In a word,

156 Assembling Your Leadership Toolbox

leadership icons are confident. Not filled with visions of morality and grandeur. Because we can always become better. Not disillusioned by ethical hubris. Because we can always do better. But serene and secure with where they are and how they seek to promote the good. Wise leaders can see deep within to be at peace with and engaging in their true cores. In taking this responsibility they encourage the confidence and trust of others who follow them.

As expressed in the aphorisms above, confidence is critical to realizing ethical leadership.

The art of leveraging your INNER Camera includes esteem and agency. Feeling good about your overall self allows you to enhance the general picture of you and your organization. Of course this needs to be balanced with a sense of humility and deference. Feeling good about your specific engagements allows you to enhance your and your organization's resilience as well as proactiveness. Of course this needs to be balanced with a sense of realism. Combine them and construct a truly formidable character capacity.

Ethical Esteem

Ethical esteem allows you to become centered in your morality.

To develop your esteem, some strategies include liking oneself more, either by acknowledging the value of one's core or increasing its value. For example:

- Find supportive others who can help you see and seek your goodness. Avoid those who instill a sense of worthlessness or demean.
- Seek out ethical mentoring and training that promote, and that can help you realize and practice, the above. Learn specific ways for how to be nicer, better, and more moral.

Other strategies might take the form of reducing reliance and dependence on others' approval. For example:

- Prioritize ethical substance over image. It is better to be good versus look good. Brand is important but not sustainable without a supportive core.
- Rely on internal calibrations versus popularity contests or poll numbers. In a sense this involves growing a thick skin. An ethical course is not always popular. But history (as well as one's conscience) rewards those who stay the course and are resolute in the right.

Still other strategies might take the form of congruency and balancing its conceptualization over time. For example, as per Kessler's (2016) *Being a True VIP*:

- Resist being too calcified (stubborn) or brittle (capricious) in your ethical esteem. Don't change your overall valuation with each episode or activity.

Instead be more cumulative. You are not horrible if you do one thing wrong or wonderful from one nice deed.

- Resist being too high (arrogant) or low (demeaning) in your ethical esteem. Instead aim for confidence without ego. Humility without worthlessness. That is, keep a sense of context.

Ethical Agency

Ethical agency allows you to take control over your morality. Not relying on luck or good fortune. Creating the good fortune. Not hoping for, but being, the moral change you seek in the word.

To develop your agency, some strategies include focusing on what is doable.

- Don't 'worry about worries' but instead 'concern oneself with concerns'. Ethical worries cannot be changed. Ethical concerns can.
- Create a strategy and a plan for ethics. Instead of being surprised or playing the victim, be proactive and get ready for moral issues before they happen.
- Being simultaneously systematic and flexible in the plan's execution. Instead of being rigid, be agile and adapt to unforeseen challenges while staying grounded in your core.

Other strategies might take the form of owning problems.

- Take responsibility. Do not blame others or waste your time and energy on complaining. Face the issues with an eye towards resolving them.
- Obtain feedback for moral growth. Do not be defensive. Similarly, do not seek aggrandizement through acolytes that blindly placate you. Instead treat your ethical journey as one of constant challenge, enlightenment, and improvement.
- Turn challenges into opportunities. Do not get down when ethical issues are not handled well. Barriers might arise. Yet with each difficulty there is a detour. Stumbling may occur. Yet with each falter there is a chance to retool.

Still other strategies might take the form of being solutions-oriented.

- Seek and use the necessary resources. Do not think that you can do everything always with no aid or assistance. Supplement your energy and strength with external catalysts. Form moral alliances, movements, and teams.
- Adopt an action and 'doing' orientation. Do not sit on the sidelines. Ignoring ethical problems and transgressions is tantamount to tacitly supporting them. Sticking your head in the sand or crossing your fingers in the corner does not make them go away.
- Deal with ethical stress (and stressful people) productively. Stress can overpower even the best of us. And few situations are more stressful than those that involve ethical quandaries. Channel that energy and stream it towards the productive.

158 Assembling Your Leadership Toolbox

Taken Together

So, what are you waiting for?
> Drive out low ethical esteem.
> Resist relying on others' likes or losing a sense of context.
> Rein in worries.
> Reduce moral helplessness by taking control.
> Instead increase your ethical confidence.
> Be more congruent.
> Grow your agency.
> Start enhancing your and others' importance.
> *UPSHOT: Wise leaders are ethically confident.*

And with Extraordinary Introspective Insight

As described in the opening section the six core tools of leadership wisdom can be seen to manifest themselves in the record of humanity's greatest successes – the achievements of the most influential real and idealized leaders who have proven themselves across a multitude of times, tasks, and locations. As such, in addition to modern relevant and complementary examples, we draw predominantly from two distinct yet complementary sources: *Time Magazine's* (TM) lists of the most influential and American Film Institute's (AFI) lists of the most heroic.

We will do this via the vehicle of an imaginary assembly of 'Invisible Counselors'. A Leadership Icon conference table to provide insights into how to look deep within oneself.

So let us call this meeting to order …

The Gavel

Here ye, here ye. I now call this LEADERSHIP ICON council to order.
> Our focus is addressing the leadership challenges of INTEGRITY.
> Our purpose is to animate the tool of ETHICS and lead with CHARAC-TER. That is, EXTRAORDINARY INTROSPECTIVE INSIGHT.

The Real

So, who might be attending as some of history's most influential ethics counselors? Let us ask them to introduce themselves (note: all biographical profiles are gleaned from many sources, including the *Encyclopedia Britannica*) and speak to the leadership tool of ethics and leading through character.

Seat One

Perhaps an architect of ethical systems.
> Like … the Buddha.

I am the founder of Buddhism, one of the major religions and philosophical systems of the world. I had a profound experience when first observing suffering. This led me towards the Four Noble Truths: the truth of suffering, the truth that suffering originates with internal cravings, the truth that these inner cravings can be eliminated, and the truth that this elimination is the result of following a methodical way or path. This Eightfold Path is constituted by right views, right aspirations, right speech, right conduct, right livelihood, right effort, right mindfulness, and right meditational attainment. As per the Buddhist Center, Buddhist ethics are about living in these loving and compassionate ways that help rather than harm. The core ethical code of Buddhism is known as the Five Precepts, and these are the distillation of its ethical principles. As per the *Oxford Handbook of World Philosophy* they require three trainings: insight, moral conduct, and mental discipline. And as per the *Stanford Encyclopedia of Philosophy* 'ethical action' is thus both an important part of the Buddhist path and an important aspect of the results said to flow from that path; someone has moral discipline when, having made a commitment to follow a certain system of moral rules, they are actually disposed to follow those rules. This form of moral discipline helps people develop self-respect, so that they are confident in appearing in any gathering. Alternatively, actions motivated by greed, hatred, and delusion have a tendency to drive those who practice them into the lower realms of suffering.

Seat Two

Plus maybe someone who has faced and managed ethical dilemmas.

Like … Katherine Graham.

I am the first female CEO of a Fortune 500 company and a Pulitzer Prize winner who published various news publications. Most notable of these is the *Washington Post*, which I transformed into one of the leading newspapers in the United States. I was especially known for supporting the *Post*'s investigation into the Watergate scandal. Under my leadership, the paper became known for its honest investigative reporting. With the publication of the Pentagon Papers and the newspaper's unrelenting investigation into unethical practices, the *Post* increased its reputation and became the most influential newspaper in the nation. My decision to do the right thing was not without controversy and enormous pressure. As per The Smithsonian I needed to weigh the paper's obligations to the truth with the potential for financial and legal turmoil. I ultimately decided to publish. My ethical stand not only defined this situation but also impacted future situations in preserving freedom of the press.

Like … Abraham Lincoln.

I am the sixteenth President of the United States, who preserved the Union during the American Civil War and brought about the emancipation of slaves. There can be no doubt of my deep and sincere devotion to the cause of personal freedom. I have spoken often on the subject. I hated slavery and the indifference

160 Assembling Your Leadership Toolbox

towards the spread of slavery because of the monstrous injustice of slavery itself and the degradation of human worth and dignity. This relates to a moral character and integrity that occupies my core. In financial dealings I paid off a partner's debts, even going beyond his legal obligation in doing so. In legal dealings I gained the nickname of 'Honest Abe' in part because of colleagues' absolute confidence that I would not tell a lie. And in my presidency I (according to Thomas Carson's book entitled *Lincoln's Ethics*) was a "singularly good and morally virtuous person" and a "morally exemplary human being" whose virtues helped him to be a great political and military leader. I made a great number of difficult and important decisions about the war and slavery under tremendous stress and pressure, and the great majority were the correct ones both morally and strategically. In the words of Frederick Douglass, "infinite wisdom has seldom sent any man into the world better fitted for his mission than Abraham Lincoln. ... The real Abraham Lincoln was as good a person as the mythical Lincoln, but also more complex, more interesting, and more human as well." And in the words of W. E. B. Du Bois, "[I] love him not because he was perfect but because he was not and triumphed ... The world is full of folk whose taste was educated in the gutter. The world is full of people born hating and despising their fellows. To them I love to say: See this man. He was one of you yet he became Abraham Lincoln. I personally revere him the more because up out of his contradictions and inconsistencies he fought his way to the pinnacles of earth and the fight was within as well as without. The scars and foibles and contradictions of the Great do not diminish but enhance the meaning of their upward struggle ... it was his true history and antecedents that proved Abraham Lincoln a Prince of men."

Seat Three

Let us also add a facilitator for considering codes of ethics.

Like ... Fyodor Dostoyevsky.

I am a Russian novelist and short-story writer best known for immensely influential works such as *Crime and Punishment*, *The Idiot*, *The Possessed*, and *The Brothers Karamazov*. It is said that my stories probe the human soul and inner states of mind. The depth and contradictoriness of my heroes have made others look shallow by comparison. And my sense of evil and my love of freedom have made my work especially relevant to a world struggling with ethical crises of war, murder, and totalitarianism. For example, in my *The Brothers Karamazov*, I imagine a fictional dialog between the Grand Inquisitor of Spain and Jesus Christ. The Inquisitor is portrayed as seeing human nature through the lens of fear and loathing. That is, cringing from freedom and responsibility, and seeing the worst of people as simple, weak, self-destructive, selfish, and evil creatures in need of a dominant dictator-like leader to obey. Alternatively, Jesus is portrayed as seeing human nature through the lens of nobility. That is, cherishing freedom and responsibility, seeing the best noble and virtuous core, as complex, strong, and capable creatures that can be benevolent and good when guided by an empowering leader.

Like … Victor Hugo.

I am a poet, novelist, and dramatist known for exploring humankind's inner struggles with evil in such novels as *Notre-Dame de Paris* and *Les Misérables*. The former has been described as touching the public consciousness by condemning a society that heaps misery on the hunchback Quasimodo and the gypsy girl Esmeralda. The latter story centers on the convict Jean Valjean, a victim of society that disparages its wretched outcasts. Valjean escapes from prisoned to become a benevolent industrialist and mayor, yet is obsessively stalked by the detective Javert and is put in positions of self-sacrifice for the good of society in general and specifically of his adopted daughter and her husband. One of the treasures implicit in *Les Misérables* is, as suggested by the above, the interplay between different ethical maturities, the exploration of authenticity and courage, and the juxtaposition of moral codes. Moreover, it is said that my morality was the source of two poems, 'La Fin de Satan' [The End of Satan] and 'Dieu' [God], both of them confrontations of the problem of evil and balancing progress with moral awareness.

Seat Four

At the table should also be a conduit for reflecting upon values and acting from principles.

Like … Muhammad Ali.

I am the greatest boxer in history, the first fighter to win the world heavyweight championship on three separate occasions. In addition, I was known for my social message of black pride and resistance to domination and for refusing induction into the army during the Vietnam War. I was inspired by the life and teachings of Mohammad who was the founder of Islam and the proclaimer of the Qur'ān, Islam's sacred scripture. And as recounted by a national newspaper about me: "In the decades to come, his country and the world would come to embrace him as an ambassador of peace and goodwill.… So it is easy to forget that … Ali 'was willing to sacrifice everything on principle'. Refusing induction, Ali cited religious reasons, specifically, the Quran's ban on Muslims fighting Christian wars, but his objection was far broader. 'My conscience won't let me go shoot my brother, or some darker people, or some poor hungry people in the mud'.… It was a humbling year for Ali, but also one of remarkable growth. Exiled from boxing, he grew bigger than the sport.… And as the anti-war movement grew, Ali became a hero … Ali also helped move black radicalism into the mainstream, Harvard professor Henry Louis Gates Jr. later wrote … (and as per Dr. King) 'He is giving up his fame … giving up millions of dollars in order to stand for what his conscience tells him is right' … (and as per Ali himself) 'There are only two kinds of men, those who compromise and those who take a stand' … (thus) as Ali's consciousness grew, so did the nation's."

162 Assembling Your Leadership Toolbox

Seat Five

And finally a philanthropist who has directed not just their wealth but also their talents towards transformative endeavors.

Like … Andrew Carnegie.

I am a Scottish-born American industrialist who led the enormous expansion of the American steel industry. I was also a philanthropist who wrote frequently about political and social matters, and my most famous article outlined what came to be called the Gospel of Wealth. This doctrine held that a man who accumulates great fortune has a duty to use his surplus for 'the improvement of mankind' in philanthropic causes. A 'man who dies rich dies disgraced'. To this end, my main trusts or charitable foundations are broadly oriented towards: (1) educational institutions, universities, and student financial aid, (2) libraries and child welfare centers, (3) cultural institutions and theaters, (4) various areas of scientific research and mechanisms for diffusing knowledge, and (5) causes such as to promote international peace and understanding.

Like … Bill Gates.

I am known in my early life as a computer programmer and entrepreneur who cofounded Microsoft Corporation, the world's largest personal computer software company. Yet in my second act I decided to redirect my time, energy, and wealth towards nobler causes. With my wife I launched what is now known as the Bill & Melinda Gates Foundation to fund global health programs. We also support libraries through the Gates Library/Learning Foundation and raised money for minority study grants through the Gates Millennium Scholars program. The foundation continues to focus on global health and global development, as well as community and education causes in the United States. For its efforts I was awarded the Presidential Medal of Freedom. Moreover, as per an article in *Business Insider* we "have been named the most generous philanthropists in the US. The philanthropists have donated more than $36 billion to charitable causes…. Through the Bill & Melinda Gates Foundation, the couple has focused on global health, education, and poverty." This is because "we are impatient optimists working to reduce inequity".

The Idealized

So, who might be attending as some of cinema's most heroic ethics counselors? The figurative icons and reflective souls who embark on a journey of self-discovery, intended or not, to find their true best selves.

Seat Six

Why not start with Rick Blaine?

Rick Blaine, in the all-time classic 1942 film *Casablanca*, is a cynical Café owner (which doubles as an upscale nightclub and gambling den) and war profiteer whose reflection leads to sacrifice his treasure for love and country. Specifically, Blaine (portrayed by Humphrey Bogart) voluntarily forfeits a valuable resource worth a lot of money to instead help his ex-lover and her husband escape from Casablanca and pursue their resistance against Nazi persecution. Overcoming his selfish, brooding suspicions the character displays extraordinary internal integrity and moral maturity when he aligns with deeper values to reflect upon and ultimately align with the struggle. Moreover, he manifests it with the confidence and agency to actually resist temptation and selfish allures that might undermine his difficult journey towards the path he knows deep down is the right one. Blaine struggles but eventually puts the good ahead of his wallet. The authentic ahead of the ego. The principled ahead of the expedient.

Seat Seven

Then maybe Will Kane.

Will Kane, in the 1952 western film *High Noon*, is a small town marshal whose ethics leads him to face down an imminent threat to the peoples under his protection. Portrayed by Gary Cooper, he is urged to simply walk away from the fight and also bearing the threat of his wife to leave him if he does not flee. The very townspeople who he supports even back down and refuse to join him, leaving him to literally as well as figuratively stand alone against evil. However, Kane, a lawful and principle-bound individual by nature, decides to stay and face the gang of violent outlaws. Kane did not default to the lower standards of others. Kane did not fall into a negative vortex of spiraling down standards. Showing courage amidst a wave of cowardice, a profound and reflective selflessness amidst a groundswell of me-first wretches, he resolutely defends the good. In this sense Marshal Kane represents the pinnacle of character and internal integrity.

Seat Eight

Further, how about the Jedi lineage from the epic *Star Wars* films?

In the 1977 first film and fourth episode of the nine-part series, *Star Wars: A New Hope* tells the story of young Luke Skywalker (portrayed by Mark Hamill) who becomes an unlikely hero of the Rebellion against the wicked Galactic Empire. He is supported by a mentor, the elder Obi-Wan Kenobi, a Jedi Master who guides Luke (and who eventually guides his protégé Rey) on how to follow his inner instinct, which helped him to use the Force to destroy the Death Star, and restore peace in the universe. Rather than relying on external stimuli, Obi-Wan teaches Luke to trust and act authentically through his core. For example, in one of the series' most memorable moments Kenobi lays down his (light-saber) sword and is killed by the evil Darth Vader so that his protégé can channel his essence to connect his inner self with the universe's overarching force and realize his destiny. Obi-Wan put the good before his own benefit. Obi-Wan looked inward and

164 Assembling Your Leadership Toolbox

similarly promoted avenues for reflection in his follower. In subsequent films Luke is guided by uber-Jedi Yoda, diminutive in physical being but colossal in innate character, to progress along his winding path and ultimately confront the evil of the 'dark side'. As per the Jedi master, some of Yoda's classic words of reflective moral wisdom are: (1) "Train yourself to let go of everything you fear to lose"; (2) "Fear is the path to the dark side. Fear leads to anger. Anger leads to hate. Hate leads to suffering"; (3) "You will know (the good from the bad) when you are calm, at peace"; (4) "Luminous beings are we ... not this crude matter"; and (5) (if you can't believe it deep down inside) "That is why you fail."

Seat Nine

And attending also is George Bailey.

George Bailey, in the 1947 Christmas drama *It's a Wonderful Life*, forgoes riches and travels much to his chagrin until a surprise visit reveals the positive impact of a noble being. Throughout each stage of his life, from adolescence to adulthood to parenthood, Bailey (portrayed by Jimmy Stewart) sacrifices himself to make others' lives better. For example, he lost his hearing one year because he saved his younger brother from drowning. Later he protects an employer from an incident that could have caused him ruin. He also canceled his traveling plans after his father's death to support his business. And he engaged in battles with the greedy Henry Potter to resist 'Potterville's' dark visions for George's beloved town and its people. George Bailey was certainly a man of internal integrity, as evidenced many times in the above flashbacks. He had an elevated moral mindset. He acted with authenticity and inspired trust. Like Luke Skywalker he forwent dreams of travel and personal adventure in favor of his devotion to the ethical high road, and where a less convenient life course more than made up for lost yearnings and riches with the priceless, long-term preservation of the lives of others around him. He displayed confidence and resoluteness in both pursuing and promoting the good. Evidencing the simple truth: Integrity and character matters.

Seat Ten (WILDCARD)

I take some publisher prerogative here and add a character that was not on the AFI list but that has made a personal impression with regard to their ethical lessons. This was a tough one. It could have been Hawkeye Pierce who brought humanity to a *M.A.S.H.* unit during the Korean conflict. It could have very well been Spike Lee's 'Mookie' who attempt to *Do the Right Thing* amidst racial strife during a scorching Brooklyn summer. For example, in the latter, Spike Lee showed how difficult it is to both figure out as well as actually do what is moral. However, we focus here on a real-life character whose life was known primarily from the theatrical depiction and brilliant portrayal by actor Liam Neeson.

The character is: Oskar Schindler.

As depicted in the 1993 film *Schindler's List*, Oskar Schindler was a war profiteer who changed his decision processes to prioritize the good over the lucrative. Instead of amassing wealth he used it to help others. Instead of orienting his productive capacity towards evil ends he sacrificed personal gain for the greater good. Set during World War II and amidst the Holocaust, the viewer witnesses Schindler's moral maturation from pleasure-seeker and profiteer who uses his skills to play the game, to paragon of virtue who instead channels his facilities and resources to save thousands of lives of those who would otherwise have been sent to concentration death camps. Though this causes him to go financially bankrupt, he is assured by the Talmudic insight that "Whoever saves one life, saves the world entire". And as per a website bearing his name (oskarschindler.com/) Schindler "rose to the highest level of humanity, walked through the bloody mud of the Holocaust without soiling his soul, his compassion, his respect for human life – and gave his Jews a second chance at life. He miraculously managed to do it and pulled it off by using the very same talents that made him a war profiteer. ... Today his name is known as a household word for courage in a world of brutality – a hero who saved hundreds of Jews from Hitler's gas chambers.... A man full of flaws like the rest of us – the unlikeliest of all role models who started by earning millions as a war profiteer and ended by spending his last pfennig and risking his life to save his Jews.... An ordinary man who even in the worst of circumstances did extraordinary things."

Even More

We might also staff our 'back-benchers' with additional most-influential nominees such as:

- Helen Keller ... and looking deep to lead on causes of ethics and disability
- Rosa Parks ... and looking deep to lead on causes of ethics and racism
- Anne Frank ... and looking deep to lead on causes of ethics and anti-Semitism
- Pelé ... and looking deep to lead on causes of ethics and the well-being of children
- Harvey Milk ... and looking deep to lead on causes of ethics and gay rights

The Upshot

During the Meeting

So ... put your ethics challenge on the table.

What do you envision these figures saying about looking deep within oneself to solve it?

When do you see calling upon them for their advice?

166 Assembling Your Leadership Toolbox

How do you see them interacting with each other?

What might the Buddha say about the integrity challenge? How might Abraham Lincoln or Katherine Graham retort? Could Victor Hugo or Fyodor Dostoyevsky add anything? And would this be supported, refuted, or amended by Muhammad Ali? And perhaps extended by Andrew Carnegie or Bill Gates?

Should we also consider the insights offered by George Bailey for reflecting and increasing character? Plus how about Will Kane? Or Jedi's Yoda, Obi-Wan Kenobi, and Luke Skywalker? And certainly we should not ignore Rick Blaine. Nor should we discount the contribution of Oskar Schindler.

In addition, would anyone from the back chime in – say, for example, Keller, Parks, Frank, or Milk?

After the Meeting

Do you see how these cases illustrate the principles of ethics-related, character-driven leadership? Morality? Authenticity? Confidence?

What do you glean from our council that might be helpful in leading like an icon to address ethics challenges that might arise in your life?

Going Forward

How might you customize the content of the council to fit your personal preferences as well as professional circumstances? Add, subtract, or amend its membership to best suit your style and needs?

How might you customize the process of the council to fit your idiosyncratic predilections and references? Use it or preside over it differently?

Lead through Character

Taken together this chapter's presentation of morality, authenticity, and confidence will allow you to enhance this leadership tool and work towards EXTRAORDINARY INTROSPECTIVE INSIGHT.

When faced with integrity and ethically related challenges it will enable you to lead a personal and professional life infused with CHARACTER. This is summarized for your convenience in Table 6.2.

Appropriately, the middle part of becoming wise is to SEE Better. And leading your organization and its people in a way so that they can also see better. We use the metaphor of (focused, accurate) CAMERAS for capturing this aspect of wisdom.

This chapter focuses on the third step in wise leadership – the INSIDE Camera of REFLECTING. It is grounded in the philosophical branch of ETHICS. It enables the wise person or organization to see DEEPER.

In a way it involves unleashing your inner ICON.

TABLE 6.2 Becoming a Leadership Icon

Leadership ICON	
Challenge	Integrity (Ethics)
Focus	Inside – Reflecting
Building a Better Core (D > I)	Morality *Mindset* *Maturity*
Crafting a Better Process (I > K)	Authenticity *Alignment* *Trust*
Leveraging a Better Capacity (K > W)	Confidence *Esteem* *Agency*
Outcome	Character: Extraordinary Introspective Insight

However, reflecting is often misunderstood and, more than this, internal limitations and external barriers often prevent us from truly feeling. So …

- Building a better reflecting *core* involves developing insight into your <u>moral</u> mindset and maturity.
- A better reflecting *process* involves honing your <u>authenticity</u> with greater alignment and trust.
- *Leveraging* your reflecting capacity involves superior <u>confidence</u> through enhanced esteem and agency.

If you do this then you will develop the CHARACTER OF A LEADER.

7

LOOKING FAR OUTSIDE YOURSELF

How to Use Your Leadership Advocate (Metaphysics) Tools

How does a leader see far beyond their self?

How do you develop the aspirational vision of a leader?

We continue to speak about seeing better. In Chapter 6 the focus was on your inner camera and looking deep inside oneself to developing extraordinary introspective insight. Here we shift the focus to your outer camera and looking far beyond oneself to developing extraordinary meaningful objectives.

Meaning is important. Literally and figuratively. In a literal sense there is no importance if there is no meaning. They are inexorably tied to one another both in substance and syntax. This suggest that a person, goal, movement, etc. will be important to the extent that they are meaningful – i.e., have value and significance of purpose. In a figurative sense leaders will not be able to lead anyone, anywhere, and for any length of time if the purpose towards which they lead them is not seen as meaningful.

Yet today we live in a world where meaning is being challenged daily.

What should be our goals? Aims? Objectives? For example, think about how these questions are debated within the (figurative as well as literal) 'wars' between societies, between faiths, among schools of thought, within institutions and organizations, as well as by slickly marketed products and services. This is where meanings' ethnocentric images and narrow prides are stirred.

And if meaning is not being challenged then it is surely being questioned. There is a profound perplexity about what if anything is inherently meaningful. School? Sports? Family? Fun? Self? Society? Work? Play? God? Country? This is where meanings' skepticisms and doubts are stoked.

And even when we want to find importance there are so many pillars from which to orient. So many different paths towards purpose(s). Which to take? Which is best? This is where meanings' multiplicities and confusions run rampant.

And finally, after we latch onto an objective, its personal relationship is often strained. The degree to which it continues to speak to one's own definitions, experiences, and desires as life unwinds and identities evolve. This is where meanings' devotions and dedications are tested.

As the prior paragraphs reveal, we are often faced with environments characterized by the following … Ethnocentrism. Skepticism. Confusion. Strain.

So, do you still want to be a leader? A wise leader?

Then you must learn to aspire like one.

One of the tools leaders must hone and wield is metaphysics. Aspiring and helping people aspire. Looking far beyond yourself and helping people look far beyond themselves. Elevating your and their meaning and sense of purpose.

But don't just take my word for it. Please consider the following insights.

To aspire is to achieve.
– James Allen

The great use of life is to spend it for something that will outlast it. /
Believe that life is worth living, and your belief will help create the fact.
– William James

It gives me a deep, comforting sense that things seen are temporal and
things unseen are eternal.
– Helen Keller

Nothing contributes so much to tranquilize the mind as a steady purpose.
– Mary Shelley

If you want to lift yourself up, lift up someone else.
– Booker T. Washington

How wonderful it is that nobody need wait a single moment before starting to
improve the world.
– Anne Frank

It does not matter much how much head (logic) and heart (aesthetics) we have if they are left to drift without a target. Without focus. Without direction. There must be a meeting of ability and opportunity. Aspiration gives our lights a place to shine. It allows us to (if you will excuse the trite-ism) 'go big' with our talents versus just packaging them up and going home. If we aim high then we unfurl, and possibly extend, ourselves to reach great heights. This is the message of James Allen.

But what do 'high', and 'big' really mean? We can start with a simple comparison – bigger and higher than ourselves. Beyond our brief flicker of existence. Beyond our miniscule arena of being. Instead of limiting ourselves to ephemeral and minute matters we can extend our impact temporally as well as geographically.

170 Assembling Your Leadership Toolbox

To discover that there is a greater meaning beyond oneself. To enact that meaning and in doing so infuse our leadership with it. This is the message of William James and of Helen Keller.

If we do this then we can attach our leadership to something more lasting. More significant. More valuable. A guiding light or north star. This helps steady ourselves. Seeing the greater horizon helps us ride out the inevitable ups and downs of life's crashing waves. Navigating by the higher stars helps us steer clearer past the fogs and disorientations of life's vast, murky seas. This is the message of Mary Shelley.

Certainly there are several potential purposes one might attach oneself to. One is to the service of others. This is true leadership. It is the embodiment of Plato's philosopher and Buddha's Bodhisattva who are not satisfied with merely seeing the light but instead dedicate themselves to helping others see it. It is perhaps this sentiment that most ably captures the difference between the wise person and the wise leader. The former leads a meaningful life. The latter also enables it for others. This is the message of Booker T. Washington.

How audacious this might sound to some. Lighting the world. Lifting humanity. Yes, it is big. But to the true leader it is not brazen as much as it is essential. They see in panoramic while others see in microscopic. They see opportunities and possibilities while others see barriers and constraints. They are invigorated and animated by the prospects of improving our common journey while others are dampened by and inhibited from such endeavors. They feel empowered to say 'yes, I can' and embrace the challenge while others feel enfeebled and cower from such aspirations. This is the message of Anne Frank.

So here we are.

Chapter 7 explains how leaders ASPIRE (i.e., not only look inside but also look OUTSIDE). It is grounded in the philosophical branch of METAPHYSICS. Developing this tool enables the wise leader and their organization to see FAR beyond themselves. In a way it involves discovering, honing, and unleashing your inner leadership ADVOCATE.

However, the true nature of the leader's aspiration is often misunderstood. More than this, individuals' internal limitations and organizations' external barriers can prevent us from truly aspiring like a proverbial leadership advocate.

So, what to do?

Coalescing what we know about leadership metaphysics provides several tools to help us in this endeavor.

In short, to be a leadership icon …

1. Building a better aspirational core involves examining the nature and elements of self that give you your ontology or perspective;
2. Crafting a better aspiring process will help you see the world more inclusively through expanded concern and duty; and
3. Leveraging your aspirational vision brings transcendence through enhanced munificence and service.

Taken together the chapter's presentation of mindfulness, collegiality, and transcendence will allow you to enhance this leadership tool and work towards EXTRAORDINARY MEANINGFUL OBJECTIVES.

When faced with meaning and mission-related challenges it will enable you to lead a personal and professional life infused with PURPOSE.

This chapter is therefore organized as follows:

- Problem: When Facing Meaning and Commitment Challenges
- Solution: Activate Your Leader 'Metaphysics' Tool
- Identity: Be a Leadership ADVOCATE
- Method: To Look Outside Yourself
- Focus: And with Extraordinary Meaningful Objectives
- Outcome: Lead though *Purpose*

When Facing Meaning and Commitment Challenges

What is this Type of Problem?

One type of challenge leaders face is 'significance' in nature. It involves meaning and mission. In essence, it demands that you develop the 'aspiration' of a leader. That you look beyond/outside yourself and see far like a leader.

An appropriate analogy for aspiring is the telescope. Leaders see the big picture. Not just out of curiosity but out of necessity. They place themselves and their endeavor within the larger context. They are embedded in layered collectives, which lie within still larger terrestrial organizations and institutions, which are then located in larger systems, galaxies, and the like. Yet this process does not make them feel insignificant but instead the opposite. As a part of something greater well beyond their mere lives and understandings. It is this that makes us part of and not isolated from each other. As per the colloquialism of my fellow Brooklynite Bernie Sanders, no matter what we believe we are all in, we are definitely all in it together.

So, ask yourself: When looking through the telescope (or perhaps at GoogleMaps or GoogleEarth) do you appreciate the vastness that you see? Are you intimidated and diminished to look further beyond yourself … or galvanized by its awe and wonder?

Can you conduct a larger exploration of meaning?

To aspire like a leader?

Net-Net: The fourth core element of management wisdom is to 'aspire'. Aspire implies that the wisest individuals, teams, organizations, and strategies demonstrate extraordinary meaningful objectives. Thus, wise actors in the professional domain are well targeted. They channel their will in positive directions. They deploy their humanity and citizenry to make themselves and their world better.

This is depicted in Figure 7.1, with emphasis added to the current topic.

FIGURE 7.1 Focus: Metaphysics and the Leadership Advocate.

So how do you know when you are facing significance and mission-related (meaning) challenges that require you to be a leadership advocate? And why are these problems so darned hard to solve?

These issues are addressed below.

How Do You Know When You Are Facing It?

You can tell if you are facing this type of challenge if you see significance and mission-related challenges. More specifically, (1) Problems of Mindfulness, (2) Problems of Collegiality, and/or (3) Problems of Transcendence. Each will be explained below.

The Need for Perspective: Dealing with Problems of Mindfulness

The foundation for building a better aspirational core involves examining your worldview. If you do not care about the nature of the world and your place in it then there is no metaphysical anchor.

In technical terms, here you have not developed an ontology and/or a perspective around it. In plain speak, you struggle with the reasons why 'I' am here and how does my 'here' relate to the whole? To see that we are all connected and that we must pay attention to this connectivity.

In these cases they indicate that we have a problem of mindfulness.

This is a Data > Information issue. Metaphysical input never makes it onto your radar screen.

Some examples: It happens when we lose our sense of personal meaning and sufficiency. When we become divorced from our professional or vocational mission and calling. When we detach from our organizational culture and vision. When we feel alienated from our societal fabric and journey. When the GPS is disabled. When 'What's the point?' supplants 'Let's roll!'

Again, as per the prior chapter, it is not my place in this book to tell you where you should locate your metaphysical core. Many seek guidance from religious systems. Other from different forms of spiritual journeys. And others from social or community dialogs. It is however my contention that without any such guideposts one can become disoriented.

The key to this is mindfulness.

As per the *OED*, mindfulness is the quality or state of being conscious or aware of something. And here that something is yourself and your place in the world.

Basically, to do this, you need to clarify your (1) Ontology and (2) Perspective.

Ontology, as per the *OED*, is a branch of metaphysics dealing with the nature of being and the set of concepts and categories that shows its properties and the relations between them. Your ontology helps you grasp the order of things in which you are a part.

Perspective, as per the *OED*, is a particular attitude towards or way of regarding something; a point of view; a true understanding of the relative importance of things; a sense of proportion. Your perspective helps you grasp the nature of your particular part in the above.

Mindful ontology and perspective arrange the world's data to form a more meaningful reality. As such they tilt the probabilities in your favor and, when facing metaphysical problems, make leadership success more likely.

The Need for Interdependence: Dealing with Problems of Collegiality

Once your metaphysical core is tended to, crafting a better aspirational process will allow you to see further in a broader and broadening way. If you cannot manage and support your core, and build and strengthen your core, then your aspirations become narrow and faint. Our guiding stars should be brightened and not dimmed. They should become more and more personal as opposed to merely pro forma. They should lift us up and help us soar higher instead of banishing us to a comatose-like routine in which we sleepwalk past each other.

In technical terms, here you do not have requisite inclusiveness or duty. In plain speak, you struggle with why do we (people, companies, countries) all relate to and rely on each other, and what is our duty in advancing our common goal or destiny during our relatively brief sojourn on this cosmic pebble?

In these cases they indicate that we have a problem of collegiality.

174 Assembling Your Leadership Toolbox

This is an Information > Knowledge issue. Metaphysical input is present but not processed well.

Some examples: It happens when we lose our sense of and care for one another. When we become selfish, myopic, and perhaps even intolerant. When compassion takes a back seat to egoism and vanity. When small-mindedness trumps mutuality and accountability.

The best leaders can reconcile their metaphysical core and create a sense of collegiality.

Collegiality, as per the *OED*, is a sense of companionship and cooperation between colleagues who share responsibility. It is often bespoken as a way of doing something that is not adversarial in purpose but respectful and kind.

Basically, to do this, you need to cultivate a sense of (1) Inclusiveness and (2) Duty.

First, inclusiveness, as per the *OED*, is the practice or policy of including people who might otherwise be excluded or marginalized, such as those who have disabilities or are members of minority groups. It recognizes that everyone is (as per Kant's categorical imperative) an end in and of themselves. This involves tolerance. And patience. And acceptance.

Second, duty, as per the *OED*, is an obligation; a responsibility. When something is done from a sense of duty it is for a higher purpose rather than for transient personal gain. Like a dutiful citizen or soldier. Like a dutiful aunt or neighbor. It involves, as per the same source, a task or action one is required to perform as part of one's job. Thus, inclusiveness implies certain duties for cultivating the interdependent relationships between beings and helping them thrive. Combined, a sense of inclusiveness and duty processes the swirling streams of information in the world and channels them in a kind and mutually responsible direction.

The Need for Wholeness: Dealing with Problems of Transcendence

Once your aspirational core is clarified and matured, and once your aspirational process is aligned and grown, then full integration of your metaphysical leadership can take place. In short, your leadership must surpass yourself. If not, then you will never cross the barrier between going to a higher place and bringing others to that higher place. Between being an enlightened person and being an enlightened leader.

In technical terms, here you do not have healthy munificence or service orientation. In plain speak, you struggle with what you should do for others, and how you as a leader can be less like a boss and more like a servant.

In these cases they indicate that we have a problem of transcendence.

This is a Knowledge > Wisdom issue. Metaphysical inputs and processes are not coupled to attaining the most meaningful and significant satisfying conclusions.

Some examples: It happens when we feel that everything we do is ultimate and everything we want is primary. When we approach our days with the sentiment that everyone should be just like me or that everyone should just focus on and care about me. When we only project our image onto the world instead of reflecting its marvels in our attitudes and actions. If you cannot see past yourself then you are not a leader. If you take more than you give and approach your role as more entitled than indebted then you are not a leader. 'Mi-mi-mi' (me-me-me) is an operatic refrain, not a wise leadership philosophy.

The best leaders can transcend themselves and help others transcend themselves.

Transcendence, as per the *OED*, involves existence or experience beyond the normal or physical level. At a higher plane of importance and significance.

Basically, to do this, you need to elevate your (1) munificence, and (2) service.

First, munificence, as per the *OED*, is the quality or action of being extremely generous. Looking beyond the self. Striving for higher order ends. Translating a mindful ontology and perspective, and a collegial sense of inclusiveness and duty, into a holistic and even benevolent super-personal vision.

Second, service, as per the *OED*, is the action of helping or doing work for someone … an act of assistance. It animates munificence. It involves the employment and use of one's abilities to be of help in illuminating and transmigrating a shared journey. Hence the phrases to be 'at someone's service' (ready to assist someone whenever possible) and to be 'in service' (available for use). Combined munificence and service complete the path towards grasping and conveying micro- and macro-universal meaningfulness.

All Together

If we do not rise to meet Mindfulness challenges, then we will not be contextualized and have a healthy perspective embedded in our leadership.

If we do not rise to meet Collegiality challenges, then we will not be connected and have a conscientious inclusivity embedded in our leadership.

If we do not rise to meet Transcendence challenges, then we will not be giving and have true superordinate service embedded in our leadership.

UPSHOT: Know when you are facing mission-related 'significance' challenges.

Activate Your Leader 'Metaphysics' Tool

As expressed in the preceding section, the primary tool leaders use to address meaning challenges is sourced from the domain of metaphysics.

Just as with the prior chapter on ethics, there are several factors which tend to get in the way of leaders becoming truly aspirational.

There follow some of the key barriers in ourselves (individual) and our environments (organizational) that impede us and our followers from addressing these types of issues.

176 Assembling Your Leadership Toolbox

Some Mindfulness Challenge Leaders Must Overcome

First, we are often biased to think within the instant and direct rather than beyond the proverbial matrix. Everyone is busy. Everyone deals with stressors. We are seldom afforded, seek, or reserve quality time to put things into perspective and ask the big questions. Instead we become so preoccupied with the daily 'who, what, when, where, and how' praxis of life that it becomes easy to lose touch with the 'why'.

A great example can be found in time management theory. It reveals that most people are so focused on the urgent that they often lose sense of the important. This is a key distinction. Urgent is what yells at you and demands your attention. Like a ringing phone or aggressive co-worker. Important is what really matters in the pursuit of your values, your dreams, and achieving greater things. Like continuing education in our chosen field or quality time with loved ones. Clearly the loudest things are not necessarily the most important. We must not confuse or conflate the two. Yet this is easier said than done.

- Leadership advocates clarify their ontology and sense of the important

In addition, we are often biased to think within the short rather than the long term. Of tactics versus strategy.

A great example can be found in sustainability theory. Particularly with the notion that it matters not just what our current standard of living is but also all of the collective, long-term quality of life. The short term is the most visible. The easiest to measure. The most directly bearing on our state. Yet as per Adam Grant we are notoriously bad at envisioning what will drive the future happiness of our future selves. And we are even worse at putting ourselves in the shoes of future generations to imagine what will impact their successes and subjective well-beings. For example, in projecting the impact of our actions on long-term financial, ecological, and human outcomes. We need to appreciate the strategic dimension across time and people. Yet, once again, this is easier said than done.

- Leadership advocates clarify their perspective and sense of relationships

Some Collegiality Challenges Leaders Must Overcome

Second, we are often biased to think in terms of 'me' rather' than 'we'. Of ethnocentric competition versus geocentric collaboration.

A great example can be found in stakeholder theory. It shows that we all have a proverbial interest in the outcomes of our efforts. That there is a mutual reliance on each other in a holistic value chain where we are all, simultaneously, each others' suppliers and each others' consumers. Where we need a minimum amount

Your Leadership Advocate (Metaphysics) Tools **177**

of inducements to impel our collective contributions. However, our selfish drivers, which have evolved over countless generations and across many millennia, act as impediments to this. This is especially true in individualistic cultures where one's success is measured against, rather than with, others. We live in one of the most individualistic times on record. And this is simultaneously one of our greatest assets and one of our greatest potential liabilities. Yes, dependence can lead to weakness. And yes, independence can foster strength. But also remember this: Interdependence is invincible.

- Leadership advocates promote interdependence and inclusiveness

In addition, we are often susceptible to the trappings of power and privilege. Of taking versus giving.

Selfish takers (perhaps you know one?) create an attitude of wanting. Conversely collegial givers can create an environment of kindness. A great example can be found in systems theory. Where complexity reigns and the chain is only as strong as its weakest link. Problems in one place can diffuse and infect the entire system. Like germs. Like diseases. That cripple their hosts. But so can solutions and enhancements. Like serums. Like solutions. That rejuvenate and recharge. And when we engage dutifully in the latter this can diffuse and lift others' akin to the process of entrainment – this is where entities are incorporated and sweep along in a common flow; where rhythmic variations in some parts of a system cause other parts to fall into positive synchrony with it.

- Leadership advocates promote mutuality of responsibility and duty

Some Transcendence Challenges Leaders Must Overcome

Third, we are often biased to create climates rife with cruel, ego-driven, callous, cut-throat, and harsh overtones. This stands in stark contrast to the aforementioned ideals of kindness, generosity, benevolence, gratitude, and magnanimity.

As per Jean-Paul Sartre's (1957) *Existentialism and Human Emotion*, consider the profound idea that our existence precedes our essence. We are not at the mercy of our nature – we can mold and shape it. We are what we become. It we want a nice, collegial, etc. world then rather than just sitting around and hoping for it we go out and actually be nice. Create it. A great example of this can be found in control theory. When we locate our fate as outside our boundaries and beyond our efforts, we are embodying what is called an 'external' locus of control. Where we hope to get lucky instead of going out and making our own luck. Where we cross our fingers rather than plan, prepare, study, train, and execute. In contrast to this when we take the initiative and the responsibility for out outcomes we are

178 Assembling Your Leadership Toolbox

said to have an 'internal' locus of control. So it does no good to simply bemoan negative climates. We have to actively build them. Yet too often too many are content complaining versus striving.

• Leadership advocates create a climate of munificence

In addition, we are often taught, and thus inclined, to think of leadership as the pinnacle of the pyramid where others act in the service of you. Instead it might be more accurate to conceptualize it in reverse where leaders serve their followers.

A great example can be found in servant leadership theory. Although this will be discussed later in greater depth, its tenets bear some introduction. As per Liden (2013):

> The focus of servant leadership is on others rather than upon self and on understanding of the role of the leader as a servant…. Self-interest should not motivate servant leadership; rather, it should ascend to a higher plane of motivation…. The servant leader's primary objective is to serve and meet the needs of others, which optimally should be the prime motivation for leadership…. Servant leaders develop people, helping them to strive and flourish…. Servant leaders provide vision, gain credibility and trust from followers, and influence.

As you can see, it makes a big difference how leaders see leadership. As having servants or being a servant. As being entitled or 'owed' by others, or owing others. As personifying the end-all be-all, or being part of something greater and larger than oneself.

• Leadership advocates lead as servants

Taken Together

As you can see, the issues of metaphysics and leadership are inexorably intertwined. So, with so many shortcomings, so many temptations, so much variability, and so much confusion, leaders must be proactive in developing their aspirational vision.

UPSHOT: *Wise leaders address metaphysical, meaning-related challenges.*

Be a Leadership ADVOCATE

The identity best befitting a metaphysical problem solver is that of a leadership advocate.

An advocate, as per the *Oxford English Dictionary*, is a person who publicly supports or recommends a particular cause or policy.

It is closely connected to the concept of VISION, defined as a mental image of what the future will or could be like and the related ability to think about or plan the future with imagination or wisdom. This gels with much thinking on the subject. For example:

As per Dan Goleman and colleagues (2002), the visionary leadership style moves people towards shared dreams and helps others to see how they fit into the big picture and view of the future. They do this by articulating a vision that takes into account and merges others' perspectives. The idea of visionary leadership (as per Westley & Mintzberg, 1989) is that it provides narrative and drama to establish a sense of story and purpose. And as per W. Glenn Rowe (2001), 'Visionary Leaders' have a distinct style and set of characteristics that sets them apart from others, including a grander proactiveness to shape ideas and the way people think about what is desirable, possible, and necessary, a larger perspective insofar as they work in, but do not belong to, organizations such that the sense of who they are does not depend on work, and a greater concern with the future of their organizations and people.

Advocates, by extension, are those who paint and lead us towards these visions.

When you picture an advocate what images come into your head?

Perhaps someone with a megaphone or placard?

A prognosticator or seer?

An opinion leader writing an op-ed column?

Someone leading a march, charge, or rally?

These are poor stereotypes and pigeonholes for sure, but they can be used as a jumping-off point for capturing the character of the advocate. And as such they may suggest ways for modeling how advocates aspire and what leaders can learn from them to aspire better.

Put more systematically, and in a manner consistent with the book's model:

- Advocates are more mindful of meaning and overarching purpose. Leadership icons therefore have the ontology and perspective to address metaphysical challenges.
- Advocates are more collegial with regard to meaning and overarching purpose. Leadership icons also have the inclusiveness and duty to address metaphysical challenges
- Advocates are more transcendent with regard to meaning and overarching purpose. Leadership icons additionally have the munificence and service to address metaphysical challenges.

Leadership advocates develop their metaphysics in these three fundamental ways.

The following offers a step-by-step map for doing this. For convenience these steps are summarized in Table 7.1. They are then illustrated as well as elaborated upon in the subsequent corresponding sections.

180 Assembling Your Leadership Toolbox

TABLE 7.1 Tools for Looking Far OUTSIDE Yourself

Better Core: Mindfulness	Clearer Ontology
	Clearer Perspective
Better Process: Collegiality	Sense of Inclusiveness
	Sense of Duty
Better Leverage: Transcendence	Elevated Munificence
	Elevated Service

To Look Outside Yourself
Step One – Building a Better Core

> *Life is available only in the present moment.*
> – Thich Nhat Hanh
>
> *Life is what happens when you are busy making other plans.*
> – John Lennon
>
> *There is more to life than increasing its speed.*
> – M. K. Gandhi
>
> *Life is not measured by the number of breaths we take, but by the moments that take our breath away.*
> – Maya Angelou
>
> *What a wonderful life I've had! I only wish I'd realized it sooner.*
> – Sidonie-Gabrielle Colette
>
> *If the doors of perception were cleansed, everything would appear as it is: infinite.*
> – William Blake
>
> *You grow up the day you have your first real laugh at yourself.*
> – Ethel Barrymore

As expressed in the above aphorisms, mindfulness is at the heart of establishing meaningful leadership.

Time is an interesting concept. The past has happened. Gone. The future has not yet happened. Speculative. All we really have is the fierce reality of the now. This is the message of Vietnamese Buddhist monk Thich Nhat Hanh and as lyricized by once-Beatle John Lennon. You can romanticize the past. You can fret about the future. But you are inexorably in the present. The only real thing. Don't waste it. For our time is finite. So why are we always rushing? Hoping for this event or that day to come? For this travail or that travel to pass? As per Mohandâs Gandhi we need to slow down and take the time to smell the proverbial roses.

Your Leadership Advocate (Metaphysics) Tools **181**

We need to appreciate it to be happy. We need to optimize it to be productive. We need to swim in it to be alive. Or if you prefer, as jested by the cinematic icon Ferris Beuller, "Life moves pretty fast, if you don't stop and look around once in a while you could miss it." We also need to focus on quality as much as quantity. On making the most of the here and now. As poet Maya Angelou reminds us, to relish the magnificent and appreciate the wondrous. We also need to appreciate the context in which these things happen. To have some perspective. As per French author Sidonie-Gabrielle Colette this involves taking the time to do the above. To gasp. To smile. To laugh. To celebrate the steps along our life course. When we see the present in and of its context, we are invited to immerse ourselves in the élan vital or vital force of its grandness. In its ongoing story and saga. In its never-ending tale. As British poet William Blake prompts us we are but chapters in the book, pixels in the picture, drops in the ocean, etc. To connect our intimate selves with this infinite is to become infinite. But we must do this with humility. Yes, with a sense of awe and appreciation. Respecting ourselves while not taking ourselves too seriously. As cleverly quipped by American actress Ethel Barrymore we need to laugh but also to laugh at ourselves. To have perspective.

Leadership ADVOCATES capture this sense of mindfulness.

Wise leaders can see far beyond themselves.

The core to becoming a better leader is this mindful clarity of ontology and perspective.

Ontology

Whether we realize it or not, we all approach the world with explicit or implicit assumptions about its nature and the very essence of the phenomena that we see (Burrell & Morgan, 1979). This is an ontology. A set of concepts and categories that can be used to shows their properties and the relations between them.

To come to grips with one's ontology is to do a few things. First, to take a position on the essence of the world – whether there is an objective reality (realism) or if everything is within our minds (idealism or nominalism). Second, to then make sense of this reality with labels. We commonly call these things categories or concepts. Third, to organize these categories into some type of (hierarchical) system to determine how they fit together with other things in the bigger picture. Fourth, to associate properties with these categories to ascribe an essence to things and understand them better. For example, we might decide that fuzzy four-legged creatures exist, and then call them dogs, and then determine that they are below us on some sort of sentient scale, and then say that they are commonly loyal and loving. Other examples might include how we make sense of nature and biology, people and organizations, or perhaps economic and business 'realities'. Today we also use these ideas to develop computer programs and approximate artificial intelligence.

Regarding the first point, existence, there is clearly an interplay between the subject (us) and the object (what we see). Our senses have evolved to detect certain

182 Assembling Your Leadership Toolbox

aspects of our world. And there is reliability between observers on the most basic of detections – sights, sounds, shapes, sizes, etc. Yet there is also some variability and relativity based on the predilections, preferences, perspectives, and peculiarities of those observing. Notwithstanding, to survive in this world it is beneficial to know where predators, cliffs, or boiling lava are and that it would be good to avoid them. To paraphrase an old philosophic saw, if you doubt the existence of reality try kicking a big rock. So: the question does not have to be extremely esoteric and intractable. Instead it can be practical. What is the best way to make sense of what we see?

- See the interplay between who we are and what we see.

Regarding the second point, labels, we use language to create categories. This is a cat and that is a dog. This is a laptop and that is a smartphone. But the labels can be confusing – e.g., are both a laptop and smartphone 'computers'? And the labels can also become complex – e.g., is something an opportunity and/or a threat? Thus we continuously hone and refine (and debate) our labels.

- Appreciate the power of labels and strive to make them more accurate and useful.

Regarding the third point, hierarchies, we arrange categories based on scales that matter to us. What is superior, similar, or inferior to this or that? Which employees, citizens, kin, etc. report to whom and who needs to listen to whom about what? For example: Connecting the very big parts of reality (galaxies, the universe, perhaps multiverses, and even beyond), connecting the very small parts of reality (quantum particles and energy), and even endeavoring to seek an inclusive language of reality to unite the above – the infinite and intimate – in a T.O.E. (theory of everything).

- Arrange labels in systems that make sense of our world.

Regarding the fourth point, essence, we then study these categories and develop theories about them. Their patterns. Their properties. Their contingencies.

- Develop hypotheses, prototypes, and models that can be used to explain, predict, and manage the concepts.

Perspective

From your ontology you can now develop perspective. A sense of proportion. Of where you stand relative to your view of reality, its concepts, its systems, and its nature. To clarify your sense of proportion and perspective, focus on locating your personal place in this greater reality. What your actions, existence, daily routines, etc. mean in the scope of things.

Some strategies include expanding perspective of space ... looking up at a systems view of the heavens. For example, and related to the above: (1) Location inside the big – Where am I? Well, here is my location: Street, City, State, Country, Planet, Solar System, Milky Way, Local Group of Galaxies, Virgo Supercluster, the Universe, the Multiverse, etc.; or (2) Location outside the small – Where are things in me? Well, here is my anatomy: Systems, Organs, etc. Drilling down further (via particle physics) ... Matter, molecules, atoms, elementary particles – leptons and quarks, etc.

- Develop and expand spatial perspective.

Other strategies might take the form of expanding perspective of time ... looking up at a systems view of eternity. For example: What time is it? In perspective of the Universe timeline, this is but a blip on the 14-billion-year-old cosmic clock. In perspective of the Earth timeline, this is but a mere nano-click on the 4.5-billion-year-old planetary clock. In perspective of the Human (*Homo Sapien*) timeline, this is but a moment on the less than half-a-million-year-old species clock. Considering the 75-ish-year average life expectancy of people today, perhaps we can have some temporal perspective.

- Develop and expand temporal perspective.

Here is a nice way to think about these together, as advocated by Albert Einstein and recently re-popularized by Astrophysicist Neil deGrasse Tyson (2017: 205–207):

> The cosmic perspective not only embraces our genetic kinship with all life on Earth but also values our chemical kinship with any yet-to-be discovered life in the universe, as well as our atomic kinship with the universe itself ... (it) flows from fundamental knowledge. But it is more than about what you know. It's also about having the wisdom and insight to apply that knowledge to assessing our place in the universe.

Leaders thus must merge their worlds with the larger world. Being in the now but also seeing the now as being in a bigger now. This is grounded. This is humble. This is mindful.

Taken Together

So: what are you waiting for?

Grow your leadership mindfulness tool.

Start enhancing your ontological core and sense of perspective core.

UPSHOT: Wise leaders are mindful of their world and their place in it.

184 Assembling Your Leadership Toolbox

Step Two – Crafting a Better Process

> *Happiness can exist only in acceptance.*
> – George Orwell
>
> *You must strive to multiply bread so that it suffices for the tables of mankind.*
> – Pope John Paul IV
>
> *We must seek, above all, a world of peace; a world in which peoples dwell together in mutual respect and work together in mutual regard.*
> – John F. Kennedy
>
> *We must build a new world – one in which the eternal dignity of man is respected.*
> – Harry S. Truman
>
> *The price of greatness is responsibility.*
> – Winston Churchill
>
> *Injustice anywhere is a threat to justice everywhere.*
> – Dr. Martin Luther King, Jr.

As expressed in the above aphorisms, collegiality is key to the process of establishing meaningful leadership.

Collegiality begins with inclusiveness. And inclusiveness begins with acceptance. Though intending a different interpretation, I take some liberties here in seeing Orwell's insight less 'Orwellian' as a surrender but instead as connoting an open-minded recognition, tolerance, and even receptivity towards others. Other people. Other points of view. Once you recognize and accept others then you can incorporate them into your calculus. To not just feast but to provide a feast. To not just see others as opponents but also as partners. As per Pope John Paul IV, to not just be provided for but also to provide. If we do this we can approximate the ideas as advocated by Kennedy and Truman. Kennedy speaks of striving towards peace, mutual respect, and mutual regard. Mutuality is key. Truman speaks of dignity. Eternal dignity. Yet these things are not given. They are earned. They are created. They are maintained. As per Sir Winston Churchill they require responsibility. And as Dr. Martin Luther King, Jr. adds, they require a broad responsibility not just to oneself but to the entire system of mutually reliant selves.

As is evident from the above, leadership ADVOCATES promote collegiality. Wise leaders can see far beyond themselves to further a sense of inclusiveness and duty.

Inclusiveness

Recall that inclusiveness is the practice or policy of including people who might otherwise be excluded or marginalized, such as those who have physical or mental disabilities and members of minority groups.

To develop your sense of Inclusiveness (see Cox, 1994), focus on diversity recognition, appreciation, and optimization. First, regarding recognition, see the combination of similarities and differences that simultaneously tie us together and make us unique. Some strategies include 'Kaleidoscope' thinking. That is, not looking at anyone, including ourselves, in single-dimension terms. Instead seeing that we can be understood as selectively overlapping across personal dimensions such as age, sex, race and ethnicity, abilities (and disabilities), religion, sexuality, intellect, emotion, physical characteristics, and the like. Also social dimensions such as roles, positions, tenures, and the like.

- Recognize diversity.

Second, regarding diversity appreciation, you can see that these divergences and differences are good. That they add richness, complexity, and depth. Or at least that they increase our potential for good as long as we can get past the barriers and challenges they bring. For example, in fighting stereotyping – the process of judging someone based solely on a perceived group to which they belong. It denies people their individuality by seeing others like everyone else in their 'category'. It happens when we put people in a group, make sweeping generalizations about the group, and blindly confirm the generalizations and apply them to all of its members. If left unchecked, stereotypes can lead to prejudices that reinforce beliefs about the superiority or inferiority of certain groups and enable discrimination.

- Appreciate diversity.

Third, regarding diversity optimization, you can actually overcome diversity's obstacles and leverage diversity's advantages. For example: In facilitating the richness of your world (workplace, network, etc.) through diversity-friendly attracting and selecting, training and developing, staffing and placing, plus compensating and retaining.

- Optimize diversity.

Duty

Recall that duty is an obligation or responsibility. Duty often comprises tasks or actions that are required as part of one's job. In turn, responsibility is the state or fact of having a duty to deal with something or of having control over someone. The state or fact of being accountable or to blame for something.

To develop your sense of duty, focus on the direction of your self-defined importance. You can feel significant and valuable by focusing solely upon yourself and an end (terminal) or, instead, as a means to elevate others (instrumental). Your efforts and energy can certainly be oriented or aimed inward, selfishly towards oneself. This is akin to the concept of 'personalized power' where people build

186 Assembling Your Leadership Toolbox

their potential to influence as their goal for narrow, individualized benefit. Alternatively, your importance can be oriented or aimed outward, as a means towards other people or larger causes. This is akin to the concept of 'socialized power' where people build their potential to influence as a resource for wider group, organizational, or even societal benefit to fulfill a larger duty.

Some strategies include stressing personal ownership and responsibility. Doing one's part. This relates to what some term organizational citizenship (cf., Podsakoff et al., 2000) or behavior that voluntarily promotes the effective functioning of the larger organization or greater cause not out of compulsion but out of discretion, choice, and commitment. These behaviors reflect a recognition of being part of a larger whole and accepting the responsibilities which that entails.

- Be a 'citizen' leader.

It can be furthered by leaders who are more 'transformational' – articulate a vision, provide an appropriate worldview, promote group goals, and support ideals such as altruism, courtesy, conscientiousness, and civic virtue.

- Be a 'visionary' leader.

Taken Together

Here is a nice way to think about these. It comes from Howard Perlmutter's classic model of diversity and our approaches to it. At the most basic level we have an ignorance of diversity. We are blind to it. This is a 'Parochial' approach where everyone is like me. A rudimentary processing of diversity, and perhaps the most common of all approaches, is that of 'Ethnocentrism' where you recognize differences but approach them like you are better than others. That your mores and methods are right whereas others are silly, under-evolved, or just plain wrong. A slightly better one is that of 'Polycentrism', or to recognize the merits of others but default to their ways like a rudderless ship or identity-less blob. That they are always right. Surpassing all of these in merit is the 'Geocentrism' approach of recognizing that (1) we are all in this together and bring different strengths to the table, and (2) we need to dedicate ourselves to learning and growing as an interdependent whole so that we can best play our parts.

There are several important actions you should consider based on this. First, to see that we are different. So, get beyond yourself. Second, to see that we are not always right. So, don't obsess on your ways. Third, to see that they too are not always right. So, don't lose yourself. Fourth, to see that we can all learn and elevate each other. So, inclusively weave together the quilt of duties and responsibilities that will warm all.

So: what are you waiting for? Grow your leadership collegiality tool. Start enhancing your metaphysical process.

UPSHOT: Wise leaders enhance inclusiveness and duty to promote collegiality.

Step Three – Leveraging a Better Capacity

> *When you learn, teach, when you get, give.*
> – Maya Angelou
>
> *What you get by achieving your goals is not as important as what you become by achieving your goals.*
> – Henry David Thoreau
>
> *We can do no great things – only small things with great love.*
> – Mother Teresa
>
> *There is no higher religion than human service. To work for the common good is the greatest creed. / The purpose of human life is to serve, and to show compassion and the will to help others.*
> – Albert Schweitzer
>
> *The destiny of the individual is to serve rather than to rule.*
> – Albert Einstein
>
> *We realize the importance of our voices only when we are silenced.*
> – Malala Yousafzai

As expressed in the above aphorisms, transcendence is the culmination of establishing meaningful leadership.

Munificence is critical to becoming transcendent. This is because giving is not a net-negative. A loss. Instead giving actually enriches the giver. As Maya Angelou explains, it increases one's capacity to do good and the reciprocal joys that come with it. And this is consistent with kindred souls echoing similar sentiments. Notable among these is Thoreau, who argued that munificence is transcendental. It elevates the person and the planet. These are strong arguments for the value of service. And they are amplified by some of humankind's most renowned servants. As explained by Mother Teresa this involves love. Great love powers great deeds and great achievements. It is the root of love that feeds the giving tree. Love makes you want to serve. Moreover, Albert Schweitzer connects this to faith and to purpose. Working for the common good as ideology. Serving as the essence of existence. Compassion as a calling. Albert Einstein extends this insofar as he highlights the intertwining of service with our fate and destiny. So, leaders must develop their aspirational capacity so as to create these transformational realities. And to do it before it is too late. Unfortunately we do not appreciate what we have until it is taken away. Until it withers. Until it cannot be impactful. This is the all-to-real lesson of Malala Yousafzai's thoughts and experiences.

188 Assembling Your Leadership Toolbox

Taken together, as is evident from the above, leadership ADVOCATES achieve transcendence in themselves and in others. Wise leaders can see and help people see far beyond themselves to achieve munificence and service.

Munificence

Recall that munificence is the quality or action of giving and being extremely generous.

To establish a climate of munificence, focus on giving, gratitude, and charity. Some strategies include a validation of giving. For example, that: (1) giving helps the recipient, (2) giving also helps the giver, and (3) giving helps the larger organization, economy, and society.

- Be a giving leader.

Other strategies might take the form of an appreciation of giving. Indeed, there is much research that validates the power of gratitude. And there are many ways to show it. For example, and very simply, journaling about things that you are grateful for or just saying 'thank you' more often and writing more thank-you notes. Counting your blessings. Focusing on the good in people and situations. In terms of research, Martin Seligman (2011) and others have validated the power of gratitude and the benefits of conducting kindness exercises.

- Be a gracious leader.

Service

Recall that service is the action of helping or doing work for someone else.

To establish a climate of service, focus on its validation, appreciation, and enhancement. For example, in terms of serving one's followers, one's customers, and one's community.

Here is a nice way to think about this. It comes from Greenleaf's (1977) model of Servant Leadership. He posits that:

> Servant leadership is based on the premise that when leaders place serving followers above everything else, followers gain self-confidence and develop trust in the leader, and proceed on a journey towards realizing their full potential. Followers respond to the support from leaders by reciprocating with behaviors that benefit the leader, coworkers, the organization, and the community in which the organization is embedded.

- Prioritize and promote service.

Further from Greenleaf:

The best test, and difficult to administer is this: Do those served grow as persons? Do they, while being served, become healthier, wiser, freer, more autonomous, and more likely themselves to become servants? And, what is the effect on the least privileged in society? Will they benefit, or at least not further be harmed?

- Enable and ensure service.

Taken Together

So: what are you waiting for?

Grow your leadership transcendence.

Start enhancing your munificence and service.

UPSHOT: Wise leaders transcend their worlds to give and to serve.

And with Extraordinary Meaningful Objectives

As described in the opening section the six core tools of leadership wisdom can be seen to manifest themselves in the record of humanity's greatest successes – the achievements of the most influential real and idealized leaders who have proven themselves across a multitude of times, tasks, and locations. As such, in addition to modern relevant and complementary examples, we draw predominantly from two distinct yet complementary sources: *Time Magazine*'s (TM) lists of the most influential and American Film Institute's (AFI) lists of the most heroic.

We will do this via the vehicle of an imaginary assembly of 'Invisible Counselors'. A Leadership Advocate conference table to provide insights into how to look far beyond oneself.

So let us call this meeting to order …

The Gavel

Here ye, here ye. I now call this LEADERSHIP ADVOCATE council to order.

Our focus is addressing the leadership challenges of SIGNIFICANCE.

Our purpose is to animate the tool of METAPHYSICS and leading for PURPOSE. That is, EXTRAORDINARY MEANINGFUL OBJECTIVES.

The Real

So, who might be attending as some of history's most influential metaphysical, purpose-oriented counselors? Let us ask them to introduce themselves (note: all biographical profiles are gleaned from many sources, including the *Encyclopedia Britannica*) and speak to the leadership tool of metaphysics and leading through purpose.

190 Assembling Your Leadership Toolbox

Seat One

Perhaps an epitome of kindness and humanity.

Like … Mother Teresa of Calcutta (and her inspiration, Jesus Christ).

I am founder of the Order of the Missionaries of Charity, a Roman Catholic congregation of women dedicated to the poor, particularly to the destitute of India, and for this I was awarded a Nobel Peace Prize. In 1946 I experienced my 'call within a call', which I considered divine inspiration to devote myself to caring for the sick and poor. Soon thereafter I moved into the slums and established a hospice where the terminally ill could die with dignity. My order also opened numerous centers serving the blind, the aged, and the disabled. Under my guidance, the missionaries built a leper colony, called Shanti Nagar (Town of Peace), in India. In the later years of my life I spoke out against divorce, contraception, and abortion. At the time of my death my order included hundreds of centers in more than 90 countries with thousands of missionaries. It is important to say here that I was inspired by Jesus Christ where the essence of his teaching (as per the *Encyclopedia Britannica*) is as such: that the kingdom would come to earth in its full power and glory, at which time God's will would be done 'on earth as it is in heaven' (Matthew 6:10). Jesus called on some people to give up everything in order to follow him (Mark 1:16–20, 10:17–31) and promised that his disciples' reward would be great in heaven. Jesus emphasized with great importance this mission and that people who accepted his message would be included in the coming kingdom.

Seat Two

Plus maybe an ideology-driven activist.

Like … Margaret Thatcher.

I am a British Conservative Party politician who became Europe's first woman prime minister. In fact at the time of my resignation I ranked as Britain's longest continuously serving prime minister. As a leader I pursued my conservative vision to accelerate the evolution of the British economy from Statism to Liberalism. To this end I advocated greater independence of the individual from the state. I also advocated an end to excessive government interference in the economy, including privatization of state-owned enterprises and the sale of public housing to tenants. I also advocated reductions in expenditures on social services such as health care, education, and housing. I also advocated limitations on the printing of money in accord with the economic doctrine of monetarism. I also advocated legal restrictions on trade unions. Thus the term Thatcherism came to refer not just to these policies but also to their seeds, which included fierce nationalism and a zealous regard for the interests of the individual.

Like … Ronald Reagan.

I am the fortieth president of the United States noted for my staunch conservative Republicanism and my fervent anticommunism. As president, I worked to

Your Leadership Advocate (Metaphysics) Tools **191**

reduce the threat of war with the Soviet Union and to encourage openness and democracy in their society. This is grounded in the idea of American exceptionalism as 'a shining city on a hill'. Aiming to restore my country to a position of prominence in the world, I called for increased defense budgets to expand and modernize the military. I also urged aggressive approaches to combating communism and totalitarianism. Following a 'supply-side' economic program I proposed massive tax cuts that I intended to stimulate the economy. In my farewell address I summarized these sentiments by saying:

"I wasn't a great communicator, but I communicated great things, and they didn't spring full bloom from my brow, they came from the heart of a great nation – from our experience, our wisdom, and our belief in the principles that have guided us for two centuries. They called it the Reagan revolution. Well, I'll accept that, but for me it always seemed more like the great rediscovery, a rediscovery of our values and our common sense."

Seat Three

Let us also add a model of service.

Like … Albert Schweitzer.

I am a mission doctor in equatorial Africa who received the Nobel Peace Prize for this work. I have held the long-standing intention to become a mission doctor in order to devote myself to philanthropic work, and after achieving my doctor of medicine set out for Equatorial Africa. There with the help of the natives I built my hospital, which I equipped and maintained from my income, and this was later supplemented by gifts from individuals and foundations in many countries. After this I turned my attention upward to larger world problems and wrote my *Philosophy of Civilization* in which I set forth my personal philosophy of 'reverence for life'. Later I returned to Africa to rebuild the hospital and aid a leper colony.

Like … Bono.

I am lead singer for the successful Irish rock band U2 and, more importantly, a prominent human rights activist. As a band we worked with Amnesty International and toured to bring attention to human rights violations and encourage fans to fight them. We also toured war-torn regions with groups seeking to help the victims of violence and poverty and focus attention on the plight of people in the less-developed world. I used my platform to further various humanitarian causes and began segueing my career to more of a global missionary. Dividing my time between fronting my band and meeting with world leaders I helped found a policy and advocacy organization that seeks to eradicate poverty, hunger, and the spread of AIDS in Africa through public awareness campaigns and in-country partnerships. That same year I appeared on the cover of *Time Magazine* with the legend 'Can Bono Save the World?'

However, if hard-pressed, we would probably award this seat to … Eleanor Roosevelt.

192 Assembling Your Leadership Toolbox

I am an American first lady and a United Nations diplomat and humanitarian. During my 12 years as first lady I pursued an unprecedented breadth of activities and advocacy of liberal causes. I instituted regular White House press conferences for women correspondents, and wire services that had not formerly employed women were forced to do so in order to have a representative present. I wrote a daily syndicated newspaper column showing particular interest in child welfare, housing reform, and equal rights for women and racial minorities. When Marian Anderson, an African American opera singer, was banned from performing in Constitution Hall I resigned my membership and arranged to hold the concert at the nearby Lincoln Memorial – the event turned into a massive outdoor celebration. On another occasion, when local officials in Alabama insisted that seating at a public meeting be segregated by race, I carried a folding chair to all sessions and carefully placed it in the center aisle. My defense of the rights of African Americans, youth, and the poor helped bring groups into government that formerly had been alienated from the political process. After my husband President Roosevelt's death, President Truman appointed me as a delegate to the United Nations where I played a major role in the drafting and adoption of the Universal Declaration of Human Rights.

Seat Four

Present as well might be a champion of social justice.

Like … Malala Yousafzai.

I am a Pakistani teenager who, while a teenager, spoke out publicly against the prohibition on the education of girls. I gained global attention when I survived an assassination attempt at age 15 and was awarded the Nobel Prize in recognition of my efforts on behalf of children's rights. I also was awarded the United Nations Human Rights Prize, became the youngest person to win the Liberty Medal recognizing strivings for people's freedom throughout the world, and was named one of *Time Magazine*'s most influential people. To further the reach of my message I co-authored a memoir, *I Am Malala: The Girl Who Stood Up for Education and Was Shot by the Taliban* and also wrote the picture book *Malala's Magic Pencil*. Later I continued to use my public profile to bring attention to human rights issues around the world. Recently, with support from the Malala Fund, I opened a girls' school in Lebanon for refugees from the Syrian Civil War.

Like … Jackie Robinson (and it's not just because I was born in Brooklyn. You got a problem with dat?).

I am the first black baseball player to play in the American major leagues where I broke the 'color line' with the Brooklyn Dodgers. Withstanding varied and vicious acts of hate and discrimination, I led the league in batting average and in stolen bases, won both Rookie of the Year and the league's Most Valuable Player awards, and led my team to a world championship. Yet some fans hurled bottles and curses at me, other players openly protested against having to play with an African American, and some even deliberately pitched balls at my head and aimed shoe spikes at my legs. However, I withstood all of this because "Plenty of times I wanted to haul off when somebody insulted me for the color of my skin, but I had to hold to myself. … The whole thing was bigger than me." After baseball I engaged in business and in civil rights activism and was a spokesperson for the National Association for the Advancement of Colored People. I eventually became the first black person to be inducted into the Baseball Hall of Fame and, posthumously, received both the Presidential Medal of Freedom as well as the honor of all of baseball retiring my number.

Seat Five

And finally, a beacon of guidance and equifinality.

Like … Mohandâs Karamchand Gandhi.

I am an Indian lawyer, politician, social activist, and writer who became the Mahatma ('Great Soul') of the nationalist movement against the British rule of India. As such, I came to be considered the father of my country, internationally esteemed for my doctrine of nonviolent protest (satyagraha) to achieve political and social progress. During my time facing racial discrimination in South Africa I made it clear that I would not accept injustice as part of the natural or unnatural order, I would defend universal human dignity. Later back in India I faced down acts of high-handedness and advocated the grievances of the long-suffering peasantry. Through boycotts, protests, and principles my message of nonviolent noncooperation movement electrified the country, broke the spell of fear of foreign rule, and led to the arrests of thousands of satyagrahis who defied laws and cheerfully lined up for prison. When violence broke out I tried to draw the warring communities out of their suspicion and fanaticism by reasoning and persuasion but eventually undertook a three-week fast to arouse the people into following the nobler path. While still a prisoner I embarked upon another fast to protest against the British government's decision to segregate the so-called untouchables (or to me the Harijans or children of God). Although my role as a political leader loomed large the mainspring of my life lay in religion. And religion for me did not mean formalism, dogma, ritual, or sectarianism. My deepest strivings were spiritual, but I did not retire to a cave in the Himalayas to meditate on the Absolute – I carried my cave with me to be upheld like a guiding beacon in the public arena.

The Idealized

So, who might be attending as some of cinema's most heroic metaphysical counselors? Archetypes who look beyond themselves to travel sometimes tumultuous journeys and find their purpose and calling.

Seat Six

Why not start with Atticus Finch?

194 Assembling Your Leadership Toolbox

Finch, in the 1962 film *To Kill a Mockingbird* based on Harper Lee's 1960 novel of the same name, is an attorney who bears great hardship, and subjects his family to the same, in order to pursue greater ideals and defend the ideal of law. Set in a small racially charged Alabama town in the early 1930s, the protagonist is a widowed lawyer (portrayed by Gregory Peck) who strives to create an atmosphere free from hatred and prejudice for his two children, 6-year-old girl Scout and 10-year-old boy Jem. As per one of the character's most memorable quotes: "You never really understand a person until you consider things from his point of view, until you climb inside of his skin and walk around in it." Atticus' motivations clearly lie with a greater external purpose – the desire to create a reality were all people are treated equally regardless of race. He can also be considered a visionary figure who aspires to bring people to this better place, both through his parenting and his layering, and though he experiences difficulty in reaching this ideal the grandeur of his character's aspiring brings us closer to it.

Seat Seven

Then maybe Terry Malloy. Or Tom Joad.

Terry Malloy in the 1954 film *On the Waterfront* is a mob enforcer who sacrifices his dreams of fame to pursue more meaningful objectives. When washed-up boxer Terry Malloy (portrayed by Marlon Brando) witnesses a contract murder he originally keeps his mouth shut but, because he could have intervened, feels responsible for the death and eventually cooperates with the authorities. As per a memorable exchange in the movie: (Terry Malloy): If I spill, my life ain't worth a nickel. (Father Barry): And how much is your soul worth if you don't? It is easy to see that Terry could have taken an easier path to a lower level place, but his strong sense of duty and justice helps him turn to a path of service and discover his greater external purpose: to not only envision the betterment of conditions on the waterfront but also deliver justice to the dock workers through his testimony.

Tom Joad in the 1940 film *The Grapes of Wrath* is the faithful crusader who is confronted by hardships in the Great Depression yet still puts duty and responsibility above comfort. In a manner similar to Terry Malloy, Joad is motivated to pursue social change and justice for the poorly treated migrants. And akin to Atticus Finch in *To Kill a Mockingbird*, his conviction to achieve equal treatment for everyone is just as powerful. As per one of Joad's most memorable quotes: "I'll be all around in the dark – I'll be everywhere. Wherever you can look – wherever there's a fight, so hungry people can eat, I'll be there."

Seat Eight

Further, let us invite Robin Hood.

Robin Hood in the 1938 film *The Adventures of Robin Hood* similarly embarks upon a quest to help the needy and overthrow a usurper to the throne in order to protect his country's honor. When an evil prince usurps the throne from King Richard the Lionhearted to whom Robin has sworn his allegiance, he robs from the wealthy oppressors to provide for his downtrodden fellow Saxons, thwarts the corrupt illegitimate monarchy, and paves the way for the triumphant return of the rightful king. As per some of the character's most memorable quotes: "I'll never rest until every Saxon in this shire can stand up free men"; "It's injustice I hate, not the Normans"; and "Men, if you're willing to fight for our people, I want you!"

Seat Nine

And we shan't forget Sergeant York.

Alvin York (portrayed by Gary Cooper) in the 1941 biographical film *Sergeant York* is a religious, family-oriented soldier who struggles with his sense of duty and service while exhibiting great valor defending his country during World War I. It is a true story of the boy who became a reluctant hero and winner of the Medal of Honor, all the while orienting himself to a higher purpose. It also highlights the idea of divine inspiration as per the occurrence of several seemingly supernatural events, such as the barrel of his rifle being split in half by lightning. In this sense York's vision is transcendent, as he believes that he is carrying out the will of God despite not fully understanding it. As per one of the movie character's most memorable exchanges: (Maj. Buxton): Do you mean to tell me that you did it to save lives? (Alvin York): Yes sir, that was why. (Maj. Buxton, amazed): Well, York, what you've just told me is the most extraordinary thing of all!

Seat Ten (WILDCARD)

I take some publisher prerogative here and add a character that was not on the AFI list but has made a personal impression with regard to their metaphysical, meaning- and significance-related lessons.

That character is Frodo Baggins, from the 2001 to 2003 film adaptations of J. R. R. Tolkien's *The Lord of the Rings* series. In this fantasy adventure which takes place in the fictional world of Middle-earth, the hobbit Frodo (portrayed by Elijah Wood) embarks upon a quest to destroy a magical artifact that if gained would grant the antagonist Sauron immeasurable powers. Frodo battles countless nasty, brutish incarnations in the journey to succeed in his mission, reach Mount Doom, and destroy the ring in the fire it was first forged in. It is particularly interesting that he is a Hobbit, characteristically carefree and fun-loving, but here this Hobbit is thrust into a more meaningful journey of discovering one's place in the order of things and pursuing it, regardless of the difficult travails it necessitates. Frodo sees the world order and his place in it. Frodo inspires collegiality, interdependence,

196 Assembling Your Leadership Toolbox

and duty in the quest of his 'Fellowship of the Ring'. Frodo pursues his higher order purpose and leads others in its pursuit. Frodo is an exemplary servant leader.

Even More

We might also staff our 'back-benchers' with additional most-influential nominees such as:

- Amadeo Giannini ... and looking far to further class mobility
- Emmeline Pankhurst ... and looking far to further voting rights
- Margaret Sanger ... and looking far to further reproductive rights
- David Ben Gurion ... and looking far to further religious security
- Walter Reuther ... and looking far to further worker dignity
- John Paul II ... and looking far to further tolerance
- the American GI ... and looking far to further freedom

The Upshot

During the Meeting

So ... put your meaning and significance challenge on the table.

What do you envision these figures saying about looking far beyond oneself to solve it?

When do you see calling upon them for their advice?

How do you see them interacting with each other?

What might Mother Teresa or Jesus say about the significance challenge? How might Ronald Reagan or Margaret Thatcher retort? Could Eleanor Roosevelt, Bono, or Albert Schweitzer add anything? And would this be supported, refuted, or amended by Jackie Robinson or Malala Yousafzai? And perhaps extended by Mahatma Gandhi?

Should we also consider the insights offered by Atticus Finch for aspiring and increasing purpose? Plus how about Terry Malloy or Tom Joad? Or Robin Hood? And certainly we should not ignore Alvin York. Nor should we discount the contribution of Frodo Baggins.

In addition, would anyone from the back chime in – say, for example, Pankhurst, Sanger, Ben Gurion, Reuther, or John Paul II?

After the Meeting

Do you see how these cases illustrate the principles of metaphysics-related, meaning-driven leadership? Mindfulness? Collegiality? Transcendence?

What do you glean from our council that might be helpful in leading like an advocate to address significant challenges that might arise in your life?

Going Forward

How might you customize the content of the council to fit your personal preferences as well as professional circumstances? Add, subtract, or amend its membership to best suit your style and needs?

How might you customize the process of the council to fit your idiosyncratic predilections and references? Use it or preside over it differently?

Lead through Purpose

Taken together this chapter's presentation of mindful perspective, dutiful collegiality, and transcendent service will allow you to enhance this leadership tool and work towards EXTRAORDINARY MEANINGFUL OBJECTIVES.

When faced with meaning and mission-related challenges it will enable you to lead a personal and professional life infused with PURPOSE. This is summarized for your convenience in Table 7.2.

This chapter focuses on the fourth step in wise leadership – the OUTSIDE Camera of ASPIRING. It is grounded in the philosophical branch of AESTHETICS. It enables the wise person or organization to become effectively stronger at what they do.

In this way it involves unleashing your inner ADVOCATE.

It is grounded in the philosophical branch of METAPHYSICS. It enables the wise person or organization to SEE FURTHER.

However, aspiring is often misunderstood, and, more than this, internal limitations and external barriers often prevent us from truly feeling. So …

- Building a better aspirating *core* involves developing <u>mindful</u> insights into your ontology and perspective.

TABLE 7.2 Becoming a Leadership Advocate

Leadership ADVOCATE	
Challenge	Significance and Mission (Metaphysics)
Focus	Outside – Aspiring
Building a Better Core	<u>Mindfulness</u>
(D > I)	*Ontology*
	Perspective
Crafting a Better Process	<u>Collegiality</u>
(I > K)	*Inclusiveness*
	Duty
Leveraging a Better Capacity	<u>Transcendence</u>
(K > W)	*Munificence*
	Service
Outcome	Purpose:
	Extraordinary Meaningful Objectives

198 Assembling Your Leadership Toolbox

- A better aspiring *process* involves honing your <u>collegiality</u> within the areas of inclusiveness and duty.
- *Leveraging* your aspiring capacity involves super-personal <u>transcendence</u> through enhanced munificence and service.

If you do this then you will develop theVISION and PURPOSE OF A LEADER.

8

PULLING PEOPLE TOGETHER

How to Use Your Leadership Maestro (Epistemology) Tools

How does a leader pull people together?

How do you develop the collaborative orientation of a leader?

These are different types of questions than those from the last four chapters.

Different from being better. From matters of logic (using your head) and becoming a leadership scientist. From matters of aesthetics (using your heart) and becoming a leadership artist.

Different from seeing better. From matters of ethics (looking inside) and becoming a leadership icon. From matters of metaphysics (looking outside) and becoming a leadership advocate.

Now we are ready to speak about the third and final part of the model. Not being better (lights). Not seeing better (camera). But doing better (action!). We will start here by focusing on PULLING people together and developing extraordinary collaborative orientation.

Think about it – which wins: A group of all stars or a tight team?

If you said a tight team then you would be right more often than not. This is because a team is a group that leverages collaboration to achieve optimum success. It is not reliant on, or limited by, any single part.

Okay, here is another one: Is the following equation correct: $2 + 2 = 4$?

If you said no then you would again be right. Not in math class but definitely in the dance of life. This is because when you put two people together with two other people you don't always get the output of exactly four people. Depending on their dynamics there could be process-loss $(2 + 2 = 3)$ or process-gain $(2 + 2 = 5)$. Have you ever been on a $2 + 2 = 3$ group? Not fun. Have you ever been on a $2 + 2 = 5$ team? Much more productive and enjoyable!

200 Assembling Your Leadership Toolbox

In a word, all teams are groups (the special types that achieve process-gain, magical 'synergy', where their whole is greater than the mere sum of their parts), but not all groups become teams.

A critical part of the leadership function is turning individual people, assets, resources, etc. into a finely oiled machine. It is the integrative function. And leaders who can pull people together enjoy greater success than those who cannot – success defined by almost any measure such as increased performance and satisfaction, as well as reduced turnover and absenteeism. This involves communication and coordinating. This involves negotiation and conflict resolution as partners. This involves creating collaborative environments that support these. In short, if you want to be a leader you must learn to coordinate and synergize like one.

However, this is much easier said than done.

We do not live in an ideal word of harmonious interactions. Why? A few reasons. First, people often rub each other up the wrong way. They do not always match or mesh. Instead the parts don't always fit. They also outright clash. They are just not naturally complementary. When our personalities, predilections, and preferences do not align we can easily but regrettably lapse into Sartre's trap of believing that 'hell is other people'. Second, people often do not communicate well. They do not speak to be understood. They do not listen to hear. Instead much of our interacting live is devoid of actual interaction marred by talking past each other and being distracted by other concerns and blinking objects. Third, people often do not settle their conflicts well. At work, at home, on social media, in the headlines. We fight. And we fight badly. This drains resources and maims partnerships. And fourth, if these were not enough, we tend not to design environments that would help the situation. Instead the disjunctive, myopic structures we form and the adversarial, cut-throat cultures we create tend to make things worse rather than better.

As the prior paragraph reveals, we are often faced with environments characterized by the following … Clashes. Miscommunications. Distractions. Draining conflicts. Antagonistic environments.

So do you still want to be a leader? A wise leader?

Then you must learn to connect and coordinate like one.

One of the tools leaders must hone and wield is epistemology. Connecting and helping people connect. Pulling people together and helping others do the same. Elevating your and their unity.

But don't just take my word for it. Please consider the following insights.

Build for your team a feeling of oneness, of dependence upon one another, and of strength to be derived by unity.
–Vince Lombardi

There is a great comfort and inspiration in the feeling of close human relationships and its bearing on our mutual fortunes. / It seems to me shallow and arrogant for

> *any man in these times to claim he is completely self-made, that he owes all his success to his own unaided efforts. Many hands and hearts and minds generally contribute to anyone's notable achievements.*
> — Walt Disney
>
> *Unity to be real must stand the severest strain without breaking.*
> — M. K. Gandhi
>
> *Do not let what you cannot do interfere with what you can do.*
> — John Wooden
>
> *Coming together is a beginning; keeping together is progress; working together is success.*
> — Henry Ford

Leaders promote unity. They take parts and create a larger whole. A new entity. This becomes evident when people begin to refer to themselves not only as individuals but as part of a collective. Not as separate parts but as an integrated whole. They stop using the word 'I' and begin using the word 'We'. As the famous sports saw goes, there is no 'I' in team. And great teams will defeat great individuals. This is the message of legendary football coach Vince Lombardi.

Leaders also promote interdependency. When you are dependent you are weak. When you are independent you are stronger. When you are interdependent, as part of a synergistic system that multiplies strengths and compensates for weaknesses, you are strongest. There is scarcely no one from which we cannot learn something. No matter how good you are, you can and will be better from the unique contributions of colleagues. This is the message of Walt Disney.

With unity and interdependency come strength. A strength that surpasses that of any of its parts. Just as many strands of fabric make for a formidable rope, and just as many components of Kevlar make for a formidable shield, a collective acting together can withstand forces that would normally overpower any of its constituents. When times are good unity is easy. When times are tough unity is essential. This is the message of M. K. Gandhi.

It is easy to be unified when everyone is similar. Similarity breeds agreement and agreement breeds harmony. Birds of a feather easily flock together. But although easier, this type of unity is not as strong as that which is forged from balanced, differentiated factors. Teams are highest performing when each member brings not the same attitudes but different, complementary outlooks. Not the same skills but different, complementary competencies. When each person plays a different part based on their particular predilections and preferences. So instead of trying to do everything we focus on our specialized roles. This is the message of John Wooden.

Yet differentiated groups only become integrated teams when the pieces of the puzzle come together. When the micro logics of each role form a macro logic and

202 Assembling Your Leadership Toolbox

synergistic, cohesive unit. So not only must leaders assemble the right parts, and maintain the flow, they must also make them sing as one voice. Just as a maestro creates the concerto from the orchestra. This is the message of Henry Ford.

So here we are.

Chapter 8 explains how leaders SYNERGIZE (i.e., PULL people together). It is grounded in the philosophical branch of EPISTEMOLOGY.

Developing this tool enables the wise leader and their organization to become WHOLE. In a way it involves discovering, honing, and unleashing your inner leadership MAESTRO.

However, the true nature of the leader's synergy is often misunderstood. More than this, individuals' internal limitations and organizations' external barriers can prevent us from truly synergizing like a proverbial leadership maestro.

So what to do?

Coalescing what we know about leadership epistemology provides several tools to help us in this endeavor.

In short, to be a leadership maestro …

1. Building a better synergistic core involves optimizing the composition and alignment of elements so as to achieve complementarity;
2. Crafting a better synergizing process will allow you to communicate well as partners and enhance conflict resolution so as to achieve interdependency; and
3. Leveraging your synergistic achievements brings greater harmony through an improved hardware (structural) and software (cultural) architecture.

Taken together, this chapter's presentation of complementarity, interdependency, and harmony will allow you to enhance this leadership tool and work towards EXTRAORDINARY COLLABORATIVE ORIENTATION.

When faced with integration and coordination-related challenges it will enable you to lead a personal and professional life infused with UNITY.

This chapter is therefore organized as follows:

*   Problem: When Facing Harmony and Teamwork Challenges
*   Solution: Activate Your Leader 'Epistemology' Tool
*   Identity: Be a Leadership MAESTRO
*   Method: To Pull People Together
*   Focus: And with Extraordinary Collaborative Orientation
*   Outcome: Lead for *Unity*

When Facing Harmony and Teamwork Challenges

What Is this Type of Problem?

One type of challenge leaders face is collaborative in nature. It involves creating teamwork. In essence, it demands that you develop the 'epistemology' of a leader.

That you SYNERGIZE (i.e., PULL people together) like a leader.

Appropriate analogies for this are the sled team and the sports team. Sled dogs that do not pull in the same direction go nowhere. This is regardless of their individual strengths. They must get on the same page. Reconcile preferences and predilections. Position themselves to make the most of their strengths and compensate for their weaknesses. And of course follow the guidance of their leader. Not everyone can be, or should be, reindeer Rudolph. Each has a role. Each complements the other.

Similarly, sports teams whose players do not fill critical roles go nowhere. All scorers with no passers make for a clunky offence. Plus someone must block and set screens. Someone must sacrifice for the overall well-being and success. And this is further exacerbated when we also consider 'unsung' heroes who play defense and do the little things which enable the stars to shine. The team-first players. The glue guys. The support crew.

So ask yourself: Do your pieces fit together? Do they make each other better or do they work against each other? Is each right for its role?

Can you synergize the parts into an integrated whole?

To unite like a leadership maestro?

Net-Net: The fifth core element of wisdom is synergy. Achieving coherent, complementary systems. Thus, wise actors in the professional domain are complete. They coordinate their efforts. They deploy their harmony and congruence to be on the same page and move to the same music.

This is depicted in Figure 8.1, with emphasis added to the current topic.

Tool #5:
When there are coordination and synergy (connection) challenges…

FIGURE 8.1 Focus: Epistemology and the Leadership Maestro.

204 Assembling Your Leadership Toolbox

So how do you know when you are facing coordination and synergy-related (connection) challenges that require you to be a leadership maestro? And why are these problems so darned hard to solve?

These issues are addressed below.

How Do You Know When You Are Facing It?

You can tell if you are facing this type of challenge if you see conscience and integrity-related challenges. More specifically, (1) Problems of Complementarity, (2) Problems of Interdependency, and/or (3) Problems of Harmony. Each will be explained below.

The Need for Synergistic Components: Dealing with Problems of Complementarity

The foundation for building a better synergistic core involves examining the selection and combination of parts that give you your teamwork potential. If you do not have the right people, or do not assign them the right parts, then there is no epistemological anchor and you are starting out from behind.

In technical terms, here you do not have a synergistic composition or alignment. In plain speak, you struggle with – What pieces will mesh best? How should they be best positioned to support one another?

In these cases they indicate that we have a problem of complementarity.

This is a Data > Information issue. Epistemological input never makes it onto your radar screen.

Some examples: When you hire people solely for their technical competence but not for their interpersonal skills – i.e., hiring the best individuals but not team players. Training people to excel at their one piece of the puzzle but without conveying an understanding and a skill-set to make it fit with others' pieces. Not prioritizing flexibility and adaptability to make pieces mesh across tasks and time.

The best leaders can identify epistemological issues and the proper tools for solving them.

Basically, you need to (1) acquire or shape 'team players' and (2) adopt or facilitate team malleability. First, the former might entail selecting or training for certain elements of personal qualities, dispositions, and approaches to working well with others. Second, the latter might entail creating or maintaining the right types of tasks and dynamics that would promote, versus inhibit, teamwork potential.

The Need for Synergistic Dynamics: Dealing with Problems of Interdependency

Once your core is high potential, crafting a better reflective process will allow you to tap this teamwork potential. If you cannot manage and support your core, and build and strengthen your core, then your potential withers and might even be lured towards other (egotistical) ends.

In technical terms, here you do not have synergistic conflict orientation or partnership. In plain speak, you struggle with – What is the best way to rely on each other and truly connect? What practices can enable us to settle disagreements in a win-win manner and become true partners?

In these cases they indicate that we have a problem of interdependence.

This is an Information > Knowledge issue. Epistemological input is present but not processed well.

Some examples: When employees talk past rather than to each other. When employees only hear but do not listen to each other. Or when they adopt adversarial rather than partner-like collaborative approaches to conflicts. Basically, when people work against versus with one another.

The best leaders can reconcile their epistemological core and create a sense of interdependency.

Basically, to do this, you need to (1) learn how to communicate well as a team, and (2) learn how to work through inevitable differences together as a cohesive team.

First, it is essential that leaders realize this basic truth – communication is more than just talking. It is an exchange of meaning between a sender and receiver. As such it involves (1) Formulating a message or translating one's thought into language; (2) Sending a message across verbal or nonverbal channels; and (3) Listening and retranslating the language into one's own thoughts. And this process repeats in multiple iterations of feedback, making each person in a communication process both an active speaker and an active listener. These will be elaborated upon later in the chapter.

Second, it is equally critical to realize that conflict is inevitable ... and it can be healthy if done in the right way. This is entirely dependent on a number of factors. For instance, if it is functional – about solving issues versus personal quibbles. If it is optimal – not too high or too low. And if it is integrative – about attending to all parties' concerns. These will also be elaborated upon later in the chapter.

The Need for Synergistic Contexts: Dealing with Problems of Harmony

Once your synergistic potential is established and cultivated, then full integration of your team-oriented leadership can take place. In technical terms, synergistic hardware or software. In plain speak, you struggle with – What structure will bring us together? What culture will bring us together?

Without the leveraging of your potential your maestro never becomes a leadership tool.

In these cases they indicate that we have a problem of harmony. Of institutionalized synchronization and concordance.

206 Assembling Your Leadership Toolbox

This is a Knowledge > Wisdom issue. Epistemological inputs and processes are not coupled to attaining the most meaningful and significantly satisfying conclusions.

Some examples: When structures are dysfunction. Like when leaders break up tasks poorly. Or when leaders put tasks together poorly. Like when leaders promote antagonistic climates. Or when they beget oppositional actions.

Basically, you need to (1) create the right formal structure – i.e., design, and (2) create the right informal structure – i.e., culture, to bring people together and unleash your teamwork potential.

First, structure is the visible hierarchy and structure of a team. Structures need to be designed for optimal differentiation, integration, centralization, and standardization. Yes – these are a lot of blah-blah-ation words. No worries, we will unpack them later in the chapter.

Second, culture is the invisible hierarchy and structure of a team. This involves establishing the right assumptions. And making them consistent with terminal and instrumental values. And reinforcing them through the right artifacts. And teaching them through the right socialization. Yes – these are a lot of technical-sounding mandate words. Again no worries, we will also unpack them later in the chapter.

All Together

If we do not rise to meet Complementarity challenges then you will have a group with individual potentials but not a team with collective potential. You will have the players but not the parts.

If we do not rise to meet Interdependency challenges then this potential is never realized. The nodes are there but not the connections between them. As such you might win some battles but not the war. You might compile impressive statistics but not win a championship.

If we do not rise to meet Harmony challenges then the micro and meso dynamics are never translated into macro success. There is no sustained teamwork. One missing part and the machine crumbles. One injury and the squad forfeits. But with a design and a culture of teamwork the coordination is imbued deeply and significantly, and almost takes on a life of its own, outlasting any temporal transitions, turnovers, or disruptions.

UPSHOT: Know when you are facing epistemology, teamwork-related challenges.

Activate Your Leader 'Epistemology' Tool

As expressed in the preceding section, the primary tool leaders use to pull people together is sourced from the domain of epistemology.

Without leadership MAESTRO tools leaders are hard-pressed to transcend different lures and predilections to create a formidable whole. As a leader you become fragmented, and this fragmentation of interests and acumens is confusing at best and, more than likely, creates a torment of conflicted ideas and intentions. It seems that you are always pulled in different directions and can never get centered. Without these tools leaders are also hard-pressed to help others and their organization transcend individualized profiles and agendas to create a formidable whole. If your organization cannot work together then no matter its collection of resources and talent it is doomed to fail when encountering a more synchronized adversary. In short, it will not have the collaboration to deal with teamwork challenges.

Leaders must thus lead for unity. But alas these are not easy tools to acquire and employ. If they were then all leaders would not have any teamwork concerns and the world would not face issues of miscommunication and be awash with dysfunctional conflicts. So, in the same economic terms used in the book's introduction but customized for this particular chapter, there is often an imbalance of the demand for unity and the supply of unity.

Here are some of the key barriers in ourselves (individual) and our environments (organizational) that impede us and our followers from addressing these types of issues.

Some Teamwork Component Challenges Leaders Must Overcome

First, and especially in highly individualistic environments, there is an inherent pressure for people to develop as entities as opposed to collectives. That is to say, we are often trained to cultivate personal competencies and less to fit within interpersonal cooperatives. Moreover, we are often assessed (grades, metrics) and rewarded for thinking about ourselves. This is compounded with selection systems that examine not role excellence but more personal excellence. If a mechanic selected, one-by-one and in isolation, the best parts based on individual performance then it would be highly unlikely that the resultant car would even run, no less hum. The parts must work together.

Common component and alignment problems include the following:

Loafers. All group members are not created alike. Some kick in whereas others coast and take advantage of others' efforts. Thus a common problem is what economists term the 'free-rider' problem. Psychologists have a more colorful term for it: social loafing. In general, people tend to loaf when (1) they are not interested and would rather be somewhere else; (2) they think the worst of co-workers and expect them to be lazy, selfish, and opportunistic so why not be that way as well; and (3) they can hide, blend in, and not be held responsible for their contributions.

- Leadership maestros balance the micro with the macro – they do not allow for too much individualism. They do not allow people to loaf.

Conformers. Loafing is a case where people blindly put the 'me' ahead of the 'we'. However, the other extreme is also a problem. Losing oneself in the group and

208 Assembling Your Leadership Toolbox

washing out one's individuality. This is called Groupthink. It is a case of over-conformity and obsession with concurrence. Groups are thus too tight … and they create more and more errors while becoming more and more confident in them. A dangerous combination.

- Leadership maestros balance the macro with the micro – they do not allow for too little individualism. They do not allow people to conform.

Isolators. Some people simply do not work well with others. One of the most common and systematic maladies is the dysfunctional specialist isolated in attitude and aptitude from those around them. They sit inside their own bubble caring only about their own frames and challenges. Often this occurs because of narrow systems that attract, select, or train people within their specialties and do not put enough emphasis on meshing with others. It is exacerbated when career ladders support this myopia at the expense of bigger-picture thinking.

- Leadership maestros balance specialism with generalism – they do not allow for too narrow a focus. They do not allow people to retreat into isolated specialties.

Floaters. These people are the opposite of isolators. Here people are too superficial and broad. The proverbial jacks-of-all-trades who master none. Always needing someone else to solve their problems. Often this occurs because of overly generalized or fast-track systems that emphasize a 'top management' orientation at the expense of familiarity with the technical cores that support it.

- Leadership maestros balance generalism with specialism – they do not allow for too broad a focus. They do not allow people to come to the party without bringing a dish.

Some Teamwork Process Challenges Leaders Must Overcome

Second, there are so many traps to good communication that it is a miracle (figuratively, but not as far-fetched as the label might suggest) that we can connect well over any length of time. Related to this, there is a propensity for those in conflict to think of each other as competitors rather than as partners. That is, approaching conflict as a bad thing or interaction as a zero-sum, win-lose battle rather than investing in positive-sum solutions to further everyone's interests.

Common communication problems include the following.

Poor encoding. Communication begins with speaking. When someone translates his or her thoughts into symbolic form – i.e., language. And communication problems begin when we do not speak well. For example, in using the wrong words. In using inappropriate jargon or technical terms. In being overly generic or vague. In not taking into account cross-cultural or cross-generational differences. It also happens when we are over-assertive and dominant in our speech, or when we are under-assertive and too withdrawn. And more than this, it can happen when we lie. Tacitly through omitting truths. Blatantly through inserting falsehoods. Or systemically through filters that warp meanings.

- Leadership maestros do not allow for distortion in the formulation (encoding) of messages. They are good talkers, and help others talk well.

Poor channel selection. Communication continues when we send messages. And problems occur when we do not choose the correct media for this transmission. For example, using overly rich media – too many meetings and conversations – when all we needed was a quick, simple directive. Or using inappropriately poor media – too many texts and emails – where lack of context obscures nuance of messages. It also happens when we do not use media skillfully. For example, in being poor tweeters, writers, or conversationalists. And further, it happens when leaders allow informal rumor grapevines to drown out truths with exaggerated fictions.

- Leadership maestros do not allow for distortion in the sending of messages. They are good with media channel selection and usage, and help others choose well.

Poor decoding. Communication is received by listeners who retranslate messages into their own thoughts. And good listening makes sure that these thoughts match those that were sent. Yet although most people claim they are good listeners very few really are. Instead we tend to listen through our own preferences and agendas. We cloud things with our prejudices and stereotypes. We are fickle and defensive in what we allow to get in. And we are often disengaged in how we do it. That is, listening is often seen as a passive action whereas it should be an active process of signaling, questioning, contemplating, and ensuring understanding.

- Leadership maestros do not allow for distortion in the receiving (decoding) of messages. They are good listeners, and help others listen well.

Poor nonverbal communication. Most of our interpersonal communication happens not with words but in their context. In their kinesics of facial expressions and gestures. In their proxemics of space and distance. In their paralanguage of pace, tone, and pause. Thus, we must also match our context with our words so as not to send mixed signals. Saying everything is okay but avoiding eye contact. Saying you care but keeping your distance. Saying you are happy but speaking in a stressed manner.

210 Assembling Your Leadership Toolbox

- Leadership maestros do not allow for nonverbal distortion. They match words with actions.

Poor supportiveness. Communication is not just about exchanging meaning. It is also about creating connections. Camaraderie. Yet even when we praise or reward, we can still do it in a negative way that creates animosity. On the flip side, done supportively we can give admonishment or punishment in a way that makes us closer. In short, when we communicate in a manner that makes people feel small, ridiculed, or belittled (disconfirming) or makes them feel like they are being attacked (creating defensiveness) then bonds are broken.

- Leadership maestros do not allow for non-supportive distortion. They build more bridges and fewer walls.

Common conflict problems include the following.

The wrong type of conflict. Most conflict is affective (versus cognitive or functional). It stresses tangential issues rather than task-completion issues. It focuses on personality or style clashes rather than connecting as a unit. In addition, it involves the interpreting of any conflict as an (affective) attack. That is, personalizing conflict too much by letting one's pride or ego get involved. Caring more about winning the fight rather than solving issues for the best outcome.

- Leadership maestros reduce affective, tangential, and personalized conflict.

The wrong amount of conflict. On the one hand, the best interactions are not zero-conflict. When this happens you get apathy. Stagnation. Boredom. On the other hand, the best interactions are also not maximum-conflict. When this happens you get chaos. Hyper-competitiveness. Sabotage. Disruption. Instead leaders need to be able to increase conflict when too low or dial it back when too high.

- Leadership maestros reduce under- and over-expressions of conflict.

The wrong form of conflict. Disagreements are seen more as win-lose battles than as win-win partnerships. For example:

Dominant, 'opera' (Me-Me-Me) conflict – caring only about self-interests and ignoring your partner's interests. Being an enemy that fights to win and create losers. Battering others to prevail.

- Leadership maestros prevent overly bullying conflict.

Submissive (You-You-You) conflict – caring only about others' interest and ignoring your own. Being a patsy or pushover that accommodates and caves in.

Your Leadership Maestro (Epistemology) Tools **211**

- Leadership maestros prevent overly submissive conflict.

Dodging conflict – sidestepping conflict out of fear. Basically, being afraid of conflict. Running away. Avoiding. Hiding. Burying one's head in the sand in the hope that it will magically disappear.

- Leadership maestros prevent too much avoidance of conflict.

Settling conflict – short-circuiting conflict with quick-fix patchwork solutions. Dealing and sacrificing for a convenient albeit suboptimal resolution. Dividing up the proverbial pie rather than growing the pie.

- Leadership maestros prevent too much placating of conflict.

Some Teamwork Context Challenges Leaders Must Overcome

Third, designing (and redesigning) organizations is more art than science. There are many dimensions to consider – for instance, centralization versus decentralization, formalization versus mutual adjustment, more or less differentiation, and integration sophistication and intensity. And more than this, the invisible dimension of culture. Their combinations, as well as variations across teams and areas, as well as suitability in different contexts and situations, can make for very complex decisions with much room for poor choices. The unbelievably large and constant number of reorganizations, bankruptcies, restructurings, and the like show how hard it is to get design right.

Common structure and culture problems include the following.

Poor design of jobs. As far back as the year 1776 Adam Smith's *The Wealth of Nations* demonstrated that prosperity and power could be gained, and sustained, by out-organizing your competition. The secret. Smart differentiation. How the division of labor divides tasks into specialized roles will make some organizations rich and keep others poor. So, when roles are poorly designed – e.g., poorly fit, confusing, redundant, overloaded, conflicting – then organizations will be poorly functioning.

- Leadership maestros differentiate well by establishing proper specializations.

Too many islands and not enough bridges. Differentiated parts must eventually be put back together if an organization is to function as a harmonious whole. Integration is the process of establishing mechanisms so that roles, tasks, functions, divisions, etc. work together and not narrowly, rigidly, against each other. It creates the connections that overcome differences in training, time orientation, mental models, job requirements and metrics, and subcultures. If you are under-integrated then leaders will witness a

212 Assembling Your Leadership Toolbox

lack of coordination and little sharing. If you are over-integrated then leaders will witness a preponderance of inefficiency, conflict, and wasted time and resources.

- Leadership maestros put things together well by matching integration to differentiation.

Under-delegation. It is tempting for leaders to centralize all decision-making power at the top of the hierarchy. It helps keep things coherent and controlled. However, it can also overload leadership and create bottlenecks that overwhelm the capacity of its centralized planners. It is seen when information gaps arise which distance decision making from the places where it needs to happen. When processes are slowed down to a crawl demanding endless rounds of approvals and reviews. When underlings are demotivated and feel like automatons. When systems fail to develop future generations of leaders. When the flow of new ideas is impinged and the creativity and innovation on which it relies are compromised. Therefore, leaders must balance centralized control with appropriate degrees of decentralization, empowering people to establish high performing systems that make the best use of resources at all levels of the hierarchy.

- Leadership maestros balance control (centralization) and freedom (decentralization).

Lack of flexibility. Organizations have rules. And for good reason. They prevent anarchy and capture best practices into standardized systems that create order, predictability, and clarity. Too few rules and you get a loss of control. However, rules come from the past and the past is not always the best predictor of the future. As such breakdowns can be seen when there is rigidity, when abiding by the policies and procedures becomes an obsessive end in and of itself, when people cannot adjust to new circumstances, and when there is a lack of flexibility and problem solving especially as things get uncertain and ambiguous.

- Leadership maestros balance standardization and flexibility.

A dysfunctional organizational 'personality'. Structure is the most visible way, but not the only way, leaders institutionalize practices. They can also shape its culture. An organization's culture is its invisible sets of shared assumptions, values, and ingrained practices that support and maintain interactions. You might see it in stories passed down from employees, in the symbols lining the walls and desks of workers, in the rites and rituals performed regularly, and even in the verbal (buzzwords) and nonverbal (how they dress, eat, interact, etc.) actions of your membership. Leaders must monitor cultures to make sure that they are guiding actions in the proper directions.

- Leadership maestros manage their 'invisible' cultures.

Taken Together

As you can see, the issues of epistemology and leadership are inexorably intertwined. With so many complementarity-, interdependency-, and harmony-related challenges leaders must be proactive in developing unity.

UPSHOT: Wise leaders address epistemology, teamwork-related challenges.

Be a Leadership MAESTRO

The identity best befitting an epistemology problem solver is that of a leadership Maestro.

A Maestro, as per the *Oxford English Dictionary*, is a distinguished conductor (person who directs the performance of an orchestra or choir) or performer of classical music.

Maestros, by extension, are those who are most skilled at creating unity.

A maestro is a conductor. A masterful conductor. And it is said that maestros do not play an instrument but instead play the orchestra. Ideally virtuosos occupy the individual seats in the orchestra pit. But without the maestro their contributions, brilliant in their own individual right though they may be, will but produce a mishmash of ill-coordinated, ill-timed noises. From the pieces the maestro assembles the puzzle. From the parts the maestro produces the whole. From the sounds the maestro makes music. They may have to speed up or slow down some parts, constrain or expand others, and even switch out some seats with lesser players if those players blend better with the team as a whole. This is often the pre-eminent charge of leaders. To take micro mastery and create macro magic.

When you picture a maestro what images come into your head?

Perhaps waving a wand with seemingly random but strategically deliberate hand movements,

And as a result complex parts coming together,

With different instruments blending,

Along with diverse virtuosos blending,

To create an emanation of beautiful music.

These are poor stereotypes and pigeonholes for sure, but they can be used as a jumping-off point for capturing the character of the maestro. And as such they may suggest ways for modeling how maestros coordinate and what leaders can learn from them to pull people together better.

Put more systematically, and in a manner consistent with the book's model:

- Maestros emphasize complementarity. Leadership maestros therefore assemble the right composition and alignment of parts to address coordination and synergy challenges.
- Maestros push interdependence. Leadership maestros therefore manage communication and conflict resolution processes as partners to also address coordination and synergy challenges.

214 Assembling Your Leadership Toolbox

TABLE 8.1 Tools for PULLING People Together

Better Core: Complementarity	Composition of Parts
	Alignment of Parts
Better Process: Interdependency	Enhanced Communication
	Enhanced Partnership
Better Leverage: Harmony	Improved Hardware (Structural Design)
	Improved Software (Cultural Design)

- Maestros seek harmony. Leadership maestros therefore design formal/ structural as well as informal/cultural systems to additionally address coordination and synergy challenges.

Leadership maestros develop their epistemology in these three fundamental ways.

The following offers a step-by-step map for doing this. For convenience these steps are summarized in Table 8.1. They are then illustrated as well as elaborated upon in the subsequent corresponding sections.

To Pull People Together

Step One – Building a Better Core

> *You're only as good as the people you hire.*
> – Ray Kroc
>
> *Associate yourself with good men if you esteem your own reputation.*
> – George Washington
>
> *The antidote for 50 enemies is one friend.*
> – Aristotle
>
> *Do I not destroy my enemies when I make them my friends?*
> – Abraham Lincoln

No matter the size of the organization, it is made up of people. If the people do not have the interpersonal orientation, and if they do not fit together, then the organization with implode. Ray Kroc knew this and embodied it when building the MacDonald's empire. And as per George Washington and Aristotle, being around good people betters you (and makes you look better to others). This is because they create virtuous cycles of positive interactions and mutually reinforcing practices that elevate all involved. Of course, not everyone needs to be your friend. And the harsh reality is that they will not be. People who work against you, either on purpose or

Your Leadership Maestro (Epistemology) Tools **215**

implicitly (because they do not know any better or never learned to act any other way), are often termed 'enemies'. Enemies oppose. They do not trust and cannot be trusted. They do not help but instead harm. They do not look to strengthen you but instead to weaken you. And the world is full of actual and potential enemies ready to pounce. So how do you convert enemies into friends? They can be compelled. They can be bribed or otherwise incentivized. But these do not last long. Only until the threat or reward expires or is surpassed by someone more threatening or lavish. Instead, and as per Lincoln, true friends can only form out of genuine acts of amity. Mutuality of goodwill. Camaraderie. This will not work with everyone but it doesn't have to. And this is especially important given Aristotle's calculus that a true friend is 50-fold the asset that an enemy is a liability.

As expressed in the above aphorisms, complementarity is at the heart of establishing synergistic leadership.

Formally stated, as found in the *OED*: Complementarity is a relationship or situation in which two or more different things improve or emphasize each other's qualities.

It is a function of composition and alignment. Composition is the nature of something's ingredients or constituents; the way in which a whole or mixture is made up. Alignment is a position of agreement or alliance.

Composition

Composition can be enhanced through synergy-oriented staffing, placement, and training. As per Richard Hackman's model of building 'true' teams it is essential for team success that its makeup enables rather than impedes teamwork.

For example, regarding Human Capital Theory (see Tarique, 2013), the recognition that people

> possess human capital … acquired from training, development, education, and other types of work and non-work learning based experiences. … Everything else equal, appropriate investments in human capital can result in increased knowledge, skills, and abilities that in turn can improve performance and productivity at various levels.

Thus, applying this to 'wise' Human Resource Management practices (as per DeNisi & Belsito, 2007), leaders must:

- Hire and place for synergy, focusing on aspects of the selection process that categorize and prioritize candidates based on relevant job criteria to provide the organization and candidate with high probabilities of success.
- Train and develop for synergy, focusing on value to both employees and organizations by cultivating as well as blending sets of complementary competencies.

216 Assembling Your Leadership Toolbox

- Appraise for synergy, where a wisdom-based approach is concerned with the content as well as with the process of performance appraisal to include employee input and account for perceptions of justice or fairness.
- Compensate for synergy, where in a wisdom-based perspective the focus should be on paying people for the extent to which they contribute valued skills or knowledge to the organizational whole and increase its potential as well as performance.

Alignment

Alignment can be enhanced through synergy-oriented roles, functions, norms, and status.

First, to mold synergistic roles. As per Fellows and Kahn (2013):

> individual behavior in social settings is governed by perceptions of role, a socially constructed position or category such as 'spouse' or 'manager' ... role theory explains how actors translate perceived societal norms and expectations into scripts for action in a given context. ... The concept of role is necessary in any system, from small groups to global economies.... It is also essential to the persistence of organizations over time; individuals may join or depart, but roles endure and establish continuity.... Thus, role theory explains why different individuals behave similarly in a social context (when they occupy the same role), as well as why the same individual may behave very differently across contexts (in playing different roles).... The ability of actors to understand their place in a role set is essential to achieving organizational objectives ... actors learn to conduct themselves as though engaging with a generalized other, a composite of the expectations of their organizational community.

As is evident from the above, the management of roles is essential if the entire case, ensemble, orchestra, etc. is to gel and interact synergistically. Some of the most critical functions for leaders in this regard are to:

- Ensure that roles are clear. This avoids role ambiguity. Like when a student does not know what is expected in an essay. Or a worker on an assignment. Or a family member in a home. People need to know what is expected of them, what is expected of others, and how these expectations come together.
- Ensure that roles are appropriate. This avoids strain or role overload when the demands of the role overwhelm the abilities of the person occupying the role. Like when a student is placed in a course well beyond their capacities. Or a worker on too difficult an assignment or demanding a client. Or a family member on too difficult a chore.

Your Leadership Maestro (Epistemology) Tools **217**

- Ensure that roles are complementary. This avoids role deficiency to ensure that they have both task roles (which establish schedules and logistics for getting things done) and maintenance roles (which provide the bonds like caring and respect for holding things together). Without task roles groups idle. Without maintenance roles they implode.
- Ensure that roles are harmonious. This avoids role conflict. Conflict can happen within roles (where expectations clash with a person's values), between roles (where expectations of one's different jobs clash, like simultaneously being a good worker, parent, friend, student, etc.), and between peoples' perceptions (where, for example, a boss or a parent might see a role differently than their worker, spouse, or child).

Second, to mold synergistic norms. As per Smith and Terry (2013):

> Social norms – or group-based standards or rules regarding appropriate attitudes and behavior – play a crucial role in shaping how we interpret our social world and how we act … for almost every workplace behavior, from which clothes to wear to whether to take a sick day when one is not ill, individuals will have an understanding of which behaviors are approved of by others and which behaviors others engage in themselves.… That is, the attitudes and behaviors that are seen to be endorsed by one's colleagues and displayed by one's colleagues will define what is seen to be appropriate – or normal – behavior within the workplace context.

As is evident from the above, the management of norms is essential. Some of the most critical functions for leaders in this regard are to:

- Establish the proper norms. This can be done by establishing them up front, by handling critical events in a consistent manner, by making clear and explicit statements of expectations, and by linking norms to desired outcomes.
- Orient the norms properly. Use them for survival for maintaining the group's cohesion. Use them for clarification for making expectations transparent. Use them for identity to establish a collective ethos and culture. Use them for achieving goals and satisfying stakeholders' critical concern.
- Guard against the downsides of norms. For example, preventing social loafing by getting them involved, creating positive expectations and an environment of teamwork, inviting critical thinking, and holding them accountable.

Taken Together

So: what are you waiting for? Grow your leadership maestro core. Start enhancing your composition and alignment.

UPSHOT: Wise leaders enhance complementarity.

218 Assembling Your Leadership Toolbox

Step Two – Crafting a Better Process

> *The single biggest problem in communication is the illusion that it has taken place.*
> – George Bernard Shaw
>
> *Whatever words we utter should be chosen with care for people will hear them and be influenced by them for good or ill.*
> – Buddha
>
> *Don't mistake politeness for lack of strength.*
> – Sonia Sotomayor
>
> *A man practicing sportsmanship is far better than a hundred teaching it.*
> – Knute Rockne
>
> *It is understanding that gives us the ability to have peace. When we understand the other fellow's viewpoint, and he understands ours, then we can sit down and work out our differences.*
> – Harry Truman
>
> *Only surround yourself with people that will lift you higher.*
> – Oprah Winfrey

George Bernard Shaw emphasizes the fidelity and completeness of the communication process. Just because you speak doesn't mean that anybody has heard anything. Similarly, if an email is sent but never opened, or if a message is posted but never read, then there is no communication. We cannot assume that just because we talk others listen. Buddha emphasizes communication impact. Words are powerful. They may not break one's bones (as do sticks and stones) but they can do great harm or promote great good. And the more powerful the speaker the more powerful the movements they can create. Justice Sonia Sotomayor reminds us about not just being accurate but also being supportive in our communication. Supportive does not mean weak. It means nice. And we can be accurate in mean or nice ways. Knute Rockne speaks to the criticality of communication and collaboration in our conflict resolution and achievement of teamwork. It is easy to speak about teamwork but much harder to practice it. Especially when it entails something that you really, really (insert as much 'reallys' here as needed) want. Harry Truman pushes us to see these collaborative, win-win solutions to conflicts as viable and shows just how important it is to develop a team-oriented mentality. He shows us a way to partnership. To look at others as partners versus rivals. Finally, Oprah Winfrey brings to this the notion that well-managed interactions are mutually reinforcing. Where you bring out the best in the other person and they bring out the best in you. Where the whole becomes greater than the sum of the parts.

As expressed in the above aphorisms, interdependence is critical for processing synergistic leadership. Formally stated, as found in the *OED*: Interdependency is the mutual dependence of two or more people or things on each other.

It is not that you and I are apart. And it is just that I need you or you need me. It happens when we would be better together. When together we can reach the pinnacle of our potential. Interdependence up and down the vertical hierarchy from the top dog to the core operator. Interdependence across the horizontal hierarchy weaving together all functions, steps, and areas of expertise.

It is a function of communication and conflict resolution. Communication is the imparting or exchanging of information by speaking, writing, or using some other medium. The successful conveying or sharing of ideas and feelings Resolution is the action of solving a problem or contentious matter. For example, the peaceful resolution of all disputes. The passing of a discord into a concord during the course of changing harmony.

Communication

In communication we speak. We send. We listen. As suggested previously, communication can therefore be enhanced through synergy-oriented speaking, sending, and listening.

To speak for synergy, try honing your:

- Language – Use precise and situation-appropriate (versus vague and insensitive) words. This includes using appropriate informal jargon and symbols. This also includes embedding the above within their proper cultural and generational contexts.
- Engagement and Assertiveness – Project communication with sufficient energy to be received but not too much energy as to be overpowering or even unbearable. For example, avoiding rudeness, yelling, and aggressiveness as well as the other extreme of shyness, whispering, and withdrawal.
- Supportiveness – Care about not just the transference of meaning but also the way communication makes people feel. For example, avoiding negative trigger words or those associated with hurtful connotations.

To send for synergy, try honing your:

- Richness – Include multiple cues (e.g., tone, visuals) to increase the chances that your message will hold its meaning. Make sure that the more complicated the message the richer your channel. Like face-to-face for complex discussions or emails and IMs for simpler directives.
- Nonverbals – Make sure words and actions gel. Like your proxemics, or how you manage distance and space. Like your paralanguage or how you manage tones and silences. Like your kinesics or how you manage facial expressions and gestures.

220 Assembling Your Leadership Toolbox

- Balance – Sync formal and informal communications. Know how to reduce information gaps. To quash rumors and manage gossip.

To listen for synergy, try honing your:

- Active listening skills – Paraphrase the messages of others to ensure that your understandings sync. It is NOT simply repeating what people say but putting things into your own words to reflect meaning. Paraphrasing is not parroting. The latter only demonstrates that you heard, and that your ears work. Not that you listened.
- Supportive listening skills – Use validating replies, own feedback, and be problem- versus person-oriented in responses to unite and create partnerships … versus making people feel defensive, small, and create animosities.

Partnership and Conflict Resolution

Resolution can be enhanced through synergy-oriented focus, magnitude, and approach. As per Bruce Tuckman's (2013) model of group development, individuals become a team – i.e., greater than the simple sum of their parts – when they can overcome their egos to form a cohesive unit, establish agreements and standards, and apply their energy supportively for interdependent problem solving. So:

- Strive for the right focus. Emphasize idea versus personality conflict. To solve problems, not snipe and gripe. Conflict should unite, not divide. Conflict should be about partnering, not playing the blame game. Wise leaders stay on task.
- Strive for the right amount. Try finding that elusive balance between too much and too little conflict. Without enough tension groups atrophy and become stagnant. With too much tension groups descend into disarray and discord. Wise leaders find that sweet spot of critical tension that sparks and animates without distracting.
- Strive for the right approach. As per Rahim and Magner (1995), try reframing conflict from distributive to integrative. Don't dominate and force your way. Don't cave in and be a doormat. Don't avoid and bury your head in the sand. And don't simply tit-for-tat compromise where nobody is really satisfied. Wise leaders strive for true win-win collaboration to invent options for joint gain and seek mutually satisfying solutions that combine perspectives for synergistic solutions.

Taken Together

So what are you waiting for? Grow your leadership maestro process. Start enhancing your communication and conflict resolution.

UPSHOT: Wise leaders enhance interdependence.

Step Three – Leveraging a Better Capacity

> *Everyone is here because he or she has a place to fill, and every piece must fit itself into the big jigsaw puzzle.*
> – Deepak Chopra
>
> *To put the world right in order, we must first put the nation in order. To put the nation in order, we must first put the family in order.*
> – Confucius
>
> *The ties of brotherhood still bind together the rich and poor in harmonious relationships.*
> – Andrew Carnegie
>
> *A company is stronger if it is bound by love rather than by fear. / Leading an organization is as much about soul as it is about systems. / Culture is intangible. It's spiritual. You can't buy it.*
> – Herb Kelleher
>
> *In order to have a winner, the team must have a feeling of unity; every player must put the team first – ahead of personal glory.*
> – Bear Bryant

Deepak Chopra reveals the importance of good design in creating harmony. Specifically, in the proper use of differentiation and the right pieces of the puzzle. Big jobs can be broken down into smaller ones. And since these pieces are different, they require different types of people to fill them where each person must fit their role and each role must fit the larger objective. Confucius further reveals the importance of good design in creating harmony within and across systems. Specifically, in the proper use of overarching integration and putting the pieces together in an orderly and consistent manner. The more you break things up, the more you need to work at putting them back together. So that they work for versus against each other. Andrew Carnegie's insight is particularly valuable for highlighting the importance of the invisible structure of culture. Rules and designs cannot cover everything and thus are necessary but not sufficient for harmony. They must also be supported by a harmonious climate or as articulated here 'brotherhood', so the bonds grow stronger and their reach wider. Herb Kelleher further emphasizes deeper elements of such a unifying culture. Culture is not just found at the surface rites and rituals. These things provide clues to it but do not define it. Culture resides in their underlying ethos. As Keller suggests, it is philosophical. In one's spiritual connections and collective souls. Casual Fridays or Employee of the Month plaques will not change a culture. But treating people with love and respect will. Bear Bryant brings these notions full circle back to

222 Assembling Your Leadership Toolbox

the chapter's goal of unity. When we design and differentiate well. When we build bridges and integrate well. When we prioritize connections. When we impress them into our very souls. Then we pull together. Become one. Become unbreakable. Become invincible.

As expressed in the above aphorisms, harmony is critical for achieving synergistic leadership.

Formally stated, as found in the *OED*: Harmony is the quality of forming a pleasing and consistent whole. The combination of simultaneously sounded musical notes to produce a pleasing effect.

It is a function of structure and culture. Structure is the (visible) arrangement of and relations between the parts or elements of something complex. The quality of being organized. Culture is the (invisible) ideas, customs, and social behavior of a particular people or society. The attitudes and behavior characteristic of a particular social group.

Unifying Structure and Design

Structure can be enhanced through synergy-oriented design of work environments. To design synergistic structures, as per Donaldson (2013), try:

- Creating collaborative functions and divisions, not antagonistic silos. This can be done through the smart differentiation of tasks and domains into areas that solve the dominant uncertainty facing the organization. For example, if it is more about how to do things, focus on functional clusters. If it is more about where to do things, focus on geographic clusters. If it is more about what things to do, focus on product/service clusters.
- Building bridges between these divisions so that they work together and not against each other. The more differentiated the pieces, the more intense integration efforts should be. When everyone is on the same page you can use less intense methods such as simple hierarchies or co-location that encourages contact both formally and casually. However, when roles put people at odds then stronger linking mechanisms are required. These might include task forces or even liaison roles and departments.
- Balancing decentralization with the need for centralized command structures. Empowerment allows for learning and flexibility, but it also introduces risks related to coordination, duplication, and consistency with overall strategic purpose. Finding the sweet spot requires constant review and adjustment. Too much freedom and things get chaotic. To many chains and things get stuck. Try establishing a dynamic process of checks and balances that allow for micro-division logic without turning it into macro-organizational nonsense (and vice versa).
- Balancing the use of rules, policies, and practices with the need for flexibility and mutual adjustment. Standardization promotes reliability and uniformity, but it also introduces greater risks related to a lack of creativity and innovation.

Again, finding the sweet spot is more art than science. Too many rules and things get bland. Too few and things get wild. Try allowing initiative while harmonizing time frames and objectives.

Unifying Culture

The informal structure, or culture, can also be enhanced and oriented to promote synergy. Culture can be understood as the shared beliefs, values, and means that interweave members' interactions with each other. It is the body of unwritten rules that everyone knows and abides by. The collection of institutionalized practices that everyone does unconsciously and automatically. The group's or organization's 'personality' that provides an identity, a stability, a sense of commitment, and a mechanism of coordination.

As per Ed Schein (2010), this culture is multi-layered. At the most surface, visible level are manifest artifacts: They include stories, rites/rituals, symbols, and language. Deeper still are underlying terminal values (what we want to be) and instrumental values (how we want to get there). Ultimately, they rest on foundational assumptions. The underlying causal beliefs about ends and means. ... How to succeed, how to live/act, and the reason for existence. Leaders thus must manage not just the tip of the proverbial iceberg but also its deep core.

To cultivate a synergistic culture, try:

- Managing its strength and direction. Stronger cultures are generally better than weaker ones. However, this is true only when the culture is positive. A powerful negative culture emphasizing the wrong values (e.g., Enron, Nazi Germany) or practices (like disrespect, selfishness, or slothfulness) can subvert the best intentions of its members.
- Managing its diffusion through socialization, or the process by which members learn and internalize the values and norms of an organization's culture. As per Jon Van Maanen and Ed Schein's (1979) socialization model there are various tactics that can be used to guide 'newcomers' to a particular role orientation, and they include various practices such as orientations and mentorships.
- Managing its subcultures. Cultures can vary across different parts of organizations. For example, different states of a union, branches of a family, or divisions of a firm such as marketing versus production, finance, and R&D. These subcultures need to integrated in a manner that preserves their ways and connects them together for greater purposes.

Taken Together

So what are you waiting for? Grow your leadership maestro capacity. Start enhancing your structure and culture.

UPSHOT: Wise leaders enhance harmony.

224 Assembling Your Leadership Toolbox

And with Extraordinary Collaborative Orientation

As described in the opening section, the six core tools of leadership wisdom can be seen to manifest themselves in the record of humanity's greatest successes – the achievements of the most influential real and idealized leaders who have proven themselves across a multitude of times, tasks, and locations. As such, in addition to modern relevant and complementary examples, we draw predominantly from two distinct yet complementary sources: *Time Magazine*'s (TM) lists of the most influential and American Film Institute's (AFI) lists of the most heroic.

We will do this via the vehicle of an imaginary assembly of 'Invisible Counselors'. A Leadership maestro conference table to provide insights into how to pull people forward.

So let us call this meeting to order …

The Gavel

Here ye, here ye. I now call this LEADERSHIP MAESTRO council to order.

Our focus is addressing the leadership challenges of COORDINATION.

Our purpose is to animate the tool of EPISTEMOLOGY and leading for UNITY. That is, EXTRAORDINARY COLLABORATIVE ORIENTATION.

The Real

So who might be attending as some of history's most influential epistemology counselors? Let us ask them to introduce themselves (note: all biographical profiles are gleaned from many sources, including the *Encyclopedia Britannica*) and speak to the leadership tool of epistemology and leading for synergy by pulling people together.

Seat One

Perhaps a champion of crafting partnerships.

Like … Nelson Mandela.

I am the first black president of South Africa. My resistance against the discriminatory system helped unify its opposition and focus forces for change. My engagement with the South African President helped finally end the country's apartheid system of racial segregation and ushered in a peaceful transition to majority rule. For this I was awarded a Nobel Peace Prize. After being released from prison I was elected president of the country's first multi-ethnic government. In office I established legislation to investigate human rights violations and launched several initiatives to expand housing, education, and economic development opportunities. I also oversaw the enactment of a new democratic constitution. After leaving public office I did not leave the public spotlight but instead remained a strong domestic as well as international advocate of peace, reconciliation, and social justice. I was also a founding member of a group of international leaders established for the promotion of conflict resolution and problem solving throughout the world.

Seat Two

Plus maybe someone who has established a supportive dynamic of interdependence.

Like … Queen Elizabeth I.

I am queen of England who served for half a century, and this time was dubbed the Elizabethan Age where we asserted ourselves vigorously as a major power in politics, commerce, and the arts. When internal divisions threatened my small kingdom, I helped unify the nation against foreign enemies. The adulation bestowed upon me for this was substantial and different than other monarchs. My methodology for bringing people together was highly successful. It emphasized, for example: (1) Discipline within ranks – Using common enemies as foils and maintaining fiscal prudence for team leadership; (2) Use of marital eligibility – Leveraging and emphasizing the importance of succession planning to team leadership; (3) Promotion of higher order goals and objectives – Appealing to collective benefits and a stated goal of policies for the good of the realm; (4) The importance of walking among the troops – Rallying the nation's spirits by demonstrating bravery and solidarity with my subjects; and (5) Self-effacement – Overt gestures of love, devotion, etc. to demonstrate solidarity of the leader and people and their mutual dependence.

Seat Three

Let us also add someone who has built structures, even an empire, to facilitate coordination.

Like … Otto von Bismarck.

I am prime minister of Prussia and founder and first chancellor of the German Empire. Once the empire was established, I pursued policies in domestic and foreign affairs that succeeded in preserving the peace in Europe for nearly two decades. When I initially became prime minister, the kingdom was considered the weakest of the five European powers. Through my leadership we became successful in uniting our resources to withstand three wars and forge a unified German Empire in the heart of Europe. When I finally left office our European center, once characterized by a weak conglomeration of small and medium-sized states, was now home to the foremost unified power on the Continent.

Like … Kemal Atatürk.

I am the founder and first president of the Republic of Turkey. I modernized and coordinated the country's legal and educational systems and encouraged the adoption of a communal way of life. I also rescued the surviving Turkish remnant

226 Assembling Your Leadership Toolbox

of the defeated Ottoman Empire at the end of World War I and used this to galvanize the populace against invading forces who sought to impose their will upon my people. You can say that I succeeded in restoring to my people pride in their historic Turkishness as well as their collective sense of accomplishment as our united nation entered into the modern world. Over the next two decades I created a state that would grow into a cohesive, viable democracy and world citizen.

Seat Four

Let us add as well a sports coach who impelled extraordinary levels of teamwork.

Like … Pat Summitt.

I am collegiate women's basketball coach at the University of Tennessee. For nearly 30 years I led the squad to 8 National Collegiate Athletic Association (NCAA) championships and compiled more wins than any other Division One college basketball coach, men's or women's, in NCAA history. As a coach I have been quoted often so please consider the following insights into my approach to team building (Summitt, 1999): (1) "To me, teamwork is a lot like being part of a family. It comes with obligations, entanglements, headaches, and quarrels. But the rewards are worth the cost"; (2) "Teamwork is what makes common people capable of uncommon results"; (3) "Teamwork is really a form of trust. It's what happens when you surrender the mistaken idea that you can go it alone and realize that you won't achieve your individual goals without the support of your colleagues"; and (4) "Teamwork doesn't come naturally. It must be taught."

Like … Herb Brooks.

I am an ice hockey player and coach who guided the U.S. men's ice hockey team to one of the greatest upsets in sports history when it defeated the Soviet Union en route to capturing the gold medal at the 1980 Winter Games in Lake Placid, N.Y. Our dramatic victory of college students defeating perhaps the mightiest squad ever assembled in the history of the sport became known as the 'Miracle on Ice'. As a coach I have been quoted often so please consider the following cinematically highlighted insights into my approach to team building (from IMDB): (1) "You wanna settle old scores, you're on the wrong team. We move forward starting right now. We start becoming a team right now! Skating, passing, flow and creativity. That is what this team is all about, gentlemen, not old rivalries. So, why don't we start with some introductions. You know, get to know each other a little bit"; (2) "When you pull on that jersey, you represent yourself and your teammates. And the name on the front (the team) is a hell of a lot more important than the one on the back (the player)! Get that through your head!"; and (3) After challenging teammates to justify their membership and loyalties, they replied … "We're a family" and "I play for the United States of America!"

Seat Five

And finally, someone adept in creating a broad-based climate of coordination.

Like ... Confucius.

I am among China's most famous teachers, philosophers, and political theorists whose ideas have influenced civilizations across East Asia. My vision for developing a community began with a holistic reflection on the human condition. My aim was to transform society by cultivating a sense of shared humanity. I therefore employ a family metaphor that applies to the broader community, the country, and even the cosmos. In this familial relationship we see together the process of becoming human as ritualistically being able to discipline oneself so to be loyal and considerate of others. It is therefore easy to understand why the Confucian 'golden rule' is 'Do not do unto others what you would not want others to do unto you'. You can say that my legacy is centered in my perspective that learning to be human is inherently, unshakably a communal enterprise. Thus, my followers have pursued learning through socialization, and defined a fully socialized member of the human community as one who has successfully sublimated his instinctual demands. Our social vision creates society not as an adversarial system based on contractual relationships but as a community of trust with emphasis on communication. Society must be organized, and each contributing member of the cooperation is obligated to recognize the existence of others and to serve the public good.

The Idealized

So who might be attending as some of cinema's most heroic epistemological counselors who bring disparate parties together for the collective good?

Seat Six

Why not start with Norma Rae Webster?

Norma Rae Webster, in the 1979 film *Norma Rae*, unites textile workers in the rural South to form a union and, together, work to remedy horrific working conditions. The film is based on the true story of Crystal Lee Sutton, an American union advocate who became famous for engaging in activism for textile workers. Portrayed by Sally Field, Webster is outspoken about the need for solidarity and is fiercely loyal to her fellow workers. She seeks to establish a collaborative culture when, for example, she refuses a wage hike if it involves selling out her fellow workers. In perhaps the movie's most famous scene, she alerts her colleagues to management's moves to silence her by writing the word 'Union' on a cardboard poster and showing it to the production line – This results in all workers uniting in partnership, joining together one after another, to halt their equipment. As we know, the word 'union' is defined as the act 'of joining or being joined, especially

228 Assembling Your Leadership Toolbox

in a political context' and as resulting in an 'association formed by people with a common interest or purpose'.

Seat Seven

Then maybe Moses.

Moses, in the 1956 film *The Ten Commandments*, depicts a former prince-turned-exile who mobilizes an opposition of oppressed masses to enable the ultimate exodus of his peoples and delivery from Egyptian slavery. The film is a dramatic re-creation of the life of Moses (portrayed by Charlton Heston) as he becomes a leader of mass appeal and exceptional coordinating acumen who is able to align multiple interest groups, translate complaints into cooperation, allay multiple setbacks and simmering frustrations, and pull people together in a singular movement. Although some see him as a towering figure standing alone, his efforts were enabled by forming a team of able colleagues to divide the work and then combining the parts to aid the whole. Moses' success as a harmonizing leader was further extended in his continuing synergistic reliance on others as well as his role in helping organize the community's religious and civil traditions.

Seat Eight

Further, let us consider Spartacus.

Spartacus in the 1960 film *Spartacus* is a former Roman slave-turned-gladiator who leads a ragtag collection of slaves in unified rebellion of their oppressive regime. Based on the historical novel of the same title by Howard Fast, the protagonist (portrayed by Kirk Douglas) is a prodigal mercenary who later deserts the Roman Army and subsequently becomes enslaved to work in a mining pit and later as a gladiator. In an incredible scene, when captured rebels are offered pardon if they will identify and turn in their leader, they instead band together to each shout "I'm Spartacus!" The maestro-like ability of Spartacus is on full display in his election as leader of the slave army, his unyielding loyalty to his fellow slaves, and the banding of them together for a common cause even in the face of personal peril.

Seat Nine

And how about Mr. Davis (Juror #8)?

Mr. Davis in the 1957 courtroom dramatic film *Twelve Angry Men* helps a collection of diverse citizens find consensus in the faithful, though less expedient, execution of their charge. The film takes great pains to depict each of the dozen panel members as very remarkably different from each other, which then makes it all the more remarkable that Mr. Davis (portrayed by Henry Fonda) could unite them. Within a jury room sweltering in summer heat and an increasingly tense cacophony of argument and counter-argument, the hero manages to point out that their diversity is complementary in seeing different parts of the case, that their practice connects versus divides them in an interdependent process, and that they can pull together to avoid a hung (divided) jury and deliver a verdict with a single, unanimous voice.

Seat Ten (WILDCARD)

I take some publisher prerogative here and add a character that was not on the AFI list but who has made a personal impression with regard to their epistemological lessons. A popular choice in the classroom is Norman Dale from the 1986 movie *Hoosiers*, and rightly so. Portrayed by Gene Hackman, the hero unites the small town team to come together and play team basketball (prioritizing passing over shooting) and advance in their state tournament. As an example, consider the following dialog:

> These six individuals have made a choice to work, a choice to sacrifice, to put themselves on the line 23 nights for the next 4 months, to represent you, this high school. That kind of commitment and effort deserves and demands your respect. This is your team.

However, here I take a slightly different route and instead examine a 'team' that promoted teamwork. The characters are Robert Shaw and John Rawlins from the 1989 movie *Glory*. It is loosely based on the Fifty-fourth Massachusetts Infantry regiment, the Union army's second all-black Union infantry regiment authorized in the wake of the Emancipation Proclamation during the American Civil War. The story involves a young white commanding officer Captain Robert Shaw (portrayed by Matthew Broderick) and the experienced black soldier John Rawlins (portrayed by Morgan Freeman) who was promoted by Shaw to assist him. In one key scene Shaw refuses his salary when his men are not afforded theirs, and in another he stakes all of his command on securing shoes for his troops. Rawlins is similarly collaborative in the mentoring of a strong-willed potential deserter and his forging of common bonds up, down, and across the troops. Together they synchronize the unit, shore up its structure, connect soldiers of discordant interests and backgrounds into a common culture of mutual partnerships, teach the men to fight in complete harmony, and in a climactic scene enable a heroic charge amidst the gallantly carried flag of the regiment.

Even More

We might also staff our 'back-benchers' with additional most-influential nominees such as:

230   Assembling Your Leadership Toolbox

- Leo Baekeland ...   and pulling together in the field of chemistry
- V. I. Lenin and Ho Chi Min ...   and pulling together in the field of politics
- Richard Rogers and Roger Hammerstein ...   and pulling together in the field of music
- T. E. Lawrence ...   and pulling together in the field of warfare
- Lech Walesa ...   and pulling together in the field of labor
- Tim Berners-Lee ...   and pulling together in the field of information systems

The Upshot

During the Meeting

So ... put your coordination challenge on the table.

What do you envision these figures saying about pulling people together to solve it?

When do you see calling upon them for their advice?

How do you see them interacting with each other?

What might Nelson Mandela say about the coordination challenge? How might Queen Elizabeth I retort? Could Atatürk or Otto von Bismarck add anything? And would this be supported, refuted, or amended by Herb Brooks or Pat Summitt? And perhaps extended by Confucius?

Should we also consider the insights offered by Norma Rae Webster for synergizing and increasing unity? Plus how about Moses? Or Spartacus? And certainly we should not ignore Fonda's Juror #8. Nor should we discount the contribution of Robert Shaw and John Rawlins.

In addition, would anyone from the back chime in – say, for example, Lenin, Rogers and Hammerstein, Lawrence, Walesa, or Berners-Lee?

After the Meeting

Do you see how these cases illustrate the principles of epistemology-related, collaboration-driven leadership? Complementarity? Interdependence? Harmony?

What do you glean from our council that might be helpful in leading like a maestro to address coordination challenges that might arise in your life?

Going Forward

How might you customize the content of the council to fit your personal preferences as well as professional circumstances? Add, subtract, or amend its membership to best suit your style and needs?

How might you customize the process of the council to fit your idiosyncratic predilections and references? Use it or preside over it differently?

Lead with Unity

Taken together this chapter's presentation of complementarity, interdependency, and harmony will allow you to enhance this leadership tool and work towards EXTRAORDINARY COLLABORATIVE ORIENTATION.

When faced with integration and coordination-related challenges it will enable you to lead a personal and professional life infused with creating UNITY. This is summarized for your convenience in Table 8.2.

The last part of becoming a wise leader that is discussed in our book is to DO Better. And leading your organization and its people in such a way that they can also do better. We use the metaphor of (well-executed) ACTION for capturing this aspect of wisdom.

This chapter focuses on the fifth step in wise leadership – SYNERGIZING. It is grounded in the philosophical branch of EPISTEMOLOGY. It enables the wise person or organization to be WHOLE at what they do.

In a way it involves unleashing your inner MAESTRO.

However, synergizing is often misunderstood and, more than this, internal limitations and external barriers often prevent us from synergizing well. So …

- Building a better synergizing *core* involves developing insight into the composition and alignment of parts for <u>complementarity</u>.
- A better synergizing *process* involves executing your <u>interdependency</u> for greater communication and conflict resolution.
- *Leveraging* your synergizing capacity involves achieving <u>harmony</u> through enhanced designs of structural/hardware and cultural/software architecture.

If you do this then you will PULL PEOPLE TOGETHER LIKE A LEADER.

TABLE 8.2 Becoming a Leadership Maestro

Leadership MAESTRO	
Challenge	Coordination (Epistemology)
Focus	Pull – Synergizing
Building a Better Core	<u>Complementarity</u>
(D > I)	*Composition*
	Alignment
Crafting a Better Process	<u>Interdependency</u>
(I > K)	*Communication*
	Partnership
Leveraging a Better Capacity	<u>Harmony</u>
(K > W)	*Hardware (Structure)*
	Software (Culture)
Outcome	Unity:
	Extraordinary Collaborative Orientation

9

PUSHING PEOPLE FORWARD

How to Use Your Leadership General (Politics) Tools

How does a leader push people forward?

How do you develop the functional execution of a leader?

In a word – Outcomes matter. Especially in leadership. If leaders do not add value then they are paper-leaders or faux-leaders at best. They are akin to the athlete who can dribble but never scores, the author who can write but never publishes, the student who studies but never passes, the coach who practices but never wins, etc.

You can be smart (logic) and spirited (aesthetics),

Reflective (ethics) and aspirational (metaphysics),

and also collaborative (epistemology),

but … in the end you have to get things done.

Eventually you have to implement plans. Execute visions. Produce results.

You must add value.

If a leader cannot cultivate excellence then they will fail.

If a leader cannot create advantage then they will lose.

If a leader cannot sustainability perform then they will fade.

Here we focus on PUSHING people forward and developing extraordinary functional application.

However, this is much easier said than done.

We live in a world where excellence is too often sacrificed at the altar of satisfaction. Where talk is seen as a proxy for action. Where just good enough is seen as good enough. Where it is okay to merely be okay and just get by.

In organizations, especially competitive ones such as businesses, excellence is essential to success. Yet people are often inefficient – burning too many resources (time, money, etc.) for too few results. And often ineffective – pursuing the wrong targets and being driven by misguided metrics. This causes advantage to diminish

Your Leadership General (Politics) Tools **233**

and ultimately disappear. And today we witness this waning across broad swaths of institutions and industries. Deteriorating operations. Declining innovation. A pronounced lack of competitiveness. Plus, adding insult to injury, over the longer term this produces vicious cycles of failing and non-competitiveness. As a result, we are not learning as fast or as well as we should. Lessons of the past are forgotten and ignored. Necessary changes are stymied in favor of familiar ruts and short-sighted intentions. Falling further and further behind. And systems (as well as jobs) become unsustainable.

As the prior paragraphs reveal, we are often faced with environments characterized by the following … Inefficiencies. Ineffectiveness. Lack of competitiveness. Myopic actions.

So do you still want to be a leader? A wise leader?

Then you must learn to execute like one.

One of the tools leaders must hone and wield is politics. Executing and helping people execute. Pushing people forward and helping others to do the same. Elevating your and their functional application and real value-added.

But don't just take my word for it. Please consider the following insights.

Winning is a habit. Unfortunately so is losing.
−Vince Lombardi

He was so learned that he could name a horse in nine languages; so ignorant that he bought a cow to ride on.
− Benjamin Franklin

Knowing is not enough; we must apply. Willing is not enough; we must do.
− Johann Wolfgang von Goethe

I have come to the conclusion that politics is too serious a matter to be left to the politicians.
− Charles de Gaulle

The world cares very little about what a man or woman knows; it is what the man or woman is able to do that counts.
− Booker T. Washington

Even if you're on the right track, you'll get run over if you just sit there.
−Will Rogers

A cold, hard fact in business, and many would say also in life, is that after all is said and done there is either performance or disappointment. Success or failure. Winning or losing. In short, outcomes are the ultimate measuring stick of leadership. They are our final arbiter and clearest metric. So regardless of how beautifully

234 Assembling Your Leadership Toolbox

the soccer and basketball players dribble during the game, it matters little unless they can put the ball in the net and actually score. If you can convert all of the previous lessons in the book into actual performance, and you do this with an expectation and a pattern of play that normalizes this, then in 'crunch time' you will prevail. Alternatively, if you never push through the pesky barriers that separate the victors from the also-rans then, sadly, when push comes to shove you will be defeated. This is the message of Vince Lombardi.

To make this leap requires an action orientation. A focus on efficient activities. But also an emphasis on effective practices. Book smart does not mean street smart. Knowledge only converts into wisdom when it is used well. So just as reading this book will not make you wise – you have to eventually put it down and actually go live it – so building your capacity and vision does not make you wise unless you can utilize them in the achievement of your goals. Not just being well. Not just seeing well. But also doing well. This is the message of Benjamin Franklin and of Johann Wolfgang von Goethe.

What we are talking about here is classically referred to as 'politics'. Politics is ideally the practical design, management, and leadership of organizations. But this is no doubt what the word means to many of our readers. Politics has taken on a negative connotation in modern times. And the word has become an insult of a sort. About talking versus doing. About corruption versus service. About paralysis ('con-gress') versus advancement ('pro-gress'). This is unfortunate and, in the humble opinion of the author, a chief cause of the wisdom deficiency that plagues our society. Politics is pragmatic and proactive, and politicians need to spend less time on the 'blame game' and more time on solving problems productively. Less time on tearing things down and more on building them up and growing them strong. This is the message of Charles de Gaulle.

Getting things done implies several things. One is in the immediate term. The fierce reality of now. In this sense it refers to operational excellence. Checking boxes. Executing punch lists. Connecting the dots. Making the machines and the processes work. Taking the idea off the paper and making it work in the laboratory and in the factory. Taking the oratory out from behind the lectern or the lecture from the ivory tower and producing the product. Making the rubber … and then making it meet the road. And this is the message of Booker T. Washington.

Getting things done also implies a longer term metric for success. In this sense it refers to learning, to change, to innovation, and to sustainability. Perennially improving in operational excellence. Adapting to and shaping ever-evolving environments (lest one become extinct à la the dinosaurs). Inventing better and better tools. And systematizing these dynamics so that we can not only optimize today's standards of living but do so while enhancing (versus sacrificing) future generations' life quality. Leaders must constantly change in order for their organizations to survive and prosper. The ash heap of history is lined with former industry leaders and titans that never grew or adapted. This is the message of Will Rogers.

So here we are.

Your Leadership General (Politics) Tools **235**

Complementing the prior chapter's discussion, Chapter 9 explains how leaders ENGAGE (i.e., not only pull people together but also PUSH people forward). It is grounded in the philosophical branch of pragmatic POLITICS (*note*: this refers to the original/broad and not contemporary/narrow definition of the term).

Developing this tool enables the wise leader and their organization to become SUCCESSFUL and attain 'real-world' results. In a way it involves discovering, honing, and unleashing your inner leadership GENERAL.

However, the true nature of the leader's engagement is often misunderstood. More than this, individuals' internal limitations and organizations' external barriers can prevent us from truly synergizing like a proverbial leadership general.

So what to do?

Coalescing what we know about leadership politics provides several tools to help us in this endeavor.

In short, to be a leadership general ...

1. Building a better engagement core involves optimizing the efficient and effective deployment of elements to achieve excellence;
2. Crafting a better engagement process will allow you to enhance operational and innovative activity to also achieve advantage, and
3. Leveraging your engagement achievements brings greater sustainability through improved feedback/learning systems and dynamic change mechanisms.

Taken together the chapter's presentation of excellence, advantage, and sustainability will allow you to enhance this leadership tool and work towards EXTRAORDINARY FUNCTIONAL APPLICATION.

When faced with efficiency and effectiveness-related challenges it will enable you to lead a personal and professional life infused with created VALUE.

This chapter is therefore organized as follows:

- Problem: When Facing Execution and Implementation Challenges
- Solution: Activate Your Leader 'Politics' Tool
- Identity: Be a Leadership GENERAL
- Method: To Push People Forward
- Focus: And with Extraordinary Functional Application
- Outcome: Lead for *Value*

When Facing Execution and Implementation Challenges

What is this Type of Problem?

One type of challenge leaders face is efficiency and effectiveness related to Execution, or value-oriented in nature. It involves achieving results. In essence, it demands that you develop the 'politics' of a leader. That you ENGAGE (i.e., PUSH people forward) like a leader.

236 Assembling Your Leadership Toolbox

It is grounded in the philosophical branch of pragmatic POLITICS.

The previous chapter discussed pulling people together and synergizing. This chapter talks about a complementary tool of pushing people forward and achieving extraordinary functional application. This is not an either-or issue. It is the harmony of pull and push that truly drives your behavior as a leader.

An appropriate analogy for thinking is the general. War is admittedly not a perfect analogy for business, though it is certainly a frequently used one. And there are some good reasons for this. They involve the assembling of logical and emotional capacities (lights). They also involve the examining of internal and external exigencies (camera). But after all is said and done they both require action. From prudent planning there must be execution. From sound strategy there must be implementation. From good intention there must be outcome. Too often what looks nice on paper doesn't actually work. But battles and business are not conducted on paper. Paraphrasing poet Robert Burns, in the arena the best laid plans of mice and men often go astray. Leaders and their organizations ultimately survive and thrive based on what they do. They have to perform. They have to win. They have to last. Reality is the final test of leadership.

So ask yourself: Do your people get results? Efficiently and Effectively? To create and sustain advantage? To win in competitive situations? Now and in the future?

Can you engage and add practical value?

To implement and execute like a leadership general?

Net-Net: The sixth core element of management wisdom is getting things done. This implies that the wisest individuals/organizations deploy their acumen and their vision in a flexible, resilient manner to create excellence, realize success, and sustain this success.

This is depicted in Figure 9.1, with emphasis added to the current topic.

So how do you know when you are facing implementation and engagement-related (execution) challenges that require you to be a leadership general? And why are these problems so darned hard to solve?

These issues are addressed below.

How Do You Know When You Are Facing It?

You can tell if you are facing this type of challenge if you see conscience- and integrity-related challenges. More specifically, (1) Problems of Excellence, (2) Problems of Advantage, and/or (3) Problems of Sustainability. Each will be explained below.

The Need for Efficiency and Effectiveness: Dealing with Problems of Excellence

The foundation of value is excellence. This is a measure of the degree to which a person or collective has performed their charge. Although the elements of

Your Leadership General (Politics) Tools **237**

Tool #6
When there are implementation and engagement (execution) challenges...

FIGURE 9.1   Focus: Politics and the Leadership General.

excellence have long been debated its reality has perpetually differentiated successes from also-rans. And its primary components are similarly stable and clear.

In technical terms, here you do not have effectiveness in ends or efficiency in means. Effectiveness means doing the right things. Ends. Targeting Efficiency means doing things right. Means. Using resources well. Thus, in plain speak, you struggle with: What is the most desirable, realistic outcome that we seek to achieve? What is the most practical, cost-effective process to achieve it?

In these cases they indicate that we have a problem of excellence.

This is a Data > Information issue. Political concerns never make it onto your radar screen.

A silly but illustrative example – A bird watcher is efficient if they scale a tree well so as to spot a rare species that nests only on the highest of branches. They are not effective, however, if they scale the wrong tree. Think about it ... How many times have you done the wrong thing well? Driven fast but in the wrong direction? Studied hard but not the material that was in the test?

The key is to do the correct things and do them in the correct way.

If you are ineffective then you cannot move things to their proper place. Is this ever you? Anyone you know? Can you see why ineffective leaders fail?

If you are inefficient then it takes too much time, energy, money, etc. to get there. Is this ever you? Anyone you know? Can you see why inefficient leaders fail?

The best leaders can walk the talk. Identify political (practical) issues of effectiveness and efficiency and the proper tools for solving them.

238 Assembling Your Leadership Toolbox

The Need for Operations and Innovations: Dealing with Problems of Advantage

Once you have a foundation of excellence, crafting a better political process will allow you to tap this potential. Put plainly, there is a difference between performing and winning. Business, as life, is competitive. It is a contact sport. It does not just happen in a vacuum or a laboratory. It happens in the messiness of real-world actualities. You must defeat your rivals who are angling for the same customer base or income stream.

In technical terms, here you do not have competitive operational or innovative practices. In plain speak, you might do things with excellence but lose ... struggling with – What will win today? What will win tomorrow?

In these cases they indicate that we have a problem of advantage.

This is an Information > Knowledge issue. Political input is present but not processed well.

An example: You create a nice product but cannot sell it. Instead everyone is buying your competitor's offering even though it is not technically as good. Why would this be? Well, there are more things that go into winning than just excellence. You might be outmaneuvered. Out-marketed. Out-positioned. Out-networked. The student with the higher grade point average does not always land the job. The poker player with the better hand does not always win the pot. The salesman with the superior technology does not always land the account. See this in the classic case of videotape recordings and the profitability of lesser VHS over the higher quality Betamax standard. See this also in the 'old' Apple languishing at the feet of clunky PCs ... until they learned to not just to be better (more excellent) but to win. Not with the eye of the scientist or artist. Not with the eye of the icon or advocate. Not even with the eye of the maestro. But as a general with the eye of the tiger.

The best leaders deliver results. They come out on top. They do this by out-producing their rivals. In a word, operations. They do this by out-inventing their rivals. In a word, innovation.

The Need for Learning and Change: Dealing with Problems of Sustainability

Once your political potential is established and cultivated then full integration of your value-creating leadership can take place.

In technical terms this is a function of dynamic learning and change management. Extending your excellence and advantage across time and space. Adapting and incorporating the newest developments to stay efficient and effective. To keep winning even when times change. Yet more often than not those on top become complacent. The champ sits on their laurels and stops training as hard as they once did. The executive sits in their office and stops reading, networking, and growing like they once did. In plain speak, you struggle with – What is needed to learn ... to remain excellent and competitive? What is needed to adapt … to expand excellence and competitiveness?

In these cases they indicate that we have a problem of sustainability.

This is a Knowledge > Wisdom issue. Political inputs and processes are not evolved to attaining the most meaningful and significantly satisfying conclusions.

Some examples: Kodak, Blackberry, Blockbuster, Sears, Xerox, Pan Am, Compaq, Borders, Polaroid, AOL, etc. The ash heap of business history. The former titans who sing about 'glory days' while watching their rivals upend and outrun them into the future.

Basically, you need to give two big hugs here. Embrace (1) learning. Embrace (2) change. There is a difference between battles and wars. Successful leaders are in it for the long haul. They stay on top. They don't remain in ruts. They learn from their mistakes. They also don't become static and obsolete. They change to continually become better versions of themselves.

All Together

If we do not rise to meet Excellence challenges then we do not have the effective or efficient foundation to perform.

If we do not rise to meet Advantage challenges then we do not have the operational and innovative posturing to transform this excellence into advantage.

If we do not rise to meet Sustainability challenges then we cannot sustain this performance or advantage.

UPSHOT: Know when you are facing politics, execution-related challenges.

Activate Your Leader 'Politics' Tool

As expressed in the preceding section, the primary tool leaders use to push people forward is sourced from the domain of politics.

Without leadership GENERAL tools leaders are hard-pressed to translate their lights and camera, even when synergized, into actual value-creating results. A leader who cannot perform, who cannot win and achieve advantage, and who cannot activate these is perhaps a leader on paper (and on the organizational chart) but not a leader in reality. And they will not last. Nor will their organizations, at least under their stewardship, if leaders cannot help others create value and attain results. As per the invisible hand of the marketplace or even the visible hand of a central authority, it will soon surrender its entrusted resources and market share to someone who can.

Leaders thus must lead for value. But alas these are not easy tools to acquire and to employ. If they were then all leaders would not have any performance concerns, face issues of sub-optimal utilization of resources both in the short term and over the longer horizon, or fade away and die. Here are some of the key barriers in ourselves (individual) and our environments (organizational) that impede us and our followers from addressing these types of issues.

240 Assembling Your Leadership Toolbox

Some Excellence Challenges Leaders Must Overcome

In terms of efficiency and effectiveness, we do not always execute in the right way. Common efficiency and effectiveness problems include the following.

We fail on costs. Spending too much money and capital. Exhausting too much manpower and energy. A popular, catch-all pseudo-solution to problems is to throw money at them. However, it cannot make people smarter or more intrinsically engaged. It cannot create character or deep-seeded meaning. Further, for those who feel that tightening the purse strings will solve problems typically are more focused on short-term metrics than on long-term objectives. Lean is a manifestation of efficient processes, not a goal in and of itself. When a leader is focused on ill-conceived infusions or nit-picky cuts then this is a sign of trouble.

- Leadership generals optimize costs.

We fail on quality. Not being reliable. Functional. Practical. There has been much written about quality in the academic, practitioner, and popular press. For example, through the work of William Edwards Deming and Joseph M. Juran, among others, Total Quality Management (TQM) methods have succeeded in improving the reliability and integrity of products, services, and their production processes. Through what has been termed the 'quality trilogy', leaders should do this by focusing on quality planning, rigorous quality control, and continuous quality improvement. Quality is a critical element of business excellence, stakeholder satisfaction, and long-term success (see Dahlgaard-Park, 2013). Yet pressures to skip steps, take short cuts, and engage in similar short-sighted practices have left organizations vulnerable to slipping standards and, subsequently, slipping reputations.

- Leadership generals optimize quality.

We fail on speed. Going too slow. Dragging our feet. Or making up for this by sloppy, haphazard scrambling that skips steps and endangers people and reputations. Core work in the field has rightly corrected the mistaken assumptions that speed is about doing the same things only faster. This results in haste, and haste brings a host of troubles. You can go faster and cut costs while increasing quality … if done correctly. Leaders who just crack the whip and hurtle out of control are dangerous. Leaders who drag their feet are less obviously but equally dangerous. It takes but a few cycles of slower operations before companies, or countries, become generations behind their competitors.

- Leadership generals optimize speed.

The above manifest themselves in many forms. For example, they can be seen in inefficient resource allocation. Poor use of physical resources (plant, property, equipment), financial resources (money, capital), human resources (people, energy, ideas), and technological resources (facilitating inputs, processes, outputs). This is also true regarding the critical resource of time. Focusing on what is urgent rather than on what is important. Being managed versus managing events. Wise leaders focus their and their organizations' energies on critical, core success factors rather than firefighting daily swings or chasing flavors of the day.

- Leadership generals optimize resources.

They can also be seen in the poor use and mismanagement of objectives. Chasing the wrong goals. Failing to establish sub-goals, milestones, and checkpoints. Or (and tell me if this sounds familiar) something called 'means–ends inversion' or 'goal displacement' where people pursue process metrics or sub-goals as though they are ends in themselves. Like a person dieting just to lose weight … not as a means to and part of a total system for getting healthier. Or a student studying just for grades … and not per se to actually learn.

- Leadership generals optimize objectives.

In summary, leadership generals must avoid efficiency and effectiveness traps.

Some Advantage Challenges Leaders Must Overcome

Second, in terms of advantage and winning with one's excellence, we do not always gain an edge in the short and long term.

In the short term, common operations problems include the following.

Not shaping the (battle-) field well. Thinking of competition on the basis of what transient products you sell or services you provide is short-sighted and destined for failure. These are but the leaves of the competitiveness tree. But they emerge from strong roots and robust trunks – i.e., 'core competencies'. Technically speaking these are the things that a person or organization do extraordinarily well and should be focusing on. The collection of skills, insights, and capabilities that represent the product of long-term tacit knowledge, learning and investment. At the firm level they represent deep-level, hard-to-replicate, knowledge-based resources and assets that provide sustainable advantage based on an underlying capacity to learn and apply new insights and skills (see Barney, 1991). When competition is miscast then you are competing on the wrong basis and fighting the wrong battles.

- Leadership generals avoid competency traps.

242 Assembling Your Leadership Toolbox

Not playing the game well. The neophyte leader focuses on one move whereas the leadership general sees performance as a function of many interdependent factors interacting dynamically. Superior performing organizations therefore shape a better fit with their environmental patterns and conditions. Strategic actions and outcomes are thus driven by interactions among the factors and decisions as opposed to being linear or isolated. This is well illustrated in complexity and game theories where competitive 'moves' must be assessed relative to what competitors and collaborators do over time and in relation to each other. When rivalry is not framed this way then you are competing at an overly simplistic level and fighting the battles wrong.

- Leadership generals avoid competitive traps.

Not tilting the odds well. Following on from the above, leaders need to manage their networks well over time to retain their edge. For example, in keeping others dependent on them by being critical, rare, and hard-to-substitute. When an organization provides a product or service that people actually need or think they need, that they cannot find elsewhere at the same level or quality, and that they cannot do without then the organization has power in the network. They will be needed. They will be profitable. To do this, leaders develop various strategies to manage two types of resource dependencies and control their access to scarce resources: Symbiotic interdependencies between an organization and its suppliers and distributors, and competitive interdependencies among organizations that compete for scarce inputs and outputs. Various strategies exist for managing them, such as co-optation, strategic alliances and joint ventures, third-party linkages, and, when warranted, mergers and takeovers.

- Leadership generals avoid network traps.

In the longer term, in terms of innovation, common problems include the following.

Mismanaging the innovation portfolio. Leaders must simultaneously compete at multiple levels. They must create things. They must create the platforms from which these things emerge. And they must create the standard for which these platforms are addressed. You should at any given time have a portfolio, or as some term it a 'pipeline', of these small, moderate, and radical advances. Yet some become so obsessed with the minutiae that they miss the next big thing (AI? Blockchain?). Or some constantly swing for the fences and solely chase radical advances so that others profit on their backs by creating incremental improvements and capturing markets.

- Leadership generals avoid innovation portfolio traps.

Mismanaging the innovation system. Leaders must avoid focusing only on the most obvious sorts of innovation: new products. In fact advantages and profits are more robustly and sustainably attained through innovations of new processes and new structures. In making things better. In designing cultures, administrative methods, and hierarchies that govern these relationships. Innovation should be thought of broadly.

- Leadership generals avoid innovation systems traps.

Mismanaging the innovation stages. Let's get this straight: Invention and innovation are not the same thing. Leaders must manage the front-end creation of ideas (invention) and achieve technical success. Guiding the fuzzy front end of scientific discovery. They must also manage the acceptance of ideas (adoption) and achieve political success. Championing and selling new ways of doing things. And they must also manage the leveraging of ideas (implementation) and achieve business success. Systematically diffusing and integrating these things up, down, and across the organization so that everyone is on the same page and commits to the same direction.

- Leadership generals avoid innovation stage traps.

Some Sustainability Challenges Leaders Must Overcome

Third, learning and change are hard.

This involves tacit and explicit elements. What is evident but also what is hard to see. It involves remembering and forgetting. What from the past can inform and what can impede excellence and success. It involves storage and transmission. How to amass broad and deep knowledge (see Chapter 4) and how to inspire change in one's team, organization, industry, and society. Overall, it requires systems thinking. This is the key important factor emphasized in Peter Senge's (1990) conceptualization of a 'learning organization' where learning becomes codified, diffused, and accumulated, and advanced.

Common learning problems include the following.

Failure of 'micro' individual learning. Leaders need to learn the 'who' and 'what' – this is basic learning, essential facts, and differentiates the informed from the ignorant. They also need to learn the 'how' – this is single-loop learning, the immediate steps, and differentiates the capable from the incompetent. They also need to learn the 'when' and 'why' – this is double-loop learning, its underlying assumptions, and differentiates the awake from the sleepwalking.

- Leadership generals avoid individual learning traps – they constantly update and refresh.

244 Assembling Your Leadership Toolbox

Failure of 'macro' organizational learning. Individual learning does not always create organizational learning (see Glynn, Georgi, & Tunarosa, 2013) because: "learning does not exclusively reside at the individual level, since learning can result from social interactions and from experiences in particular contexts or situations. Over time, the new repertoire of knowledge and actions can become embedded in the organization's routines and practices." A way of enhancing this is by maintaining an organization's overall 'absorptive capacity' (think about a good sponge) to assess both what is needed to know and then to actually learn it. Such absorptive capacity depends on the depth as well as breadth of accumulated knowledge, as well as the ability to transfer it across and within sub-units in the organization.

- Leadership generals avoid organizational learning traps – they enable others to constantly update and refresh.

Related to this, managing change and achieving sustainability is hard. It involves overcoming the barriers to change. It involves facilitating the drivers to change. It involves not taking the change far enough. Common change problems include the following.

Insufficient forces or impetus for change. Here leaders do not respond to competitive and technological pressures to match, counter, or exceed their rivals in one or more critical performance metrics. Or they do not respond to environmental and institutional pressures related to political (policy or regime), economic (supply or demand), or legal (statutory or regulatory) conditions. Or they do not respond to social and demographic pressures related to workforce (diversity and readiness) or cultural (attitudes and practices) trends. They can address these through Organizational Development (OD) techniques to promote change via counseling, sensitivity training, process consultation, and similar interventions.

- Leadership generals avoid impetus traps – they ignite change.

Immovable barriers or obstacles to change. Here leaders do in fact recognize the aforementioned pressures but cannot respond because they are stopped. By organizational resistances from its structure (stable patterns), culture (values and norms), or strategy (vision and commitment). By group resistances from its norms, cohesiveness, sub-unit orientations, power struggles, or even dysfunctions such as groupthink or social loafing. By individuals' resistances from their cognitive biases, selective perceptions, habits and personalities, or general fears of insecurity and uncertainty. Thus, they must counter resistors across these levels.

- Leadership generals avoid resistance traps – they enable change.

Limited scope of change. Here leaders do not change enough. This highlights the power of inertia and the different degrees of change (see Corbo, 2013):

Change is incremental or evolutionary when it is piecemeal and gradual, that is, when only a few elements transform either in a minor or a major way ... (alternatively) it is discontinuous or revolutionary only when quantum changes radically shape many elements of structure ... change is traditionally modeled as a punctuated equilibrium process in which long periods of incremental movement are interrupted by brief periods of cataclysmic adjustment.

To make sure that change is appropriate leaders can turn to the tools of action research (see Argyris, Putnam, & Smith, 1985). It begins with the diagnoses of current and desired states. It then plots what types of actions would be necessary to get from the former to the latter. It follows through this with a thorough evaluation and assessment of progress along with appropriate, continuous adjustments.

- Leadership generals avoid restriction traps – they spread change.

UPSHOT: Wise leaders address politics and execution-related challenges.

Be a Leadership GENERAL

The identity best befitting a political problem solver is that of a leadership GENERAL.

A general, as per the *Oxford English Dictionary*, is a person having overall authority. A commander of an army, or an army officer of very high rank.

Generals, by extension, are those charged (and hopefully most skilled) and engaged in advancing agendas for excellence, for advantage, and for victory.

When you picture a leadership general what images come into your head?

Perhaps a sword-wielding stately figure atop a horse?

With medals dripping from their lapel?

Huddled with advisors over maps?

Moving men and manpower to defend and gain terrain?

Or perhaps a down-and-dirty fighter with gritty fingernails and a thousand-mile stare?

Leading the charge up a hill or onto the battlefield?

Generals connote visions of battles and warfare. Of weapons. And weapons are tools for achieving objectives. They are often hard. Steely. They are often explosive. Potent. However, in a less literal sense they also convey a get-it-done approach to the world. One removed from esoteric arguments and abstract figures but instead in the real world of human lives. Blood. Territory. Consequences. Power. Prosperity. Of establishing, maintaining, and cultivating, and advancing the city-state ... i.e., the 'polis'.

246 Assembling Your Leadership Toolbox

TABLE 9.1 Tools for PUSHING People Forward

Better Core: Excellence	Enhanced Effectiveness
	Enhanced Efficiency
Better Process: Advantage	Superior Operations
	Superior Innovation
Better Leverage: Sustainability	Elucidated Learning
	Institutionalized Change

These are poor stereotypes and pigeonholes for sure, but they can be used as a jumping-off point for capturing the character of the general. And as such they may suggest ways for modeling how generals execute and what leaders can learn from them to push people forward amidst the messy praxis of life's ebbs and flows.

Put more systematically, and in a manner consistent with the book's model:

- Generals emphasize excellence. Leadership generals therefore have the efficiency and effectiveness to address real-world politics challenges.
- Generals push advantage. Leadership generals therefore execute an operational and innovation agenda to also address real-world politics challenges.
- Generals seek not just short-term wins in battles but long-term victory and defensible sustainability. Leadership generals therefore manage as well as institutionalized learning and change to additionally address real-world politics challenges.

Leadership generals develop their political wisdom in these three fundamental ways.

The following offers a step-by-step map for doing this. For convenience these steps are summarized in Table 9.1. They are then illustrated as well as elaborated upon in the subsequent corresponding sections.

To Push People Forward

Step One – Building a Better Core

The quality of a person's life is in direct proportion to their commitment to excellence, regardless of their chosen field of endeavor.
−Vince Lombardi

With regard to excellence, it is not enough to know, but we must try to have and use it.
− Aristotle

> *The secret of joy in work is contained in one word: excellence. To know how to do something well is to enjoy it.*
> – Pearl S. Buck

> *Nine-tenths of wisdom consists in being wise in time. / Do what you can with what you have where you are.*
> – Theodore Roosevelt

> *A pint of sweat will save a gallon of blood.*
> – George Patton

> *The question isn't who is going to let me; it's who is going to stop me.*
> – Ayn Rand

> *We can do anything we want if we stick to it long enough.*
> – Helen Keller

We return to the field-general, legendary Green Bay Packer coach (and namesake for the National Football League championship trophy) Vince Lombardi. This is true in military encounters but also in dance, debate, or business battles. Excellence expands options of what you can do in playing 'offense' and 'defense'. It also makes tools more potent. For example, excellence in marksmanship turns a U.S. Marine and his rile into, as per General John Pershing, "the deadliest weapon in the world", whereas the same weapon would be wasted in the hands of an amateur. As per Aristotle and Pearl Buck excellence improves the lives of the leader and by extension their followers. Yet the way you apply excellence depends on timing and circumstances. Leaders must be resourceful. Teddy Roosevelt was keen to do this and conveys that the right thing to do shifts within and across battles. Excellence must be proactive. General George Patton conveys the role of preparation in being excellent. And more than this, it must be consistent and persistent. Even tenacious. Ayn Rand and Helen Keller convey the role of determination in being excellent.

Formally stated, as found in the *OED*: Excellence is the quality of being outstanding or extremely good. An outstanding feature or quality.

It is essentially a function of efficiency and effectiveness.

Efficiency

Efficiency means *'Doing Things Right'*. It is manifest in the ratio of the useful work performed by a machine or in a process to the total energy expended or heat taken in. Efficiency can be enhanced through leadership interventions aimed at better implementation of strategies, such as:

- Streamlining Operations. Leaders need to prudently manage complex, interdependent systems of people, processes, and technology to maximize value for its stakeholders. As per Jeffrey Liker (2004), this is done through lean enterprises to ensure that they are able to meet short-term value delivery goals while simultaneously shaping subsequent iterations and long-term operations. A lean enterprise requires leaders to consider all facets of life cycles in an integrative fashion, eliminating waste and ensuring efficient performance of each area as well as the larger system.

- Reducing Operational Constraints. As per Eliyahu M. Goldratt (Goldratt & Cox, 2004), continuous process improvement involves addressing the weakest links in systems' collection of interrelated and independent processes as measured by metrics such as profit performance, component throughput, inventory, and operating expenses.
- Improving Quality. As per Joseph Juran (1992), leaders need to create value for the customer via the 'quality trilogy' of (1) quality planning, to establish a system development plan to meet quality standards, (2) quality control, to provide a monitoring process to take corrective actions when necessary, and (3) quality improvement, to find better and more efficient ways of doing things.
- Minimizing Transactions. Leaders need to optimize exchanges within as well as between organizations. As per Oliver Williamson (1975), this is done by making sure that economic transactions are governed through lowest cost structural, financial, legal, and logistical arrangements where 'efficiency is the best strategy'.
- Maximizing Control. As per Max Weber (1947), leaders need to establish formal authority mechanisms to ensure that they are based on principles of science and rationality. Moreover, as per Chester Barnard (1938), these need to be supplemented with informal mechanisms to ensure sufficient employee engagement and contributions.

Effectiveness

Effectiveness means '*Doing the right things*'. It is manifest in the degree to which something is successful in producing a desired result. Effectiveness can be enhanced through leadership interventions aimed at better formulation of strategies, such as:

- Enhancing Vision. This involves establishing goals and objectives that are simultaneously aligned with both the external environment as well as the internal capacity of the organization. Popularly known as SWOT analysis (see Helms, 2013), leaders can better leverage strengths to realize new opportunities and mitigate weaknesses that might slow progress or magnify threats.
- Heightening Focus. Leaders not only need to keep their organizations' strategic priorities straight, they also need to keep their own priorities in order. This entails prioritization, or as per Steven Covey (1989), putting first things first. They spend more time, and their best time, on truly important items

that drive success versus constantly being distracted by firefighting minor/peripheral issues.

- Improving Planning. As per Kenneth Andrews (1971), leaders need to assess what businesses a company should be in by proactively plotting patterns of objectives, purposes, and goals. Then they need to align elements of the organization so as to enable success within these defined areas.

Taken Together

Leadership is the force that binds together the critical success factors for excellence at all levels of the organizations. This comes from Tom Peters and colleagues' model and subsequent programs of excellence characteristics. In addition, a primary element of both the 'EFQM Excellence Model' and 'Baldrige Performance Excellence Program' is (now act surprised): Leadership. While it is easy to get lost in the labels and technical terminology, the message is clear. Excellence is important. it is multi-faceted. And it is the purview of leaders to promote it.

So what are you waiting for? Grow your leadership general tool. Start enhancing your leadership execution core.

UPSHOT: Wise leaders are effective and efficient in the pursuit of excellence.

Step Two – Crafting a Better Process

> *There is no security in this life, only opportunity. / In war, you win or lose, live or die – and the difference is just an eyelash. / In war there is no substitute for victory.*
> – Douglas MacArthur
>
> *My attitude has always been … if it's worth playing, it's worth playing to win.*
> – Bear Bryant
>
> *I'm a great believer in luck, and I find that the harder I work the more I have of it.*
> – Thomas Jefferson
>
> *Pennies do not come from heaven. They have to be earned here on earth. / I do not know anyone who has got or gotten to the top without hard work.*
> – Margaret Thatcher
>
> *Farming looks mighty easy when your plow is a pencil and you're a thousand miles from a cornfield.*
> – D. D. Eisenhower
>
> *Nothing will work unless you do.*
> – Maya Angelou

250 Assembling Your Leadership Toolbox

> *Once a year, go someplace you've never been before.*
> – Dalai Lama
> *A comfort zone is a beautiful place, but nothing ever grows there.*
> – Unknown
> *What would life be if we had no courage to attempt anything?*
> –Vincent Van Gogh
> *Those who dare to fail greatly can achieve greatly.*
> – Robert F. Kennedy

There are many ideas conveyed in the above box. More so than in others from the book. Perhaps this is because this theme is so resonant among leaders.

Excellence increases options and establishes a platform for performance. But it does not guarantee results. The best-armed militias or best-funded firms do not always triumph. Races are run against others. Sports are played against active defenders and attackers. Profits are pursued against capable rivals. Battles are fought against combatants. As per General George MacArthur excellence provides potential but no guarantees or inherent security. And in the end there is no 'A for effort' or 'participation trophies'. You win or you lose. Period.

And the sports equivalent is similarly comparable. Nobody recognizes or remembers second place. This is gleaned from Alabama legendary coach Bear Bryant. So how to win? Cross your fingers and hope for it? Sit there and wait for it? Ask nicely for it? No, winning must be earned and victory must be taken. Not with luck, as per Thomas Jefferson. Not from gifts, as per Margaret Thatcher. Not from detachment, as per Dwight Eisenhower. Not from coasting, as per Maya Angelou. It comes from hard work. Pushing oneself and one's followers forward through obstacles and apathy, across trials and tribulations, and sweating the sweat of champions. It also comes from working smart. Finding better ways. Innovating. As per the Dalai Lama this requires experimentation. As per Vincent Van Gogh this requires exploration beyond current capacities. As per Robert Kennedy this requires daring and the willingness to fail. After all, muscled are strengthened by tearing (workouts) and ideas are strengthened through testing (debate). Nothing grows in a comfort zone. So we must invent and reinvent. Create and re-create. Innovate. Triumph.

Formally stated, as found in the *OED*: Advantage is a condition or circumstance that puts one in a favorable or superior position. The opportunity to gain something; to benefit or profit.

It is essentially a function of operations and innovation.

Operational Competitiveness

Operations is an active process; a discharge of a function. An organized activity involving a number of people.

Operational competitiveness can be enhanced through leadership interventions such as:

- Improving position. As per Michael Porter (1980), leaders can identify, create, and sustain a competitive advantage over rivals in an industry by occupying a unique position so as to generate supra-normal rents. They do this by (1) identifying the primary forces in an industry that determine the structural attractiveness of a position, (2) locating themselves within an advantageous niche, and then (3) utilizing an appropriate strategy to create competitive advantage in that niche such as cost leadership or differentiation.
- Fortifying the core. As per C. K. Prahalad and Gary Hamel (1990), advantageous positions must be supported with 'core competencies' – bundles of skills, insights, and capabilities that enable organizations to create, innovate, and deliver value to their stakeholders. Leaders must shape and guide their cultivation through dynamic routines, hard-to-replicate tacit knowledge, and their cumulative path-dependent development.
- Strengthening the value chain. Again by Michael Porter (1985), and digging deeper within an organization's activities, leaders must oversee their organization's primary and support activities so that they can be engaged for customer value creation and competitive advantage. By optimizing each activity so that each component adds value to the final product, leaders can outperform competitors and maximize profits.
- Reinforcing the platform. Once more from Michael Porter (1990), organizations should also strengthen their global 'home base'. These attributes catalyze advantage and the competitiveness of industries and organizations within it – e.g., factor and demand conditions, related and supporting industries, rivalry, and the role of government.

Innovative Competitiveness

Operations are clearly important to creating advantage. But so is their innovation. Innovation is the process applying creativity to invent and update, as well as implement and diffuse, new and useful ideas. It is evident in new products, new processes, and even new structures and strategies to support them.

Innovative competitiveness can be enhanced through leadership interventions such as:

- Encouraging entrepreneurship. This can be done through: (1) Promoting an "entrepreneurial orientation" (Lumpkin & Dess, 1996) of innovativeness, risk taking, and proactiveness, as well as aggressiveness and autonomy in pursuing them for improving long-term organizational performance; and (2) "Pursuing entrepreneurial opportunities" (Alvarez & Barney, 2007) for exploiting competitive imperfections in markets when information about technology, demand, or other determinants of competition in an industry are not widely understood.

252 Assembling Your Leadership Toolbox

- Increasing the speed of innovation. As per Kessler and Chakrabarti (1996), this involves arranging sets of strategic and structural characteristics so as to quickly respond to market demands, accelerate the timeliness of product entry, and improve customer satisfaction. This achieves several benefits such as increased profitability, better margins and market share, favorable industry standards, and preferred distribution channels.
- Balancing the portfolio of innovation. This involves simultaneously pursuing different types (see Henderson & Clark, 1990) of innovative activities such as radical innovations that usher in new paradigms, platform innovations that alter either design or component functionality, and incremental innovations which extend the performance of existing offerings in small but meaningful ways.
- Optimizing the stages of innovation. As per Andy Van de Ven (2013), leaders need to attend to different demands at different stages of the innovation journey: (1) Invention of a novel idea; (2) Developing the idea from an abstract concept into an operational reality; and (3) Implementing the idea and diffusing the innovation across users.

Taken Together

So what are you waiting for? Grow your leadership general tool. Start enhancing your leadership-execution process.

UPSHOT: Wise leaders optimize advantage through the operational and innovative performance of their organizations.

Step Three – Leveraging a Better Capacity

I don't think much of a man who is not wiser today than he was yesterday.
– Abraham Lincoln

If I had to live my life again, I'd make the same mistakes, only sooner.
– Tallulah Bankhead

I am not afraid of storms for I am learning how to sail my ship.
– Louisa May Alcott

One day, in retrospect, the years of struggle will strike you as the most beautiful.
– Sigmund Freud

Sometimes you win, sometimes you learn.
– John Maxwell

Don't find fault. Find a remedy.
– Henry Ford

> *It is better to light a candle than curse the darkness.*
> – Eleanor Roosevelt

> *Be the change that you want to see in the world.*
> – Mohandâs Gandhi

> *We cannot choose our external circumstances, but we can always choose how we respond to them.*
> – Epictetus

> *Neither a wise man nor a brave man lies down on the tracks of history to wait for the train of the future to run over him.*
> – D. D. Eisenhower

> *You cannot expect to achieve new goals or move beyond your present circumstances unless you change.*
> – Les Brown

When we stop learning we stop living. This is because wisdom is more of a process than a thing. It is continuously enhanced or diminished. Thus, as per Abraham Lincoln we must be continuous, perpetual, even resolute learners. If you are standing still then you will be passed by someone who is not. Complementing this are insights gleaned from Tallulah Bankhead, Louisa May Alcott, Sigmund Freud, and John Maxwell. Mistakes are not bad things to be feared – they are opportunities to learn. All great leaders have failed. This is why they are great leaders. Storms are not bad things to be feared – they are opportunities to learn. They force us to develop new capacities, leverage old capacities in new ways, and find a way. Struggle is not a bad thing to be feared – it is an opportunity to test oneself and learn, Losing is not a bad thing to be feared – it is an opportunity to reveal and correct weaknesses.

Related to this is the notion of problem solving. Not crying and playing the pity game. Not finger pointing and playing the blame game. But working problems, learning, and changing. Henry Ford tells us that business is not about (informal, negative) politics and avoiding issues. Instead it is about (formal, positive) politics and owning issues. Eleanor Roosevelt cautions against a victim mentality and instead, in her avocation, to act. If you want light, then light something. And if you want change then, as per Mohandâs Gandhi, change things. It is an ancient but perennial point as given voice by Epictetus. We cannot control everyone and everything around us. But we can control how we face them. Not per se the stimulus but definitely our response.

This leads to the inevitability of change. It is as they say the only constant in life. For better or worse we operate in a VUCA world. That is, a business climate that is simultaneously Volatile, Uncertain, Complex, and Ambiguous. However,

254 Assembling Your Leadership Toolbox

in order to end up on the positive side of the curve leaders must understand the changes confronting them and apply the appropriate tools to manage them. And it is easier said than done. This notion is captured well by Robert F. Kennedy, Jr.: "Progress is a nice word, but change is its motivator, and change has its enemies." It is also evident in Niccolò Machiavelli's warning that: "There is nothing more difficult to handle, more doubtful of success, nor more dangerous to manage, than to put oneself at the head of introducing a new order of things." Thus, the insights of Eisenhower and Brown here are particularly germane. As well as the lamentation by Mark Twain, "Nobody likes change except a wet baby." Well, perhaps nobody except a wet baby AND a wise leader.

Formally stated, as found in the *OED*: Sustainability is the ability to be maintained at a certain rate or level.

There are multiple dimensions of sustainability, hence different targets for a development strategy. Two of the most important are learning and change.

Improved Learning/Elucidation

Learning is the acquisition of knowledge or skills through study, experience, or being taught. Learning is institutionalized when it is established as a convention or norm in an organization or culture. Institutionalized learning can be enhanced through several leadership interventions (see *Encyclopedia of Management Theory*, Appendix-B) such as via:

- Action Learning, with techniques to "develop organizational members' competencies in the process of solving real, difficult management issues".
- Business Process Reengineering, where "dramatic business improvement can be accomplished with radical process redesign that is supported by information technology".
- Double-Loop Learning, whereby "entrenched assumptions and governing values inform peoples' theory-in-use which influences their action strategies; deep reflection on this underlying reasoning process questions the status quo and enables productive change".
- Experiential Learning, promoting "creative tension among four learning modes – based on dual dialectics of grasping and transforming experience – within a dynamic learning cycle that is responsive to contextual demands".
- Promoting Learning Organization, showing that "learning involves more than transferring information; it is embedded in ongoing social interactions and cyclical, multilevel practices and routines by which organizations notice, interpret, and manage their experience".

Improved Change/Institutionalization

Change is the act or process through which something becomes different. The substitution of one thing for another. An alteration or modification.

A new or refreshingly different experience. Similar to learning, change is institutionalized when it is established as a convention or norm in an organization or culture.

As per Kurt Lewin's (1951) force field analysis, leaders need to: (1) unfreeze old habits to generate a need and urgency for change; (2) move the organization by shifting trajectories towards the new, preferred, and intended state; and (3) refreeze and stabilize the new state, institutionalizing policies, practices, and/or procedures. Institutionalizing this change can be enhanced through leadership models and associated interventions (see *Encyclopedia of Management Theory*, Appendix-B) such as via:

- Continuous and Routinized Change – This shows leaders that "revolutions are not necessary for organizational development; continuous, routinized change shifts the focus from 'change' to 'changing' through an ongoing mixture of reactive and proactive modifications guided by purposes at hand".
- Process Theories of Change – This shows leaders that they "need to understand how and why organizational change unfolds over time and the different motors or mechanisms that drive the process".
- Punctuated Equilibrium Model – This shows leaders that "the process of organizational change is marked by long periods of incremental or evolutionary change 'punctuated' by sudden bursts of radical or revolutionary change; each needs to be managed differently".
- Quantum Change – This shows leaders that "large-scale change should be carried out rapidly across an organization's structures, systems, and values when initiating or responding to a transformative event".
- Strategies for Change – This shows leaders that "gaining organizational alignment with an external environment where change seems the only constant requires managers and leaders to implement systematic strategies for change".

Taken Together

Here is a nice way to think about the above. It comes from Elkington's (1997) Triple-Bottom-Line. He encouraged leaders to simultaneously optimize change around three interlinked dimensions of value: People, Profits, and Planet. This enables organizational sustainability for their long-term survival to ensure that their own business models remain valid and adaptable, as well as works to extend the life expectancy of their overlapping ecosystems, enveloping societies, and vitalizing economies.

So what are you waiting for? Grow your leadership general tool. Start enhancing your leadership-executing leverage.

UPSHOT: Wise leaders learn and change to sustain their excellence and advantage.

256 Assembling Your Leadership Toolbox

And with Extraordinary Functional Application

As described in the opening section the core tools of leadership wisdom can be seen to manifest themselves in the record of humanity's greatest successes – the achievements of the most influential real and idealized leaders who have proven themselves across a multitude of times, tasks, and locations. As such, in addition to modern relevant and complementary examples, we draw predominantly from two distinct yet complementary sources: *Time Magazine*'s (TM) lists of the most influential and American Film Institute's (AFI) lists of the most heroic.

We will do this via the vehicle of an imaginary assembly of 'Invisible Counselors'. A Leadership General conference table to provide insights into how to push people forward.

So let us call this meeting to order …

The Gavel

Here ye, here ye. I now call this LEADERSHIP GENERAL council to order.

Our focus is addressing the leadership challenges of EXECUTION.

Our purpose is to animate the tool of POLITICS and leading for VALUE. That is, EXTRAORDINARY FUNCTIONAL APPLICATION.

The Real

So who might be attending as some of history's most influential political counselors? Let us ask them to introduce themselves (note: all biographical profiles are gleaned from many sources, including the *Encyclopedia Britannica*) and speak to the leadership tool of politics and leading for synergy by pushing people forward.

Seat One

Perhaps we should start with someone of action.

Like … Theodore (Teddy) Roosevelt.

I am the twenty-sixth President of the United States. But there is much more to my story. I was also many other things, including: (1) An active soldier who organized the volunteer cavalry known as the Rough Riders that charged up Kettle Hill during the Spanish–American War. (2) An active executive who expanded the powers of the presidency, engaged the nation in world politics, trust-busted by breaking up monopolies, initiated the building of the Panama Canal to expand shipping, and turned my office into a 'bully pulpit' to confront challenges fiercely and publicly (this is supported in a letter where I wrote: "I believe in a strong executive; … While President, I have been President, emphatically; I have used every ounce of power there was in the office. … I do not believe that any President ever had as thoroughly good a time as I have had, or has ever

Your Leadership General (Politics) Tools **257**

enjoyed himself as much."). (3) An active diplomat, winning the Nobel Peace Prize for mediating an end to the Russo–Japanese War and creating the Forest Service to set aside almost five times as much land as all of my predecessors combined. Overall I championed and executed a highly active leadership approach embodied in my famous saw "Speak softly and carry a big stick".

Seat Two

Plus maybe someone focused, even obsessed, with bottom-line results.

Like Thomas Alva Edison.

I am one of the most prolific and venerated inventors-executives that the world has ever known. Some people call me the 'Wizard of Menlo Park' because of the quantity as well as quality of my impact, not the least of which is ushering in the modern age of electricity. I also created and ran the world's first industrial research laboratory and earned a world record 1,000-plus patents. My labs produced many inventions, including the phonograph, the carbon-button transmitter for telephones and microphones, the incandescent lamp, a generator of unprecedented efficiency, the first commercial electric light and power system, and key elements of motion-picture devices and equipment. Unlike some scientists who were content with producing new ideas, I insisted on taking them to reality and actually building them as a machine shop operator and small manufacturer. As a leader it was my approach to never question whether something might be done, only how.

Seat Three

Let us also add a master of seeking victory on the (literal as well as proverbial) battlefield. Among history's most revered generals there are certainly a few who stand out.

Like … Alexander the Great.

I am among the greatest and most skilled generals that the world has known. Operationally, I am supremely versatile in the combined use of different arms and also in adapting my tactics to the diverse challenge of varied enemies and the vastly different battlefields on which I engaged (and defeated) them. Strategically, I am unparalleled in my ability to exploit the chances that arise in the fog of battle and know how to act decisively to seize victory and avoid defeat. For example, my innovative use of cavalry and infantry was especially effective. As a statesman I successfully brought many advances to civilization and spread its influence to create a political as well as economic and cultural 'organization' of unprecedented size. And I also facilitated the establishment of a new coinage to accelerate commerce and trade and maintain the vibrancy of my large empire.

Like … Dwight Eisenhower.

I am a five-star general who rose to supreme commander of the Allied forces in Western Europe during World War II. In this role I directed many operations,

258 Assembling Your Leadership Toolbox

including the assault of Sicily and North Africa, and then launched the Normandy Invasion, the largest amphibious attack in history. After these successes I retired from active duty as the most popular and respected soldier in the country. Then I became president of Columbia University in New York City and published a book that made me a wealthy man. And oh yes, I was then elected as President of the United States where I worked hard at achieving peace by constructing collective defense agreements backed by massive military might. These actions checked the spread of communism and ultimately led to the defeat of new and related threats.

Like … Napoleon Bonaparte.

I am undoubtedly one of the most celebrated figures in world history and a key architect in Western civilization, with many of my reforms leaving lasting marks on the institutions of France and of much of Europe. Yes I was a brilliant general, and statistically am ranked by historians as one of if not the greatest to ever live. But my actions go far deeper than this. I also revolutionized the practice of military organization. I sponsored the Napoleonic Code, the prototype of later civil law codes. I reorganized our education systems. I established a successful accord with the papacy. And in the wake of my many victories I also left many durable institutions, the 'granite masses' upon which our modern society has been built: the administrative system of the prefects, the legal and judicial system, the Banque de France and the country's financial organization, the centralized university, and the military academies.

Like … Master Sun Tzu.

I am the author of the Chinese classic and renowned *The Art of War*, the earliest and perhaps greatest treatise on war and military science. My codified thoughts and action principles have been characterized as the essential systematic guide to strategy and tactics for rulers, commanders, and leaders of organizations. In it I provide insight on strategy and tactics, momentum and patience, maneuvers and the effect of terrain on battles, the use of information and disinformation, and deployments and movements. In an age of constant conflict and competition – military, business, and political – I show how to adapt to situations as well as control situations for advantage and ultimate victory. Because of the inherent unpredictability of battle I emphasize the use of flexible strategies and tactics. This is summarized in the axiom "Know the enemy and know yourself, and you can fight a hundred battles with no danger of defeat".

Seat Four

At the table as well there should probably be someone from the corporate world who is an operational titan as well as an innovative guru.

Like … Henry Ford.

I am an industrialist and businessman who revolutionized factory production with my innovative assembly-line methods. I was the creative force behind the

Your Leadership General (Politics) Tools **259**

development of the automobile and its related industries that generated unprecedented product and wealth. It also changed the economic and social character of the world both directly, through its impact on transportation, and indirectly, through the mass production factories that enabled it. Some say that I was a key catalyst in the rise of the middle class and the (sub)urbanization of society, not to mention the massive construction of superhighway systems. I certainly spent most of my life making headlines, and yes they were both good and bad, but at least I actively took stands and was never passive or indifferent.

Like ... Walt Disney.

I am a celebrated corporate magnate who founded and ran one of the world's largest entertainment conglomerates. And this has brought me renown in many ways. I am famous as a motion-picture and television producer and showman, as a pioneer of animated cartoon films and the creator of many classic characters, and as the meticulous planner of the Disneyland empire – its structure, its culture, and its strategic expansion – which began as a massive amusement park near Los Angeles but then grew to several others across the country such as the massive Walt Disney World in Florida. Today my parks have extended all over the world from Paris to Tokyo. And their gift shops sell my merchandise with amazing velocity. It has been said that my imagination and my execution were key ingredients for the successful Disney brand that has brought much joy (and earned many dollars) from 'children of all ages'.

Seat Five

And finally let us add a modern practitioner of technical excellence, learning, and change.

Like ... Jeff Bezos.

I am an entrepreneur and one of the world's richest people who played a key role in the growth of e-commerce as the founder and chief executive officer of Amazon. Under my guidance the company has become the largest retailer on the World Wide Web. It began as an online bookstore but systematically expanded to music and videos, then consumer products and apparel, and then nearly any commercially available product imaginable. The company, known for its hard-driving culture and innovative policies, has since incorporated web services, a cloud-computing service that eventually became the largest such service in the world. It also released its own products such as e-reader 'Kindle' with wireless connectivity. Now we even make our own television shows and movies with our Studios division.

Like ... Mark Zuckerberg.

I am a computer programmer who as a college student co-founded Facebook, the world's pre-eminent social networking site. As its CEO I piloted its growth to more than a billion users and amassed a net worth in multiples of this. Our site has many components that expand and grow with the changes in the industry, and in the larger world, to continually enhance its users' experience. For example, some

260 Assembling Your Leadership Toolbox

include Timeline, Status, and NewsFeed. Users can also chat with each other and send each other private messages. Users can also signal their approval of content on Facebook with the Like button. Facebook has since become one of the most lucrative advertising destinations and most powerful political influencers. It has been used to impact presidential elections, rally protesters, organize events, and power uprisings. Our economic model has since evolved to earn much capital through advertising and sales of third-party applications.

Like ... Sergey Brin and Larry Page.

We are the founders of Google, the most visited Internet site in the world where more than 70 percent of worldwide online search requests are handled. Our company's name has become so ubiquitous that it is now used as a verb. Our mission is nothing less than "to organize the world's information and make it universally accessible and useful". To do this we complement Google search with functionalities such as Gmail (email), Google Maps (navigation), Google Drive (storage), Google Docs (productivity), Google Calendar (scheduling), and Google Translate (communication). To accommodate this unprecedented growth we built a headquarters nicknamed the Googleplex and an infrastructure of data centers around the world, each of them containing several hundred thousand servers. Google has since reorganized itself to become a subsidiary of the holding company Alphabet Inc., which includes Internet search, advertising, apps, and maps, as well as the mobile operating system Android and the video-sharing site YouTube.

The Idealized

So who might be attending as some of cinema's most heroic political figures excelling at their craft and create advantage to get the job done? Seat Six

Why not start with James Bond?

James Bond debuted in the 1962 film *Dr. No* as the prototypical international spy who uses his skills to resourcefully defeat terrorists, foreign agents, and similarly cast villains. Since then his character has been featured in a number of movies and been played by a variety of characters, most notably (at least according to me) Sean Connery. In this premier movie the action takes place largely in Jamaica. Overall, throughout his adventures, Bond is the archetypical instrument. He is highly trained, ensuring maximal effectiveness and efficiency in his operations. In addition to his silky-smooth excellence, Bond has access to innovative equipment and devices that multiply his performance and give him an edge over his competitors. He is also adept at adapting and, after learning about a foe, changing his tactics to suit the scene. Thus, he always achieves results, accomplishing the primary objective no matter the formidability of the challenge.

Seat Seven

Then maybe let us invite Ellen Ripley.

Ellen Ripley is the pilot officer and space warrior who, in the 1979 film *Alien*, uses her skills to resourcefully defeat very scary extraterrestrial monsters. Ripley (portrayed by Sigourney Weaver) is a formidable hero. And she must be to save mankind from the existential threat of a seemingly unstoppable enemy. She is regimented and performance focused in her operations, following protocol and dismissing other extraneous considerations in favor of a focused, pragmatic 'what-will-work' approach. She is effective in her planning and innovative in her ad-libbing during the proverbial 'fog of battle'. She uses what is at her disposal and creates what is needed but is not. She is capable of making hard choices and carrying them through to achieve desired results. For example, in using the ignition from one of the engine exhausts to dislodge the Alien from an escape shuttle.

Seats Eight and Nine

Further, we should not forget crime-fighters like Zorro and Philip Marlow.

Diego Vega, a.k.a. Zorro, is the swashbuckler who, starting in the 1949 film *The Mark of Zorro*, uses his skills to resourcefully defeat ruthless oppressors. The plot follows Don Vega under the guise of 'Zorro' (portrayed by Tyrone Power), a masked man who defends the commoners suffering under a corrupt establishment. An excellent swordsman, he combines this technical skill with ingenuity to gain advantage over the oppressors and continuously out-strategize and out-fight them. His moves are lightning fast and precise. And more than this, his psychological dueling is equally as impressive.

Philip Marlow is the detective who, in the 1946 film *The Big Sleep*, similarly uses his skills to resourcefully defeat crafty criminals. Marlowe's (portrayed by Humphrey Bogart) method and execution during his investigation is both impressive and unmatched. He takes action when actions are necessary, although his weapon of choice is not the sword but the gun.

Seat Ten (WILDCARD)

I take some publisher prerogative here and add a character that was not on the AFI list but has made a personal impression with regard to their practical, politic-related lessons. This was a hard choice, as a case could be made for several resourceful characters.

For example, in the *Die Hard* series commencing in 1988, NYC police officer John McClane, Sr. (portrayed by Bruce Willis) battles an army of terrorists occupying a Los Angeles tower through superb and inventive interventions that leverage his excellence as an officer with resourcefulness and clever guerrilla combat. Similarly in the *Kill Bill* series commencing in 2003, elite assassin Beatrix 'The Bride' Kiddo (portrayed by Uma Thurman) tracks down and eliminates the former members of her squad who turned on her,

262 Assembling Your Leadership Toolbox

changing approaches each time – à la Bruce Lee's classic character whose jumpsuit she symbolically wears – to overcome the different skill-sets of her foes.

In a related genre, for example, in the *Home Alone* series commencing in 1990, young Kevin McCallister (portrayed by Macaulay Culkin) crafts a series of strategies and accompanying booby traps to repel stronger, more seasoned burglars. Related to this in the 1986 film *Ferris Bueller's Day Off*, the crafty high school senior Ferris Bueller (portrayed by Matthew Broderick) uses his ingenuity to avoid going to school and getting caught by a pursuant and determined principle.

However, in going a little different direction here …

The selection is: Andy Dufresne.

Andy Dufresne, played by Tim Robbins as the protagonist in the 1994 film adaptation of Stephen King's *Shawshank Redemption*, uses his skills to resourcefully defeat a sadistic warden and his prison staff. As a young, successful vice president of a bank he was wrongfully charged with murder and received two life sentences in Shawshank Prison. Here, adapting his financial acumen he gains exemption from manual labor and escapes harassment by his fellow inmates. He also uses them to build a prison library. Then using his skills as a hobbyist stone shaper he spends nearly two decades secretly tunneling behind a poster on his cell wall to escape from the Prison. He simultaneously uses his chess-playing skills to craft a plan for withdrawing the Warden's ill-gotten gains from local banks and then crosses the Mexican border to settle on a beautiful beach.

Even More

We might also staff our 'back-benchers' with additional most-influential nominees such as:

- The Wright Brothers … and pushing forward in the field of aviation
- Willis Carrier … and pushing forward in the field of engineering
- David Sarnoff … and pushing forward in the field of media
- Stephen Bechtel … and pushing forward in the field of construction
- Ray Kroc … and pushing forward in the field of food service
- William Levitt … and pushing forward in the field of real estate
- Estée Lauder … and pushing forward in the field of business
- Thomas Watson … and pushing forward in the field of computing
- Akio Morita … and pushing forward in the field of consumer products
- Pete Rozelle … and pushing forward in the field of sports and entertainment

The Upshot

During the Meeting

So … put your execution challenge on the table.

What do you envision these figures saying about pushing people forward to solve it?

When do you see calling upon them for their advice?

How do you see them interacting with each other?

What might Teddy Roosevelt say about the execution challenge? How might Thomas Edison retort? Could Sun Tzu, Alexander the Great, Dwight Eisenhower, or Napoleon Bonaparte add anything? And would this be supported, refuted, or amended by Walt Disney or Henry Ford? And perhaps extended by Jeff Bezos, Mark Zuckerberg, or Sergey Brin and Larry Page.

Should we also consider the insights offered by James Bond for engaging and getting the job done? Plus how about Ellen Ripley? Or Zorro? And certainly we shouldn't ignore Philip Marlow. Nor should we discount the contribution of Andy Dufresne.

In addition, would anyone from the back chime in – say, for example, Carrier, Sarnoff, Kroc, Lauder, Morita, or Rozelle?

After the Meeting

Do you see how these cases illustrate the principles of politics-related, results-driven leadership? Excellence? Advantage? Sustainability?

What do you glean from our council that might be helpful in leading like a general to address execution challenges that might arise in your life?

Going Forward

How might you customize the content of the council to fit your personal preferences as well as professional circumstances? Add, subtract, or amend its membership to best suit your style and needs?

How might you customize the process of the council to fit your idiosyncratic predilections and references? Use it or preside over it differently?

Lead with Functional Value

Taken together this chapter's presentation of excellence, advantage, and sustainability will allow you to enhance this leadership tool and work towards EXTRAORDINARY FUNCTIONAL APPLICATION.

When faced with efficiency and effectiveness-related challenges it will enable you to lead a personal and professional life infused with creating VALUE. This is summarized for your convenience below in Table 9.2.

264 Assembling Your Leadership Toolbox

TABLE 9.2 Becoming a Leadership General

Leadership GENERAL	
Challenge	Execution (Politics)
Focus	Push – Engaging
Building a Better Core (D > I)	Excellence *Effectiveness* *Efficiency*
Crafting a Better Process (I > K)	Advantage *Operations* *Innovation*
Leveraging a Better Capacity (K > W)	Sustainability *Learning Systems* *Cybernetic Change*
Outcome	Value: Extraordinary Functional Application

This chapter focuses on the sixth and final step in wise leadership – EXECUTING. It is grounded in the philosophical school of POLITICS. It enables the wise person or organization to be ENGAGED in what they do.

In a way it involves unleashing your inner GENERAL.

However, executing is often misunderstood and, more than this, internal limitations and external barriers often prevent us from executing well. So …

- Building a better engaging *core* involves developing effectiveness and efficiency for excellence.
- A better engaging *process* involves executing your advantage through greater operation and innovation.
- *Leveraging* your engaging capacity involves achieving sustainability through enhanced learning and change.

If you do this then you will PUSH PEOPLE FORWARD LIKE A LEADER.

PART III

Leveraging Your Leadership Success

10

A SELECTION GUIDE FOR THE WISE LEADER

Customizing Your Leadership Approach

Part I of this book (Chapters 1–3) was about making the case for leadership wisdom and presenting a model of wise leadership. A case firmly rooted in philosophic insight and grounded in core leadership research. But more than this, a case that at the same time is consistent with perennial, seminal leadership issues as well as and highly relevant to its cutting-edge challenges. The model of wise leadership was then shown to address these issues. With a set of clearly defined, complementary components. Each focusing on a corresponding leadership competency. So the pieces fit together well. In a way that is straightforward and compelling. And easy to use.

Hopefully you have now bought into the program. You know the 'why' of leadership wisdom.

Part II of this book (Chapters 4–9) was about providing the means for leadership wisdom – a.k.a. the 'Leadership Toolbox. Detailing three corresponding sets of tools. The figurative lights-camera-action of leadership. Each necessary but none sufficient for sustainable leadership success. And they represent three dynamic dialectics. Head and heart. Leading with sagacity and spirit. Inside and outside. Leading for character and meaning. Pull and push. Leading through unity and value.

Hopefully you now have a better idea about what it takes. You know the 'what' of leadership wisdom.

Here, Part III of the book (Chapters 10–12) is all about the practical realities of using these tools. In essence it seeks to provide a set of directions for using the aforementioned ingredients. The 'where' and 'when' of leadership wisdom. Or, to extend the cooking analogy, to walk you through, step by step, concocting the proverbial 'Secret Sauce'.

Chapter 10 discusses the initial and most basic direction in using your 'Leadership Toolbox' – choosing the right tool. We will start by delineating the reasons leaders need to be agile by customizing their approach. We will follow this with a customizable

268 Leveraging Your Leadership Success

checklist for assessing where you stand and a mechanism for improvement. We will then detail, section by section, the negative implications of choosing the wrong tool for a situation. For example, being a scientist when a maestro is needed or being a general when an advocate is needed. We will then outline a user-friendly contingency 'if-then' framework/map for enhancing leadership fit and facilitating alignment between leadership tools and leadership challenges.

So, net-net, at the end of this chapter you can get to work immediately – this week, this day, this minute – on enhancing your adeptness.

Simply put, the plan for investing your time in Chapter 10 is to process and master the following:

- The Importance of Agility and Customization
- Sizing Yourself Up
- Summoning the Skill and the Will
- What Happens When You Are the 'Wrong' Type of Leader
- Taken Together: Aligning the Gears
- Implications and Issues Going Forward

The Importance of Agility and Customization

Imagine hearing the following stories around the office break-room or seeing them pop up as social media posts.

As you read the cases ask yourself: *What is most lacking, and thus what type of leadership is most needed, in each of these scenarios?* To this end check one box for each story.

Case 1

My boss is an idiot. Completely over their head. No understanding. They are clueless about the nuts-and-bolts of the business. They just don't get it. I mean, where is the intellect? They can't even figure things out for themselves so how are they going to help us figure things out? Like when we were facing the deadline yesterday they didn't even have a basic comprehension of the issues. Shouldn't they have learned this a long time ago? How did they ever get promoted to boss? Yes, I agree. They could not pick up the major clues and identify what was important. And more than this, they have terrible judgment. I mean, talk about a penchant for making irrational decisions. And not having a creative bone in their body. We wish they could use their head a lot better and help us out here with some intelligence-based leadership.

QUESTION: What type of leadership problem is this?

- ❑ Understanding Problem – Poor Logic/Scientist (Head)
- ❑ Energy Problem – Poor Aesthetics/Artist (Heart)
- ❑ Integrity Problem – Poor Ethics/Icon (Inside)

Customizing Your Leadership Approach **269**

- ❑ Meaning Problem – Poor Metaphysics/Advocate (Outside)
- ❑ Synergy Problem – Poor Epistemology/Maestro (Pull)
- ❑ Execution Problem – Poor Politics/General (Push)

ANSWER: This is essentially an …

- ☑ Understanding Problem – Poor Logic/Scientist (Head)

Case 1 contrasts the ignorant versus expert leader.

Simply put the leader lacks understanding.

Recall from Chapter 4 that there are several tell-tale signs that you are facing this type of challenge: Problems of Comprehension (What do I need to know? What do I need to know about it?); Problems of Assessment (What are the essential facts? How do they relate to each other?); and Problems of Judgment (What is the most rational way of dealing with this? What is the most creative way of dealing with this?).

This highlights a typical situation where, as a leader, you need to invoke your Leadership SCIENTIST Tool by tapping into your inner logic to use your head … and help your people use theirs.

When doing this we can, through extraordinary intellectual prowess, lead with sagacity.

Case 2

My boss is a jerk. Completely icy and distant. No spirit. They are detached from what makes us tick and what inspires us. They just don't care about our feelings or well-being. I mean, where is the connection? They can't even manage their own emotions so how are they going to help us manage our emotions? Like when we were facing the deadline yesterday they didn't even have a basic sensitivity or empathy for what we were going through. Shouldn't they have developed this a long time ago? How did they ever get promoted to boss? Yes, I agree. They could not promote any positivity or upbeat attitude. And more than this, they have terrible motivation skills. I mean, talk about the lack of any magnetism or inspiration. And not having a charismatic bone in their body. We wish they could use their hearts a lot better and help us out here with some passion-based leadership.

QUESTION: What type of leadership problem is this?

- ❑ Understanding Problem – Poor Logic/Scientist (Head)
- ❑ Energy Problem – Poor Aesthetics/Artist (Heart)
- ❑ Integrity Problem – Poor Ethics/Icon (Inside)
- ❑ Meaning Problem – Poor Metaphysics/Advocate (Outside)
- ❑ Synergy Problem – Poor Epistemology/Maestro (Pull)
- ❑ Execution Problem – Poor Politics/General (Push)

270 Leveraging Your Leadership Success

ANSWER: This is essentially an …

☑ Energy Problem – Poor Aesthetics/Artist (Heart)

Case 2 contrasts the apathetic versus caring leader.

Simply put the leader lacks inspiration.

Recall from Chapter 5 that there are several tell-tale signs that you are facing this type of challenge: Problems of Awareness (Sensitive?, Empathetic?); Problems of Attitude (Sense of Positivity? Pluralism?); and Problems of Inspiration (Enhanced Motivation? Influence?).

This highlights a typical situation where, as a leader, you need to invoke your Leadership ARTIST Tool by tapping into your inner aesthetics to use your heart … and help your people use theirs.

When doing this we can, through extraordinary emotive capacity, lead with spirit.

Case 3

My boss is a sleazebag. Completely unprincipled and cut-throat. No fundamental honesty or decency. I wouldn't trust them further than I could throw them. They do not seem to have any core values. They will do anything they want no matter how depraved and corrupt. I mean, where is the moral compass? They can't even look deep inside themselves and manage their own ethics so how are they going to help us see deep within ourselves and manage our ethics? Like when we were facing the deadline yesterday they didn't even have a basic maturity in assessing what is good versus bad. Shouldn't they have developed this a long time ago? How did they ever get promoted to boss? Yes, I agree. They could not promote any authenticity or openness about our agenda. And more than this, they projected personal insecurity and a lack of confidence in doing the right thing. I mean, talk about the absence of any real sense of self-esteem. And not having a reflective bone in their body. We wish they could help us out here by showing some character and principle-based leadership.

QUESTION: What type of leadership problem is this?

❑ Understanding Problem – Poor Logic/Scientist (Head)
❑ Energy Problem – Poor Aesthetics/Artist (Heart)
❑ Integrity Problem – Poor Ethics/Icon (Inside)
❑ Meaning Problem – Poor Metaphysics/Advocate (Outside)
❑ Synergy Problem – Poor Epistemology/Maestro (Pull)
❑ Execution Problem – Poor Politics/General (Push)

ANSWER: This is essentially an …

☑ Integrity Problem – Poor Ethics/Icon (Inside)

Customizing Your Leadership Approach **271**

Case 3 contrasts the corrupt versus honorable leader.

Simply put the leaders lacks character.

Recall from Chapter 6 that there are several tell-tale signs that you are facing this type of challenge: Problems of Morality (Moral Mindset? Maturity?); Problems of Authenticity (Tight Alignment? Enhanced Trust?); and Problems of Confidence (Appropriately High Esteem? Agency?).

This highlights a typical situation where, as a leader, you need to invoke your Leadership ICON Tool by tapping into your ethics to see deep inside yourself … and help your people see deep inside themselves as well.

When doing this we can, through extraordinary introspective insight, lead with character.

Case 4

My boss is a puppet. Completely adrift and without purpose. No fundamental meaning or goals. I wouldn't follow them further than I could throw them. They do not seem to have any overarching commitment. They will do anything they are told no matter where it leads and whom it serves. I mean, where is the direction? They can't even look very far beyond themselves and manage their own meaning so how are they going to help us see far beyond ourselves and manage our meaning? Like when we were facing the deadline yesterday they didn't even have a basic view of our role in the grand scheme of things. Shouldn't they have developed this a long time ago? How did they ever get promoted to boss? Yes, I agree. They could not convey any duty or responsibility about our overarching aims and objectives. And more than this, they projected personal short-sightedness and a lack of perspective. I mean, talk about the absence of any real sense of significance. And not having a service-oriented bone in their body. We wish they could help us out here by showing some direction and vision-based leadership.

QUESTION: What type of leadership problem is this?

- ❑ Understanding Problem – Poor Logic/Scientist (Head)
- ❑ Energy Problem – Poor Aesthetics/Artist (Heart)
- ❑ Integrity Problem – Poor Ethics/Icon (Inside)
- ❑ Meaning Problem – Poor Metaphysics/Advocate (Outside)
- ❑ Synergy Problem – Poor Epistemology/Maestro (Pull)
- ❑ Execution Problem – Poor Politics/General (Push)

ANSWER: This is essentially a …

- ☑ Meaning Problem – Poor Metaphysics/Advocate (Outside)

Case 4 contrasts the disoriented versus big-picture leader.

Simply put the leader lacks vision.

272 Leveraging Your Leadership Success

Recall from Chapter 7 that there are several tell-tale signs that you are facing this type of challenge: Problems of Mindfulness (Clear Ontology? Healthy Perspective?); Problems of Collegiality (Inclusiveness? Duty?); and Problems of Transcendence (Munificence? Service?).

This highlights a typical situation where, as a leader, you need to invoke your Leadership ADVOCATE Tool by tapping into your metaphysics to see far beyond yourself ... and help your people see far beyond themselves as well.

When doing this we can, through extraordinary principled objectives, lead with purpose.

Case 5

My boss is an egomaniac. Completely go-it-alone. Lots of individual instructions but no prioritization of teamwork or actual synergy. They do not seem to have any care about cooperation or building unity. I mean, where is the organization and coordination that we all desperately need? They just can't make us whole. Like when we were facing the deadline yesterday we basically all went our separate ways and didn't even have a trace of structure in the way that we did things. Shouldn't they have developed this a long time ago? How did they ever get promoted to boss? Yes, I agree. They could not promote any satisfying resolutions to our conflicts and did not create any interdependency or a mutually reinforcing climate. And more than this, the way they carry themselves fosters a not-so-subtle sense of discord and an obvious lack of partnership. I mean, working alone we sometimes did fine but, when we met together, geez talk about the absence of any harmony in our collective actions and an inability to get on the same page. We wish they could encourage some real collaboration-based leadership and help us pull together here.

QUESTION: What type of leadership problem is this?

- ❑ Understanding Problem – Poor Logic/Scientist (Head)
- ❑ Energy Problem – Poor Aesthetics/Artist (Heart)
- ❑ Integrity Problem – Poor Ethics/Icon (Inside)
- ❑ Meaning Problem – Poor Metaphysics/Advocate (Outside)
- ❑ Synergy Problem – Poor Epistemology/Maestro (Pull)
- ❑ Execution Problem – Poor Politics/General (Push)

ANSWER: This is essentially a ...

- ☑ Synergy Problem – Poor Epistemology/Maestro (Pull)

Case 5 contrasts the divisive versus integrative leader.

Simply put the leader lacks collaboration.

Recall from Chapter 8 that there are several tell-tale signs that you are facing this type of challenge: Problems of Complementarity (Composition? Alignment?);

Customizing Your Leadership Approach **273**

Problems of Interdependency (Communication? Win-Win Partnership?); and Problems of Harmony (Hardware Structure? Software Culture?).

This highlights a typical situation where, as a leader, you need to invoke your Leadership MAESTRO Tool and draw from epistemology to pull people together … and help your people pull themselves together as well.

When doing this we can, through extraordinary collaborative orientation, lead for unity.

Case 6

My boss is a paper tiger. Completely ineffectual. Lots of ideas but no prioritization of their execution or actually implementing the plans. They talk a good game but do not seem to have any care about building the excellence or skill to accomplish our objectives. I mean, where is the practicality and results-oriented pragmatism that we desperately need? They just can't seem to get things done. Like when we were facing the deadline yesterday we basically all worked to our own levels and didn't even have a trace of efficiency or effectiveness in the way we did things. Shouldn't they have developed this a long time ago? How did they ever get promoted to boss? Yes, I agree. They could not create any source of strategic advantage for us and did not cultivate any proficiency in how we operate or innovate. And more than this, the way they carry themselves fosters a not-so-subtle sense of frailty and an obvious lack of resiliency or sustainability. I mean, talk about the absence of any learning in our collective actions and an inability to get ahead of or adapt to the changes in our industry. We wish they could encourage some real performance-based leadership and help us push forward here.

QUESTION: What type of leadership problem is this?

- ❏ Understanding Problem – Poor Logic/Scientist (Head)
- ❏ Energy Problem – Poor Aesthetics/Artist (Heart)
- ❏ Integrity Problem – Poor Ethics/Icon (Inside)
- ❏ Meaning Problem – Poor Metaphysics/Advocate (Outside)
- ❏ Synergy Problem – Poor Epistemology/Maestro (Pull)
- ❏ Execution Problem – Poor Politics/General (Push)

ANSWER: This is essentially an …

- ☑ Execution Problem – Poor Politics/General (Push)

Case 6 contrasts the ineffectual versus pragmatic leader.

Simply put the leader lacks execution.

Recall from Chapter 9 that there are several tell-tale signs that you are facing this type of challenge: Problems of Excellence (Effectiveness? Efficiency?); Problems of Advantage (Operations? Innovation); and Problems of Sustainability (Learning Systems? Change?).

274 Leveraging Your Leadership Success

This highlights a typical situation where, as a leader, you need to invoke your Leadership GENERAL Tool by tapping into your inner politics to push people forward ... and help your people push themselves forward as well.

When doing this we can, through extraordinary functional application, lead for value.

Sizing Yourself Up

So how did you do on the above quiz? Were you able to see what was most lacking, and thus what type of leadership was most needed, in each of the scenarios?

Now turn the spotlight around and please ask yourself: *Where do I personally stand on each of these scenarios?* To this end complete Table 10.1 by circling one number in each row.

The Selection Issues

Table 10.1 prompts several questions related to selecting the best leadership tool. Here are some particularly powerful ones.

TABLE 10.1 So ... Where Do You Stand?

	Your Assessment						
Issue	*LOW*						*HIGH*
Judgment Challenge	Weak Understanding	1	2	3	4	5	Sagacity
Inspiration Challenge	Weak Motivation	1	2	3	4	5	Spirit
Moral Challenge	Unclear Principles	1	2	3	4	5	Character
Meaning Challenge	Unclear Significance	1	2	3	4	5	Purpose
Teamwork Challenge	Poor Harmony	1	2	3	4	5	Unity
Implementation Challenge	Poor Execution	1	2	3	4	5	Value

Row One

This is based in Chapter 4, The Mind of a Leader, and is illustrated in Case 1 ('My boss is an idiot').

Can you identify a judgment challenge when you see one?

Is it evident where and when a lack of understanding is the problem?

Do you know how to use logic-related tools?

Taking on the identity of a leadership scientist?

To use your head?

And lead with sagacity?

Row Two

This is based in Chapter 5, The Heart of a Leader, and is illustrated in Case 2 ('My boss is a jerk').

Can you identify an emotional challenge when you see one?
Is it evident where and when a lack of inspiration is the problem?
Do you know how to use aesthetic-related tools?
Taking on the identity of a leadership artist?
To use your heart?
And lead with spirit?

Row Three

This is based in Chapter 6, Looking Deep Inside Yourself, and is illustrated in Case 3 ('My boss is a sleazebag').

Can you identify a moral challenge when you see one?
Is it evident when a lack of principles is the problem?
Do you know how to use ethics-related tools?
Taking on the identity of a leadership icon?
To see deep within yourself?
And lead through character?

Row Four

This is based in Chapter 7, Looking Far Outside Yourself, and is illustrated in Case 4 ('My boss is a puppet').

Can you identify a meaning challenge when you see one?
Is it evident where and when a lack of significance is the problem?
Do you know how to use metaphysics-related tools?
Taking on the identity of a leadership advocate?
To see far beyond yourself?
And lead through purpose?

Row Five

This is based in Chapter 8, Pulling People Together, and is illustrated in Case 5 ('My boss is an egomaniac').

Can you identify a teamwork challenge when you see one?
Is it evident where and when a lack of harmony is the problem?
Do you know how to use epistemology-related tools?
Taking on the identity of a leadership maestro?
To pull people together?
And lead for unity?

276 Leveraging Your Leadership Success

Row Six

This is based in Chapter 9, Pushing People Forward, and is illustrated in Case 6 ('My boss is a paper tiger').

Can you identify an implementation challenge when you see one?
Is it evident where and when a lack of execution is the problem?
Do you know how to use politics-related tools?
Taking on the identity of a leadership general?
To push people forward?
And lead for value?

The Selection Scoring and Implications

So How Did You Do?

Here is a way of interpreting your self-assessments:

- If you scored a five on any of these then you know how and when to use this tool. It will still require constant honing and periodic maintenance but the foundation is there.
- If you scored a three or four on any of these then there is still some meaningful work to be done.
- If you scored a one or two on any of these then there is a dangerous gap in your leadership style that will require a more serious adjustment.

Leaders need both the skill and the will to customize their emphasis and match their identity to their dominant challenge.

The Skill

Skill is a question of ability. You must be able to do these things.

First, the ability to develop and deploy each of the tools as described in the previous section. Second, the 'meta' ability to (1) read situations, and (2) switch styles. Whereas chapters 4 to 9 discussed the former we now consider the latter.

How can a leader 'read' situations? What skill is required?
Environmental scanning. Of situations. Of people.
How can a leader 'adapt' to situations? What skill is required?
A stable core, or nucleus.
A full toolbox, or orbitals.

The Will

Will is a question of desire. You must be willing to do these things.

Customizing Your Leadership Approach **277**

First, the desire to develop and deploy each of the tools as described in the previous section. Second, and similar to the prior paragraph, the 'meta' desire to (1) read situations, and (2) switch styles. Whereas chapters 4 to 9 discussed the former we now consider the latter.

Why would a leader want to 'read' situations?

A drive to succeed. A drive to sustainably succeed.

And a realization that it is needed for the furtherance of each of these, especially in today's dynamic, complex, hyper-competitive environment.

Why would a leader want to adapt to situations?

Again, a drive to succeed in both the short and long term.

And again a realization that it is needed for the furtherance of each of these.

Summoning the Skill and the Will

Table 10.2 depicts various combinations of skill and will. It is helpful in the abstract for seeing the possibilities. But more important it is helpful to diagnose oneself and one's leadership situation/needs.

TABLE 10.2 Do You Have the Skill and the Will?

SKILL WILL	Low	High
Low	1 Mistaken (Wrong)	3 Misguided (Blind)
High	2 Misplaced (Lame)	4 Actual (Success)

Quadrant 1

If you are both LOW in skill and LOW in will then you risk being a *MISTAKEN* leader.

This is the kind version of the label; the more direct one is that you are the proverbial hot mess or smoldering dumpster fire of a leader. There exists neither the ability to do the job nor the desire to do it. In other words, you can't and you won't. Clueless. Anemic.

In a word, at this time you are the wrong person for the job. Short-term performance and long-term prospects will be bleak. The result will likely be failure for you and for those in your charge.

You should NOT be a leader if you have neither the skill nor the will to evoke the appropriate leadership tools to solve the core leadership challenges. Much must change.

Do you know anyone who is (not) leading in this quadrant?

Is it you?

278 Leveraging Your Leadership Success

Quadrant 2

If you are LOW skill but HIGH in will then you are a *MISPLACED* leader.

The drive is there but the proverbial body cannot cash the checks that you are writing. In other words, you will but you can't. Aware but incapable.

This is a frustrating situation both for the prospective leader and for their followers. Good intentions by themselves do not lead to good outcomes.

The likely result is well-intentioned but lame leadership. The problem is a lack of potency. Weak but well-intentioned efforts. You try to do the right things but do them in the wrong way. Simply put, at this time you are over your head. Capacity must change.

Do you know anyone who is (partially) leading in this quadrant?

Is it you?

Quadrant 3

If you are HIGH skill but LOW in will then you are a *MISGUIDED* leader.

The capacity is there but there is no energy or intention. In other words, you can but you won't. Strong but oblivious.

This is also an unpleasant situation for both for the prospective leader and their followers. However, it is due to a different reason than the above. Resources are wasted or deployed in the wrong directions.

The result is high potential but ultimately blind leadership. The problem is a lack of direction. Strong but off-target efforts. You do the wrong things really well. Simply put, at this time you are out of step. Intentionality must change.

Do you know anyone who is (partially) leading in this quadrant?

Is it you?

Quadrant 4

If you are both HIGH in skill and HIGH in will then you are an *ACTUAL* leader.

There exists both the ability to do it and the desire to do it. In other words, you can and you will. Aware and capable.

In a word, you are the right person for the job in every sense – short-term performance and long-term prospects are bright. The likely results will skyrocket into that rare air of sustainable success.

Do you know anyone who is (actually) leading in this quadrant?

Is it you?

Taken Together

So … Which of these four people are you?

It is important to know who you are because different interventions are appropriate for each quadrant. One needs major surgery. Four benefits more from

Customizing Your Leadership Approach **279**

tweaking and a tune-up. Two and three require more focused remedies but the focus is critical. A capable person does not need re-teaching – they need orienting. A well-intentioned person does not need re-motivating – they need the skill-sets.

Notwithstanding, it should be evident that the key to wise leadership is to marshal both the skill along with the will to lead well.

With regard to the will – drive and determination – it is my hope that after nine chapters you are on board. You have self-selected, or been nudged, into the program. If not then please feel free to circle back.

With regard to the skill – capacity and resources – it is my hope that the prior chapters have also provided you with at least a fundamental grasp of the core principles of the model.

This chapter will 'amp them up' by discussing the method of selecting the right tool.

And, following this, Chapter 11 will further amp up the method of optimizing them by focusing on the capitalization of strengths. And the final chapter (Chapter 12) will correspondingly amp up the method of sustaining them by focusing on the mitigation of threats.

So let us now turn to the issue of selection.

What Happens When You Are the 'Wrong' Type of Leader

It is the central contention of this book that leaders develop the skill and the will to MATCH the right tool to the right job. It is not enough to understand the model (Part I) and stock the toolbox (Part II). You need to be willing and able to adapt.

In other words, to develop and evoke the appropriate type of leadership identity for the dominant challenge at hand.

A lot of bad things can happen when this does not occur. Here is an overview of the reckonings different mismatches bring. As an ill-timed … scientist, artist, icon, advocate, maestro, and general. They are illustrated in Table 10.3.

Can you identify where any leaders (or even you) have resided? Why they succeeded or failed?

So be forewarned. To first avoid these situations. And then to know how to move away from incompatibilities when necessary.

The Ill-Emphasized Scientist

Your Leadership SCIENTIST tool should be matched to COGNITIVE challenges.

Here you apply this logic-based identity to solve thinking and understanding-related issues with SAGACITY. If you try to be a scientist at the wrong time, then you do not solve the dominant problem. For example,

TABLE 10.3 (Mis)Matching Leadership Tools to Leadership Challenges

Challenge: Tool:	Cognitive Challenges	Affective Challenges	Integrity Challenges	Significance Challenges	Connection Challenges	Execution Challenges
Scientist	**SAGACITY**	Disinterested	Hazardous	Arbitrary	Disputed	Abstract
Artist	Distorted	**SPIRIT**	Twisted	Aimless	Fractioned	Chaotic
Icon	Lax	Resigned	**CHARACTER**	Absorbed	Divisive	Helpless
Advocate	Feeble	Submissive	Herd-Like	**PURPOSE**	Discordant	Frustrated
Maestro	Foolish	Inertial	Malicious	Apathetic	**UNITY**	Futile
General	Erroneous	Antagonistic	Dishonorable	Hollow	Inconsistent	**VALUE**

Sagacity does not solve affective challenges. It does not provide motivation. If you lead like a scientist when an artist is needed, then ... you will just perpetuate disinterest. Never win them over. Scratch deeper and deeper but never hit the itch.

Sagacity does not solve integrity challenges. It does not provide moral guidance. If you lead like a scientist when an icon is needed, then ... you can even make things more hazardous insofar as greater ability is available for questionable ethical pursuits.

Sagacity does not solve significance challenges. It does not provide meaning. If you lead like a scientist when an advocate is needed, then ... your superior ability remains arbitrary, scattered, and ill-focused. You might be driving your people faster but in the wrong direction.

Sagacity does not solve connection challenges. It does not pull things together. If you lead like a scientist when a maestro is needed, then ... you just prompt further adversity and disputes among increasingly stronger rivals. Wars are not settled, only escalated.

Sagacity does not solve execution challenges. It does not provide engagement. If you lead like a scientist when a general is needed, then ... you just increase the unused, wasted abstract potential that never translates into results. More and more latent power sits around, is poorly deployed, or is under-utilized while the planning and the debating never end.

As you can see, leadership scientists are successful when the issues are about better comprehending situations with a breadth and depth of knowledge, assessing them through sharper perception and keener intuition; and making judgments that are rational and creative. This logical tool is highly effective in these situations. It is less so, even ineffective, in others. And as the above also suggests it can be dangerous.

If logic is the only instrument in your toolbox then you are a one-trick pony whose star will fade when situations are more complex and their challenges change. You might do well when facing narrowly defined cognitive-related challenges. However, your leadership success will not be complete or sustainable.

The Ill-Emphasized Artist

Your Leadership ARTIST tool should be matched to AFFECTIVE challenges.

Here you apply this aesthetic-based identity to solve feeling and inspiration-related issues with SPIRIT. If you try to be an artist at the wrong time, then you do not solve the dominant problem. For example,

Spirit does not solve cognitive challenges. It does not provide knowledge and understanding. If you lead like an artist when a scientist is needed, then ... you may distort reality, but at an even more animated or intense level. And by better inspiring less logical followers you can actually make the problem worse.

Spirit does not solve integrity challenges. It does not provide moral guidance. If you lead like an artist when an icon is needed, then ... you just twist the

282 Leveraging Your Leadership Success

proverbial moral compass even further askew. And by better inspiring less ethical followers you can actually make the problem worse.

Spirit does not solve significance challenges. It does not provide meaning. If you lead like an artist when an advocate is needed, then … you remain aimless, surging adrift further and faster. And by better inspiring less oriented followers you can actually make the problem worse.

Spirit does not solve connection challenges. It does not pull things together. If you lead like an artist when a maestro is needed, then … you just add friction, or fuel, to an already raging fire. And by better inspiring less cohesive, fractioned followers you can actually make the problem worse.

Spirit does not solve execution challenges. It does not provide engagement. If you lead like an artist when a general is needed, then … you just create more chaos. And by better inspiring less effective followers you (yes, you probably guessed it) can actually make the problem worse.

As you can see, leadership artists are successful when the issues are about showing a sensitive and empathetic emotional awareness; projecting a positive and pluralistic attitude; and inspiring others through motivation and influence. This aesthetic tool is highly effective in these situations. It is less so, even ineffective, in others. And as the above also suggest it can be dangerous.

If aesthetics is the only instrument in your toolbox, then you are a one-trick pony whose star will fade when situations are more complex and their challenges change. You might do well when facing narrowly defined affective-related challenges. However, your leadership success will not be complete or sustainable.

The Ill-Emphasized Icon

Your Leadership ICON tool should be matched to INTEGRITY challenges.

Here you apply this ethics-based identity to solve moral and principle-related issues with CHARACTER. If you try to be an icon at the wrong time, then you do not solve the dominant problem. For example,

Character does not solve cognitive challenges. It does not provide knowledge and understanding. If you lead like an icon when a scientist is needed, then … your results might be a benign, yet lax and ill-informed, set of intentions.

Character does not solve affective challenges. It does not provide motivation. If you lead like an icon when an artist is needed, then … your results might be a resigned non-energized set of intentions.

Character does not solve significance challenges. It does not provide meaning. If you lead like an icon when an advocate is needed, then … your results might be a self-absorbed, ill-guided set of intentions.

Character does not solve connection challenges. It does not pull things together. If you lead like an icon when a maestro is needed, then … your results might be a divided, poorly aligned set of intentions.

Character does not solve execution challenges. It does not provide engagement. If you lead like an icon when a general is needed, then … your results might be a helpless, poorly implemented set of intentions.

As you can see, leadership icons are successful when the issues are dependent on having a moral mindset and maturity, approaching things authentically with alignment and trustworthiness, and having enough confidence through esteem and agency to do the right thing. This ethical tool is highly effective in these situations. It is less so, even ineffective, in others. And as the above also suggest it can be dangerous.

If ethics is the only instrument in your toolbox, then you are a one-trick pony whose star will fade when situations are more complex and their challenges change. You might do well when facing narrowly defined integrity-related challenges. However, your leadership success will not be complete or sustainable.

The Ill-Emphasized Advocate

Your Leadership ADVOCATE tool should be matched to SIGNIFICANCE challenges.

Here you apply this metaphysics-based identity to solve meaning and mission-related issues with PURPOSE. If you try to be an advocate at the wrong time, then you do not solve the dominant problem. For example,

Purpose does not solve cognitive challenges. It does not provide knowledge and understanding. If you lead like an advocate when a scientist is needed, then … you might just create a feeble wanting to go somewhere but not knowing how.

Purpose does not solve affective challenges. It does not provide motivation. If you lead like an advocate when an artist is needed, then … you might create a submissive wanting to go somewhere that is not sufficiently energized or invigorated.

Purpose does not solve integrity challenges. It does not provide moral guidance. If you lead like an advocate when an icon is needed, then … you might just create a herd-like rush wanting to go somewhere but without reflection or grounding.

Purpose does not solve connection challenges. It does not pull things together. If you lead like an advocate when a maestro is needed, then … you might just create a discord-ridden set of wanting to go somewhere that is not cohesive or reconciled.

Purpose does not solve execution challenges. It does not provide engagement. If you lead like an advocate when a general is needed, then … you might just create a spectacular flop because the frustrated wanting to go somewhere cannot be translated into concrete action plans or action steps.

As you can see, leadership advocates are successful when the issues are about mindfully developing the ontology and perspective on one's place in the world, finding the collegiality to do so with a sense of inclusiveness and of responsibility,

284 Leveraging Your Leadership Success

and marshaling the transcendence to put them into action with munificence and through service. This metaphysical tool is highly effective in these situations. It is less so, even ineffective, in others. And as the above also suggest it can be dangerous.

If metaphysics is the only instrument in your toolbox, then you are a one-trick pony whose star will fade when situations are more complex and their challenges change. You might do well when facing narrowly defined meaning-related challenges. However, your leadership success will not be complete or sustainable.

The Ill-Emphasized Maestro

Your Leadership MAESTRO tool should be matched to CONNECTION challenges.

Here you apply this epistemology-based identity to solve integration and coordination-related issues with UNITY. If you try to be a maestro at the wrong time, then you do not solve the dominant problem. For example,

Unity does not solve cognitive challenges. It does not provide knowledge and understanding. If you lead like a maestro when a scientist is needed, then … you might magnify the folly by putting more people behind it.

Unity does not solve affective challenges. It does provide motivation. If you lead like a maestro when an artist is needed, then … you might magnify the inertia by stagnating more people within it.

Unity does not solve integrity challenges. It does not provide moral guidance. If you lead like a maestro when an icon is needed, then … you might magnify the malice by corrupting more people for it.

Unity does not solve significance challenges. It does not provide meaning. If you lead like a maestro when an advocate is needed, then … you might magnify the apathy by exiling more people from it.

Unity does not solve execution challenges. It does not provide engagement. If you lead like a maestro when a general is needed, then … you might magnify the futility by obstructing more people from it.

As you can see, leadership maestros are successful when the issues are complementarity and establishing the ideal composition and alignment of parts, interdependency, and developing processes of good communication and conflict resolution, and harmony through the design of facilitating architectures both formal (structure) and informal (culture). This epistemological tool is highly effective in these situations. It is less so, even ineffective, in others. And as the above also suggest it can be dangerous.

If epistemology is the only instrument in your toolbox, then you are a one-trick pony whose star will fade when situations are more complex and their challenges change. You might do well when facing narrowly defined teamwork-related challenges. However, your leadership success will not be complete or sustainable.

The Ill-Emphasized General

Your Leadership GENERAL tool should be matched to EXECUTION challenges.

Here you apply this politics-based identity to solve efficiency and effectiveness-related issues with VALUE. If you try to be a general at the wrong time, then you do not solve the dominant problem. For example,

Value does not solve cognitive challenges. It does not provide knowledge and understanding. It enables active dependence because behaviors are no more informed. If you lead like a general when a scientist is needed, then ... you can actually make the problem worse because increasing movement and commitment to erroneous, ill-informed actions might magnify their mistakes.

Value does not solve affective challenges. It does not provide motivation. It enables active revolt because behaviors are no more energized. If you lead like a general when an artist is needed, then ... you can actually make the problem worse because increasing movement and commitment to unappealing actions might magnify antagonism and distaste for those actions.

Value does not solve integrity challenges. It does not provide moral guidance. It enables active evil because behaviors are no more ethical. If you lead like a general when an icon is needed, then ... you can actually make the problem worse because executing a series of increasingly immoral actions upon immoral actions might magnify how dishonorable one becomes.

Value does not solve significance challenges. It does not provide meaning. It enables active indifference because behaviors are no more purposeful. If you lead like a general when an advocate is needed, then ... you can actually make the problem worse because executing a series of increasingly hollow actions upon hollow actions might magnify how lost one becomes.

Value does not solve connection challenges. It does not pull things together. It enables active disharmony and inconsistency because behaviors are no more synergized. If you lead like a general when a maestro is needed, then ... you can (yes, you probably guessed it) actually make the problem worse because pushing vicious circles of conflicting, inconsistent actions upon inconsistent actions might magnify discord and result in implosion.

As you can see, leadership generals are successful when the issues are about excellence via the cultivation of efficiency and effectiveness, advantage via high-performing operations and high-impact innovation, and sustainability via institutionalized learning and the management of change. This political tool is highly effective in these situations. It is less so, even ineffective, in others. And as the above also suggest it also can be dangerous.

If politics is the only instrument in your toolbox, then you are a one-trick pony whose star will fade when situations are more complex and their challenges change. You might do well when facing narrowly defined execution-related challenges. However, your leadership success will not be complete or sustainable.

Taken Together: Aligning the Gears

One way of conceptualizing this is to imagine two complementary GEARS or wheels of (1) Leadership tools, and (2) Leadership challenges. Each leadership wheel is calibrated along the six dimensions of leadership wisdom and each challenge wheel is calibrated along the corresponding six dimensions of leadership challenges.

Over TIME – Wise leaders should thereby orient themselves to aligning the wheels (1) statically, and (2) dynamically so that alignment can be optimized in both the immediate and long term. Regarding a static snapshot of the gears aligning: It is good to match problems with their best mechanisms to generate solutions. Regarding a dynamic cinema of the gears continually aligning: It is better to do this constantly and consistently.

Across LEVELS – Wise leaders should also align them (1) individually, and (2) institutionally so that alignment can be optimized within both the micro and across the macro context. Regarding individual alignment: The leader matches their identity to solve their dominant challenges. Regarding institutional alignment: The organization (business, government, family, etc.) rotates and deploys their leaders' identities to solve their dominant challenges. They can do this in myriad ways. Of course this is easiest when a firm develops leaders in a manner that they are high in all capacities and can diagnose the means for appropriately deploying them. However, this is not always the case. This will be discussed further in the forthcoming chapters.

Such a static-dynamic and individual-institutional wisdom-based approach helps us appreciate that wise leadership is, at its philosophical core, essentially a mega/meta-competency which involves (1) the meta-monitoring skills for

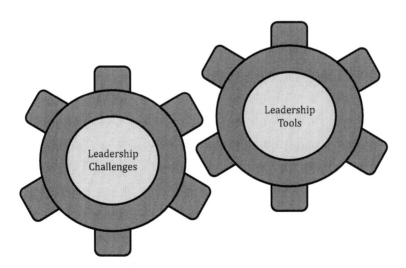

FIGURE 10.1 Customizing Your Approach (Aligning the Gears).

Customizing Your Leadership Approach **287**

leaders to make sense of the dominant situational elements and role identities, and (2) the corresponding mega-heuristics to activate and execute appropriate wise leadership tools for facilitating sustainable personal and professional success.

Meta-monitoring … the skill and will to identify what is needed.

Mega-heuristics … the skill and will to become what is needed.

If we combine <u>ALL SIX</u> of the aforementioned dimensions we can see how synergistic, alacritous application of these tools can address their corresponding tasks.

For example, but not exclusively, consider the following cases (while keeping in mind that these individuals are not perfect – just relatively well-rounded and agile in their leadership approaches). They certainly present happier stories than those used to open this chapter.

Case A

This man relentlessly walked a path to truth. He was not the largest of men. In fact he was physically small and not terribly athletic. He was smart but there were others who achieved higher marks. He did not come from great wealth or royalty. However, he had something that none of this could buy – a constant drive to learn and grow as well as an enlightened sense of responsibility to use his abilities in the service of others. He went to school and became a lawyer. What he found on his journey was that education was important but not sufficient to find his calling and succeed both as a person and as an agent of something bigger.

When confronting problems of understanding, he needed to constantly develop his intelligence and broaden it to rub up against life. Rational problems faced him – he needed to hone his judgment. To decipher legal nuance. Creative problems also faced him – he needed to hone his imagination. To upend a stronger foe. He also needed to marry this formidable head with a constantly developing heart. To see the strivings of real people, their dreams and their challenges, and connect with this in a holistic, spiritual sense.

He needed to look inward, deep within himself, in his 'great soul', to get in touch with his core. To not take ethical short cuts and do bad things in pursuit of the good. He needed to look outward to find his place in the grander scheme of things. To place current challenges in their proper context. To unite the intensely personal stories of those in his charge with the callings of his faith and his spirituality.

And he also needed to act. To become unified and whole as well as bring his colleagues, fellow citizens, and stakeholders together. To encourage teamwork. To strengthen a culture. To form a country. And not just talk the walk but actually walk the talk. Get off the hilltop and into the arena of human affairs. Implement what was imagined. Adjust to what was planned. Innovate beyond what was thought possible. Achieve what was thought unattainable.

Later this tiny man would supersede his limitations and cast off his chains, both externally as well as internally imposed, to become one of the true lions of

288 Leveraging Your Leadership Success

history. A leader among leaders. Reaching the pinnacle of personal development and helping millions ascend with him. You see, he did things that most people do not or cannot dedicate themselves to do. And more than this, he did things that most leaders – leaders in politics, business, social group, or family – do not or cannot do for their followers. He loved and lived wisdom. He made himself and others better.

Question – Who is this person?

Answer – *Mohandâs Gandhi*

Case B

It is patently unfair to compare someone with Gandhi. However, we do not need to be Gandhi to be wise – we need to approximate the principles embedded in his actions. To be genuine seekers and faithful practitioners of the craft. Let us also be careful about not denegrating the present. Wisdom need not be thought of as some ancient quality that is only available to people with togas. It can also be clad in a business suit. Or in this case khakis and a nice collared shirt.

He was a smart guy. So smart that he got into one of the best schools in the land. However, he did not finish this school. Instead he sought different learning opportunities and growth challenges. What was unmistakable were his formidable abilities to think and reason, his inquisitive mind. What lay deeper under the surface, or perhaps was not yet as developed, were a huge heart and desire to do good. A dream about helping others grow and achieve. An ability to inspire followers not with the charisma of Gandhi but in a slightly yet also understated way.

He was able to see that doing good was just as important as amassing money. Thus he pledged to give it away. But not just his money – also his time and his talents in the pursuit of something greater. For transcendental aims such as global health ("to harness advances in science and technology to save lives in developing countries"), global development ("to identify and fund the delivery of high-impact solutions that can reduce health inequities and give everyone the opportunity to lead healthy, productive lives"), global opportunity ("to understand the underlying causes of poverty and develop evidence-based solutions that can be delivered at scale"), global learning ("to support the development of innovative solutions in education that are unlikely to be generated by institutions working alone and that can trigger change on a broader scale"), and global advocacy ("to promote public policies that advance our work, build strategic alliances with governments and the public and private sectors, and foster greater public awareness of urgent global issues") (see www.gatesfoundation.org/What-We-Do).

And he certainly has a passion for doing. He did not invent everything he used, but he did add significant parts, and he knew when to borrow, adapt, and integrate what made the most sense. Not entirely dissimilar to the riddle of the sphinx … as an industry 'lad' he learned to crawl – become stronger. As a professional young man in the dawn of the information age he learned to see the possibilities, the combinations, the hopes, and the potential of newer and better means. Now as a 'senior' statesman he is utilizing his formidable abilities and treasures to strategically as well as innovatively address some of the world's most troublesome problems. He synergistically combines the elements of leadership as he once combined the elements of the computer.

Question – Who is this person?

Answer – *Bill Gates*

Implications and Issues Going Forward

In this chapter we presented the first of three sets of instructions for leveraging your leadership success.

A selection guide for the wise leader. To customize your leadership approach. With guidelines for diagnosing, targeting, and adapting your leadership.

It presented a rationale for the importance of agility and customization. It further highlighted this with a series of cases and scenarios.

The chapter also helped you size up and score yourself on the component leadership tools. And requested that you summon the skill and the will to use them well. With warnings about what happens when you are the 'wrong' type of leader.

Taken together, it showed how aligning the gears could enable more successful and sustainable leadership.

So …

The core message here is to employ this as a personal selection assessment and checklist. As a template and planning aid in being the right type of leader at the right time.

For using the tools well.

Of course the tools must also remain sharp.

The next chapter will discuss just how to do this.

11

AN OPTIMIZATION GUIDE FOR THE WISE LEADER

Growing Your Leadership Strengths

In the previous chapter you learned how to best match your 'Leadership Toolbox' tools to the dominant challenge facing you. This first direction offered you a selection guide for choosing the right tool and customizing your leadership approach.

In this chapter you will learn to better hone or sharpen your tools.

This is your second direction – To fortify them. To temper their steel. To make sure that, when you do need to unfold each of them, they will not break or buckle. In a word, that when needed your leadership tools are powerful enough to do the job. We will do this by offering you an optimization guide for growing your leadership strengths.

Here we will first describe the reasons why leaders need to fully maximize and leverage their tools' power. We will then show the negative implications of not fully exploiting their advantages. For example, not being a sage enough scientist or unifying enough maestro.

We will then outline and describe a user-friendly best-practices framework/ map for maximizing leadership strengths.

Finally, we will conclude with a personalizable checklist for doing this.

Simply put, the plan for investing your time in this chapter is to process and master the following:

- Dynamic Leadership Competencies
- Growing the Self: Maximizing Your Tools
- Growing Others: A Leadership 'Talent Management' Program
- Implications and Issues

Dynamic Leadership Competencies

So how did you do on each of the Leadership Identity tests in Chapter 10?

How sharp are your tools?

Use Table 11.1 to record your summary scores, at least how they were assessed at that one particular point in time (and of course feel free to update this appropriately, like a running status tally, as you grow them over time).

If you ranked 'high' (H) in a particular tool – i.e., you are really good at this and can act very well as a leader in this capacity – then put a mark score in the top (green) row.

If you ranked 'moderate' (M) in a particular tool – i.e., you are okay at this and can do some things as a leader in this capacity – then put a mark in the middle (yellow) row.

If you ranked 'low' (L) in a particular tool – i.e., you are not good at this and cannot act all that well as a leader in this capacity – then put a mark in the bottom (red) row.

Are you perfect? Probably not.

Can you be better? Undoubtedly so! (Hint: We all can.)

So let us review your personal scorecard.

What is in the green? At the tip-top of the green?

What is in the yellow?

What is in the red? At the very bottom of the red?

To remind you, there are two main reasons why people do not optimize their tools. The first reason has to do with competency. The tool is not developed. Some folks' knives are just sharper and some folks' pliers are just stronger. That is why they can cut or grip better. The second reason has to do with skill. The techniques for using the tool are not developed. Some folks can cut better or grip better even using the same (or even an inferior) tool.

Those who refuse to strengthen and leverage their tools, or who are complacent with their capacity and skill-set, are the ones who fail. Their leadership is NOT sustainable.

Will you stock your toolbox with better tools? Will you learn how to better use them?

Growing Oneself: Maximizing Your Toolbox

The modern leader must have a deep/wide portfolio of tools and the ability to use them well. Each must be at least at a MINIMUM (yellow or higher) level of competency. This is because when a challenge surfaces you must be able to at least do something about it.

Ideally you will build up to an OPTIMAL (score approximating 5) level of competency so that you can not just do the job but do it masterfully.

Yet this is frequently not the case. Partly because we tend to inspire and select the wrong types of leaders. Ones who are good at getting the job but not

292 Leveraging Your Leadership Success

TABLE 11.1 So … How Sharp Are Your Tools?

	LIGHTS *Being – A resource to empower*		CAMERA *Seeing – A guide to direct*		ACTION *Doing – An agent to accomplish*	
	HEAD: Tool 1	*HEART:* Tool 2	*INSIDE:* Tool 3	*OUTSIDE:* Tool 4	*PULL:* Tool 5	*PUSH:* Tool 6
High (Green)						
Moderate (Yellow)						
Low (Red)						

necessarily at doing the job. In a word, the leaders we need tend not to be the leaders we want. This explains why some people care more about getting the leadership glory and less about living the leadership story.

This prescient insight is gleaned from one of philosophy's most seminal thinkers, Plato, as compellingly conveyed in perhaps his most seminal work, *The Republic*. And as suggested earlier in the book but detailed here, its message is as elucidating as it is alarming.

Timeless Toolbox Problems

On the one hand, Plato argues that we need wise leaders who are true philosophers – individuals broadly learned enough to see beyond shifting superficialities that, by developing the requisite skill and will, realize those higher principles that enable sustainable success. However, on the other hand, he points out that we are not inclined to want or choose leaders who are true philosophers. This is because they are also the people we often least relate to and identify with (Ashforth & Mael, 1989). Since they necessarily seem, see, and act so different they are typically ill-regarded and unpopular. And if this is not disheartening enough then brace yourself – it gets even worse. Even if by some chance or fleeting fancy a true lover of wisdom were to be selected as a leader then Plato contends that their wise tenure would not remain so for long. Instead they would lamentably, but likely, be corrupted by the socially institutionalized nature of the role, seduced by vicious cycles of its dysfunctional rewards contingencies, or unseated if resistant to either of these.

This is consistent with David Winter's (1987) seminal study of U.S. presidents, where he found that the surface appeal of leaders was differentiated from the ultimate greatness or performance of leaders. The former is sourced from the congruence or match between the leader and that of their contemporary society; the latter is more a function of the leader themselves and not associated with societal congruence. In short, and again, it is concluded that leader appeal and leader performance are two different things. And the caution remains consistent across

Growing Your Leadership Strengths **293**

the ages: That the wisdom necessary to be a leader actually runs counter to those attributes often required for becoming a leader.

This difference between leader appeal and leader wisdom – just getting elected versus actually getting the job done – is specifically illustrated through two stories from *The Republic* (see Project Gutenberg EBook of *The Republic*, 2008: Books VI and VII): (1) The 'Ship of Fools', and (2) The 'Cave of Ignorance'.

In the (Leadership) 'Ship of Fools' in Book VI of *The Republic*, Plato illustrates the difference between leadership capacity and electability.

> The sailors are quarrelling with one another about the steering – every one is of opinion that he has a right to steer, though he has never learned the art of navigation and cannot tell who taught him or when he learned, and will further assert that it cannot be taught, and they are ready to cut in pieces any one who says the contrary. They throng about the captain, begging and praying him to commit the helm to them ... (yet) the true pilot must pay attention to the year and seasons and sky and stars and winds, and whatever else belongs to his art, if he intends to be really qualified for the command of a ship, and that he must and will be the steerer, whether other people like or not.... Now in vessels which are in a state of mutiny and by sailors who are mutineers, how will the true pilot be regarded? Will he not be called by them a prater, a star-gazer, a good-for-nothing?

So applying this to practical matters,

> Then suppose you now take this parable to the gentleman who is surprised at finding that philosophers have no honor in their cities; explain it to him and try to convince him that their having honor would be far more extraordinary.... The ruler who is good for anything ought not to beg his subjects to be ruled by him; although the present governors of mankind are of a different stamp; they may be justly compared to the mutinous sailors, and the true helmsmen to those who are called by them good-for-nothings and star-gazers.... For these reasons, and among men like these, philosophy, the noblest pursuit of all, is not likely to be much esteemed by those of the opposite faction.

This message – of the difference between being and becoming a leader – is reinforced by Plato in Book VII of *The Republic* through the parable of the (Leadership) 'Cave of Ignorance'. Here he represents wisdom as an upward journey out of ignorance, no longer unnaturally constrained to seeing manipulated shadows of partial realities but instead to behold the proverbial light. Yet when those enlightened dare to venture back into the cave to help lead those still imprisoned and unenlightened, this is how this wise leader is regarded (hint: not well) by their prospective constituents:

Imagine once more, I said, such an one coming suddenly out of the sun to be replaced in his old situation; would he not be certain to have his eyes full of darkness.... And if there were a contest, and he had to compete in measuring the shadows with the prisoners who had never moved out of the den ... would he not be ridiculous? Men would say of him that up he went and down he came without his eyes; and that it was better not even to think of ascending; and if any one tried to loose another and lead him up to the light, let them only catch the offender, and they would put him to death.

Therefore, Plato posits the solution as to compel the wisest to re-enter the cave, struggle against these systemic obstacles, and take up the mantle of leadership:

Then, I said, the business of us who are the founders of the State will be to compel the best minds to attain that knowledge which we have already shown to be the greatest of all – they must continue to ascend until they arrive at the good; but when they have ascended and seen enough they must ... be made to descend again among the prisoners in the den. ... Wherefore each of you, when his turn comes, must go down to the general underground abode, and get the habit of seeing in the dark. When you have acquired the habit, you will see ten thousand times better than the inhabitants of the den, and you will know what the several images are, and what they represent, because you have seen the beautiful and just and good in their truth. And thus our State ... will be administered in a spirit unlike that of other States, in which men fight with one another about shadows only and are distracted in the struggle for power.

Altogether, when considering systems that both obstruct or corrupt wise leaders, the above insights into the divide are intriguing. The masses are generally obsessed with the ephemeral and superficial. They live in the cave of shadows, they do not trust those who 'see the light' and are hostile to these alleged lunatics. Moreover, even if a wise leader might ascend to a position of leadership they would be compelled and rewarded in ways that run counter to, and even corrupt, their elucidation. Net-net: Organizational systems tend to select the wrong people and motivate them in the wrong ways. We don't always get the (wise) leaders we need.

These observations raise serious questions about a fundamental and perhaps systemic misalignment: Are the candidates who select for leadership positions the same people who can perform to the level of the expectations of those who selected them? Are they even the best people for these roles? Are the skills required to meet selection criteria for leadership positions compatible with the competencies of successful leaders? For instance, some research (cf., Atwater et al. 1999; Eagly & Karau, 2012; Nevickaa et al., 2011; Smith & Foti, 1998) has tied leader emergence to different factors (e.g., narcissism, dominance) than leader

Growing Your Leadership Strengths **295**

effectiveness while others have explored how the two become asymmetrical in terms of role congruity and prejudice.

And there is also evidence that these processes might entail entirely different dynamics altogether. For example, according to Hogg's (2001) review of a social identity theory of leadership, leaders may emerge and sustain their position on characteristics divorced from effectiveness (e.g., based on "the defining features of a common and distinctive ingroup" where they "assimilate themselves to these"). Thus a danger of this is that

> leadership becomes increasingly based on prototypicality rather than leader schemas or intrinsic status characteristics ... this can degrade decision-making processes.... Rather than basing leadership on leader schemas that generally contain optimal situation and task-specific leadership prescriptions, a situation can exist where there is a powerful leader who embodies a group prototype that does not prescribe optimal decision-making procedures.

Moreover, and as classically construed in 1975 by Kerr, even well-qualified and well-intentioned leaders might still be led astray by corrupt reward contingencies endemic to the leadership position which provide greater support to those that actually act less effectively (e.g., speak in terms of elusive generalities, look out for themselves, prioritize image over substance, and focus on short-term visible (versus long-term sustainable) growth). The synchronicity between leadership selection and execution criteria is absolutely critical for organizations of all types – from governments and businesses to social institutions and specialized associations. Thus the calling for choosing/developing Plato's archetypal Philosopher King, which from a multicultural perspective is also aligned with the Buddhist concept of the 'Bodhisattva' (Silk, 2019) who has taken the steps to attain enlightenment but remains dedicated to the service of others.

Modern Challenges in (Wise) Leadership Education and Development

In terms of education and development, a wisdom-based approach suggests ways of helping potential leaders (1) understand content-related leadership issues, (2) bring together its often confusing and contradictory paradigms, and (3) process its fundamental insights in a clear, relatable, and consistent manner.

For not sailing on a proverbial ship of fools.

And instead better aligning leader appeal and success.

For not wallowing in a proverbial cave of ignorance.

And instead better choosing, attracting, and being wise leaders.

As per Benjamin and O'Reilly (2011: 453, 471):

296 Leveraging Your Leadership Success

evidence for the failures in leadership abound.... If we want our graduates to flourish, it is imperative that we help them acquire the skills, abilities, attitudes, and knowledge required to do so.... By identifying specific challenges that young managers face and creating teaching materials that help students confront these challenges, extract the appropriate learning, and make the necessary psychological transitions, we can improve the relevance and the rigor of leadership development in the business school context.

These might be approximated by leadership educators through an approach that, as per Kessler (2017), combines all elements of the educational 'triumvirate' of cognitive (intellectual), affective (motivational), and conative (skill-based) growth.

First, by promoting gist-based instruction to wise leadership. A gist is a holistic representation or main thrust of a theory or literature (Suddaby, Hardy, & Huy, 2011). It helps ground efforts in established, time-tested practices. Gist-based instruction centered on such wisdom-based themes would help clarify theories' core insights, relationships, and principles and better allows students to integrate their lessons. These opportunities might also be useful for deconstructing classroom exercises or analyzing business cases about why individuals fail at becoming and/or being leaders.

- Wise leaders grasp the fundamental gists of the wisdom model.

Second, by using these gists to then foster customization through personalized opportunities for wise leadership. This relates to 'whole-person' learning (Hoover et al., 2010) by focusing on the unique alignment of a person's various wisdom-based role identities and then helping each individual map them onto their particular collections of leadership states and circumstances. Not everyone will relate to or use the wisdom model in the same way. Or in the same order. Or with the same emphases. Or through the same style. Or at the same level. Or to the same ends. Instead each person must customize the lessons to their predilections and preferences as well as particular areas of engagement.

- Wise leaders personalize the wisdom model and adapt it to their lives.

Third, and finally, by using these customized gists to then encourage coaching opportunities for wise leadership. Drawing from Whitmore's (2009) classic 'GROW' model, students might be given hands-on opportunities to actually develop the wisdom-sourced competencies associated with each philosophical aspect. For instance, to systematically, synergistically foster core leadership competencies in the previously defined areas utilizing an integrated, measurable, customizable, coaching platform via the following sequence: (1) Goal, asking: Where do you want to be? This entails defining desired ends based on the Wise Leadership model and establishing appropriate educational objectives; (2) <u>R</u>eality, asking: Where are you now? This entails establishing current states along each of the above dimensions and customizing a developmental profile of needs; (3) <u>O</u>ptions, asking: What could you do? This entails laying out the best mechanisms and plans to bridge the gaps between desired goals and actual states; and (4) <u>W</u>ill, asking: What are you going to do? This entails the process of getting things done – undertaking real actions and measuring actual results – for personal and professional success.

Ultimately it is intended that, through a grounded and personalized coaching process, the aspirant wise leader would be moved from: (1) Passive Ineffectiveness – Not knowing why they are having problems, to (2) Active Ineffectiveness – Understanding the key factors and reasons to address them, to (3) Active Effectiveness – Short-term learning of best practices and applying of appropriate tools, to (4) Passive Effectiveness – Deep, long-term transformation into sustainably successful individuals.

- Wise leaders master strategies and techniques for applying the wisdom modl.

Growing Others: An (Organizational) Talent Management Program

This chapter therefore presents core principles for 'optimizing' leadership along all of the aforementioned dimensions. In the language of leadership practitioners and academics, this is therefore the Talent Management or Human Resources section of the chapter related to developing people and organizational competencies.

In the short term, it allows you and your organization to 'up your game'.

In the medium term, it allows you and your organization to find help with a deficiency that is proving stubborn to develop.

In the longer term, it allows you and your organization to forge systematic strategies for…. Getting leadership talent; Growing leadership talent; Deploying leadership talent; and Retaining leadership talent.

So … Here are some best practices for tapping into and cultivating leadership strengths.

But First, Some Background

Drawing from the work of Kessler (2020), the strategic use of Global Talent Management (GTM) is contingent upon the organizational objectives and the positions which possess a disproportional amount of leverage to facilitate them – i.e., leaders. According to scholars Collings and Mellahi (2009), this involves all

> activities and processes that involve the systematic identification of key *positions* which differentially contribute to the organization's sustainable

competitive advantage, the development of a talent *pool* of high potential and high performing incumbents to fill these roles, and the development of a differentiated human resource *architecture* to facilitate filling these positions with competent incumbents and to ensure their continued *commitment* to the organization.

There are no positions more 'key' than in leadership. This is consistent with how Huselid and colleagues (2005) describe these positions as exhibiting a "disproportionate importance to a company's ability to execute some parts of its strategy and second ... the wide variability in the quality of the work displayed among the employees in these positions". It also aligns with Becker and Huselid's (2006) arguments that the most economically valuable human capital is that deployed in the execution of an organization's strategic direction.

Therefore, we focus our attention on developing those most able to directly (via performance) and indirectly (via design) define and perform them. Whereas we ascribe to Lepak and Snell's (1999) arguments regarding the degree of uniqueness in positions, and in their proposition of a typology for clarifying these differences (e.g., knowledge-based vs. job-based) we depart slightly here to add the consideration of previously discussed leadership-oriented 'wisdom-based' positions.

As per Dries (2003), the wisdom-based approach to developing leadership talent is in line with its various theoretical perspectives: Human resources management (HRM) in viewing leadership wisdom as resource-based capital that is defined via organizational contributions; I/O psychology in viewing leadership wisdom as something to be acquired, appraised, and cultivated among differentiated personnel; Educational psychology in viewing leadership wisdom as a rare form of 'giftedness' applied in domain-specific excellence; Vocational psychology in viewing leadership wisdom as a dynamic crystallization and expression of one's evolving identity; Positive psychology in viewing leadership wisdom as a vehicle for personal as well as organizational enhancement and actualization; and Social psychology in viewing leadership wisdom as inexorably intertwined with its organizational and professional context.

Taken together, and drawing from prior insights herein that (1) Leadership is a contingent behavior that can be developed, plus (2) Enhanced development must incorporate the various dimensions of wise leadership, we can now say that (3) Developing globally talented leaders involves efforts across the international human resources management (IHRM) spectrum. More specifically, again as per Tarique and Schuler (2010: 124), "global talent management is about systematically utilizing IHRM activities ... to attract, develop, and retain individuals ... consistent with the strategic directions of the multinational enterprise in a dynamic, highly competitive, and global environment". Thus our independent variable is IHRM, our dependent variable is Wise Leadership, and our mediating variable (i.e., the remaining focus of our chapter) is wise leadership development principles and practices. In short, if a GTM program seeks to develop (versus attract or retain) wisdom in its leaders then it must speak to each of these interwoven dimensions of talent.

To be sure, these dimensions do in fact align with a broad swath of GTM competencies as described in multiple reviews (cf., Jokinen, 2005; Kim & McLean, 2015) and research (cf., Baltes & Staudinger, 2000; Boyatzis, Goleman, & Rhee, 2000; Brake, 1997; Goldsmith & Walt, 1999; Gregersen, Morrison, & Black, 1998; Harris & Moran, 1987; Jordan & Cartwright, 1998; Kets deVries & Florent-Treacy, 2002; Meldrum & Atkinson, 1998; Rhinesmith, 1996; Rosen, 2000; Spreitzer, McCall, & Mahoney, 1997; Srinivas, 1995; Sternberg, 2003). For example: Leadership *logic* is discernible in discussions on enhancing fluid intelligence, cognitive skills, thinking, learning, and intellectual capacity. Leadership *aesthetics* is discernible in discussions on transformation and motivation, sensitivity, empathy, and emotional intelligence. Leadership *ethics* is discernible in discussions on character, courage, and integrity. Leadership *metaphysics* is discernible in discussions on complexity, uncertainty, ambiguity and their relationships to the self, and human spirituality and existence. Leadership *epistemology* is discernible in discussions on managing communication, teamwork, partnerships, relationships, and social processes. Leadership *politics* is discernible in discussions on business literacy and acumen, competitiveness, technical proficiency and savvy, and success orientation.

All in all these findings can be reconciled within our rubric as per the meta-insights that global leaders see the 'big picture', that these elements will be required to varying degrees according to the circumstances, and that some are more coherently demonstrated by outstanding leaders and that these competencies can be identified, assessed, and developed (cf., Brownell & Goldsmith, 2006; Chakraborty, 1995; McKenna, Rooney, & Boal, 2009; Kim & McLean, 2015).

Developing Wise Leadership Talent

Drawing from Kim and McLean's (2015) framework for developing global leadership competency we can distinguish requisite practices that address some of these dimensions more than others. More specifically, by extracting and then reconciling examples from their review, we might glean strategies for: (1) Developing logically oriented competencies via enhanced knowledge, critical thinking, intelligence, inquisitiveness, mental mapping, and cognitive attributes; (2) Developing aesthetically oriented competencies via enhanced compassion, motivational processes, intrinsic engagement, and sensitivity to differences; (3) Developing ethically oriented competencies via enhanced self-awareness, honesty and integrity, balancing tensions, asking tough questions, and instilling trust; (4) Developing metaphysically oriented competencies via enhanced tolerance of ambiguity and articulations of vision and mission; (5) Developing epistemologically oriented competencies via enhanced interpersonal skills, teamwork, open communications, networking, social competencies and capital,

300 Leveraging Your Leadership Success

TABLE 11.2 Strengthening Your Leadership Wisdom 'Talent'

Activity Dimension	Getting	Growing	Deploying	Retaining
Logic	Leadership Scientists	Thinking and Understanding Competencies	Meeting Cognitive Challenges	Assess and Reward Sagacity
Aesthetics	Leadership Artists	Feeling and Inspiration Competencies	Meeting Affective Challenges	Assess and Reward Spirit
Ethics	Leadership Icons	Moral and Principles Competencies	Meeting Integrity Challenges	Assess and Reward Character
Metaphysics	Leadership Advocates	Meaning and Mission Competencies	Meeting Significance Challenges	Assess and Reward Purpose
Epistemology	Leadership Maestros	Integration and Coordination Competencies	Meeting Connection Challenges	Assess and Reward Unity
Politics	Leadership Generals	Efficiency and Effectiveness Competencies	Meeting Execution Challenges	Assess and Reward Value

and relationship management; and (6) Developing politically oriented competencies via enhanced business skills, adaptability, organizing expertise, and technical competencies.

Thus in this section we come full circle in synthesizing the complementary literatures of leadership, wisdom, and GTM. In doing this we derive and propose the following multi-dimensional and multi-stage model of global leadership talent management organized around major (but not necessarily linear) human resource challenges; this is summarized in Table 11.2: Getting talent (via recruitment and selection), growing talent (via training and development), deploying talent (via staffing and placement), and retaining talent (via assessment and compensation practices).

Cultivating Leadership LOGIC Talent

How might an organization enhance the logic 'talent' of its leadership? Here global leaders must overcome barriers to sound reasoning and rationality to discover the hidden truth of situations. Globalization expands the information to be processed and the subsequent knowledge required for processing it.

Modern firms are thus charged with (1) Acquiring global leadership *scientists* either proven or with its particular proclivity, who can best make sense of the complexities of the global landscape. Tip … How to spot a leadership scientist: Any major (not just STEM) as long as they are versed in appropriately accessing and applying core insights/models/gists from their professional field's pedagogy. For example, they know what the core theories are and are comfortable with using them. And they are good at conveying this (i.e., teaching) to help others understand things better.

Moreover, they must continuously (2) Develop the requisite *thinking and understanding competencies* to keep up with its single and double loop shifts. Tip … How to develop a leadership scientist: Send them to continuing education and workshops. Enroll them in online opportunities via MOOCs, distance learning, and certification programs.

As per seminal contingency perspectives the best leadership scientists should be dynamically (3) Placed up, down, and across the hierarchy in leadership positions when the dominant challenges are of a *cognitive* nature. In the event that current and immobile leadership resources are entrenched in positions ill-fit for their competencies then requisite support staff and resources should be provided to compensate for logical shortcomings. Tip … How to place a leadership scientist: Look for front-line areas where people come in direct contact with information and problems.

All the while this process should be (4) Energized throughout the HR process with an appraisal and compensation system that can evaluate/reward intellectual criteria to continually enhance, systematically retain, and by extension potentially institutionalize global leadership *sagacity*. Tip … How to reward a leadership scientist: Focus on knowledge-based merit pay considering credential-based assessments.

Cultivating Leadership AESTHETICS Talent

How might an organization enhance the aesthetic 'talent' of its leadership? Here global leaders must overcome barriers to emotional well-being and joy to discover the hidden beauty of situations. Globalization expands the diversity of needs and the subsequent emotional range required for engagement.

Modern firms are thus charged with (1) Acquiring global leadership *artists*, either proven or with a particular proclivity, who can best motivate a global workforce and network. Tip … How to spot a leadership artist: Any major (not just Liberal Arts) as long as they are passionate about the field and their passion is infectious.

Moreover, they must continuously (2) Develop the requisite *feeling and inspiration* competencies to keep up with its single and double loop shifts. Tip … How to develop a leadership artist: Send them to interact where encounters are most intense and energy levels are highest.

As per seminal contingency perspectives the best leadership artists should be dynamically (3) Placed up, down, and across the hierarchy in leadership positions when the dominant challenges are of an *affective* nature. In the event that current and immobile leadership resources are entrenched in positions ill-fit for

302 Leveraging Your Leadership Success

their competencies then requisite support staff and resources should be provided to compensate for affective shortcomings. Tip … How to place a leadership artist: Look for areas where people come in direct contact with people such as customers or clients.

All the while this process should be (4) Energized throughout the HR process with an appraisal and compensation system that can evaluate/reward affective criteria to continually enhance, systematically retain, and by extension potentially institutionalize global leadership *spirit*. Tip … How to reward a leadership artist: Focus on *esprit-de-corps*-based merit pay considering emotions such as happiness, vitality, and wellness.

Cultivating Leadership ETHICS Talent

How might an organization _enhance_ the aesthetic 'talent' of its leadership? Here global leaders must overcome barriers to reflection by looking inside one's self to discover a greater sense of right and wrong and the nature of being good. Globalization expands the criteria to be considered and the subsequent prudence required for assessment.

Modern firms are thus charged with (1) Acquiring global leadership *icons*, either proven or with a particular proclivity, who can best ground global initiatives. Tip … How to spot a leadership Icon: See how people act (nobly?) when what they want runs counter to what is right. Especially when they think that they can get away with it.

Moreover, they must continuously (2) Develop the requisite *moral and principle-based* competencies to keep up with its single and double loop shifts. Tip … How to develop a leadership Icon: Allow people to rub up against life replete with all of its ethical ugliness and quandaries. When they work their way through predicaments and dilemmas they develop, and own, their principles.

As per seminal contingency perspectives the best leadership icons should be dynamically (3) Placed up, down, and across the hierarchy in leadership positions when the dominant challenges are centered on integrity. In the event that current and immobile leadership resources are entrenched in positions ill-fit for their competencies then requisite support staff and resources should be provided to compensate for *integrity* shortcomings. Tip … How to place a leadership Icon: Look for areas where people come in direct contact with vague or ill-regulated situations especially when there are large human, ecological, etc. consequences.

All the while this process should be (4) Energized throughout the HR process with an appraisal and compensation system that can evaluate/reward integrity criteria to continually enhance, systematically retain, and by extension potentially institutionalize global leadership *character*. Tip … How to reward a leadership Icon: Focus on ethics-based merit pay considering support for core organizational/ corporate values.

Growing Your Leadership Strengths **303**

Cultivating Leadership Metaphysics Talent

How might an organization enhance the metaphysical 'talent' of its leadership? Here global leaders must overcome barriers to aspiration by looking outside one's self to discover a greater sense of mission and importance and the nature of one's place in the world. Globalization expands the perspectives to be considered and the subsequent equifinality required for reconciliation.

Modern firms are thus charged with (1) Acquiring global leadership *advocates*, either proven or with a particular proclivity, who can best orient global initiatives. Tip … How to spot a leadership Advocate: They are long-term, mission-driven and know where they are going, plus they can orient other people to go there as well.

Moreover, they must continuously (2) Develop the requisite *meaning and mission-based* competencies to keep up with its single and double loop shifts. Tip … How to develop a leadership Advocate: Give them exposure beyond their roles to see the bigger picture, where each part fits into it, and how larger systems can be aligned in pursuit of greater ideals.

As per seminal contingency perspectives the best leadership advocates should be dynamically (3) Placed up, down, and across the hierarchy in leadership positions when the dominant challenges are centered on *significance*. In the event that current and immobile leadership resources are entrenched in positions ill-fit for their competencies then requisite support staff and resources should be provided to compensate for aspirational shortcomings. Tip … How to place a leadership Advocate: Look for areas where a sense of purpose is important, such as jobs or tasks where control/oversight is limited, failures and setbacks are common, and people need to keep their eyes on the prize.

All the while this process should be (4) Energized throughout the HR process with an appraisal and compensation system that can evaluate/reward significance criteria to continually enhance, systematically retain, and by extension potentially institutionalize global leadership *purpose*. Tip … How to reward a leadership Advocate: Focus on long-term advancement of objectives with five-, ten-, etc. -year calibrated-based merit pay considering mission-specific progress rather than transactional variations in the day-to-day performance of their individual task lists.

Cultivating Leadership Epistemology Talent

How might an organization enhance the epistemological 'talent' of its leadership? Here global leaders must overcome barriers to communication and coordination to use a common language for achieving a synergistic system. Globalization expands the literal as well as figurative languages to be considered and the subsequent fluency required for synthesis.

Modern firms are thus charged with (1) Acquiring global leadership *maestros*, either proven or with a particular proclivity, who can best synthesize global

304 Leveraging Your Leadership Success

capacities. Tip … How to spot a leadership Maestro: They don't just say that they are team players but, when assessed, say, in job samples or through background records, actually can put together a team, defer their personal credit for team glory, and support collective efforts.

Moreover, they must continuously (2) develop the requisite *integration and coordination* competencies to keep up with its single and double loop shifts. Tip … How to develop a leadership Maestro: Practice good communication (not just talking but also listening, and not just their accuracy but also their supportiveness). Work through conflict management techniques and win-win approaches that perpetuate partnerships. Learn how to design structures and cultures that work.

As per seminal contingency perspectives the best leadership Maestros should be dynamically (3) Placed up, down, and across the hierarchy in leadership positions when the dominant challenges are centered on *connection*. In the event that current and immobile leadership resources are entrenched in positions ill-fit for their competencies then requisite support staff and resources should be provided to compensate for collaboration shortcomings. Tip … How to place a leadership Maestro: Look for areas where teamwork is especially critical. This is particularly important when there are greater threats to teamwork such as prejudices and stereotypes, as well as poor tolerances and capitalization of diversity.

All the while this process should be (4) Energized throughout the HR process with an appraisal and compensation system that can evaluate/reward connection criteria to continually enhance, systematically retain, and by extension potentially institutionalize global leadership *unity*. Tip … How to reward a leadership Maestro: Focus on integration, interdependency, and the harmonic alignment of followers. Consider using collectivist-based merit pay, taking into account pooled or averaged metrics that encourage cooperation and citizenship behavior.

Cultivating Leadership Politics Talent

How might an organization enhance the political 'talent' of its leadership? Here global leaders must overcome barriers to performance to use pragmatic strategies for achieving 'real-world' results. Globalization expands the competitive dynamics to be considered and the subsequent functionality required for performance.

Modern firms are thus charged with (1) Acquiring global leadership *generals*, either proven or with a particular proclivity, who can best leverage global capacities. Tip … How to spot a leadership General: They get results. Period. Using a basketball analogy that a dear friend once shared with me, they don't just dribble and pass pretty – they actually go to the hoop and score.

Moreover, they must continuously (2) Develop the requisite *efficiency and effectiveness* competencies to keep up with its single and double loop shifts. Tip … How to develop a leadership General: There are techniques for increasing the

Growing Your Leadership Strengths **305**

operational and innovative performance of people – these should be trained, practiced, and mastered. For example, employing resource utilization algorithms and product development funnels.

As per seminal contingency perspectives the best leadership generals should be dynamically (3) Placed up, down, and across the hierarchy in leadership positions when the dominant challenges are centered on *implementation*. In the event that current and immobile leadership resources are entrenched in positions ill-fit for their competencies then requisite support staff and resources should be provided to compensate for performance shortcomings. Tip … How to place a leadership General: Look for areas where outcomes trump process. Where it matters less how the sausage is made, just that it is made. Especially when there are real-time learning and adjustments that must be undertaken and cannot be pre-designed or pre-ordained.

All the while this process should be (4) Energized throughout the HR process with an appraisal and compensation system that can evaluate/reward execution criteria to continually enhance, systematically retain, and by extension potentially institutionalize global leadership value *enhancement*. Tip … How to reward a leadership General: Focus on results-based merit pay considering excellence, advantage, and sustainability. Does it make us outstanding? Does it help us win? Will it help us survive and prosper?

Taken Together: Leadership Wisdom Talent

Integrating the above, organizations are ultimately charged with transitioning to a more holistic GTM strategy along both temporal and proximal dimensions.

Regarding time, there must be short- and long-term leadership wisdom strategies. In the present, talent will be utilized and optimized to current dominant challenges. In the future, talent will be evolved and adapted as challenges shift in their nature and importance.

For example, in each of the above areas challenges can change over time and come in and out of the forefront. For each leader they must be educated as to the development of each dimension as well as the diagnosis and deployment of consistent behaviors as per relevant contingencies. Across the talent pool of leaders they must be flexibly positioned and pooled via an institutionalized system to enable the most appropriate internal leadership to meet the most pressing external needs. If the above strategies are realized then a global talent management system can facilitate wise leadership with (as per previously discussed) a meta-heuristic alacrity to synthesize competencies and balance approaches to fluidly address complex, dynamic challenges.

Regarding level, first from an INDIVIDUAL perspective you can utilize and enhance the wisdom template for exploring how to become a wise leader. For example: How does one best learn leadership logic, ethics, metaphysics, epistemology, and politics? What leadership positions and teams best highlight

306 Leveraging Your Leadership Success

complementary competencies? How can one best adapt their leadership by shifting the deployment of these competencies to differentially fit, and dynamically adapt to, globally complex and ever-changing situations?

From an INTERPERSONAL perspective you can utilize and enhance the wisdom template for exploring how to help others become wise leaders. Implicit in this direction are curricular (i.e., where should leadership be taught) and pedagogical (i.e., how should leadership be taught) issues. For example: Are universities well positioned to produce wise leaders? Are corporate programs well positioned to supplement or substitute for them?

From an ORGANIZATIONAL perspective you can utilize and enhance the wisdom template for exploring how to design wise contexts. This may include consideration of structural and cultural variables to create facilitative systems. This is consistent with Hays (2007) that organizational wisdom can be institutionalized insofar as it is not a thing per se but the embodiment of a dynamic, complex system. For example, as per Lawrence (2007), analogy between the functioning of the human brain and wise corporate governance: What vertical and horizontal arrangements best inspire and facilitate (the dimensions of) leadership wisdom among and across their component members? What organizational policies, practices, and socialization methods best enhance, combine, and diffuse these arrangements?

From a STRATEGIC perspective you can utilize and enhance the wisdom template for exploring how to advance a wise agenda. This may include consideration of programmatic initiation and implementation issues across different HR activities. For example, how might organizations best manage: The getting of leadership wisdom via recruitment and selection?; The growing of leadership wisdom via training and development?; The institutionalizing of leadership wisdom via staffing and placement?; and The sustaining of leadership wisdom via appraisal and compensation?

Taken together, when conceived across these levels of analysis, it is useful to draw upon complexity theory (Ganco, 2013) and its insights into understanding the criticality of building a wise leadership system. In a nutshell:

> Overall organizational performance is assumed to be a function of the performance contributions of all decisions that the organization makes.... Superior performing organizations are those that achieve a better fit with the external environment or discover a better solution to a problem. The organizational performance is emergent in the sense that it cannot be deduced from the analysis of each organizational unit in isolation but rather depends on the interactions within the system as a whole.... When the interdependencies are dense, however, even changing a small number of decisions can have a dramatic effect (positive or negative) on the overall organizational performance as the focal decision may affect the performance of many other decisions.

Growing Your Leadership Strengths **307**

Thus foolishness in any parts of the talent management system, particularly critical ones related to leadership, can undermine wisdom when decisions are increasingly tied together and dependent upon one another.

So what to do? A nice way to answer this adapts the classic 'dynamic capability' model (Teece, 2013) to wise leadership. In a nutshell:

> Dynamic capabilities are the firm's ability to integrate, build, and reconfigure internal and external resources to address and shape rapidly changing business environments.... The strength of a firm's dynamic capabilities determines the speed and degree to which the firm's idiosyncratic resources/competences can be aligned and realigned to match the opportunities and requirements of the business environment. Strong dynamic capabilities are the basis for the sustained competitive advantage displayed by a handful of firms that have endured for decades even as they have shifted the focus of their activities.

So for example:

> Dynamic capabilities can usefully be thought of as comprised of three primary clusters of competences (1) identification and assessment of an opportunity (sensing); (2) mobilization of resources to address an opportunity and to capture value from doing so (seizing); and (3) continued renewal (transforming).... Complementarities need to be constantly managed (reconfigured as necessary) to achieve evolutionary fitness.

In this, leaders need to first 'sense' the nature of their different challenges.

Then to 'seize' on these opportunities to acquire, develop, deploy, and reward the appropriate leadership competencies to address them.

Then to constantly repeat the above to 'transform' leadership systems when needed and to perpetually align them with their larger ecosystems.

By doing this you can maximize not just your own wise leadership but also others' (and your larger organization's) leadership talent and collective wisdom toolboxes.

Implications and Issues

In this chapter we presented the second of three sets of instructions for leveraging your leadership success. An optimization guide for the wise leader. To bolster your leadership approach.

It presented a rationale for the importance of continuously and dynamically growing your leadership competencies.

308 Leveraging Your Leadership Success

We spoke about this in terms of growing the self and maximizing your personal tools. One of the lessons is that focus should be placed not just on the skills for becoming a leader but also on those for actually being a leader.

We also spoke about this in terms of growing others and establishing a leadership 'talent management' program. In terms of getting the talent. Developing the talent. Deploying the talent. And retaining the talent. Within wise leadership-systems.

So …

The core message here is to use this as a personal optimization assessment and checklist. As a template and planning aid in honing your tools. Fortifying them. Tempering their steel. Making sure that, when you do need to unfold each of them, they will not break or buckle. That when needed your leadership tools are powerful enough to do the job.

For growing leadership strengths.

Of course there are also threats that can undermine or erode the very fabric of these tools. Thus they must also be maintained.

The next chapter will discuss just how to do this.

12

A MAINTENANCE GUIDE FOR THE WISE LEADER

Trouble-Shooting Your Leadership Exposures

The third direction in using your 'Leadership Toolbox' is to continuously refine and care for your tools.

As any craftsman or do-it-yourselfer knows all too well, if your tools are not maintained then they will (figuratively as well as literally) lose their edge.

Times change and our tools must change with them for us to adapt, survive, and thrive.

In this chapter, we will first describe the reasons why leaders need to trouble-shoot and minimize their tools' long-term exposures.

We will then show the negative implications of not fully evolving to address their potential disadvantages. For example, not taking account of three big leadership changes: technological advances, globalization dynamics, and institutional shifts.

We will then outline and describe a user-friendly developmental framework (in other words, a map) for minimizing leadership erosion.

Finally, we will conclude with a personalizable checklist for doing this.

Simply put, the plan for investing your time in this chapter is to process and master the following:

- Erosion versus Evolution
- Major Forces – Opportunities AND Threats
- Technology and Leadership
- Globalization and Leadership
- Institutions and Leadership
- Your Personal Trouble-Shooting Checklist

310 Leveraging Your Leadership Success

Erosion versus Evolution

Let's start with an incredibly easy multiple-choice test.
Which of these words sounds better to you?

a. Erosion
b. Evolution

If you are like most people then the first word – Erosion – brings to mind more negative ideas and feelings, whereas the latter word – Evolution – is seen as more positive. But why is this the case?

According to the *Oxford English Dictionary* (OED), the word '*erosion*' refers to the gradual destruction or diminishing of something. Like when wind or water erodes the strength of a structure. Like when opposition erodes the support of a policy or strategy. Erosion happens when outside changes reduce the effectiveness of what once worked. This is extremely relevant to our conversation because the environment that leaders operate in has never witnessed such velocity and magnitude of change as it is now seeing in our modern times.

Contrary to this, the word '*evolution*' is defined by this same source as the gradual development of something. Basically, it refers to moving along with the environment so that one can continue to survive and thrive in a world characterized by constant, often tumultuous change.

Pushing this even further, evolution suggests a proactive approach to your personal leadership development.

> Proactive – A positive, getting-out-ahead of inevitable changes approach.

This stands in stark contrast to a reactive or inactive approach to leadership development (do you see yourself here or perhaps some people you know?):

> Reactive – A lagging, after-the-fact, if it ain't broke then don't fix it approach.
>
> Inactive – A passive, lazy and stubborn, my way or the highway approach.

So the heading of this section refers to the attitude you adopt as a leader, and the sets of choices that go along with it, when facing a world awash with change. Will they smash you like a wave … or will you get up and surf the wave?

There is a Darwinian dynamic at play here. One where inevitable variations shake things up and select the next generation of leaders. Those who refuse to move are the ones who are unsurprisingly displaced by the waves of change. Their leadership is a flash-in-the-pan and will not last. Their leadership is a temporary fit

Trouble-Shooting Leadership Exposures **311**

and NOT sustainable. Alternatively, those who adapt with the times are the ones who will experience lasting success and be able to lead in whatever conditions they find themselves.

In the short term, evolution improves your resilience to spikes of change. You can handle the twists and turns better because you have anticipated them. In the longer term, evolution improves your rejuvenation to arcs of change. You can flourish in the new environments because you have changed with them and can lead appropriately.

So what are these changes in which leaders must maintain their tools? A complete accounting would comprise a separate book or even encyclopedic series. However, the main thrust can be represented by three potent forces.

They offer Opportunities … and leaders must know how to jump all over them.

They also offer Threats … and leaders must know how to navigate their minefields.

And they are as follows.

Major Forces – Opportunities and Threats

There are many sources of change leaders face. However, we focus here on a representative 'big three' to pay special attention to:

- Technology – Process: How do we do things?
- Globalization – Location: Where and why do we do things?
- Institutionalization – Governance: Who influences when we do things?

Technology is a matter of leadership method or process. Its instruments and its implements. It impacts how we do things. As technology changes so do the methods in how we do our jobs.

Globalization is a matter of leadership environment or location. Its culture and its context. It impacts where and why do we do things. As cultures change so do the contexts that we do our jobs in.

Institutionalization is a matter of leadership rulebooks or governance. Its authority and its sanction. It impacts who determines and oversees the things we are allowed to do and when we are allowed to do them. As institutions change so do the definitions of our jobs.

All of these changes are like streams – constantly flowing and occasionally surging. As such they each represent both an opportunity and a threat. Opportunities to seize initiatives and sustainably succeed. Or threats that can overwhelm you, render you irrelevant, and ultimately fail.

And all of these streams are changing both incrementally (single loop, within paradigms) and radically (double loop, between paradigms).

312 Leveraging Your Leadership Success

During normal times change is flowing. It is incremental and evolutionary. It is piecemeal and gradual. It involves minor improvements to a few elements in a routinized, predictable way. Tweaking the parameters of the game. This challenges leaders to approach work from the same platform but in slightly different ways. Therefore, they must continuously take these into account when executing their jobs and trying to figure things out, motivate, be moral and purposeful, pull people together, and push people forward.

But these are not normal times. Change also surges. It can be discontinuous and revolutionary. And we are increasingly experiencing these paradigm-challenging shifts. Of a quantum nature. Where many elements change. Radically reshaping the playing field. Dramatically altering the rules of the game. This challenges leaders to loop back not just once but twice to question the very assumptions of the platforms themselves. Not just to make better phones (or telegraphs, letters, or fax machines) but to redefine the nature of media and communication. Not just to make better cars (or buggies, bicycles, or stage-coaches) but to redefine the meaning of distance and transportation. Not just to make better computers (or abaci, punch cards, or calculators) but to redefine the notion of exploration and computation. Therefore, they must also be prepared to reconceptualize and reimagine their jobs when trying to figure things out, motivate, be moral and purposeful, pull people together, and push people forward.

Change can therefore be viewed as a sort of punctuated equilibrium process in which long periods of small, incremental single-loop adaptations are periodically disturbed by intense periods of cataclysmic double-loop adjustment. Each represents a different exposure that leaders must take into account and guard against. When the deep structure of technology, culture, and institutions remains intact versus when it is dismantled. When systems are updated versus destroyed. When frontrunners are familiar versus when they seemingly come out of nowhere to supplant the old guard.

The impact of these exposures on leadership is illustrated in Table 12.1, with each detailed in the following discussions.

TABLE 12.1 So ... Where Are You Exposed (And What Are the Dangers)?

	Single-Loop (Streaming) Threat	Opportunity for Resilience	Double-Loop (Surging) Threat	Opportunity for Rejuvenation
Technological/ Network	Obstructed	➜ Smooth	Obsolete	➜ Reimagine
Global/ Cultures	Narrow	➜ Expand	Naive	➜ Elevate
Societal/ Institutions	Rejected	➜ Negotiate	Repugnant	➜ Partner

Technology

Newsflash 1 – How we do things is changing.

Technological transformations are driving this change.

Technology is an often-misunderstood word. It simply means the way in which we convert inputs into outputs for accomplishing tasks. An abacus or sundial is (low) technology. So are a (medium) calculator and a (higher) spreadsheet. So are the latest analytical tools embedded in (even higher) artificial intelligence and machine learning.

Changes in technology are altering networks. As such they can be viewed as threats to your leadership … or opportunities to strengthen and evolve your leadership.

Single-loop change in technology involves improvements to current systems or platforms. If threatened with immediate technological conflict then your leadership is in danger of becoming *OBSTRUCTED*. What you do simply will not work as well anymore. You must therefore learn the new tools. How to work the latest program or device. In essence, you must *SMOOTH* the road to change (i.e., update your skills) for better alignment with the new reality. This provides an immediate opportunity to keep your existing leadership alive while technology transitions.

Double-loop change in technology involves transitions to new systems or platforms. If threatened with evolving technological conflict then your leadership is in danger of becoming perpetually obstructed and increasingly *OBSOLETE*. What you do is simply not done anymore. You must therefore travel through multiple iterations of change and learn the new paradigms. How to approach the different process and mindset. In essence, you must *REIMAGINE* the direction of change (i.e., transform your mindset) for better alignment with the vastly new reality. This provides an ongoing opportunity to enhance your future leadership after technology transitions.

Globalization

Newsflash 2 – Where and why we do things is changing.

Global/cultural transformations are driving this change.

Globalization is also an often-misunderstood word. It simply means the figurative shrinking of distances where we are more interdependent on one another regardless of physical geography. This is in contrast to being independent (no relationships or impacts) or dependent (one-way relationships or impacts).

Changes in globalization and the interrelation of cultures can be viewed as threats to your leadership … or opportunities to strengthen and evolve your leadership.

Single-loop change in globalization involves improvements to current systems or platforms. If threatened with immediate globalization conflict then your leadership is in danger of becoming *NARROW*. The way you do things will not work

314 Leveraging Your Leadership Success

as well in some places. Perhaps because you do not see differences and are ignorant of cultural differences. Perhaps because you feel that your way is always better than other peoples' ways and are arrogant about cultural differences. You must therefore learn the new cultures. How to work within the local climates. In essence, you must *EXPAND* the road to change (i.e., update your cultural intelligence) for better alignment with the new reality. This provides an immediate opportunity to keep your existing leadership alive while global networks transition.

Double-loop change in globalization involves transitions to new systems or platforms. If threatened with evolving globalization conflict then your leadership is in danger of becoming perpetually narrow and increasingly *NAIVE*. What you do, even if once deemed acceptable, is simply not done anymore on the world stage. You must therefore travel through multiple iterations of change and learn the new global paradigms. How to approach the different process and mindset. In essence, you must *ELEVATE* the direction of change (i.e., transform your mindset) for better alignment with the vastly new reality. This provides an ongoing opportunity to enhance your future leadership after global transitions.

Institutions

Newsflash 3 – Who determines when we do things is changing.

Institutional transformations are driving this change.

Institution is, like the prior two terms, also often misunderstood. It does not refer simply to a stigmatized mental care facility. It is actually a more encompassing term referring to governing bodies and organizations that set and regulate policies relating to such areas as economics, politics, and law.

Changes in institutions can be viewed as threats to your leadership … or opportunities to strengthen and evolve your leadership.

Single-loop change in institutions involves improvements to presiding systems or platforms. If threatened with immediate institutional conflict then your leadership is in danger of becoming *REJECTED*. The way you do things simply will not be allowed to work anymore. They may be deemed inappropriate or ruled illegal. Against the current political will. Against the current economic consensus. Against the current legal dicta. You must therefore learn the new changes in institutions. How to work within the sovereign local frameworks. In essence, you must *NEGOTIATE* the road to change for better alignment with the new reality. This provides an immediate opportunity to keep your existing leadership alive while global institutions transition.

Double-loop change in institutions involves transitions to new systems or platforms. If threatened with evolving institutional conflict then your leadership is in danger of becoming perpetually rejected and increasingly *REPUGNANT*. What you do, even if at one time seen as benign or merely tolerated, is seen as deeply offensive and deemed fundamentally unacceptable under (nearly) any circumstances. It is not just illegal, it is antithetical to the core. You must therefore travel through multiple iterations of change and learn the new institutional paradigms. How to approach the different process and mindset. In essence, you must *PARTNER* with these institutions in the direction of change (i.e., transform your mindset) for better alignment with the vastly new reality. This provides an ongoing opportunity to enhance your future leadership after institutional transitions.

Taken Together

Are you sold on the importance of maintenance?

Improving your immediate leadership success through short-term resilience?

Improving your ongoing leadership success through long-term rejuvenation?

Good. Because we do not have a choice in whether these things happen. They are happening now and occurring at accelerating velocities. Whether you, or I, like it or not.

In Chapter 10 we discussed the growing *complexity* of the leader's landscape and the importance of choosing the right tool. This was about crafting a wise leadership strategy.

In Chapter 11 we discussed the growing *competitiveness* of the leader's landscape and the importance of strengthening their tools. This was about playing offense.

Now …

In Chapter 12 we will discuss the growing *dynamism* of the leader's landscape and the importance of maintaining and adapting their tools. This is about playing defense.

Technology and Leadership

> The factory of the future will have only two employees, a man and a dog. The man will be there to feed the dog. The dog will be there to keep the man from touching the equipment.
>
> *(Warren Bennis)*

There are many ways that technological change influences leadership success, both in the short and long term. And as the opening quote to this section suggests, they will change the nature of work and the way it is led. Perhaps not in the literal sense put forth by Warren Bennis but certainly consistent with the spirit of his prod that leaders need to be aware of and prepare for them. Here are some of the most impactful.

Your TECHNOLOGICAL Leadership Exposures

1 Power: Doing More Faster

The most obvious way in which technology impacts leadership is its ability to transform the band-width of a leader's activities. Their communication is not limited to one-on-one sequential interactions but instead can reach employees instantaneously and simultaneously. Computers and their merged machineries have exponentially greater computational power than their prior generations. And their arc is increasing in pitch. What once took an entire room of machinery to do can now be done within the confines of a teenager's backpack or back pocket.

As an illustration, consider the impact of *artificial intelligence* upon leadership. How will this change how we think, feel, reflect, aspire, coordinate, and execute?

Today, and for the foreseeable tomorrows, leaders must update their leadership to gel with the increased power of computers.

2 Embeddedness: Integrated with Everyday

A second way in which technology impacts leadership is its ubiquity and the ability to improve the impact of a leader's activities. Their processing power is not constrained by human limitations but instead enhanced with machine-processing power and learning capacity. Just as it was probably unimaginable for our great grandparents to visualize the vast sway of computers in our lives today, it is probably equally if not more difficult for us to imagine the world that our great grandchildren will inhabit. Technology in our accessories, woven into the (figurative as well as literal) fabrics of our lives, and even into our bodies and heads.

As an illustration, consider the impact of *wearable and imbedded devices* on leadership. How will this change how we think, feel, reflect, aspire, coordinate, and execute?

Today, and for the foreseeable tomorrows, leaders must update their leadership to gel with the increased penetration of computers.

3 Networking: Links, Webs, and Systems

A third way in which technology impacts leadership is its connectivity and the ability to improve the impact of a leader's activities. Their relationships are not constrained by personal familiarities but instead enhanced with verifiable trust networks and record keeping. In a word, everything is increasingly symbiotic and connected. This means immediate, short-term hyperlinks and wikis. This means constructed, medium-term intra- and inter-nets. This also means distributed, long-term virtual trust networks that store and retain the aforementioned while increasingly blurring the boundaries between organizations over time.

As an illustration, consider the impact of *block chain* and similar transactional exchange mechanisms upon leadership. How will this change how we think, feel, reflect, aspire, coordinate, and execute?

Today, and for the foreseeable tomorrows, leaders must update their leadership to gel with the increased connectivity and networking of computers.

Upshot

You must maintain your leadership edge amidst technological changes.

Leadership in an increasingly high-powered world must leverage this force. Leadership in an increasingly embedded world must acclimatize to this ubiquity. Leadership in an increasingly networked world must merge in this interconnectivity. Thus the modern leader must harness and leverage, incorporate and acclimatize, as well as flow and merge with its evolving reality. For example:

Understanding like a scientist – Technology will challenge our understanding and the prevailing Leadership Logic. So … Will we be able to figure out how things work, or get lost in its futuristic machineries?

Motivating like an artist – Technology will challenge our enthusiasm and the prevailing Leadership Aesthetics. So … How can we get jazzed about it and through it, or will it sap our desire and joy?

Reflecting like an icon – Technology will challenge our morals and the prevailing Leadership Ethics. So … Should we do all of the things it enables us to do, or are some things better left undone?

Aspiring like an advocate – Technology will challenge our meaning and the prevailing Leadership Metaphysics. So … Do we like where it is taking us, or do we not want to go to some places?

Coordinating like a maestro – Technology will challenge our connections and the prevailing Leadership Epistemology. So … Will it link us, or will it isolate and separate us into rival camps?

Executing like a general – Technology will challenge our performance metrics and the prevailing Leadership Politics. So … Will it make us more effective and give us an edge, or render our advantages obsolete?

STRATEGIES For Mitigating Your Technological Leadership Exposures

The above are good questions. Here are some ways to go about confronting them.

Technology and Leadership Logic

Technology effects, and is affected by, the Leadership <u>Scientist</u> tool.

Accept that it brings the leader more data, more information, and more knowledge. Also accept that it does not necessarily bring them more wisdom. For this, technology must be used to increase versus obscure *understanding*.

To enlighten us versus dumb us down. To free us versus overwhelm us. To make us more capable and flexible versus more rigid and programmed. As an example, do you use Google to become stronger or, by relying on it so much, become weaker?

318 Leveraging Your Leadership Success

Leaders must therefore avoid chasing technology as an end and instead use it as a means to better meet their primary scientist-related challenges.

To enhance breadth and depth of comprehension.

To enhance perception and intuition.

To enhance rationality and creativity.

Technology and Leadership Aesthetics

Technology effects, and is affected by, the Leadership <u>Artist</u> tool.

Accept that it brings the leader more opportunities for outreach and customization. Also accept that it does not necessarily bring them more inspiration. For this, technology must be used to increase versus dissipate *energy*.

To animate us versus dampen or alienate us. To make us more versus less excited. To make us masters of versus slaves to the screen. As an example, does using your smartphone make you more or less joyous and vibrant?

Leaders must therefore avoid chasing technology as an end and instead use it as a means to better meet their primary artist-related challenges.

To enhance human sensitivity and empathy.

To enhance positivity and pluralism.

To enhance motivational and inspiration.

Technology and Leadership Ethics

Technology effects, and is affected by, the Leadership <u>Icon</u> tool.

Accept that it brings the leader more opportunities for reflection, assessment, and probes. Also accept that it does not necessarily bring them more internal grounding. For this, technology must be used to increase versus dissipate *integrity*.

To bring out our best versus our worst. To make us more versus less introspective. To elevate us as people of character versus debase us as small-minded, biased caricatures. As an example, does your use of social media make you behave more, or less, principled?

Leaders must therefore avoid chasing technology as an end and instead use it as a means to better meet their primary icon-related challenges.

To enhance morality.

To enhance authenticity.

To enhance esteem, agency, and confidence.

Technology and Leadership Metaphysics

Technology effects, and is affected by, the Leadership <u>Advocate</u> tool.

Accept that it brings the leader more opportunities for accessing and targeting objectives. Also accept that it does not necessarily them bring more external purpose. For this, technology must be used to increase versus dissipate *meaning*.

To enlarge versus limit our horizons. To make us dream bigger versus smaller. To make us less versus more selfish and ego-oriented. To elevate versus diminish our larger sense of significance. As an example, do you use your laptop, computer, or tablet to become more or less mindful (in the moment) and transcendent (of the big picture)?

Leaders must therefore avoid chasing technology as an end and instead use it as a means to better meet their primary advocate-related challenges.

To enhance ontology and perspective.

To enhance collegiality and inclusiveness.

To enhance munificence and service.

Technology and Leadership Epistemology

Technology effects, and is affected by, the Leadership <u>Maestro</u> tool.

Accept that it brings the leader more opportunities for coordination, association, and relationship building. Also accept that it does not necessarily bring them more communication or connection. For this, technology must be used to increase versus dissipate *harmony*.

To work out versus exacerbate our conflicts. To bond versus fracture. To make us less versus more isolated. To supplement versus substitute for human contact. To bring us together versus drive us apart. As an example, do you use the Internet to become more, or less, connected to other people?

Leaders must therefore avoid chasing technology as an end and instead use it as a means to better meet their primary maestro-related challenges.

To enhance complementarity and alignment.

To enhance interdependency and partnership.

To enhance connective structure and culture.

Technology and Leadership Politics

Technology effects, and is affected by, the Leadership <u>Politics</u> tool.

Accept that it brings the leader more opportunities for getting things done better, cheaper, and faster. Also accept that it does not necessarily bring them more efficiency or effectiveness. For this, technology must be used to increase versus dissipate *execution*.

To enlarge versus limit our competitiveness. To help versus hinder our learning. To make us more versus less innovative. To raise versus diminish our viability and marketability. As an example, do you use machines and other highly automated resources to become more, or less, effective and sustainable?

Leaders must therefore avoid chasing technology as an end and instead use it as a means to better meet their primary general-related challenges.

320 Leveraging Your Leadership Success

To enhance excellence.
To enhance advantage.
To enhance adaptivity.

Globalization and Leadership

> In today's interconnected and globalized world, it's now commonplace
> for people of different world views, faiths and races to live side by side.
> It's a matter of great urgency, therefore, that we find ways to cooperate
> with one another in a spirit of mutual acceptance and respect.
>
> *(Dalai Lama)*

There are many ways in which global/cultural change influences leadership success, both in the short and long term. And as the opening quote to this section suggests, they will change the nature of work and the way it is led. Both in deep-seeded and practical ways as the Dalai Lama rightly observes (and, interestingly enough, communicated transnationally via Twitter). Here are some of the most impactful.

Your GLOBAL Leadership Exposures

1 Geography: A Smaller World

The most obvious way in which globalization impacts leadership is its ability to transform the location of a leader's activities.

There is a new global reality. A more integrated and interdependent world economy characterized by the rapid flow of resources, information, goods and services, capital, and people. And this does not vary based on whether you want it to be so. It is here. It is not going away. And it is not receding. This is making the term 'global leadership' redundant – there is simply no other kind.

Leaders must address themselves to a global market of broad tastes and preferences. Served by global production with varying factor costs. Fueled by global technology that is lowering the costs of transportation and data processing while expanding the reach of communication networks and mass media. Thus they must interact with global institutions that manage and promote interdependencies. With global firms and multinational enterprises (MNEs) that cross and overlap countries. Which create a global economy ripe with trade, investment, job creation (as well as loss and displacement), and wealth creation.

Today, and for the foreseeable tomorrows, leaders must update their leadership to gel with the increased diffusion within and across places.

2 Culture/Tradition: A Blended World

A second way in which globalization impacts leadership is its ability to transform the scope of a leader's activities.

Across the planet there exist different path-dependent, taken-for-granted, life-guiding assumptions about how to think and act. That is to say, different cultures. And these cultures bring with them varied mores and folkways that alter the routines of personal and professional practices. Therefore, wise leaders need to cultivate cross-cultural literacy – a comprehension of how cultural differences across and within nations can affect the way in which business is practiced.

They do this, as per the research of Chris Earley (Earley & Ang, 2003), through the development of a 'cultural intelligence' (CQ). This involves a meta-cognitive, deep understanding of the places and peoples of the world. This also involves a motivation and willingness to positively engage in and with them. And this additionally involves a behavioral alacrity and skill-set to do this well.

Today, and for the foreseeable tomorrows, leaders must update their leadership to gel with the increased layering and nuance of locations.

3 Topography: A Flatter and Spiky World

A third way in which globalization impacts leadership is its ability to transform the (a)symmetry of a leader's activities.

There is, as per Thomas Friedman (2005), a 'flattening' across the world where leveling playing fields are creating unprecedented levels of competition and coordination. However, there also remains, as per Richard Florida (2008), an unevenness or 'spikiness' across these horizons where the world map is better represented as topographical and textured. There are scattered and concentrated hot spots for different technologies, different competencies, and different focuses. And they are shifting. Imagine trying to map, let alone traverse, mountain ranges that rise and fall unpredictably as well as dramatically.

Thus leaders need to identify the degrees to which they must be responsive to as well as coordinating these global forces (Bartlett & Ghoshal, 1989). Should leadership approaches be customized for each distinct location or standardized across common cultures and markets? And if so, how? Should value leadership activities be simultaneously coordinated on a global and regional basis or idiosyncratic on a country-by-country basis? And if so, how? Make no mistake about it, today the pressure on leaders to be transnational is greater than ever. To target and adapt strategies. To develop and share competencies. To promote global learning.

Today, and for the foreseeable tomorrows, leaders must update their leadership to gel with the increased complexity of globalization.

Upshot

Globalization is increasing the level of uncertainty that leaders must deal with.

You must maintain your leadership edge amidst cultural changes.

Leadership in an increasingly uncertain world must leverage its increasing complexity, dynamism, and richness. Leadership in an increasingly interconnected world

322 Leveraging Your Leadership Success

must acclimatize through appropriate responsiveness, assimilation, and amalgamation. Leadership in an increasingly challenged world must merge its concerns with those of peoples (poverty), profits (jobs), and the planet (environment). Thus the modern leader must leverage uncertainties, acclimatize to interdependencies, and merge with larger realities.

Understanding like a scientist – Globalization will increasingly highlight that we have different understandings and Leadership Logics. So ... Will cultures change what we know, or will we remain ignorant and prejudicial of others' knowledge?

Motivating like an artist – Globalization will increasingly highlight that we have different motivations and Leadership Aesthetics. So ... Will cultures change why we work, or will convention trump enlightenment?

Reflecting like an icon – Globalization will increasingly highlight that we have different morals and Leadership Ethics. So ... Will cultures change what is right and good, or will we be rigid and perhaps even xenophobic in our sense of morality?

Aspiring like an advocate – Globalization will increasingly highlight that we have different meanings and Leadership Metaphysics. So ... Will cultures change our goals and ends, or will we pursue different or perhaps contradictory and conflicting paths?

Coordinating like a maestro – Globalization will increasingly highlight that we have different connections and Leadership Epistemologies. So ... Will cultures change our methods of communication, or will we talk at and past (rather than with) each other?

Executing like a general – Globalization will increasingly highlight that we have different performance metrics and Leadership Politics. So ... Will cultures change our means to productivity, or will we hunker down (and reject everything 'not-invented-here') rather than learn, improve, and evolve?

STRATEGIES For Mitigating Your Global Leadership Exposures

The above are good questions. Here are some ways to go about confronting them.

Globalization and Leadership Logic

Globalization effects, and is affected by, the Leadership <u>Scientist</u> tool.

Accept that it brings the leader more diverse mythology and path-dependent history.

Also accept that, unless used well, it does not necessarily bring them greater truth. For this, culture must be approached in a way that increases versus obscures *understanding.*

As an example, consider Geert Hofstede's (2001; as per Garibaldi de Hilal, 2003) cultural dimension of Uncertainty Avoidance (UA).

Trouble-Shooting Leadership Exposures **323**

What is it? It indicates to what extent a culture programs its members to feel either comfortable or anxious when processing incomplete information and making judgments about things that are not known. Why is it important? It manifests itself in decision rules, rituals, regulations, and planning. How should you adjust? UA tends to be higher in East and Central European countries, in Latin countries, in Japan and in German-speaking countries, lower in English speaking, Nordic and Chinese culture countries.

So … Wise leaders must therefore avoid treating culture as irrelevant myth. Instead, they need to balance facets of its global logic and judgment to understand better and meet their primary scientist-related challenges.

To enhance global comprehension.

To enhance global perception and intuition.

To enhance global rationality and creativity.

Globalization and Leadership Aesthetics

Globalization effects, and is affected by, the Leadership <u>Artist</u> tool.

Accept that it brings the leader more diverse energies. Also accept that, unless used well, it does not necessarily bring them greater motivations or encouragements. For this, culture must be approached in a way that increases versus obscures *inspiration*.

As an example, consider Hofstede's cultural dimension of Indulgence versus Restraint.

What is it? Indulgent societies allow relatively free gratification of human desires related to enjoying life and having fun, whereas restrained societies control this more by means of strict social norms and de-emphasis on leisure. Why is it important? It relates to the prioritization of different pleasures and the means for pursuing happiness. How should you adjust? Indulgence tends to prevail in North and South America, in Western Europe, and in parts of Sub-Sahara Africa. Restraint prevails in Eastern Europe, in Asia, and in the Muslim world. Mediterranean Europe occupies a middle position on this dimension.

So … Wise leaders must therefore avoid treating culture as extraneous to spirit. Instead, they need to balance facets of its global pleasures and inspirations to energize better and meet their primary artist-related challenges.

To enhance global sensitivity and empathy.

To enhance global positivity and pluralism.

To enhance global motivation and influence.

Globalization and Leadership Ethics

Globalization effects, and is affected by, the Leadership <u>Icon</u> tool.

Accept that it brings the leader more diverse principles. Also accept that, unless used well, it does not necessarily bring them greater morality. For this, culture must be approached in a way that increases versus obscures *integrity*.

324 Leveraging Your Leadership Success

As an example, consider Hofstede's cultural dimension of Quantity versus Quality of life.

What is it? More stereotypical masculine (assertive) versus feminine (caring) societies emphasize different values between the genders. Why is it important? In quantity-oriented, masculine countries there is a more aggressive, competitive, and materialistic ethic whereas in quality-oriented, feminine countries there is more equality, camaraderie, and appreciation. How should you adjust? Masculinity is generally high in Japan, in German-speaking countries, and in some Latin countries like Italy and Mexico; it is moderately high in English-speaking Western countries; it is low in Nordic countries and moderately low in some Latin and Asian countries like Chile, Korea, and Thailand.

So ... Wise leaders must therefore avoid treating culture as background noise. Instead, they need to balance facets of its global ethics and morals to elevate character and better meet their primary icon-related challenges.

To enhance global morality.

To enhance global authenticity.

To enhance global confidence.

Globalization and Leadership Metaphysics

Globalization effects, and is affected by, the Leadership <u>Advocate</u> tool.

Accept that it brings the leader more diverse ambitions. Also accept that it does not necessarily bring them greater commonality of purpose. For this, culture must be approached in a way that increases versus obscures *meaning.*

As an example, consider Hofstede's cultural dimension of Long-Term vs. Short-Term Orientation.

What is it? Consistent with a Confucian work dynamism, it relates to the relative time frame in which meaning and success are assessed. Why is it important? In short-term-oriented cultures the hear-and-now and bottom line tend to be major concerns, and leaders judge and are judged by these metrics. In long-term oriented societies, businesses work towards gradually building up strong positions in their markets and assess success not by immediate results but by overarching progress and patterns. How should you adjust? Generally, long-term-oriented countries are East Asian countries, followed by Eastern and Central European countries. A medium-term orientation is found in South and North European and South Asian countries. Shorter term-oriented countries are the U.S.A. and Australia; Latin American, African, and Muslim countries.

So ... Wise leaders must therefore avoid treating culture as disorientation. Instead, they need to balance facets of present- and future-global significances to elevate meaning and better meet their primary advocate-related challenges.

To enhance global ontology and perspective.

To enhance global collegiality and inclusiveness.

To enhance global munificence and service.

Globalization and Leadership Epistemology

Globalization effects, and is affected by, the Leadership Maestro tool.

Accept that it brings the leader more, and more diverse, moving parts. Also accept that it does not necessarily bring them greater wholeness. For this, culture must be approached in a way that increases versus obscures *harmony*.

As an example, consider Hofstede's cultural dimension of Individualism vs. Collectivism.

What is it? Individualism is the degree to which people are loosely coupled from others and think of themselves as independent entities, whereas on the opposite end Collectivism is the degree to which people in a society think of themselves and are tightly integrated as cohesive and loyal groups. Why is it important? In individualistic cultures employees are expected to act according to their own interest, and the relationship between employee and employer is primarily through the invisible hand of business transactions. In a collectivistic culture, an employer hires not an individual but a group member, so actively cultivating trust and loyalty is of critical importance. How should you adjust? Individualism tends to prevail in developed and Western countries, while collectivism tends to prevail in less developed, Latin American and Eastern countries.

So … Wise leaders must therefore avoid treating culture as separation. Instead, they need to balance facets of its global coordination mechanisms (the 'me' with the 'we') to improve harmony and better meet their primary maestro-related challenges.

To enhance global complementarity and alignment.
To enhance global interdependency and partnership.
To enhance global connective structure and culture.

Globalization and Leadership Politics

Globalization effects, and is affected by, the Leadership Politics tool.

Accept that it brings the leader more, and more diverse, potential. Also accept that, unless used well, it does not necessarily bring them greater performance. For this, culture must be approached in a way that increases versus obscures *execution*.

As an example, consider Hofstede's cultural dimension of Power Distance (PD).

What is it? Power Distance is the extent to which members of organizations and institutions accept and expect that formal power be distributed unequally. Why is it important? Subordinates in low PD countries tend to prefer a consultative type of leader who gets things done by sharing power, while subordinates in high PD countries tend to see as more effective, and thus are more accepting of, paternalistic leaders who wield it more centrally and autocratically. How should you adjust? Power Distance tends to be higher for East European, Latin, Asian, and African countries and lower for Germanic and English-speaking Western countries.

326 Leveraging Your Leadership Success

So ... Wise leaders must therefore avoid treating culture as a barrier or handicap. Instead, they need to balance facets of its global control with empowerment to improve execution and better meet their primary general-related challenges.

To enhance global excellence.

To enhance global advantage.

To enhance global adaptiveness.

Institutions and Leadership

> Leadership and learning are indispensable to each other.
>
> *(John F. Kennedy)*

Institutions are important. They shape the organizations and the people who operate within them. As per institutional theory it explains how macro pressures shape micro actions. That leaders are subject to pressures of governments, pressures of markets, and pressures of laws that force them to adapt their practices in order to achieve, and maintain, legitimacy.

For example, as per Paul DiMaggio and Walter Powell (1983), organizations and their leaders often face three different types of isomorphic (i.e., conformity) pressures from their larger institutional environments: (1) Coercive isomorphism and the need to appear legitimate to powerful regulators such as the state − these tend to be explicitly articulated and enforced through mandates for obeying rules or policies. (2) Normative isomorphism and the demand to appear legitimate to respected networks − these tend to be more implicitly advanced through professional practices and standards. (3) Finally, mimetic isomorphism and the desire to be consistent with more experienced, successful leaders and organizations − these tend to be even more informal and context-specific.

In short, there are many ways in which institutional factors weigh on leadership success. And as the opening quote to this section suggests, they will change the nature of work and the way it is led. Therefore, as per President Kennedy, there must be a dynamic harmony between the ways in which leaders lead and the confluence of the various dimensions which comprise their contexts. Here are some of the most impactful.

Your INSTITUTIONAL Leadership Exposures

1 Politics and Governments: Expansive

The most obvious way in which institutions impact leadership is in the enormity of its ability to transform a leader's activities. And no organization or their leaders is bigger than the government(s) which oversee, enable, and endorse (or not) their activities.

There are many different ilks of governmental systems operating across the world. Each influences leadership practices and success differently. And among these there are many variations and frequently shifting cycles of acceptance.

For example, here are a few of the major ones (see Hill, 2013): (1) Democracy – A political system in which the right to govern is granted by the people and the act of governing is of the people. It is fundamentally based on the assumption that a citizen populace should be involved in decision making either directly or through elected agents. (2) Totalitarian – A political system in which the right to govern and the act of governing is separated from the people. Here one person or one party exercises (near) total control over all spheres of public activity. Different forms of totalitarianism exist, including: (a) Communist – based in single party rule, (b) Theocratic – based in single religious rule, and (c) Tribal – based in single community or clan rule. (3) Hybrid – Many variations entailing different blends of democratic and totalitarian modes.

What is the prevailing trend? Some contend that democracy might be 'on the march'. In other times and places there may be shifts towards authoritarianism. So it depends on when and where you are reading this.

Today, and for the foreseeable tomorrows, leaders must update their leadership to gel with different and evolving political climates. Adapting to the political environment begets amiable leadership. Opposing the political environment results in antagonistic leadership.

2 Laws and Regulations: Transnational

A second way in which institutions impact leadership is the comprehensiveness of its dominion in the ability to legislate or regulate a leader's activities.

There are many different types of legal systems operating across the world. Each influences leadership practices and success differently by mandating the content and associated obligations of the legal codes, the process by which they are enforced, and the adjudication mechanisms available for obtaining compliance and redress.

For example, here are a few of the major ones (see Hill, 2013): (1) Common law – Laws are based on tradition, precedent, and custom. It tends to be a relatively flexible and adaptable system. (2) Civic law – Laws are based on detailed sets of laws organized into codes. It tends to be a more stable and less adversarial system. (3) Theocratic law – Laws are based on religious teachings.

Each of the above has vastly different ways of dealing with matters essential to leadership and business. For example, these codes bring to bear varied policies and procedures regarding the issues of transactions and executing contracts, defending property rights, fighting corruption, protecting intellectual property, and ensuring personal safety.

Today, and for the foreseeable tomorrows, leaders must update their leadership to gel with the particular and shifting nuances of legal systems. Adapting to the legal environment begets permitted leadership. Opposing the legal environment results in prohibited leadership (and jail, fines, etc.).

328 Leveraging Your Leadership Success

3 Economic Systems and Engines: Indispensable

A third way in which institutions impact leadership is the commercial and financial power of its ability to transform a leader's activities.

There are many different types and blends of economic systems operating across the world. For example, here are a few of the major ones (see Hill, 2013): (1) Market economies – Productive activities are wholly or mostly privately owned. Production and prices are determined by the interaction of supply and demand. Resources are allocated by the invisible hands of the competitive marketplace often under the rubric of free and fair competition. (2) Command economies – Productive activities are wholly or mostly controlled by public officials and bureaucrats. Production and prices are determined by government planners. Resources are allocated by the visible hands of the government, often under the rubric of what is 'good for society'. (3) Mixed economies – Select sectors of the economy are orchestrated by private ownership and free market mechanisms whereas other sectors are under state ownership and government planners.

Again, it is important to note that each of the above has vastly different ways of dealing with matters essential to leadership practices and success. Such as their impact on organization, on strategy, and on operations.

Today, and for the foreseeable tomorrows, leaders must update their leadership to gel with the active and emergent engines of economic systems. Adapting to the economic environment begets fluid leadership. Opposing the economic environment results in clunky, awkward leadership.

Upshot

You must consider the appropriateness of your leadership edge amidst institutional changes. The modern leader must account for, manage, and align with evolving institutional realities.

Understanding like a scientist – Institutions will increasingly shape our understandings and attempt to guide our Leadership Logic. So … What knowledge and means of understanding will be sanctioned/promoted by the overarching system(s)? Will we be consistent or run afoul of these?

Motivating like an artist – Institutions will increasingly shape our inspirations and attempt to guide our Leadership Aesthetic. So … What motivations and paths to happiness will be sanctioned/promoted by the overarching system(s)? Will we be consistent or run afoul of these?

Reflecting like an icon – Institutions will increasingly shape our morals and attempt to guide our Leadership Ethic. So … What standards of right and wrong will be sanctioned/promoted by the overarching system(s)? Will ours be in line with or contradict them?

Aspiring like an advocate – Institutions will increasingly shape our meanings and attempt to guide our Leadership Metaphysic. So … What perspectives, goals, and aspirations will be sanctioned/promoted by the overarching system(s)? Will ours be in line with or contradict them?

Coordinating like a maestro – Institutions will increasingly shape our connections and attempt to guide our Leadership Epistemology. So … What communication architectures and means of interacting will be sanctioned/promoted by the overarching system(s)? Will they work or not with our methods?

Executing like a general – Institutions will increasingly shape our functioning and attempt to guide our Leadership Politics. So … What performance metrics and means of operating, innovating, and executing will be sanctioned/promoted by the overarching system(s)? Will they work or not with our methods?

STRATEGIES For Mitigating Your Institutional Leadership Exposures

The above are good questions. Here are some ways to go about confronting them.

Institutions and Leadership Logic

Institutions effect, and are affected by, the Leadership <u>Scientist</u> tool.

Accept that it brings the leader more input into decisions. Also accept that it does not necessarily bring them better decisions and more intellectual clarity. For this, institutions must be managed in a way that increases versus obscures *understanding*.

As an example, consider the varied approaches taken by institutions towards the validity and power of science as a field. With regard to evolution. Climate change. Artificial intelligence. And how are these factored into government, economic, and legal systems?

So … Wise leaders thus not only need to be trained, they also need to be educated to better manage data-information-knowledge trends into wisdom and meet their primary scientist-related challenges.

To enhance institutional comprehension.

To enhance institutional perception and intuition.

To enhance institutional rationality and creativity.

Institutions and Leadership Aesthetics

Institutions effect, and are affected by, the Leadership <u>Artist</u> tool.

Accept that it brings the leader more emotional influencers. Also accept that it does not necessarily bring them better inducements and greater passion. For this, institutions must be managed in a way that increases versus obscures *energy*.

As an example, consider the varied approaches taken by institutions towards money and the meaning of wages, affluence, wealth creation, and capital distribution. What levels are desired? Promoted? How should financial resources be

330 Leveraging Your Leadership Success

pursued? Dispersed? Regulated? And how are these are factored into government, economic, and legal systems?

So … Wise leaders thus need to manage incentives to better meet their primary artist-related challenges.

To enhance institutional sensitivity and empathy.

To enhance institutional positivity and pluralism.

To enhance institutional motivational and inspiration.

Institutions and Leadership Ethics

Institutions effect, and are affected by, the Leadership <u>Icon</u> tool.

Accept that it brings the leader more ethical standard bearers and adjudicators. Also accept that it does not necessarily bring them better codes and more moral clarity. For this, institutions must be managed in a way that increases versus obscures *integrity*.

As an example, consider the varied approaches taken by institutions towards the nature and meaning of freedom. Of speech. Assembly. Worship. The press. Ownership. Are these seen as good things? Virtues to cultivate or vices to remedy? And how is this factored into government, economic, and legal systems (and does legal mean the same thing as ethical)?

So … Wise leaders thus need to manage freedoms to better meet their primary icon-related challenges.

To enhance institutional morality.

To enhance institutional authenticity.

To enhance institutional confidence.

Institutions and Leadership Metaphysics

Institutions effect, and are affected by, the Leadership <u>Advocate</u> tool.

Accept that it brings the leader more definitions of importance and purpose. Also accept that it does not necessarily promote enlightened ends and more vision clarity. For this, institutions must be managed in a way that increases versus obscures *meaning*.

As an example, consider the varied approaches taken by institutions towards ideology and belief. Are people encouraged and allowed to aspire? To pursue spirituality in their own ways and on their own terms? To find and define their significance and value? Or does loyalty trump principles? Dogma drown out devotion? And how are these factored into government, economic, and legal systems?

So … Wise leaders thus need to manage spirituality to better meet their primary advocate-related challenges.

To enhance institutional ontology and perspective.

To enhance institutional collegiality and inclusiveness.

To enhance institutional munificence and service.

Trouble-Shooting Leadership Exposures **331**

Institutions and Leadership Epistemology

Institutions effect, and are affected by, the Leadership <u>Maestro</u> tool.

Accept that it brings the leader more integration mechanisms. Also accept that it does not necessarily promote better collaboration, increased synchronicity, and more coordinative clarity. For this, institutions must be managed in a way that increases versus obscures *harmony.*

As an example, consider the varied approaches taken by institutions towards community and family. What priority is given to the maintenance of harmonious homes, neighborhoods, organizations, and societies? To what extent is there complementarity? Mutuality? Respect? Partnership? Especially between opposing parties. Or is an aggressive 'us-versus-them' culture cultivated and perpetuated? And how are these are factored into government, economic, and legal systems?

So … Wise leaders thus need to manage community to better meet their primary maestro-related challenges.

To enhance institutional complementarity and alignment.

To enhance institutional interdependency and partnership.

To enhance institutional connective structure and culture.

Institutions and Leadership Politics

Institutions effect, and are affected by, the Leadership <u>Politics</u> tool.

Accept that it brings the leader more assets and raw productive power. Also accept that it does not necessarily promote better operational methods, more innovation, and increased performance clarity. For this, institutions must be managed in a way that increases versus obscures *execution.*

As an example, consider the varied approaches taken by institutions towards innovation, enterprise, and entrepreneurial activity. Basically, in defining the role of the leader and their organizations. Are outcomes valued as much as processes? Pragmatism as much as the pedantic? Efficiency as much as appearance? Resourcefulness as much as regulation? The new as much as the conventional? Invention as much as the traditional? And how are these factored into government, economic, and legal systems?

So … Wise leaders thus need to manage initiative to better meet their primary general-related challenges.

To enhance institutional excellence.

To enhance institutional advantage.

To enhance institutional learning and change.

Your Personal Trouble-Shooting Checklist

Table 12.2 presents a practical template and planning aid for the reader to use to minimize leadership erosion.

332 Leveraging Your Leadership Success

TABLE 12.2 A Trouble-Shooting Checklist

	Technological Resilience and Rejuvenation	Global Resilience and Rejuvenation	Institutional Resilience and Rejuvenation
Head/Logic	Think Stronger	Think Broader	Think Consistently
Heart/Aesthetics	Inspire Stronger	Inspire Broader	Inspire Consistently
Inside/Ethics	Reflect Stronger	Reflect Broader	Reflect Consistently
Outside/Metaphysics	Aspire Stronger	Aspire Broader	Aspire Consistently
Pull/Epistemology	Synergize Stronger	Synergize Broader	Synergize Consistently
Push/Politics	Engage Stronger	Engage Broader	Engage Consistently

Technological Change

So ask yourself:

Can wisely incorporating technology help me to ... Think or inspire better? Reflect or aspire better? Synergize or engage better?

Is technological change a barrier to my leadership in the short term? Or am I a technologically resilient leader?

In the long term will it surpass me and, if not accounted for, make me fail? Or will I perpetually be a technologically rejuvenated leader?

Wisely evolving your leadership with changes in technology can prevent your tools' erosion by keeping them STRONG. In the short term if you smooth over its process-related obstructions to your leadership, and in the long term by continuously reimagining their technical possibilities to avoid obsolescence.

Global/Cultural Change

So ask yourself:

Can wisely embracing globalization help me ... Think or inspire better? Reflect or aspire better? Synergize or engage better?

Is cultural change a barrier to my leadership in the short term? Or am I a globally resilient leader?

In the long term will it surpass me and, if not accounted for, make me fail? Or will I perpetually be a globally rejuvenated leader?

Wisely evolving your leadership with changes in globalization can prevent your tools' erosion by keeping them BROAD. In the short term if you expand its context-related limits to your leadership, and in the long term by continuously elevating their cultural applicability to avoid naivety.

Institutional Change

So ask yourself:

Can wisely working with institutions help me ... Think or inspire better? Reflect or aspire better? Synergize or engage better?

Is economic, political, and legal change a barrier to my leadership in the short term? Or am I an institutionally resilient leader?

In the long term will it surpass me and, if not accounted for, make me fail? Or will I perpetually be an institutionally rejuvenated leader?

Wisely evolving your leadership with changes in institutions can prevent your tools' erosion by keeping them CONSISTENT. In the short term if you negotiate its governance-related assessments of your leadership, and in the long term by continuously partnering with their societal interests to avoid revolution.

Taken Together

Paraphrasing the insights of Winston Churchill, we must recognize that success is never final nor is failure necessarily fatal. This is why most leaders do not last. They do not recognize that they must perpetually maintain their tools and adapt to their world.

So, to summarize the chapter's (and, since it is our final chapter, the entire book's) ultimate, cumulative message:

If you ...

1. Discover Your Leadership Wisdom (from Part I), using the model's core components and contingencies ...
2. Assemble Your Leadership Toolbox (from Part II), dynamically applying its wisdom-based instruments and identities ...
3. Leverage Your Leadership Success (from Part III), based on selection, optimization, and maintenance guidelines ...

Then you can be an effective leader in any situation!

APPENDIX A

BIBLIOGRAPHY

Adams, S. (1996). *The Dilbert Principle: A Cubicle's-Eye View of Bosses, Meetings, Management Fads & Other Workplace Afflictions*. New York: Harper Collins.

Allen, S. (2017). Ten Ways to Encourage People to Give More. Greater Good Science Center at UC Berkeley. Retrieved from https://greatergood.berkeley.edu/article/item/ten_ways_to_encourage_people_to_give_more.

Allison. G. T., & Zelikow, P. (1972). *Essence of Decision: Explaining the Cuban Missile Crisis*. Boston, MA: Little, Brown.

Alvarez, S. A., & Barney, J. B. (2007). Discovery and Creation: Alternative Theories of Entrepreneurial Action. *Strategic Entrepreneurship Journal*, 1(1–2): 11–26.

American Film Institute (2019 search). Greatest Movie Heroes. Retrieved from www.afi.com/afis-100-years-100-heroes-villians/.

Anderson, P. (1990). *Great Quotes from Great Leaders*. Lombard, IL: Successories Publishing.

Andrews, K. A. (1971). *The Concept of Corporate Strategy*. Burr Ridge, IL: Dow-Jones-Irwin.

Andrews, R. (1989). *The Concise Columbia Dictionary of Quotations*. New York: Columbia University Press.

Appelbaum, L., & Paese, M. (2001). What Senior Leaders Do: The Nine Roles of Strategic Leadership. Retrieved from www.hr.com/en/communities/organizational_development/ddi-insight-what-senior-leaders-do-the-nine-roles-_eacxu3d7.html.

Ardelt, M. (2000). Intellectual Versus Wisdom-Related Knowledge: The Case for a Different Kind of Learning in the Later Years of Life. *Educational Gerontology*, 26: 771–789.

Ardelt, M. (2004). Wisdom as Expert Knowledge System: A Critical Review of a Contemporary Operationalization of an Ancient Concept. *Human Development*, 47: 257–285.

Argyris, C., Putnam, R., & Smith, D. M. (1985). *Action Science: Concepts, Methods and Skills for Research and Intervention*. San Francisco, CA: Jossey-Bass.

Ashforth, B. E., & Mael, F. (1989). Social Identity Theory and the Organization. *Academy of Management Review*, 14(1): 20–39.

Atwater, L. E., Dionne, S. D., Avolio, B., Camobreco, J. F., & Lau, A. W. (1999). A Longitudinal Study of the Leadership Development Process: Individual Differences Predicting Leader Effectiveness. *Human Relations*, 52(12): 1543–1562.

Bibliography   335

Audi, R. (1999). *Cambridge Dictionary of Philosophy* (2nd edn). Cambridge: Cambridge University Press.

Avolio, B. J., & Gardner, W. L. (2005). Authentic Leadership Development: Getting to the Root of Positive Forms of Leadership. *The Leadership Quarterly*, 16(3): 315–338.

Baltes, P. B., & Staudinger, U. M. (2000). Wisdom: A Metaheuristic (Pragmatic) to Orchestrate Mind and Virtue toward Excellence. *American Psychologist*, 55: 122–136.

Baltes, P. B., & Kunzmann, U. (2004). The Two Faces of Wisdom: Wisdom as a General Theory of Knowledge and Judgment about Excellence in Mind and Virtue vs. Wisdom as Everyday Realization in People and Products. *Human Development*, 47: 290–299.

Bandura, A. (2013). Social Cognitive Theory. In E. H. Kessler (Ed.) *Encyclopedia of Management Theory*. Thousand Oaks, CA: Sage.

Barnard, C. (1938/1968). *The Functions of the Executive*. Cambridge, MA: Harvard University Press.

Barney, J. B. (1991). Firm Resources and Sustained Competitive Advantage. *Journal of Management*, 17: 99–120.

Bartlett, C. A., & Ghoshal, S. (1989). *Managing Across Borders: The Transnational Solution*. Cambridge, MA: Harvard Business School Press.

Bass, B. M. (1985). *Leadership and Performance Beyond Expectation*. New York: Free Press.

Bass, B. M., & Stogdill, R. M. (1990). *Bass & Stogdill's Handbook of Leadership: Theory, Research, and Managerial Applications* (3rd edn). New York: Free Press.

Becker, B., & Huselid, M. A. (2006). Strategic Human Resource Management: Where Do We Go from Here? *Journal of Management*, 32: 898–925.

Belasen, A., & Frank, N. (2008). Competing Values Leadership: Quadrant Roles and Personality Traits. *Leadership & Organization Development Journal*, 29(2): 127–143.

Benjamin, B., & O'Reilly, C. (2011). Becoming a Leader: Early Career Challenges Faced by MBA Graduates. *Academy of Management Learning & Education*, 10(3): 452–472. (Quote from pp. 453 and 471.)

Bettin, P. J., & Kennedy, J. K. (1990). Leadership Experience and Leader Performance: Some Empirical Support at Last. *The Leadership Quarterly*, 1(4): 219–228.

Bierly. P. E., Kessler, E. H., & Christensen, E. W. (2000). Organizational Learning, Knowledge, and Wisdom. *Journal of Organizational Change Management*, 13(6): 595–618.

Bill & Melinda Gates Foundation (accessed 2019). www.gatesfoundation.org/.

Bill & Melinda Gates Foundation (accessed 2019). What We Do. Retrieved from www.gatesfoundation.org/What-We-Do.

Blackburn, S. (2016). *The Oxford Dictionary of Philosophy* (3rd edn). Oxford: Oxford University Press.

Blake, R. R., & Mouton, J. S. (1964). *The Managerial Grid*. Houston, TX: Gulf Publishing.

Blake, R. R., & Mouton, J. S. (1982). Theory and Research for Developing a Science of Leadership. *Journal of Applied Behavioral Science*, 18: 275–291.

Bluck, S., & Gluck, J. (2005). People's Implicit Theories of Wisdom. In R. Sternberg & J. Jordan (eds) *A Handbook of Wisdom: Psychological Perspectives* (pp. 84–109). New York: Cambridge University Press.

Boyatzis, R. E., Goleman, D., & Rhee, K. (2000). Clustering Competence in Emotional Intelligence: Insights from the Emotional Competence Inventory (ECI)s. In R. Bar-On & J. D. A. Parker (eds) *Handbook of Emotional Intelligence* (pp. 343–362). San Francisco, CA: Jossey-Bass.

Boyce, L. A., Zaccaro, S. J., & Wisecarver, M. Z. (2010). Propensity for Self-Development of Leadership Attributes: Understanding, Predicting, and Supporting Performance of Leader Self-Development. *The Leadership Quarterly*, 21(1): 159–178.

336 Appendix A

Brake, T. (1997). *The Global Leader: Critical Factors for Creating the World Class Organization.* Chicago, IL: Irwin.

Brewer, M. B., & Hewstone, M. (eds.) (2004). *Self and Social Identity.* New York: Blackwell.

Brown, M. E., Treviño, L. K., & Harrison, D. A. (2005). Ethical Leadership: A Social Learning Perspective for Construct Development and Testing. *Organizational Behavior and Human Decision Processes,* 97: 117–134.

Brownell, J., & Goldsmith, M. (2006). Meeting the Competency Needs of Global Leaders. *Human Resource Management,* 45(3): 309–336.

Bülow, L. (2009). The Oscar Schindler Story. Retrieved from www.oskarschindler.com.

Burke, W. W. (1994). *Organization Development: A Process of Learning and Changing* (2nd edn). Reading, MA: Addison-Wesley.

Burns, R. (1785). To a Mouse, On Turning Her Up in her Nest, with the Plough. Retrieved from www.poetryfoundation.org/poems/43816/to-a-mouse-56d222ab36e33.

Burrell, G., & Morgan, G. (1979). *Sociological Paradigms and Organisational Analysis.* London: Routledge.

Cameron, K. S., Dutton, J. E., & and Quinn, R. E. (eds) (2003). *Positive Organizational Scholarship: Foundations of a New Discipline.* San Francisco, CA: Berrett-Koehler Publishers.

Cameron, K. S., Quinn, R. E., DeGraff, J., and Thakor, A. (2006). *Competing Values Leadership: Creating Value in Organizations.* Northampton, MA: Edward Elgar.

Campbell, D. T. (1969). Ethnocentrism of Disciplines and the Fish Scale Model of Omniscience. In M. Sherif & C. W. Sherif (Eds.) *Interdisciplinary Relationships in the Social Sciences* (pp. 328–348). Chicago, IL: Aldine.

Carroll, A. B., & Shabana, K. M. (2010). The Business Case for Corporate Social Responsibility: A Review of Concepts, Research and Practice. *International Journal of Management Reviews,* 12: 85–105.

Chakraborty, S. K. (1995). Wisdom Leadership: Leading Self by the Self. *Journal of Human Values,* 1(2): 205–220.

Choi, Y., & Van de Ven, A. (2013). Stages of Innovation. In E. H. Kessler (Ed.) *Encyclopedia of Management Theory.* Thousand Oaks, CA: Sage.

Clayton, B. R. (2010). *Buddhist Ethics. The Oxford Handbook of World Philosophy.* Oxford: Oxford University Press.

Collings, D. G., & Mellahi, K. (2009). Strategic Talent Management: A Review and Research Agenda. *Human Resource Management Review,* 19(4): 304–313.

Collins, J. (2001a). *Good to Great: Why Some Companies Make the Leap … And Others Don't.* New York: HarperCollins.

Collins, J. (2001b). Level 5 Leadership. *Harvard Business Review,* 79(1): 66–78.

Conger, J. A., & Kanungo, R. N. (1998). *Charismatic Leadership in Organizations.* Thousand Oaks, CA: Sage.

Cooper, C. D., Scandura, T. A., & Schriesheim, C. A. (2005). Looking Forward but Learning from our Past: Potential Challenges to Developing Authentic Leadership Theory and Authentic Leaders. *The Leadership Quarterly,* 16(3): 475–493.

Corbo, L. (2013). Continuous and Routinized Change. In E. H. Kessler (Ed.) *Encyclopedia of Management Theory.* Thousand Oaks, CA: Sage.

Covey, S. (1989). *The 7 Habits of Highly Effective People.* New York: Free Press.

Cox, T. (1994). *Cultural Diversity in Organizations.* San Francisco, CA: Berrett-Koehler Publishers.

Crainer, S. (1998). *The Ultimate Book of Business Quotations*. New York: AMOCOM.

Crew, B. (2018). This Timeline Shows the Entire History of the Universe, and Where It's Headed. Science Alert. Retrieved from www.sciencealert.com/timeline-shows-the-entire-history-of-the-universe-and-how-it-ends.

Csikszentmihalyi, M. (1988). The Flow Experience and Its Significance for Human Psychology. In M. Csikszentmihalyi & I. S. Csikszentmihalyi (Eds.) *Optimal Experience: Psychological Studies of Flow in Consciousness* (pp. 15–35). New York: Cambridge University Press.

Daft, R. L. (2014). *The Leadership Experience* (6th edn). Stamford, CT: Cengage Learning.

Dahlgaard-Park, S. M. (2013). Total Quality Management. In E. H. Kessler (Ed.) *Encyclopedia of Management Theory*. Thousand Oaks, CA: Sage.

Dalai Lama (2018). Quote via Twitter, 2:31 a.m., June 8, 2018. Retrieved from https://twitter.com/DalaiLama/status/1005019375957471232.

Day, D. V., Fleenor, J. W., Atwater, L., Sturm, R. E., & Mckee, R. A. (2014). Advances in Leader and Leadership Development: A Review of 25 Years of Research and Theory. *The Leadership Quarterly*, 25: 63–82.

Deaux, K., & Perkins, T. (2001). The Kaleidoscopic Self. In C. Sedikides & M. B. Brewer (Eds.) *Individual Self, Relational Self, and Collective Self: Partners, Opponents, or Strangers?* (pp. 299–313). Mahwah, NJ: Erlbaum.

Den Hartog, D. N., House, R. J., Hanges, P. J., Antonio Ruiz-Quintanilla, S., Dorfman, P. W., et al. (1999). Culture Specific and Crossculturally Generalizable Implicit Leadership Theories: Are Attributes of Charismatic/Transformational Leadership Universally Endorsed? *Leadership Quarterly*, 10(2): 219–252.

DeNisi, A. S., & Belsito, C. A. (2007). Strategic Aesthetics – Wisdom and Human Resource Management. In E. H. Kessler & J. R. Bailey (Eds.) *Handbook of Organizational and Managerial Wisdom* (pp. 261–273). Thousand Oaks, CA: Sage.

Diamond, A. (2017). What the Post Gets Right (and Wrong) About Katherine Graham and the Pentagon Papers. Smithsonian. Retrieved from www.smithsonianmag.com/smithsonian-institution/what-the-post-gets-right-wrong-katharine-graham-pentagon-papers-180967677/#r4xj2PY6GCmPhUxB.99.

DiMaggio, P. J., & Powell, W. W. (1983). The Iron Cage Revisited: Institutional Isomorphism and Collective Rationality in Organizational Fields. *American Sociological Review*, 48:147–160.

Dinh, J., Lord, R., Garnder, W., Meuser, J., Liden, R. C., & Hu, J. (2014). Leadership Theory and Research in the New Millennium: Current Theoretical Trends and Changing Perspectives. *The Leadership Quarterly*, 25 (1): 36–62.

Donaldson, L. (2013). Organizational Structure and Design. In E. H. Kessler (Ed.) *Encyclopedia of Management Theory*. Thousand Oaks, CA: Sage.

Dries, N. (2003). The Psychology of Talent Management: A Review and Research Agenda. *Human Resource Management Review*, 23: 272–285.

DuBrin, A. J. (2018). *Leadership: Research Findings, Practice, And Skills* (9th edn). Cengage Learning.

Durant, W. (1961). *The Story of Philosophy: The Lives And Opinions Of The Greater Philosophers*. New York: Washington Square Press.

Durant, W. (2014). *Fallen Leaves*. New York: Simon & Shuster.

Eagly, A. H. (2005). Achieving Relational Authenticity in Leadership: Does Gender Matter? *The Leadership Quarterly*, 16(3): 459–474.

Eagly, A. H., & Karau, S. J. (2012). Role Congruity Theory of Prejudice Toward Female Leaders. *Psychological Review*, 109(3): 573–598.

338 Appendix A

Earley, P. C., & Ang, S. (2003). *Cultural Intelligence: An Analysis of Individual Interactions across Cultures*. Palo Alto, CA: Stanford University Press.

Einstein, A. (2015). *The Philosophy of Albert Einstein: Writings on Art, Science, and Peace*. New York: FallRiver Press.

Elder, G. H. (1985). *Life Course Dynamics: Trajectories and Transitions*. Ithaca, NY: Cornell University Press.

Elkington, J. (1997). *Cannibals with Forks: The Triple Bottom Line of 21st Century Business*. Oxford: Capstone/John Wiley & Sons.

Emerson, R. W (1967). *Self-Reliance*. White Plains, NY: Peter Pauper Press.

Encyclopedia Britannica (2019). Retrieved from www.britannica.com.

Fellows, S., & Kahn, W. A. (2013). Role Theory. In E. H. Kessler (Ed.) *Encyclopedia of Management Theory*. Thousand Oaks, CA: Sage.

Fiedler, F. E. (1967). *A Theory of Leadership Effectiveness*. New York: McGraw-Hill.

Fiedler, F. E., & Garcia, J. E. (1987). *New Approaches to Effective Leadership: Cognitive Resources and Organizational Performance*. New York: Wiley.

Florida, R. (2008). *Who's Your City?* New York: Basic Books, Penguin Random House LLC.

Forbes Nonprofit Council (2017). Nine Ways Nonprofits Can Increase Community Engagement. Forbes. Retrieved from www.forbes.com/sites/forbesnonprofitcouncil/2017/10/17/nine-ways-nonprofits-can-increase-community-engagement/#1aa524227799.

Friedman, T. L. (2005). *The World Is Flat: A Brief History of the Twenty-first Century*. New York: Farrar, Straus & Giroux.

Fryer, B. (2007). The Ethical Mind: A Conversation with Psychologist Howard Gardner. *Harvard Business Review*, March: 51–56.

Fuller, R. B. (1982). *Critical Path*. New York: St. Martin's Press.

Gaines, J. (2014). Science Explains Why Girls Went So Crazy for The Beatles. Business Insider. Retrieved from www.businessinsider.com/science-explains-why-girls-went-so-crazy-for-the-beatles-2014-2.

Galli, E. B., & Müller-Stewens, G. (2012). How to Build Social Capital with Leadership Development: Lessons from an Explorative Case Study of a Multibusiness Firm. *The Leadership Quarterly*, 23(1): 176–201.

Ganco, M. (2013). Complexity Theory and Organizations. In E. H. Kessler (Ed.) *Encyclopedia of Management Theory*. Thousand Oaks, CA: Sage.

Gardner, W. L., Avolio, B. J., Luthans, F., May, D. R., & Walumbwa, F. (2005). Can You See the Real Me? A Self-Based Model of Authentic Leader and Follower Development. *The Leadership Quarterly*, 16(3): 343–372.

Garibaldi de Hilal, A. V. (2003). Cultural Values. In E. H. Kessler (Ed.) *Encyclopedia of Management Theory*. Thousand Oaks, CA: Sage.

Gelb, M. J. (2000). *How to Think Like Leonardo da Vinci: Seven Steps to Genius Every Day*. New York: Dell.

George, W. (2011). Why Leaders Lose Their Way. *Harvard Business Review*. Retrieved from https://hbr.org/2011/06/why-leaders-lose-their-way.html.

George, W. W. (2015). *Discover Your True North*. New York: Wiley.

George, W. W., & Sims, P. (2007). *True North: Discover Your Authentic Leadership*. San Francisco, CA: Jossey-Bass.

Glynn, M. A., Giorgi, S., & Tunarosa, A. (2013). Learning Organization. In E. H. Kessler (Ed.) *Encyclopedia of Management Theory* (pp. 440–444). Thousand Oaks, CA: Sage.

Bibliography **339**

Goldratt, E. M., & Cox, J. (2004). *The Goal: A Process of Ongoing Improvement* (3rd edn). Great Barrington, MA: North River Press.

Goldsmith, M., & Walt, K. (1999). New Competencies for Tomorrow's Global Leader. *CMA Management*, December/January: 20–24.

Goleman, D., Boyatzis, R., & Mckee, A. (2002). *The New Leaders – Transforming the Art of Leadership into the Science of Results*. Boston, MA: Little, Brown.

Goodman, C. (2017). Ethics in Indian and Tibetan Buddhism. *Stanford Encyclopedia of Philosophy*. Retrieved from https://plato.stanford.edu/entries/ethics-indian-buddhism/.

Google (2019). Retrieved from google.com.

Graen, G. B., & Uhl-Bien, M. (1995). Development of Leader–Member Exchange (LMX) Theory of Leadership over 25 Years: Applying a Multi-level Multi-domain Perspective. *The Leadership Quarterly*, 6: 219–247.

Grant, A. (2014). *Give and Take: Why Helping Others Drives Our Success*. London: Penguin Books.

Gray, S. (2006). *The Mind of Bill James: How a Complete Outsider Changed Baseball*. New York: Doubleday.

Green, S. G., & Mitchell, T. R. (1979). Attributional Processes of Leaders in Leader–Member Interactions. *Organizational Behavior and Human Performance*, 23: 429–458.

Greenleaf, R. K. (1977). *Servant Leadership: A Journey into the Nature of Legitimate Power and Greatness*. New York: Paulist Press.

Gregersen, H. B., Morrison, A. J., & Black, J. S. (1998). Developing Leaders for the Global Frontier. *Sloan Management Review*, Fall: 21–32.

Hackman, J. R. (2002). *Leading Teams: Setting the Stage for Great Performances*. Cambridge, MA: Harvard Business Review Press.

Hammond, C. (2016). How Do Charities Encourage Us to Part with Our Cash? As Claudia Hammond Finds, There Are Some Proven Ways to Appeal to People's Better Natures. BBC. Retrieved from www.bbc.com/future/article/20160914-five-ways-to-encourage-generosity.

Hannah, S. T., & Avolio, B. J. (2011). Leader Character, Ethos, and Virtue: Individual and Collective considerations. *The Leadership Quarterly*, 22: 989–994.

Harari, Y. N. (2015). *Sapiens: A Brief History of Humankind*. New York: Harper Collins (pp. 415–416).

Harris, P. R., & Moran, R. T. (1987). *Managing Cultural Differences*. Houston, TX: Gulf Publishing.

Hawking, S., & Mlodinow, L. (2010). *The Grand Design*. New York: Bantam Books.

Hays, J. M. (2007). Dynamics of Organizational Wisdom. *Journal of Global Strategic Management*, 1: 17–35.

Helms, M. M. (2013). SWOT Analysis Framework. In E. H. Kessler (Ed.) *Encyclopedia of Management Theory*. Thousand Oaks, CA: Sage.

Henderson, R. M., & Clark, K. B. (1990). Architectural Innovation: The Reconfiguration of Existing Product Technologies and the Failure of Established Firms. *Administrative Science Quarterly*, 35: 9–30.

Hersey, P. H., Blanchard, K. H., & Johnson, D. E. (2009). *Management of Organizational Behavior* (9th edn). Englewood Cliffs, NJ: Prentice Hall.

Hill, C. (2013). *International Business: Competing in the Global Marketplace* (9th edn). New York: McGraw Hill.

Hill, N. (2003/1937). *Think and Grow Rich* (15th edn). London: Penguin.

Hirst, G., Mann, L., Bain, P., Pirola-Merlo, A., & Richter, A. (2004). Learning to Lead: The Development and Testing of a Model of Leadership Learning. *The Leadership Quarterly*, 15(3): 311–327.

340 Appendix A

Hitt, M. A., Beamish, P. W., Jackson, S. E., & Mathieu, J. E. (2007). Building Theoretical and Empirical Bridges across Levels: Multilevel Research in Management. *Academy of Management Journal,* 50: 1385–1399.

Hofstede, G. (2001). *Culture's Consequences: Comparing Values, Behaviors, Institutions and Organizations Across Nations.* Thousand Oaks, CA: Sage.

Hogg, M. A., (2001). A Social Identity Theory of Leadership. *Personality and Social Psychology Review,* 5(3): 184–200.

Hogg, M. A., Terry, D. J., & White, K. M. (1995). A Tale of Two Theories: A Critical Comparison of Identity Theory with Social Identity Theory. *Social Psychology Quarterly,* 58(4): 255–269.

Hooijberg, R., & Choi, J. (2000). Which Leadership Roles Matter to Whom? An Examination of Rater Effects on Perceptions of Effectiveness. *The Leadership Quarterly,* 11: 341–364.

Hoover, J. D., Giambatista, R. C., Sorenson, R. L., & Bommer, W. H. (2010). Assessing the Effectiveness of Whole Person Learning in Pedagogy in Skill Acquisition. *Academy of Management Learning & Education,* 9: 192–203.

House, R. J. (1996). Path-Goal Theory of Leadership: Lessons, Legacy, and a Reformulated Theory. *The Leadership Quarterly,* 7(3): 323–352.

Howe, D. W. (2008). Honest Abe: Abraham Lincoln and the Moral Character. Foreign Policy Research Institute. Retrieved from www.fpri.org/article/2008/06/honest-abe-abraham-lincoln-and-the-moral-character/.

https://flowingdata.com/2012/10/09/history-of-earth-in-24-hour-clock/.

Huselid, M. A., Beatty, R. W., & Becker, B. E. (2005). "A Players" or "A Positions?": The Strategic Logic of Workforce Management. *Harvard Business Review,* December: 110–117.

Hutchison, E. D. (2010). *Dimensions of Human Behavior: The Changing Life Course* (4th edn). Thousand Oaks, CA: Sage.

Ilies, R., Morgeson, F. P., & Nahrgang, J. D. (2005). Authentic Leadership and Eudaemonic Well-being: Understanding Leader–Follower Outcomes. *The Leadership Quarterly,* 16(3): 373–394.

Internet Movie Database (accessed 2019). Bill Murray – Biography – Personal Quotes. IMDb. Retrieved from www.imdb.com/name/nm0000195/bio?ref_=nm_dyk_qt_sm#quotes.

Internet Movie Database (accessed 2019). Miracle (2004) – Kurt Russell as Herb Brooks. IMDb. Retrieved from www.imdb.com/title/tt0349825/characters/nm0000621.

Isaacson, W. (2008a). *Einstein: His Life and Universe.* New York: Simon and Schuster.

Isaacson, W. (2008b). *Steve Jobs.* New York: Simon and Schuster.

Jokinen, T. (2005). Global Leadership Competencies: A Review and Discussion. *Journal of European Industrial Training,* 29(3): 199–216.

Jordan, J., & Cartwright, S. (1998). Selecting Expatriate Managers: Key Traits and Competencies. *Leadership & Organization Development Journal,* 19(2): 89–96.

Joullie, J. (2016). The Philosophical Foundations of Management Thought. *Academy of Management Learning & Education,* 15(1): 157–179.

Judge, T. A., & Piccolo, R. F (2004). Transformational and Transactional Leadership: A Meta-Analytic Test of Their Relative Validity. *Journal of Applied Psychology,* 89: 755–768.

Juran, J. M. (1992). *Juran on Quality by Design.* New York: The Fess Press.

Kahn, W. A., & Fellows, S. (2013). Role Theory. In E. H. Kessler (Ed.) *Encyclopedia of Management Theory.* Thousand Oaks, CA: Sage.

Katz, D., & Kahn, R. L. (1978). *The Social Psychology of Organizations* (2nd edn). New York: John Wiley & Sons.

Kennedy, J. F. (1955). *Profiles in Courage.* New York: Harper.

Kennedy, J. F. (1963). Remarks Prepared for Delivery at the Trade Mart in Dallas, TX, November 22, 1963 [Undelivered]. Retrieved from www.jfklibrary.org/archives/other-resources/john-f-kennedy-speeches/dallas-tx-trade-mart-undelivered-19631122.

Kenworthy, C. (2015). *Shoot Like Spielberg: The Visual Secrets of Action, Wonder and Emotional Adventure*. Michael Wiese Productions.

Kerr, S. (1975). On the Folly of Rewarding A, While Hoping for B. *Academy of Management Journal*, 18(4): 769–783.

Kerr, S., & Jermier, J. M. (1978). Substitutes for Leadership: Their Meaning and Measurement. *Organizational Behavior and Human Performance*, 22: 375–403.

Kessler, E. H. (2010). *Management Theory in Action: Real Work Lessons for Walking the Talk*. New York: Palgrave Macmillan.

Kessler, E. H. (2013a). Appendix B – Central Management Insights. In E. H. Kessler (Ed.) *Encyclopedia of Management Theory*. Thousand Oaks, CA: Sage.

Kessler, E. H. (2013b). *Encyclopedia of Management Theory*. Thousand Oaks, CA: Sage.

Kessler, E. H. (2013c). Reader's Guide. In E. H. Kessler (Ed.) *Encyclopedia of Management Theory*. Thousand Oaks, CA: Sage.

Kessler, E. H. (2016). *Being a True VIP: Managing Importance in Yourself and Others*. New York: Palgrave Macmillan.

Kessler, E. H. (2017). The Triumphant Triumvirate: Synergistically Realizing the Purposes of a University Through a Core Management Course. *Journal of Management Education*, 41(6): 794–816.

Kessler, E. H. (Forthcoming, 2020). A Wisdom-Based Approach for Developing Global Talented Leaders. In I. Tarique *Companion to Talent Management*. New York: Routledge.

Kessler, E. H., & Chakrabarti, A. K. (1996). Innovation Speed: A Conceptual Model of Context, Antecedents and Outcomes. *Academy of Management Review*, 21(4): 1143–1191.

Kessler, E. H., & Bailey, J. R. (2007). *Handbook of Organizational and Managerial Wisdom*. Thousand Oaks, CA: Sage.

Kessler, E. H., & Bartunek, J. M. (2014). Designing Management Maps and Apps: Insights for Discovering and Creating Our Management Realities. *Academy of Management Review*, 39: 234–243.

Kets de Vries, M. F. R., & Florent-Treacy, E. (2002). Global Leadership from A to Z: Creating High Commitment Organizations. *Organizational Dynamics*, 295(309): 1–16.

Kim, J., & McLean, G. N. (2015). An Integrative Framework for Global Leadership Competency: Levels and Dimensions. *Human Resource Development International*, 18(3): 235–258.

King Jr., M. L. (1963). Letter from Birmingham Jail. Retrieved from https://swap.stanford.edu/20141218230016/http://mlk-kpp.01.stanford.edu/kingweb/popular_requests/frequentdocs/birmingham.pdf.

Kirkpatrick, S. A., & Locke, E. A. (1991). Leadership Do Traits Matter. *Academy of Management Executive*, 5: 48–60.

Kohlberg, L. (1969). Stage and Sequence: The Cognitive-Developmental Approach to Socialization. In D. A. Goslin (Ed.) *Handbook of Socialization Theory and Research* (pp. 347–480). Skokie, IL: Rand McNally.

Kotecki, P. (2018). Bill and Melinda Gates Were Just Named the Most Generous Philanthropists in America — Here Are Their Biggest Projects. Business Insider. Retrieved from www.businessinsider.com/biggest-projects-of-generous-philanthropists-bill-and-melinda-gates-2018-8.

Kotter, J. (1990). What Leaders Really Do? *Harvard Business Review*, 3: 103–111.

342 Appendix A

Kouzes, J. M., & Posner, B. Z. (2011). *Credibility: How Leaders Gain and Lose It, Why People Demand It* (2nd edn). San Francisc-o, CA: Jossey-Bass.

Kouzes, J. M., & Posner, B. Z. (2012). *The Leadership Challenge: How to Make Extraordinary Things Happen in Organizations* (5th edn). San Francisco, CA: Jossey-Bass.

Kramer, R. M. (2013). Self Concept and Theory of the Self. In E. H. Kessler (Ed.) *Encyclopedia of Management Theory* (pp. 682–686). Thousand Oaks, CA: Sage.

Kulman, L. (2007). Walter Isaacson Discusses 'Einstein'. NPR. Retrieved from www.npr.org/2007/07/09/11749884/walter-isaacson-discusses-einstein.

Lawrence, P. E. (2007). Institutionalizing Wisdom in Organizations. In E. H. Kessler & J. R. Bailey (Eds.) *Handbook of Organizational and Managerial Wisdom* (pp. 43–60). Thousand Oaks, CA: Sage.

Leary, M. R., & Tangney, J. P. (Eds.) (2003). *Handbook of Self and Identity*. New York: Guilford Press.

Lepak, D. P., & Snell, S. A. (1999). The Human Resource Architecture: Toward a Theory of Human Capital Allocation and Development. *Academy of Management Review*, 24: 31–48.

Lepak, D. P., & Snell, S. A. (2002). Examining the Human Resource Architecture: The Relationship among Human Capital, Employment, and Human Resource Configurations. *Journal of Management*, 28: 517–543.

Lewin, K. (1951). *Field Theory in Social Science*, edited by D. Cartwright. New York: Harper & Bros.

Liden, R. C. (2013). Servant Leadership. In E. H. Kessler (Ed.) *Encyclopedia of Management Theory* (pp. 698–702). Thousand Oaks, CA: Sage.

Liden, R. C., Wayne, S. J., Zhao, H., & Henderson, D. (2008). Servant Leadership: Development of a Multidimensional Measure and Multilevel Assessment. *The Leadership Quarterly*, 19: 161–177.

Liker, J. K. (2004). *The Toyota Way: 14 Management Principles from the World's Greatest Manufacturer*. New York: McGraw-Hill Professional.

Loehr, J., & Schwartz, T. (2005). *The Power of Full Engagement: Managing Energy, Not Time, Is the Key to High Performance and Personal Renewal*. New York: Free Press.

Lord, R. G., & Hall, R. J. (2005). Identity, Deep Structure and the Development of Leadership Skill. *The Leadership Quarterly*, 16: 591–615.

Lumpkin, G. T., & Dess, G. G. (1996). Clarifying the Entrepreneurial Orientation Construct and Linking It to Performance. *Academy of Management Review*, 21: 135–172.

Marshall-Mies, J. C., Fleishman, E. A., Martin, J. A., Zaccaro, S. J., Baughman, W. A., & McGee, M. L. (2000). Development and Evaluation of Cognitive and Metacognitive Measures for Predicting Leadership Potential. *The Leadership Quarterly*, 11(1): 135–153.

Martinko, M. J., & Gardner, W. L. (1987). The Leader/Member Attribution Process. *Academy of Management Review*, 12: 235–249.

Mastin, L. (2009). Where in the Universe Is the Earth? Retrieved from www.physicsoftheuniverse.com/where-in-the-universe-is-the-earth.html.

Mayer, R. C. (2013). Trust. In E. H. Kessler (Ed.) *Encyclopedia of Management Theory* (pp. 904–907). Thousand Oaks, CA: Sage.

McCorvey, J. J. (2015). The Key to Oprah Winfrey's Success: Radical Focus. Fast Company. Retrieved from www.fastcompany.com/3051589/the-key-to-oprah-winfreys-success-radical-focus.

McGregor, D. M. (1960). *The Human Side of Enterprise*. New York: McGraw-Hill.

McKenna, B., Rooney, D., & Boal, K. B. (2009). Wisdom Principles as a Meta-Theoretical Basis for Evaluating Leadership. *The Leadership Quarterly*, 20(2): 177–190.

Meldrum, M., & Atkinson, S. (1998). Is Management Development Fulfilling Its Organizational Role? *Management Decision*, 36(8): 528–532.

Merriam Webster Dictionary (2019). Retrieved from www.merriam-webster.com/.

Michie, S., & Gooty, J. (2005). Values, Emotions, and Authenticity: Will the Real Leader Please Stand Up? *The Leadership Quarterly*, 16(3): 441–457.

Miller, D. (2002). Successful Change Leaders: What Makes Them? What Do They Do that Is Different? *Journal of Change Management*, 2(4): 359–368.

Miller, K. D. (2019). 14 Health Benefits of Practicing Gratitude According to Science. Positive Psychology. Retrieved from https://positivepsychology.com/benefits-of-gratitude/.

Mooallem, J. (2016). Inside the Mind of Steven Spielberg, Hollywood's Big, Friendly Giant. Wired. Retrieved from www.wired.com/2016/06/steven-spielberg-the-bfg/.

Moretti, J. (2010). *Frommer's Florence, Tuscany, and Umbria* (7th edn). Hoboken, NJ: Wiley Publishers.

Mumford, M., Marks, M. A., Connelly, M. S., Zaccaro, S. J., & Reiter-Palmon, R. (2000a). Development of Leadership Skills: Experience and Timing. *The Leadership Quarterly*, 11(1): 87–114.

Mumford, M., Zaccaro, S. J., Johnson, J. F., Diana, M., Gilbert, J. A., & Threlfall, K. (2000b). Patterns of Leader Characteristics: Implications for Performance and Development. *The Leadership Quarterly*, 11(1): 115–133.

Mumford, T. V., Campion, M. A., & Morgeson, F. P. (2007). The Leadership Skills Strataplex: Leadership Skill Requirements across Organizational Levels. *The Leadership Quarterly*, 18(2): 154–166.

Nevickaa, B., De Hoogha, A. H. B., Van Vianena, A. E. M., Beersmaa, B., & McIlwain, D. (2011). All I Need Is a Stage to Shine: Narcissists' Leader Emergence and Performance. *The Leadership Quarterly*, 22(5): 910–925.

Northouse, P. G. (2018). *Leadership Theory and Practice* (8th edn). Thousand Oaks, CA: Sage.

Noy, N. F., & McGuinness, D. L. (2000). Ontology Development 101: A Guide to Creating Your First Ontology. Stanford University. Retrieved from https://protege.stanford.edu/publications/ontology_development/ontology101-noy-mcguinness.html.

Oxford English Dictionary (2019). Retrieved from www.oed.com/.

Perlmutter, H. V. (1969). The Tortuous Evolution of the Multinational Corporation. *Columbia Journal of World Business*, January/February: 9–18.

Peters, T., & Waterman, R. (1982). *In Search of Excellence – Lessons from America's Best-Run Companies*. New York: Harper and Collins Publishers.

Peterson, C., & Seligman, M. E. P. (2004). *Character Strengths and Virtues: A Handbook and Classification*. New York: Oxford University Press.

Pfeffer, J. (1993). Barriers to the Advancement of Organizational Science: Paradigm Development as a Dependent Variable. *Academy of Management Review*, 18: 599–620.

Pfeffer, J. (2015). *Leadership BS: Fixing Workplaces and Careers One Truth At A Time*. New York: Harper Collins.

Pirson, M. (2017). What is Humanistic Management? International Humanistic Management Association. Retrieved from http://humanisticmanagement.international/what-is-humanistic-management/.

Plato's Republic (Release date: August 27, 2008). The Project Gutenberg EBook of *The Republic* by Plato. Project Gutenberg – www.gutenberg.org. Translator: B. Jowett.

Pluchik, R. (1980). *Emotions: A Psychoevolutionary Synthesis*. New York: Harper & Row.

Plutchik, R. (1988). The Nature of Emotions: Clinical Implications. In M. Clynes & J. Panksepp (Eds.) *Emotions and Psychopathology*. Boston, MA: Springer.

344 Appendix A

Podsakoff, P. M., MacKenzie, S. B., & Bommer, W. H. (1996). Meta-Analysis of the Relationships between Kerr and Jermier's Substitutes for Leadership and Employee Job Attitudes, Role Perceptions, and Performance. *Journal of Applied Psychology*, 81: 380–399.

Podsakoff, P. M., MacKenzie, S. B., Paine, J. B., & and Bachrach, D. G. (2000). Organizational Citizenship Behaviors: A Critical Review of the Theoretical and Empirical Literature and Suggestions for Future Research. *Journal of Management*, 26(3): 513–563.

Porter, M. E. (1980). *Competitive Strategy: Techniques for Analyzing Industries and Competitors*. New York: Free Press.

Porter, M. E. (1985). *Competitive Advantage: Creating and Sustaining Superior Performance*. New York: Free Press.

Porter, M. E. (1990). *The Competitive Advantage of Nations*. New York: Free Press.

Posner, B. Z., & Schmidt, W. H. (1992). Values and the American Manager: An Update. *California Management Review*, 34(3): 80–94.

Pralahad, C. K., & Hamel, G. (1990). The Core Competence of the Corporation. *Harvard Business Review*, 68(4): 79–93.

Quinn, R. E., & Rohrbaugh, J. (1983). A Spatial Model of Effectiveness Criteria: Toward a Competing Values Approach to Organizational Analysis. *Management Science*, 29: 363–377.

Rahim, A., & Magner, N. (1995). Confirmatory Factor Analysis of the Styles of Handling Interpersonal Conflict: First-Order Factor Model and Its Invariance across Groups. *Journal of Applied Psychology*, 80(1): 122–132.

Rath, T. (2007). *StrengthsFinder 2.0*. New York: Gallup Press.

Rath, T., & Conchie, B. (2009). *Strengths-Based Leadership*. New York: Gallup Press.

Reichard, R. J., & Johnson, S. K. (2011). Leader Self-Development as Organizational Strategy. *The Leadership Quarterly*, 22(1): 33–42.

Reis, C. (2015). *Careers and Talent Management: A Critical Perspective*. New York: Routledge.

Rhinesmith, S. H. (1996). *A Manager's Guide to Globalization: Six Skills for Success in a Changing World*. New York: McGraw-Hill.

Roberts, L. M., Spreitzer, G., Dutton, J. E., Quinn, R. E., Heaphy, E. D., & Barker, B. (2005). How to Play to Your Strengths. *Harvard Business Review*, 2005 issue. Retrieved from https://hbr.org/2005/01/how-to-play-to-your-strengths.

Rolling Stone (2018). How the Beatles Took America: Inside the Biggest Explosion in Rock & Roll History. *Rolling Stone*. Retrieved from www.rollingstone.com/music/music-features/how-the-beatles-took-america-inside-the-biggest-explosion-in-rock-roll-history-244557/.

Ronald Reagan Presidential Foundation & Institute (accessed 2019). January 11, 1989 – Reagan Quotes and Speeches. Retrieved from www.reaganfoundation.org/ronald-reagan/reagan-quotes-speeches/farewell-address-to-the-nation-2/.

Rosen, R. H. (2000). What Makes a Globally Literate Leader? *Chief Executive*, April: 46–48.

Routledge Encyclopedia of Philosophy (2019). Retrieved from www.rep.routledge.com/.

Rowe, G. (2001). Creating Wealth in Organizations: The Role of strategic leadership. *Academy of Management Executive*, 15(1): 81–94.

Sanders, E. P., & Pelikan, J. J. (accessed 2019). Jesus. In *Britannica*. Retrieved from www.britannica.com/biography/Jesus.

Sartre, J. P. (1957). *Existentialism and Human Emotion*. New York: Philosophical Library.

Scandura, T. A., & Lankau, M. J. (1996). Developing Diverse Leaders: A Leader–Member Exchange Approach. *The Leadership Quarterly*, 7(2): 243–263.

Schein, E. H. (2010). *Organizational Culture and Leadership* (4th edn). San Francisco, CA: John Wiley & Sons.

Schein, E. H. (2011). Douglas McGregor: Theoretician, Moral Philosopher or Behaviorist? An Analysis of the Interconnections between Assumptions, Values and Behavior. *Journal of Management History*, 17: 156–164.

Seldes, G. (1985). *The Great Thoughts*. New York: Ballantine Books.

Seligman, M. (2011). *Flourish: A Visionary New Understanding of Happiness and Well-Being*. New York: Atria Paperback.

Senge, P. M. (1990). *The Fifth Discipline: The Art and Practice of the Learning Organization*. New York: Currency Doubleday.

Shotter, J., & Tsoukas, H. (2014). In Search of Phronesis: Leadership and the Art of Judgment. *Academy of Management Learning & Education*, 13(2): 224–243.

Silk, J. A. (Accessed 2019). Bodhisattva. In *Britannica*. Retrieved from www.britannica.com/topic/bodhisattva.

Smith, A. (1981/1776). *An Inquiry into the Nature and Causes of the Wealth of Nations*, Volumes I and II, edited by R. H. Campbell and A. S. Skinner. Indianapolis: Liberty Fund.

Smith, D. (2015). *How to Think Like Einstein*. London: Michael O'Mara.

Smith, J. A., & Foti, R. J. (1998). A Pattern Approach to the Study of Leader Emergence. *The Leadership Quarterly*, 9(2): 147–160.

Smith, J. R., & Terry, D. J. (2013). Norms Theory. In E. H. Kessler (Ed.) *Encyclopedia of Management Theory* (pp. 508–5011). Thousand Oaks, CA: Sage.

Snyder, M. (1979). Self-Monitoring Processes. In L. Berkowitz (Ed.) *Advances in Experimental Social Psychology* (Vol. 12, pp. 86–128). New York: Academic Press.

Spreitzer, G. M., McCall, M. W., & Mahoney, J. (1997). The Early Identification of International Executive Potential. *Journal of Applied Psychology*, 82(1): 6–29.

Srinivas, K. M. (1995). Globalization of Business and the Third World: Challenge of Expanding the Mindsets. *Journal of Management Development*, 14(3): 26–49.

Stanford Encyclopedia of Philosophy (2019). Retrieved from https://plato.stanford.edu/.

Staudinger, U. M., & Gluck, J. (2011). Psychological Wisdom Research: Commonalities and Differences in a Growing Field. *Annual Review of Psychology*, 62: 215–241.

Staudinger, U. M., Dörner, J., & Mickler, C. (2005). Wisdom and Personality. In R. Sternberg & J. Jordan (Eds) *Handbook of Wisdom: Psychological Perspectives* (pp. 191–219). New York: Cambridge University Press.

Sterling, R. W., & Scott, W. C. (1985). *Translation of The Republic by Plato*. New York: W. W. Norton & Company.

Sternberg, R. J. (Ed.). (1990). *Wisdom: Its Nature, Origins, and Development*. New York: Cambridge University Press.

Sternberg, R. J. (1995). A Triarchic View of "Cognitive Resources and Leadership Performance". *Applied Psychology: An International Review*, 44: 29–32.

Sternberg, R. J. (2003). WICS: A Model of Leadership in Organizations. *Academy of Management Learning and Education*, 2(4): 386–401.

Sternberg, R. J. (2008). The WICS Approach to Leadership: Stories of Leadership and the Structures and Processes that Support Them. *The Leadership Quarterly*, 19(3): 360–371.

Stets, J. E., & Burke, P. J. (2000). Identity Theory and Social Identity Theory. *Social Psychology Quarterly*, 63(3): 224–237.

Stevenson, B. E. (1967). *The Home Book of Quotations: Classical and Modern*. New York: Dodd, Mead & Company.

Stewart, D., & Blocker, H. G. (1987). *Fundamentals of Philosophy*. New York: Macmillan.

Stogdill, R. M. (1974). *Handbook of Leadership: A Survey of the Literature*. New York: Free Press.

346 Appendix A

Strang, S. E., & Kuhnert, K. W. (2009). Personality and Leadership Developmental Levels as Predictors of Leader Performance. *The Leadership Quarterly*, 20(3): 421–433.

Strube, M. J., & Garcia, J. E. (1981). A Meta-Analytic Investigation of Fiedler's Contingency Model of Leadership Effectiveness. *Psychological Bulletin*, 90(2): 307–321.

Suddaby, R. (2003). Institutional Theory. In E. H. Kessler (Ed.) *Encyclopedia of Management Theory* (pp. 379–384). Thousand Oaks, CA: Sage.

Suddaby, R., Hardy, C., & Huy, Q. N. (2011). Where Are the New Theories of Organization? *Academy of Management Review*, 36: 236–246.

Summitt, P. (1999). Reach for the Summit (p. 131). Crown Publishing Group. Retrieved from www.azquotes.com/author/19881-Pat_Summitt/tag/teamwork.

Sutton, C. (accessed 2019). Subatomic Particle – Four Basic Forces. In *Britannica*. Retrieved from www.britannica.com/science/subatomic-particle/Four-basic-forces.

Tannenbaum, R., & Massarik, F. (1950). Participation By Subordinates in the Managerial Decision-Making Process. *Canadian Journal of Economics and Political Science*, 16: 408–418.

Tannenbaum, R., & Schmidt, W. H. (1973). How to Choose a Leadership Pattern (With Retrospective Commentary). *Harvard Business Review*, 51: 162–180.

Tarallo, M. (2018). The Art of Servant Leadership. SHRM. Retrieved from www.shrm.org/resourcesandtools/hr-topics/organizational-and-employee-development/pages/the-art-of-servant-leadership.aspx.

Tarique, I. (2013). Human Capital Theory. In E. H. Kessler (Ed.) *Encyclopedia of Management Theory* (pp. 343–346). Thousand Oaks, CA: Sage.

Tarique, I., & Schuler, R. S. (2010). Global Talent Management: Literature Review, Integrative Framework, and Suggestions for Further Research. *Journal of World Business*, 45: 122

Teece, D. (2013). Dynamic Capabilities. In E. H. Kessler (Ed.) *Encyclopedia of Management Theory* (pp. 221–224). Thousand Oaks, CA: Sage.

Thaler, R. H., & Sunstein, C. R. (2009). *Nudge: Improving Decisions About Health, Wealth and Happiness*. New York: Penguin.

The Buddhist Centre (accessed 2019). What Are Buddhist Ethics About? The Buddhist Centre. Retrieved from https://thebuddhistcentre.com/text/ethics.

The Oxford Dictionary of Quotations (1979). Oxford: Oxford University Press.

The Pluralism Project (accessed 2019). From Diversity to Pluralism. Harvard University. Retrieved from http://pluralism.org/encounter/todays-challenges/from-diversity-to-pluralism/.

The Rubik Zone (accessed 2019). Number of Combinations. Retrieved from www.therubikzone.com/number-of-combinations/.

The Shawshank Wiki (accessed 2019). Andy Dufresne. Fandom. Retrieved from https://shawshank.fandom.com/wiki/Andy_Dufresne.

Thomas, M. L., Bangen, K. J., Palmer, B. W., Martin, A. S., Avanzino, J. A., Depp, C. A., Glorioso, D., Daly, R. E., & Jeste, D.V. (2017). A New Scale for Assessing Wisdom Based on Common Domains and a Neurobiological Model: The San Diego Wisdom Scale (SD-WISE). *Journal of Psychiatric Research*, 108, January 2019, pp. 40–47. DOI: 10.1016/j.jpsychires.2017.09.005.

Thompson, G., & Vecchio, R. P. (2009). Situational Leadership Theory: A Test of Three Versions. *The Leadership Quarterly*, 20: 837–848.

Thorpe, S. D. (2000). *How to Think Like Einstein: Simple Ways to Break the Rules and Discover Your Hidden Genius*. Sourcebook.

Time Magazine Most Influential (2019). Retrieved from https://time.com.

Bibliography **347**

Treviño, L. K., Hartman, L. P., & Brown, M. (2000). Moral Person and Moral Manager: How Executives Develop a Reputation for Ethical Leadership. *California Management Review*, 42(4): 128–142.

Tsoukas, H. (1994). What is Management? An Outline of a Metatheory. *British Journal of Management*, 5: 289–301.

Tuckman, B. W. (2013). Group Development. In E. H. Kessler (Ed.) *Encyclopedia of Management Theory* (pp. 318–322). Thousand Oaks, CA: Sage.

Tuttle, R. H. (accessed 2019). Human Evolution. In *Britannica*. Retrieved from www.britannica.com/science/human-evolution.

Tyson, N. D. (2017). *Astrophysics for People in a Hurry*. New York: W. W. Norton and Company (pp. 205–207).

University of Michigan (accessed 2019). About – Center for Positive Organizations. University of Michigan Ross School of Business. Retrieved from https://positiveorgs.bus.umich.edu/about/.

University of Michigan (accessed 2019). Reflected Best Self Exercise™. University of Michigan Ross School of Business. Retrieved from https://positiveorgs.bus.umich.edu/cpo-tools/rbse/.

U.S. Citizenship and Immigration Services (accessed 2019). Citizenship Rights and Responsibilities. USCIS. Retrieved from www.uscis.gov/citizenship/learners/citizenship-rights-and-responsibilities.

Van Maanen, J., & Schein, E. H. (1979). Toward a Theory of Organizational Socialization. In B. M. Staw (Ed.) *Research in Organizational Behavior* (Vol. 1, pp. 209–264). Greenwich, CT: JAI Press.

Warren Bennis Quotes (n.d.). BrainyQuote.com. Retrieved December 14, 2019, from BrainyQuote.com Website: www.brainyquote.com/quotes/warren_bennis_402360.

Watt, W. M., & Sinai, N. (accessed 2019). Muhammad. In *Britannica*. Retrieved from www.britannica.com/biography/Muhammad.

Wayne, S. J., Shore, L. M., & Liden, R. C. (1997). Perceived Organizational Support and Leader–Member Exchange: A Social Exchange Perspective. *Academy of Management Journal*, 40: 82–111.

Weber, M. (1947). *The Theory of Social and Economic Organization*, translated by A. M. Henderson & T. Parsons. Glencoe, IL: Free Press.

Weber, M. (1968). *Economy and Society* (3 vols), edited by Guenter & Wittich. New York: Bedminister (original work published in 1925).

WebMD (accessed 2019). Meditation, Stress, and Your Health. Retrieved from www.webmd.com/balance/guide/meditation-natural-remedy-for-insomnia#1.

WebMD (accessed 2019). What Mindfulness Can Do For You. Retrieved from www.webmd.com/balance/guide/what-is-mindfulness#1.

Weick, K. E. (2007). Foreword. In E. H. Kessler & J. R. Bailey (Eds.) *Handbook of Organizational and Managerial Wisdom* (pp. ix–xiii). Thousand Oaks, CA: Sage.

Westley, F., & Mintzberg, H. (1989). Visionary Leadership and Strategic Management. *Strategic Management Journal*, 10: 17–32.

Whetten, D. A., & Cameron, K. S. (2015). *Developing Management Skills* (9th edn). Harlow, Essex: Pearson.

Whitmore, J. (2009). *Coaching for Performance: GROWing Human Potential and Purpose: The Principles And Practice Of Coaching And Leadership*. Boston, MA: Nicholas Brealey.

Williamson, O. E. (1975). *Markets and Hierarchies, Analysis and Antitrust Implications: A Study in the Economics of Internal Organization*. New York: Free Press.

348 Appendix A

Winter, D. G. (1987). Leader Appeal, Leader Performance, and the Motive Profiles of Leaders and Followers: A Study of American Presidents and Elections. *Journal of Personality and Social Psychology*, 52(1): 196–202.

Wofford, J. C., & Liska, L. Z. (1993). Path-Goal Theories of Leadership: A Meta-Analysis. *Journal of Management*, 19(4): 857–876.

Wolfson, A. (2018). Muhammad Ali Lost Everything in Opposing the Vietnam War. But in 1968, He Triumphed. *USA Today*. Retrieved from www.usatoday.com/story/news/2018/02/19/1968-project-muhammad-ali-vietnam-war/334759002/.

Wong-Ming Ji, D. J. (2013). Force Field Analysis and Model of Planned Change. In E. H. Kessler (Ed.) *Encyclopedia of Management Theory* (pp. 287–291). Thousand Oaks, CA: Sage.

Yukl, G. A. (1989). Managerial Leadership: A Review of Theory and Research. *Journal of Management*, 15: 251–289.

Yukl, G. A. (2002). A Hierarchical Taxonomy of Leadership Behavior: Integrating a Half Century of Behavior Research. *Journal of Leadership and Organizational Studies*, 9(1): 15–32.

Yukl, G. A. (2012). *Leadership in Organizations* (8th edn). Harlow, Essex: Pearson.

Zaccaro, S. J. (2007). Trait-Based Perspectives of Leadership. *American Psychologist*, 62: 6–16.

Zacharatos, A., Barling, J., & Kelloway, E. K. (2000). Development and Effects of Transformational Leadership in Adolescents. *The Leadership Quarterly*, 11(2): 211–226.

APPENDIX B

SUMMARY OF CORE WISE LEADERSHIP TOOLS

TOOL	CHALLENGE	FOCUS	BUILDING A BETTER CORE	CRAFTING A BETTER PROCESS	LEVERAGING A BETTER CAPACITY	OUTCOME	
Leadership SCIENTIST (Logic) Tool	Cognitive	Head – Thinking	Comprehension *Breadth* *Depth*	Assessment *Perception* *Intuition*	Judgment *Rational* *Creative*	Extraordinary Intellectual Prowess	Sagacity
Leadership ARTIST (Aesthetics) Tool	Affective	Heart – Feeling	Awareness *Sensitivity* *Empathy*	Attitude *Positivity* *Pluralism*	Inspiration *Motivational* *Influential*	Extraordinary Emotive Capacity	Spirit
Leadership ICON (Ethics) Tool	Integrity	Inside – Reflecting	Morality *Moral Mindset* *Moral Maturity*	Authenticity *Alignment* *Growth*	Confidence *Esteem* *Agency*	Extraordinary Introspective Insight	Character
Leadership ADVOCATE (Metaphysics) Tool	Significance	Outside – Aspiring	Mindfulness *Ontology* *Perspective*	Collegiality *Inclusiveness* *Duty*	Transcendence *Munificence* *Service*	Extraordinary Meaningful Objectives	Purpose
Leadership MAESTRO (Epistemology) Tool	Coordination	Pull – Synergizing	Complementarity *Composition* *Alignment*	Interdependency *Communication* *Partnership*	Harmony *Hardware/Structure* *Software/Culture*	Extraordinary Collaborative Orientation	Unity
Leadership GENERAL (Politics) Tool	Execution	Push – Engaging	Excellence *Effectiveness* *Efficiency*	Advantage *Operations* *Innovation*	Sustainability *Learning Systems* *Cybernetic Change*	Extraordinary Functional Application	Value

APPENDIX C

SAMPLE SYLLABUS FOR A WISE LEADERSHIP PROGRAM

1	INTRODUCTION – Overview of Objectives and Design		

DISCOVERING YOUR LEADERSHIP WISDOM			
2	The PROBLEM	Chapter 1	Stupid Smart People: *The Importance of Leadership*
3	The JOURNEY	Chapter 2	Paths for Exploring Leadership: *What We Know about Leadership*
4	The SOLUTION	Chapter 3	A Model of 'Wise' Leadership: *How We Can Elevate Leadership*

ASSEMBLING YOUR LEADERSHIP TOOLBOX			

LIGHTS			
5	HEAD	Chapter 4	Becoming a Leadership SCIENTIST: *Using Your Logic Tools*
6	HEART	Chapter 5	Becoming a Leadership ARTIST: *Using Your Aesthetics Tools*

CAMERA			
7	INSIDE	Chapter 6	Becoming a Leadership ICON: *Using Your Ethics Tools*
8	OUTSIDE	Chapter 7	Becoming a Leadership ADVOCATE: *Using Your Metaphysics Tools*

ACTION			
9	PULL	Chapter 8	Becoming a Leadership MAESTRO: *Using Your Epistemology Tools*
10	PUSH	Chapter 9	Becoming a Leadership GENERAL: *Using Your Politics Tools*

LEVERAGING YOUR LEADERSHIP SUCCESS			
11	SELECTION	Chapter 10	Dealing with Complexity: *Customizing Your Leadership Approach*
12	OPTIMIZATION	Chapter 11	Dealing with Dynamism: *Growing Your Leadership Strengths*
13	MAINTENANCE	Chapter 12	Dealing with Uncertainty: *Trouble-Shooting Your Leadership Exposures*
14	CONCLUSION – Synthesis of Insights and Final Projects		

APPENDIX D

EXERCISES TO PRACTICE WISE LEADERSHIP

Levels of Leadership

How can Wise Leadership tools be applied at the following levels of leadership?

TABLE 1

Leading a ...	Head	Heart	Inside	Outside	Pull	Push
Nuclear or Extended Family						
Social Club or Athletic Team						
Business Organization						
School or University						
Nonprofit Institution						
Professional Association						
City, State, or Region						
Government Agency						
Sovereign Country						
International Alliance						
Global Movement						

352 Appendix D

DOMAINS OF LEADERSHIP

How can Wise Leadership tools be applied to address the following 'global risks' (as identified by the World Economic Forum)?

TABLE 2

Addressing ...	Head	Heart	Inside	Outside	Pull	Push
Adverse Consequences of Technological Advances						
Asset Bubbles/Financial Crisis in A Major Economy						
Biodiversity Loss and Ecosystem Collapse						
Climate Change and Extreme Weather						
Critical Infrastructure Breakdown						
Cyber-Attacks						
Data Fraud or Theft						
Government Corruption and Accountability						
Lack of Education, Opportunity, and Employment						
Large-Scale Conflict/Wars						
Large-Scale Involuntary Migration						
Man-Made and Environmental Disasters						
Natural Disasters						
Poverty and Inequality						
Religious Conflicts						
Spread of Infectious Diseases						
Terrorist Attacks						
Water or Food Crises						
Weapons of Mass Destruction						

INDEX OF NAMES

Adams, Scott 63
Alcott, Louisa May 252
Alexander the Great 257
Ali, Muhammad 161
Allen, James 169
Allison, Graham 29
American GI 196
Andrews, Kenneth 249
Angelou, Maya 180, 187, 249
Appelbaum, Loren 44
Ardelt, Monika 18
Argyris, Chris 245
Aristotle 24, 51, 88, 96, 214, 246
Atatürk, Kemal 225

Bacon, Francis 96
Baekeland, Leo 230
Baggins, Frodo 195
Bailey, George 164
Bailey, James 57
Balboa, Rocky 131
Ball, Lucille 133
Baltes, Paul 18
Bandura, Albert 45
Bankhead, Tallulah 252
Barnard, Chester 248
Barrymore, Ethel 180
Bass, Bernard 36, 37
Bechtel, Stephen 262
Beethoven, Ludwig van 128
Belasen, Alan 43
Ben Gurion, David 196

Bennis, Warren 315
Bentham, Jeremy 53
Berners-Lee, Tim 230
Bezos, Jeff 259
Blaine, Rick 162
Blake, Robert 39
Blake, William 88, 180
Blanchard, Ken 39
Blocker, H. Gene 51
Bonaparte, Napoleon 258
Bond, James 260
Bono 191
Brando, Marlon 133
Brewer, Marilynn 45
Brin, Sergey 260
Brontë sisters 127
Brooks, Herb 226
Brown, Les 253
Bryant, Paul "Bear" 221, 249
Buber, Martin 151
Buck, Pearl S. 247
Buddha 73, 158, 218
Bueller, Ferris 262
Buffett, Warren 152

Cameron, Kim 38
Campbell, Joseph 117
Carnegie, Andrew 162, 221
Carnegie, Dale 106, 122
Carrier, Willis 262
Carroll, Archie 153
Chaplin, Charlie 133

354 Index of Names

Chinese proverb 119
Chipping, Charles Edward (Mr. Chips) 132
Chopra, Deepak 221
Churchill, Winston 126, 137, 184, 333
Colette, Sidonie Gabrielle 180
Collins, Jim 38
Confucius 155, 221, 227
Conger, Jay 37
Covey, Steven 74, 248
Cox, Taylor 185
Crick, Francis 102
Curie, Marie 99

Da Vinci, Leonardo 97
Dalai Lama 117, 250, 320
Dale, Norman 229
Darwin, Charles 99
Davis, Mr. (Juror #8) 228
de Gaulle, Charles 233
Deaux, Kay 45
Deming, William Edwards 240
Descartes, Rene 54
Dickinson, Emily 119
DiMaggio, Paul 326
Dinh, Jessica 56
Disney, Walt 155, 201, 259
Donaldson, Lex 222
Dostoyevsky, Fyodor 160
Dufresne, Andy 262
Durant, Will 5, 11–12, 16
Dylan, Bob 133

Earley, Chris 321
Edison, Thomas Alva 257
Einstein, Albert 93, 98, 187
Eisenhower 249, 253, 257
Elder, Glen 75
Elizabeth I, Queen 225
Elkington, John 255
Emerson, Ralph Waldo 75
Epictetus 117, 253

Fellini, Federico 121
Fermi, Enrico 102
Fiedler, Fred 36
Finch, Atticus 194
Fleming, Alexander 102
Florida, Richard 321
Ford, Henry 155, 201, 252, 258
Foucault, Michel 55
Frank, Anne 165, 169
Frank, Nancy 43

Franklin, Benjamin 88, 96, 152, 233
Franklin, Aretha 133
Frege, Gottlob 51
Freud, Sigmund 102, 252
Friedman, Thomas 321
Fuller, Buckminster 10

Gandhi, Mohandas K. 137, 155, 180, 195, 202, 253, 288
Gardiner, Howard 141
Gates, Bill 162, 289
George, Bill 37, 63, 142
Giannini, Amadeo 196
Goddard, Robert 102
Godel, Kurt 102
Goethe, Johann Wolfgang von 233
Goffman, Erving 46
Gogh, Vincent van 250
Goldratt, Eliyahu 248
Graen, George 38
Graham, Katherine 159
Graham, Martha 133
Green, Stephen 38
Greenleaf, Robert 37
Gunderson, Marge 101

Hackman, Richard 215
Hamel, Gary 251
Hammerstein, Roger 230
Harari, Yuval Noah 11
Hawking, Stephen 34
Hegel, Georg 54
Henson, Jim 133
Hersey, Paul 39
Hill, Napoleon 68
Ho Chi Minh 230
Hobbes, Thomas 55
Hofstede, Geert 322–326
Hogg, Michael 46, 295
Holmes, Oliver Wendell 74
Holmes, Sherlock 101
House, Robert 37
Hubble, Edwin 102
Hugo, Victor 161
Hume, David 55
Hunting, Will 101

James, Bill 100
James, William 169
Jeanneret, Charles-Édouard (Le Corbusier) 102
Jefferson, Thomas 137, 249
Joad, Tom 194

Index of Names **355**

Jobs, Steve 98
John Paul II, Pope 196
John Paul IV, Pope 184
Johnson, Samuel 155
Jones, Indiana 100
Juran, Joseph M. 240, 248

Kahn, Robert 46
Kane, Will 163
Kant, Immanuel 52–53
Katz, Daniel 46
Kelleher, Herb 221
Keller, Helen 106, 165, 169, 247
Kennedy, John F. 122, 152, 184, 324
Kennedy, Robert F. 250, 254
Kerr, Steve 39, 63, 295
Kessler, Eric 57, 156, 252, 296
Keynes, John Maynard 102
Kiddo, Beatrix "The Bride" 261
King, Dr. Martin Luther, Jr. 107, 126,
    148, 151, 184
Kirkpatrick, Shelley 44
Kohlberg, Lawrence 141, 151
Kouzes, James 41
Kramer, Roderick 45
Kroc, Ray 148, 214, 262
Kubrick, Stanley 130

Lao Tsu 17
Lauder, Estée 262
Lawrence, T.E. 230
Leakey, Louis and Mary 102
Leary, Mark 45
Lenin, V.I. 230
Lennon, John 128, 180
Levitt, William 262
Lewin, Kurt 255
Liker, Jeffrey 248
Lincoln, Abraham 137, 159, 214, 252
Locke, Edwin 44
Locke, John 54
Loehr, Jim 106
Lombardi, Vince 200, 233, 246
Lord, Robert 56

Machiavelli, Niccolo 55, 254
Malloy, Terry 194
Mandela, Nelson 224
Marlow, Philip 261
Maslow, Abraham 93
Maxwell, John 252
McCallister, Kevin 262
McCarthur, Douglas 249

McCartney, Paul 128
McClane, John 261
McGregor, Douglas 37
Michelangelo 2
Milk, Harvey 165
Mill, John Stuart 53
Miller, David 43
Milton, John 73
Morita, Akio 262
Moses 228
Mother Teresa of Calcutta 187, 190
Mouton, Jane 39
Mozart, Wolfgang Amadeus 128
Murray, Bill 133

Newton, Sir Isaac 97
Nietzsche, Friedrich 54

Orwell, George 184

Paese, Matthew 44
Page, Larry 260
Pankhurst, Emmeline 196
Parks, Rosa 165
Parsons, Talcott 46
Patton, George 91, 247
Peale, Norman Vincent 106
Pele 165
Perlmutter, Howard 186
Peters, Tom 249
Pfeffer, Jeffrey 63
Piaget, Jean 102
Plato 21, 24, 52, 62, 74, 98, 293
Popper, Karl 55
Porter, Michael 251
Posner, Barry 41
Powell, Walter 326
Prahalad, C.K. 251

Rafael 21
Rahim, M. Afzalur 220
Rand, Ayn 247
Rath, Tom 41
Rawlins, John 229
Rawls, John 56
Reagan, Ronald 190
Reuther, Walter 196
Ripley, Ellen 260
Robin Hood 195
Robinson, Jackie 192
Rockne, Knute 121, 218
Rodgers, Fred (Mr.) 133
Rogers, Richard 230

356 Index of Names

Rogers, Will 233
Roosevelt, Eleanor 191, 253
Roosevelt, Theodore (Teddy) 148, 247, 256
Rousseau, Jean-Jacques 56, 93
Rozelle, Pete 262
Russell, Bertrand 52

St. Anselm 54
Sakharov, Andrei 133
Salk, Jonas 102
Sanger, Margaret 196
Sarnoff, David 262
Sartre, Jean-Paul 137, 177
Schein, Ed 223
Schindler, Oskar 164
Schopenhauer, Arthur 52
Schwartz, Tony 106
Schweitzer, Albert 91, 187, 191
Senge, Peter 243
Shakespeare, William 128
Shane 131
Shaw, George Bernard 218
Shaw, Robert 229
Shelley, Mary 169
Shockley, William 102
Sinatra, Frank 133
Smith, Adam 211
Smith, Jefferson (Mr.) 132
Socrates 52, 152
Sotomayor, Sonia 218
Spartacus 228
Spencer, Diana (Lady Di) 133
Spiderman 137
Spielberg, Steven 130
Spinoza, Baruch 54
Spock, Mr. 101
Starling, Clarise 100
Sternberg, Robert 18
Stewart, David 51
Stogdill, Ralph 56
Stravinsky, Igor 133
Summitt, Pat 226
Sun Tzu 258

Tannenbaum, Robert 38
Tennyson, Alfred Lord 117

Tesla, Nikola 98
Thaler, Richard 150
Thatcher, Margaret 190, 249
Thich Nhat Hanh 180
Thoreau, Henry David 91, 187
Tibbs, Virgil 100
Tolstoy, Leo 107, 127
Truman, Harry S. 91, 119, 184, 218
Tuckman, Bruce 220
Turing, Alan 99
Turkish proverb 88
Twain, Mark 148, 254

Unknown (quote) 250

Van de Ven, Andrew 252
Vito, Mona Lisa 101
Von Bismarck, Otto 225

Walesa, Lech 230
Walton, Sam 129
Washington, Booker T. 169, 233
Washington, George 117, 152, 214
Watson, James 102
Watson, Thomas 262
Wayne, Bruce (Batman) 101
Weber, Max 37, 248
Webster, Norma Rae 227
Weick, Karl 17
Whitehead, Alfred North 52
Wilde, Oscar 119
Williamson, Oliver 248
Wilson, Woodrow 148
Winfrey, Oprah 129, 218
Winter, David 293
Wittgenstein, Ludwig 55, 102
Wooden, John 93, 137, 201
Wright Brothers 262

Yoda 164
York, Sergeant Alvin 195
Yousafzai, Malala 187, 192
Yukl, Gary 56

Zorro 261
Zuckerberg, Mark 259

INDEX OF SUBJECTS

Action Learning 254
Active Listening 220
Actual Leader 278
Advantage 238, 241, 250
Advocate 178
Aesthetics 37, 52, 58
Agency 75
Agility and Customization 268
Alignment 216, 286
American Film Institute's 'Greatest Movie Heroes' 68
Antagonistic Environments 200
Approaches to Leadership 33–34
Artificial Intelligence 77, 316
Artist 116
Aspire 170
Assembly of 'Invisible Counselors' 68
Assessment 79, 83
Attitude 111, 114
Attribution 84
Attribution Model of Leadership 39
Authentic Leadership 38
Authenticity 142
Awareness 109

Block Chain 316
Bodhisattva 295
Business Process Reengineering 254

Centralization 212
Change 244, 254
Channel Selection 209

Character 61, 167, 282
Charismatic Theory of Leadership 38
Checklists 150
Clashes 200
Coaching 296–297
Cognitive Resource Theory 37
Collegiality 174, 176
Communication 208–210, 219
Competency Traps 242
Competing Values Framework 38
Competitive Traps 242
Complementarity 204, 215
Complexity 73
Complexity Theory 306
Composition 215
Comprehension 77, 82
Comprehension: Breadth 89; Depth 90
Confidence 143
Confirmation 83
Conflict 210, 220
Conformers 207
Confusion 169
Context 84
Contingency Theory of Leadership 39
Continuous and Routinized Change 255
Control 248
Core Competencies 251
Costs 240
Creative Capacities (and Decision Making) 94
Cultivating Wise Leadership: Aesthetics Talent 301; Epistemology Talent 303;

358 Index of Subjects

Cultivating Wise Leadership: *continued*
    Ethics Talent 302; Logic Talent 30;
    Metaphysics Talent 303; Politics
    Talent 304
Cultural Intelligence 321
Culture 223, 320

Data 15
Decentralization 212
Decision Trees 150
Decoding 209
Delegation 212
Differentiation 211
Distorted Confidence 137
Distractions 200
Double Loop Learning 254
Duty 174, 185
Dynamism 73
Dynamic Capability Model 307
Dynamic Leadership Competencies 291

Economic Systems 328
Education (vs. Training) 22–23
Effectiveness 248
Efficiency 247
Emotional and Motivation Challenges 61
Emotions: Attentiveness 109;
    Attitude 114; Awareness 113;
    Channeling 111
Emotional Intelligence 107
Empathy 113, 114, 118
Emphasis 84
Encoding 208
Energy 105, 270
Engagement 219
Entrepreneurship 251
Epistemology 38, 54, 58
Erosion 310
Escalation 85
Ethical Agency 157
Ethical Alignment 153
Ethical Courage 143, 146
Ethical Esteem 156
Ethical Outlook 141, 145
Ethical Practices 142, 145
Ethics 37, 52, 58
Ethnocentrism 169
Evolution 310
Excellence 236, 240, 247
Execution and Implementation
    Challenges 62, 235, 273
Expectations 115
Experiential Learning 254

Extraordinary: Collaborative Orientation
    62; Emotive Capacity 61; Functional
    Application 62; Intellectual Prowess
    61; Introspective Insight 61; Principled
    Objectives 62

Flexibility 212
Floaters 208
Flow 115
Force Field Analysis 255
Framing 83

General 245
Geography 320
Gists 296
Globalization 314, 326
Goal Setting 115
Government 327

Halo Effect 84
Harmony 205
Harmony and Teamwork Challenges
    62, 202
Head 60
Heart 60
Heart of a Leader 105, 116, 135
Heuristics 82
Human Brain 77
Human Capital 215
Human Resource Management 215, 298
Hypercompetitive 73

Identity Theory 45
Idiocy 11
Ill-Emphasized: Advocate 283; Artist 281;
    General 285; Icon 282; Maestro 284;
    Scientist 279
Imagination 85
Immaturity 137
Inactive 310
Inauthenticity 137
Inclusiveness 174, 184
Individual Learning 243
Influential 124
Information 15
Innovation 242, 252
Inside 60
Inspiration 111
Institutionalization 254, 314, 326
Integration 212
Integrity 270
Interdependence 173, 204
Intuition 92

Index of Subjects **359**

Isolators 208
Isomorphism 326

Job Design 115
Judgment 80, 84

Kaleidoscopic Self 45
K.I.D. 12
Knowledge 16

Language 219
Leader–Member Exchange 39
Leadership 29–30, 56
Leadership Advocate 62, 197
Leadership Artist 61, 135
Leadership Categories 33
Leadership Chronologies 31
Leadership Competencies 34
Leadership Continuum Theory 39
Leadership Education and Development 295
Leadership General 62, 264
Leadership Icon 61, 167
Leadership Identities 45
Leadership Maestro 62, 231
Leadership Practices 39
Leadership Roles 40
Leadership Scientist 61, 103
Leadership Selection (versus Success) 292
Learning Organization 254
Legal Systems 327
Level-5 Leadership 38
Lights-Camera-Action 60
Listening 220
Loafers 207
Logic 36, 51, 57
Looking Deep Inside 136, 148
Looking Far Outside 168, 180

Maestro 213
Maintenance Guide 309
Managerial (Leadership) Grid 39
Manipulated Salience 83
Matching 115
Meaning 168, 271
Meaning and Commitment Challenges 62, 171
Mega-Heuristics 287
Meta-Monitoring 287
Meta-Theoretical Perspective 35
Metaphysics 38, 53, 58
Mind of a Leader 73, 88, 104
Mindfulness 173, 176, 181
Miscommunications 200

Misguided Leader 278
Misplaced Leader 278
Mistaken Leader 277
Moral and Value Challenges 61, 139
Moral Blindness 137
Moral Compass 136
Moral Maturity 151
Moral Mindset 149
Morality 141
Motivation and Inspirational Challenges 114
Motivation 122
Multinational Enterprise (MNE) 320
Munificence 175, 188

National Platform 251
Network Traps 242
Nonverbal Communication 209, 219
Norms 217
Nudges 150

Ontology 173, 181
Operational Competitiveness 250
Operational Constraints 248
Operations 247
Opportunities and Threats 311
Optimization Guide 290
Organizational Culture 212
Organizational Development (OD) 244
Organizational Learning 244
Outside 60

Partnership 220
Path–Goal Theory of Leadership 38
People-Related Role Behaviors 40
Perception 91
Perspective 173, 182
Philosopher King 296
Philosophy 49–51
Planning 250
Plato's Cave 21, 293–295
Plato's Ship of Fools 292–294
Pluralism 121
Politics 39, 55, 59, 236
Positivity 120
Power 124
Proactive 310
Process Theories of Change 255
Production-Related Role Behaviors 40
Projection 82
Pull 60
Pulling People Together 199, 214, 231
Punctuated Equilibrium Model 255
Purpose 62, 282

360 Index of Subjects

Push 60
Pushing People Forward 232, 246, 264

Quality 240, 248
Quantum Change 255

Rational Capacities (and Decision
  Making) 94
Rationalization 84
Reactive 310
Reasoning and Judgment Challenges 61
Reflective Capacity 136
Reinforcement 115
Relationship-Oriented Role Behaviors 40
Richness 219
Role Theory 46
Roles 216

Sagacity 61, 279
San Diego Wisdom Scale 42
Satisficing 85
Scientist 86
Selection Guide 267
Selective Attention 83
Self-Absorption 137
Selfhood 45
Sensitivity 113, 114, 118
Servant Leadership 38, 178
Service 175, 188
Situational Theory of Leadership 39
Skepticism 169
Skill and Will 277
Social Identity Theory 45
Socialization 223
Specialization 211
Speed 240
Spirit 61, 281
Spirited Workforce 111
Standardization 212
Stereotyping 82
Strain 169
Strategic Position 251
Strategies for Change 255
Structure and Design 211, 222
Substitutes for Leadership 39
Supply and Demand (of Wisdom) 20

Supportiveness 210, 219
Sustainability 238
Sustainability Challenges 243
SWOT Analysis 249
Synergistic: Components 204; Contexts
  205; Dynamics 204
Synergy 199, 272

Talent Management 298
Task-Oriented Role Behaviors 40
Team 199
Teamwork Challenges: Component 207;
  Context 211; Process 208
Technology 313, 315
Theory X and Y 38
Thinking and Understanding
  Challenges 76
Time 180
Time Magazine's 'Most Influential' 68
Total Quality Management (TQM) 240
Tradition 320
Trait Theory of Leadership 37
Transactions 248
Transcendence 175, 177
Transformational Theory of Leadership 38
Triple-Bottom-Line 255
Trouble-Shooting Checklist 332
Trust 154
Turning Points 75

Uncertainty 73
Understanding Problem 269
Unity 62, 284

Value 62, 285
Value Chain 251
Vision 179, 198
VUCA 253

Whole-Person Learning 296
Wholeness 174
Wisdom 16, 49
Wisdom Cycle 23
Wisdom Ladder 22
Wise Leadership Model 61
Wise Leadership Tools 59